W9-CZR-807

CHINA'S QUEST
FOR GREAT
POWER

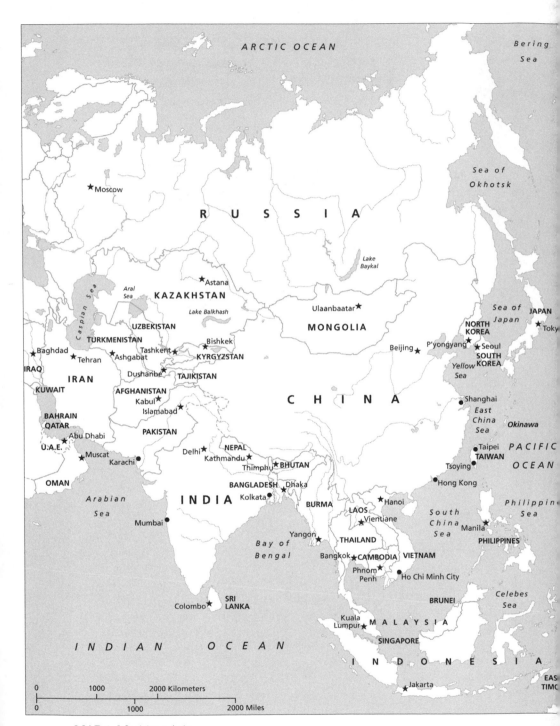

MAP 1. Maritime Asia

CHINA'S QUEST FOR GREAT POWER

Ships, Oil, and Foreign Policy

BERNARD D. COLE

NAVAL INSTITUTE PRESS
Annapolis, Maryland

This book has been brought to publication with the generous assistance of Marguerite and Gerry Lenfest.

Naval Institute Press
291 Wood Road
Annapolis, MD 21402

Library of Congress Cataloging-in-Publication Data
Names: Cole, Bernard D., date, author.
Title: China's quest for great power : ships, oil, and foreign policy / Bernard D. Cole.
Description: Annapolis, Maryland : Naval Institute Press, 2016.
Identifiers: LCCN 2016027911| ISBN 9781612518381 (hardback) |
    ISBN 9781682471456 (epub) | ISBN 9781682471456 (mobi)
Subjects: LCSH: Sea-power—China. | Energy policy—China. | Energy security—
    China. | National security—China. | China—Foreign relations—21st century. |
    BISAC: HISTORY / Military / Naval.
Classification: LCC VA633 .C648 2016 | DDC 355/.033551—dc23
    LC record available at https://lccn.loc.gov/2016027911

Maps created by Chris Robinson.

♾ Print editions meet the requirements of ANSI/NISO z39.48-1992
(Permanence of Paper).
Printed in the United States of America.

24 23 22 21 20 19 18 17 16   9 8 7 6 5 4 3 2 1
First printing

CONTENTS

ILLUSTRATIONS

PREFACE

The People's Republic of China (PRC) was established on 1 October 1949, when the Chinese Communist Party (CCP) took power in Beijing following nearly a century of civil war and foreign invasions. China had, in the words of Mao Zedong, finally "stood up." That announcement was followed by brutally enforced land redistribution, the Korean War, episodes of fanatical socialization, the disastrous Great Leap Forward, and the barbaric and chaotic Great Proletarian Cultural Revolution.

It was only following Mao's death in 1976, a period of governmental confusion, and the imprisonment of the "Gang of Four" led by Mao's widow that Deng Xiaoping was able to take power in 1978 and launch China onto a sea of economic modernization, social sanity, and relative political regularity. Even during Deng's reign, China was rent by the social unrest of the spring of 1989, which culminated in the June Tiananmen Square massacre.

Since approximately 1980, however, China has established an overall record of economic modernization unique in history, lifting hundreds of millions of its people out of poverty. China has modernized its military, focusing on the People's Liberation Army (PLA), as its dramatically increasing gross domestic product (GDP) has provided the necessary financial resources. All services and branches of the military have benefited, but the navy, air force, and the new Rocket and Strategic Support Forces now hold pride of place in China's military priorities. The navy in particular is seizing the headlines, as the May 2015 defense department white paper depicts China's future navy as a global force with far-reaching strategic missions.

This book focuses on China's primary national security concerns. These include achieving world-class economic and military status; both of these goals require national energy security. Hence, Beijing is pursuing national security based on these three objectives.

ACKNOWLEDGMENTS

This book marks an important stage in my efforts to gain an understanding of some facets of the PRC. That process began at the University of Washington in 1970, where I benefited from studying with George Taylor, Robert J. C. Butow, Winston Hsieh, James Townsend, and others. Since then I have learned a great deal from many China experts. At the risk of omitting someone, I thank Kenneth Allen, Jeffrey Bader, Thomas Bickford, Dennis Blasko, Leah Bray, Scott Bray, Richard Bush, Michael Byrnes, Tai-ming Cheung, Warren Cohen, Thomas Christenson, Cortez Cooper, John Corbett, Thomas Christensen, Peter Dutton, Karl Eikenberry, Andrew Erickson, David Finkelstein, Taylor Fravel, Chas Freeman, Bonnie Glaser, Paul Godwin, Lonnie Henley, Charles Hooper, Linda Jakobson, Roy Kamphausen, James Kraska, Nan Li, Michael McDevitt, Frank Miller, Bernard Moreland, Jonathan Odom, Douglas Paal, Raul Pedrozo, Susan Puska, Alan Romberg, Stapleton Roy, Phillip Saunders, Christopher Sharman, Michael Swaine, Scot Tanner, and Larry Wortzel. This manuscript was read all or in part by Kenneth Allen, Thomas Bickford, George Eberling, Andrew Erickson, Eric McVadon, and Christopher Yung.

Any errors of facts or omission are of course solely my responsibility.

I owe many thanks to Susan Brook, Susan Corrado, Judy Heise, Rick Russell, and the staff at the Naval Institute Press, who are true professionals and very supportive. Patti Bower was a wonderful editor. I also note the superb leadership of Vice Adm. Peter Daly, USN (Ret.).

Cynthia Watson once again served as my most important editor, inspiration, and loving support.

This book is dedicated to the memory of Ellis Joffe, a pioneer in the study of China's military and a generous, gracious human being.

ACRONYMS AND ABBREVIATIONS

A2/AD	anti-access / area denial
AAW	anti-air warfare
ADB	Asian Development Bank
ADIZ	air defense identification zone
AEW	airborne early warning
AIIB	Asian Infrastructure Investment Bank
AIP	air-independent propulsion
APEC	Asia Pacific Economic Cooperation
ASBM	antiship ballistic missile
ASCM	antiship cruise missiles
ASEAN	Association of Southeast Asian Nations
ASUW	antisurface warfare
ASW	antisubmarine warfare
bbl	billion barrels
bcm	billion cubic meters
BRICS	Brazil, Russia, India, China, South Africa
CCP	Chinese Communist Party
CMC	Central Military Commission
CNOOC	China National Overseas Oil Company
CNPC	China National Petroleum Company
CV	multipurpose aircraft carrier
DDG	guided-missile destroyer

DOC	Declaration on the Conduct of Parties in the South China Sea
DPP	Democratic Progressive Party
EEZ	exclusive economic zone
EIA	Energy Information Agency
ESF	East Sea Fleet
EU	European Union
FAO	Foreign Affairs Office
FBM	fleet ballistic missile
FDI	foreign direct investment
FFG	guided-missile frigate
FTA	free trade agreement
GDP	gross domestic product
ICBM	intercontinental ballistic missile
IMF	International Monetary Fund
IPR	intellectual property rights
JAM-GC	Joint Concept for Access and Maneuver in the Global Commons
km	kilometers
LNG	liquefied natural gas
LSG	leading small group
LTE	low-tide elevation
mbl	million barrels
MLP	mobile landing platform
MOFA	Ministry of Foreign Affairs
MOOTW	military operations other than war
MR	military region
mt/y	million tons per year
NCO	noncommissioned officer
NEO	noncombatant evacuation operation
nm	nautical mile
NOC	national oil company
NSF	North Sea Fleet
OBOR	one belt, one road
OMTE	*Outline for Military Training and Evaluation*
PBSC	Politburo Standing Committee

PGM	precision-guided munitions
PLA	People's Liberation Army
PLAAF	PLA Air Force
PLAN	People's Liberation Army Navy
PRC	People's Republic of China
RAS	replenishment at sea
SAR	search and rescue
SCO	Shanghai Cooperation Organization
Sinopec	China National Petrochemical Corporation
SLOC	sea line(s) of communications
SOA	State Oceanographic Administration
SOE	state-owned enterprise
SOF	Special Forces
SS	submarine
SSBN	nuclear-powered ballistic-missile submarine
SSF	South Sea Fleet
SSN	nuclear-powered attack submarine
tcf	trillion cubic feet
UAV	unmanned aerial vehicle
UNCLOS	United Nations Convention on the Law of the Sea
WTO	World Trade Organization

INTRODUCTION

This book examines China's national security policy formulation and implementation by looking at three major elements—foreign policy, energy security, and naval power—that are interactive and major influences on China's future. The focus is maritime; the scope is the navy, energy, economy, and diplomacy, all at the strategic level.

The People's Republic of China (PRC) was established on 1 October 1949, when the Chinese Communist Party (CCP) took power in Beijing following nearly a century of civil war and foreign invasions. China had, in the words of Mao Zedong, finally "stood up." That announcement was followed by brutally enforced land redistribution, the Korean War, episodes of fanatical socialization, the disastrous Great Leap Forward, and the barbaric and chaotic Great Proletarian Cultural Revolution.

It was only following Mao's death in 1976, a period of governmental confusion, and the imprisonment of the "Gang of Four" led by Mao's widow that Deng Xiaoping was able finally to take power in 1978 and launch China onto a sea of economic modernization, social sanity, and relative political regularity.[1] Even during Deng's reign, China was rent by the social and political unrest of early 1989, which culminated in the June Tiananmen Square massacre.

Since approximately 1980, however, China has established an overall record of striking economic modernization unique in history, lifting hundreds of millions of its people out of poverty. China has modernized its military, focusing on the People's Liberation Army (PLA), as its dramatically

1

increasing gross domestic product (GDP) has provided the necessary financial resources. All services and branches of the military have benefited, but the navy, air force, Rocket and Strategic Forces may be gaining prominence in China's military priorities. The navy in particular is seizing the headlines, as the May 2015 Ministry of National Defense white paper depicts China's future navy as a global force, with far-reaching strategic missions.

A significant driver of those missions is support for China's continued economic well-being, particularly ensuring a secure source of the energy resources required to drive the economy. This book's title refers to China's modernizing navy and search for energy security. Both should be supported by an effective foreign policy, and both should support that policy, which combines "hard" and "soft" elements of the global power wielded by Beijing. Foreign policy formulation and execution thus form the third leg of the triad of twenty-first-century Chinese strategy and stature examined in this book.

Defining "national security policy" is an important starting point. In China, that phrase includes concerns considered in the United States to be domestic issues. Chinese "grand strategy" does not differentiate categorically between internal and external issues. This work focuses primarily on the external factors in policy formulation.

Different, sometimes competing, views of China's future are offered by both American and Chinese analysts, who often draw on the same record and sources to support their different positions. The overarching question is whether China will displace the United States as the world's leading power. That in turn raises the question of definition, of course; China is widely forecast to surpass the United States in economic terms, but forecasts of dramatic military power shifting are less firmly offered.[2] Some naval analysts foresee a Chinese navy more powerful than that of the United States, for instance, but they usually overlook the mission responsibilities of each: the U.S. Navy is tasked as a global force while for the foreseeable future—at least through the middle of the twenty-first century—the Chinese navy will remain primarily an East Asian regional force.[3]

One view of future U.S.-Chinese relations is the theory that a rising power inevitably will come into conflict with the current global power. The most vociferous American advocate of this problematic thesis is the political scientist John Mearsheimer. His Chinese counterpart may be Colonel Zhao Jingfang, an assistant professor at China's National Defense University.[4]

Mearsheimer argues that conflict is inevitable as China approaches the United States in global power; Zhao argues, "A tremendous power shift is underway in the world's politics and economy today which is manifested prominently in China's rise and the relative U.S. decline."[5] While asserting that crises are inevitable between the two nations, Zhao is more optimistic than Mearsheimer about Beijing and Washington being able to prevent outright conflict. Perhaps the most measured and, hence, likely conclusion is provided by two American scholars, Adam Liff and John Ikenberry, whose recent analysis concluded that history "demonstrates that not all cases of rising powers end tragically. No outcome is inevitable."[6]

A third, probably unquantifiable, measure of global power in addition to economic and military strengths is the sociopolitical strength that China and the United States possess. Some Beijing analysts may offer their current economic-political model, "socialism with Chinese characteristics," as an alternative to American democratic capitalism for other nations to emulate, but there is little evidence of the international attractiveness of this concept.

Chinese analysts and opinion writers generally disclaim ambition to "replace the United States," but the history of the rise and fall of great empires does not support this professed lack of purpose.[7] A slightly but importantly different question was recently offered under the headline "China Working to Dominate Sea Routes as U.S. Loses Interest."[8] Apart from the fallacious assumption of U.S. policy and intentions, this topic more reflects Beijing's concerns about ensuring energy imports from abroad than it does ambition to surpass the United States as a global maritime power.

China emerged from the twentieth century on a course of growing economic wealth and maritime power not seen since the U.S. phenomenon in the late nineteenth and early twentieth centuries. A decade and a half into the twenty-first century, Beijing requires, first, reliable access to the energy resources for continued economic growth and, second, the foreign policies to enable the nation to navigate safely toward its goals of economic growth and international stability.

Domestic concerns form the bedrock of China's national concerns and underlie external issues. For example, maritime sovereignty issues are not just naval concerns but also affect the population's views of the CCP legitimacy.

China published two relevant documents in 2015. The defense white paper on military strategy appeared in May, and the government announced in June it had enacted a new national security law. The first of these papers clearly expressed Beijing's belief that a modernizing People's Liberation Army Navy (PLAN) was required to sustain the country's growing economy.[9]

The paper offered a clear explanation of President Xi Jinping's "China Dream," based on a national strategic goal of "building of a moderately prosperous society in all respects by 2021," when the CCP will celebrate its centenary, to be followed by "a modern socialist country that is prosperous, strong, democratic, culturally advanced and harmonious by 2049 when the People's Republic of China (PRC) marks its centenary." A strong military is declared necessary "as part of the Chinese Dream" to make the country safe and secure.[10]

The national security law is effectively a command from President Xi to maintain the primacy of CCP rule throughout Chinese society. The law bolsters the power of the domestic security apparatus and the military. "Security" is emphasized in all societal areas, from culture to education to cyberspace. The law includes defending national security on international seabeds, in the polar regions, and in cyberspace and outer space.

Xi's view of the PLA may be reflected in his September 2015 announcement of the first step in what is likely to be an extensive reorganization of the military to make it "leaner and meaner." He announced a 300,000 personnel cut in the 2.3-million-strong PLA. A Ministry of National Defense spokesperson then announced the reduction will "mainly target troops equipped with outdated armaments, administrative staff, and non-combatant personnel," with the purpose of optimizing "the structure of the Chinese forces." The "end of 2017" was given as the target date for completing the reduction.[11]

Zheng Shuna, deputy director of the legislative affairs commission of the National People's Congress, recently described China's national security situation as "increasingly grim," saying "from the inside we are dealing with the double pressure of maintaining political security and social stability." She added that both internal and external elements of national security were "more complicated than at any other time in history."[12] This was a startling opinion, given the past quarter-century or more of China's remarkable development.

This confused view, if commonly shared, supports a Beijing goal of diminishing Washington's dominance at sea, a possible policy discussed in the examination of China's maritime strategy (chapter 3). That strategy may involve nothing more than expanding the distance between its coast and its effective foreign naval power, based on its natural desire to improve its capability to enforce and defend its insular claims in the East and South China Seas. As expressed in China's 2015 military strategy, however, it includes the goal of exercising maritime power worldwide.[13]

The 2015 defense white paper is the first published by Beijing to focus on military strategy; it is particularly notable for addressing China's modernizing navy, with an emphasis on global responsibilities for securing the country's worldwide economic interests, particularly energy resources. The defense white paper is composed of six sections:

I.   The national security situation, with "the primary security" coming "from the ocean";
II. Missions and strategic tasks of China's armed forces, with a focus on safeguarding "overseas investment interests," protecting "the lives and property of Chinese living abroad," and ensuring "the resource supplies of Chinese companies and expansion of their product markets";
III. Strategic guideline of active defense, with a "transformation" of maritime strategy from "offshore waters defense" to one including "open seas protection," and "strategic [nuclear and conventional] deterrence and counterattack";
IV. Building and development of China's armed forces, with "the focus of winning informationalized local wars";
V.   Preparation for military struggle, in which the usual Chinese words about only fighting in defense are seriously qualified by the concept of active defense, with the navy becoming a "maritime power" in "every corner of the globe"; and
VI. Military and security cooperation.[14]

The May 2015 strategy features a near-nefarious view of the United States. There is no doubt about who Beijing means in the strategy white paper when it criticizes "some states" while more directly blaming the United States for inciting China's sovereignty disputants in the East and South China Seas. The United States' "provocative military activities taking place at a very high frequency" are criticized, as is U.S. interference with Chinese "normal military activities."[15]

In sum, China's 2015 military strategy assumes a worldview that is curiously bifurcated, with both a beneficent international situation weakened by specific threats. The CCP Politburo highlighted this latter view earlier in the year. The Politburo said that "currently international developments are turbulent and volatile and our country is undergoing profound economic and social changes. . . . Social conflicts are frequent and overlapping, and security risks and challenges, both foreseeable and hard to anticipate, are unprecedented. . . . There must be constant strengthening of a sense of peril. . . . [The military must] strive to create high-quality, professional national security forces."[16] The question of which of these views prevails obviously is key to gaining an understanding of national security policy formulation in Beijing. The likely answer is that both factor into Chinese policymaking on domestic and foreign fronts. This in turn raises the issue of the Chinese view of national security policies—they are viewed as far more united than divided between domestic and foreign issues.

A final element in Beijing's view of the United States is the classic Chinese view that before the early nineteenth century China was the central country in Asia, if not in the world. Many facts support that view, but it seems to overlook the development of the Westphalian order, imposed globally by the West.[17] That order remains in effect for the most part, despite U.S. advocates of the "responsibility to protect," which has contributed to a quarter-century of continuous and, for the most part, profitless U.S. military interventions in the Middle East.[18]

Beijing's goal likely is not to surpass or supplant the United States per se but rather to reestablish its country and culture as central to the region and possibly to the world. In other words, it demands respect, deference, and global influence, not domination. President Xi's October 2015 speech at the United Nations included his announcement of expanded Chinese financial and personnel support for the organization's global peacekeeping missions, a notable step in Beijing's assumption of major power responsibilities.[19] This book addresses how China's current triple-headed drive for a modern navy, energy security, and an effective foreign policy supports that goal.

That drive will have to continue dealing with the strong U.S. presence in Asia. As discussed recently by the former U.S. Chief of Naval Operations, Adm. Jonathan Greenert, the United States has "been engaged for more than seventy years in the Asia-Pacific region," and this will not change. Greenert noted that "five of America's top-fifteen trading partners" and "five U.S. treaty allies—Japan, South Korea, the Philippines, Australia, and Thailand—are located in the region."[20]

Background

Securing global energy resources and deploying a modern navy are two of the key elements contributing to China's foreign policy formulation.

The ruling CCP came to power in October 1949 after a long civil war. That victory resulted essentially from the dissatisfaction of the Chinese people after nearly a half-century of chaos preceding and following the 1911 fall of the Qing Dynasty. The CCP was able to impose order and institute immediate improvement to the daily economic and social life of much of China's population.

The party's continued legitimacy depends on its ability to continue ensuring order and societal improvements. Mao Zedong's successor, Deng Xiaoping, initiated an economic revolution in China in the early 1980s that embraced a form of capitalism within the CCP's reach, often called "socialism with Chinese characteristics," as mentioned earlier.

China since has risen to become the world's second-largest economy, built on an unspoken covenant between the CCP government and the populace: the former enhances opportunities for Chinese citizens to achieve an ever-improving standard of living; in return, the people leave governing to the party. This understanding appears to be effective.

An ensured secure supply of energy is a primary ingredient in maintaining China's remarkable economic growth and prosperity. Imported petroleum products form an increasing share of that supply. These imports come largely from Southwest Asia, the Middle East, and sub-Saharan Africa. All of them depend on maritime transportation over long sea lines of communication (SLOC). In view of this maritime dependence, Beijing has been building a modern navy, whose mission it is, among other things, to safeguard the SLOCs on which the nation depends for energy imports.

Hence, the need constantly to acquire new energy sources and the need for a navy able to safeguard that energy's transport to China form two important elements underlying China's foreign policies. Those policies of course involve other nations, ranging from the United States to many of the world's oil-producing countries.

Few if any of the earth's continental spaces are either unexplored or not included in recognized national polities. The globe's vast maritime expanses fall into a very different category. They are for the most part by definition and treaty categorized as the "maritime commons" or "high seas," or "international waters." However they are named, they are areas without commonly or legally acknowledged ownership or national sovereignty.

That state of affairs subsumes the absolute dependence on the seas for national and international economic viability, a fact tempting to the more powerful nations concerned about ensuring that reliance is not imposed upon. The United States, Japan, India, and China are leaders in both dependence and concerns about maintaining the accessibility and security of the maritime commons.

Those concerns were for a century or more ensured by the so-called Pax Britannica imposed by Great Britain's Royal Navy during the 1815–1914 period, a role fulfilled by the U.S. Navy since World War II, three-quarters of a century ago. China now is challenging that "Pax Americana," albeit perhaps incidentally rather than by design. That is evidenced to a degree by China's development of a modern navy, capable of conducting assured operations on twenty-first-century oceans. However, that navy currently is being built and deployed at a moderate pace, with specifically prioritized strategic situations clearly in mind—Taiwan, the "three seas" (Yellow, East China, and South China Seas) that form the western Pacific littoral, and the SLOCs reaching across the Indian Ocean to the energy-rich regions of the Middle East.

The other side of the coin of China's emerging, potentially dominant, global maritime presence is its merchant fleet, from graving dock to far-flung commercial routes. Paul Kennedy and Alfred Thayer Mahan wrote a century apart, but both recognized that global maritime powers relied for their vital economic strength on sea power, both naval and commercial.[21] Measuring the importance of global SLOCs in the twenty-first century often focuses on transporting energy resources, but these are just one part of the overwhelming dependence on all international economic interactions, especially in China's case.

This vital seaborne trade is measurable and accessible; in other words, vulnerable, since 80 percent or more of maritime traffic transits a relatively few geographic choke points. These include the Bab-el-Mandeb, the passage from the Indian Ocean to the Red Sea; the Strait of Hormuz, which is the entrance to the Persian Gulf; the Cape of Good Hope; the Malacca and Singapore Straits, linking the Indian Ocean and the South China Sea; the Panama Canal, connecting the Pacific and Atlantic Oceans; the Suez Canal, between the Mediterranean and Red Seas; and the Mediterranean's western outlet, the Strait of Gibraltar. Perhaps less important in terms of transit loading but not in terms of national and regional reliance are the Turkish Straits / Bosphorus at the Mediterranean's eastern end; the English Channel; the Northern Sea Route to Baltic waters; the potentially open Northwest Passage, as climate change continues causing the retreat of arctic ice; and the western Pacific seas already mentioned, plus the seas of Japan and Okhotsk.

The vital role filled by maritime cables is an area of maritime dependence seldom noted by analysts; they warrant notice since the cables carry so much of international communications. An unwelcome example of maritime cables' importance came in 2011, when the massive Fukushima earthquake in Japan caused several seabed landslides, interfering with the operation of nearby cables. Similarly, a 2006 earthquake in Taiwan severely damaged communications cable linking Taiwan, Hong Kong, and many areas of coastal China.[22]

Seaborne commerce rests on the ships that transport it, of course, but these in turn depend on the shore-based infrastructure of dockyards, cargo ports, personnel training and employment facilities, and governmental regulation and safeguarding. China is among the world leaders in the national registration of merchant ships.

China has a long history as a maritime power. Its best-known operations were the early fifteenth-century voyages of Zheng He, a Muslim eunuch who led fleets of large ships as far as Africa and the Persian Gulf. Although his fleets followed trading routes already frequently used, these were not primarily commercial voyages; rather, the renowned admiral conducted voyages that combined exploration with—despite the revisionist claims of current Chinese apologists—demonstration of Ming dynasty China's military power. Hence, the well-armed expeditions included large contingents of soldiers that impressed and intimidated at every port of call as well as intervened in political contests in Southeast Asia and sought to suppress piracy.

Despite these and other notable periods of great maritime power, China has historically been a continental power, with land forces typically defending against threats from the northern and western reaches of Asia. However,

Chinese leadership's primary concerns are focused daily on the nation's domestic priorities and problems. The overwhelmingly number one goal is maintaining the CCP in power, but that in turn means simply keeping the Chinese people satisfied with their current economic and social situation and, even more important, confident that they have the potential to improve those conditions.

The party's legitimacy and durability are of particular concern to China's leadership, a concern possibly intensified since Xi Jinping became the country's leader in 2012. Concerns about corruption by CCP officials has long been recognized as a source of popular discontent with the party; by the end of 2014, more than 100,000 officials reportedly had been punished for corruption as a result of Xi's ongoing campaign.[23]

Another important focus under Xi has been the increasingly loud campaign to avoid infiltration of "Western values" into China's education system and culture. This has been as significant as the concern about corruption linked to monetary gain. Minister of Education Yuan Guiren told an education conference in January 2015, "Young teachers and students are key targets of infiltration by enemy forces. . . . We must, by no means, allow into our classrooms material that propagates Western values."[24] This twenty-first-century campaign echoes the mid-nineteenth-century campaign by prominent Chinese reformers who coined the slogan "Western science, Chinese culture"; those reform movements did not succeed.[25]

Hence, the question of how China's officials are going to seal their nation from "Western values" is both intriguing and disturbing. One obvious avenue is to ensure that society is ruled not by the "rule of law" but by "rule by the Party." The political and economic implications are huge if China hopes to continue modernizing and increasing its global power status.

These and similar steps reflect the Chinese leadership's likely problem with maintaining its population's continued faith in the ability of the CCP to rule: maintaining economic growth and sustaining optimism. China has scored remarkable economic growth over the past three decades or more, measured in double-digit GDP annual increases. The announced 2014 GDP growth of approximately 7 percent is still impressive but a cause of concern to Beijing, which has instituted several reforms to encourage continued economic expansion.[26] Several problems dog the flourishing economy, including a housing "bubble" and an unpredictable stock market.

These modernization efforts almost certainly will conflict with the concomitant drive to prevent or at least control the influence of Western "values" on Chinese policy. One 2014 government announcement of grants for "social-science research," for instance, included seven of the top ten projects "dedicated to analyzing Xi's speeches," rather than some more constructive topics.[27] A final concern in Beijing—one that directly affects and links economic growth, energy security, and political stability—is the gross air, water, and ground pollution afflicting China.

The international economic arena, where China already wields major influence, offers one venue for replacing Western influence. The October 2014 establishment of the Asian Infrastructure Investment Bank (AIIB) in Beijing seems an obvious step to challenge, if not replace, the Western-organized international financial framework that emerged from the 1944 Bretton Woods conference. The United States and its allies have dominated this construct, based on the World Bank, International Monetary Fund, and eventually the Asian Development Bank.

The AIIB may have originated in China's desire to provide an Asian-based alternative, but it has attracted members from around the world, more than fifty as of October 2015. The United States apparently views the AIIB as a threat to the world economy it has long dominated, but Washington has been unable to halt or even slow the AIIB's development, a sign of Beijing's increasing importance in that economy.[28]

The AIIB is just one of a series of potentially significant moves to provide China with increased roles in the international economic system. Other steps include the much-touted "new silk road" and the "maritime silk road," more formally titled the "21st Century Maritime Silk Route Economic Belt." Collectively, these two avenues for Chinese geoeconomic and geopolitical influence are called "one belt, one road."

Xi Jinping announced the establishment of these initiatives in October 2013, including a US$40 billion fund for investing in the countries lying along the "roads."[29] What is most significant about Xi's determination to redefine the international economic paradigm through the AIIB and to focus on China's economic expansion to the west is that it represents Beijing's determination to act as a global rule maker, not merely accepting rules established by the United States and its allies.[30]

An even more recent addition to this initiative has been Beijing's announcement of a US$46 billion investment fund to establish an "economic corridor" with Pakistan.[31] These efforts to China's west strive for economic gain but are inherently political in nature; they represent Beijing's assumption that its efforts will not suffer from the political unrest lying at or near the surface of many of the Central Asian nations that form the "road," and they represent stakes in the unspoken but very real contest with Moscow for garnering economic benefits and political control in that region.[32]

These aspects are examined in later chapters as we survey economic conditions in China, the future improvement of which depends in turn on the government's ability to maintain the security of the energy sector.

A Maritime Power

Asia's inherently maritime environment retains the characteristics addressed by the Western naval theorists of the late nineteenth century. At the same time, this environment is subject to the rapidly changing technology of the twenty-first century, a phenomenon pursued by all Asian nations to the degree permitted by their resources and possible participation in maritime disputes. For instance, the number of Asian navies with significant submarine flotillas continues to grow. The United States, Russia, Japan, China, and India have been joined by North Korea, South Korea, Indonesia, Vietnam, Singapore, Malaysia, and Pakistan with submarine forces of note.

Additionally, the Asian maritime picture continues to be affected by the enormous political and social developments that followed, first, the end of the Cold War in 1990 and, second, the changes in the conduct of international relations following the events of 11 September 2001 (9/11) and the subsequent "war on terrorism" declared by Washington.

These changes are characterized by complexity and ambiguity in the current security environment. The SLOCs remain a focal point of maritime security concerns, "transporting 90 percent of intercontinental trade." These vital sea routes contribute to preserving peace, enhancing international security and stability, and feeding billions of people. SLOCs contribute significantly to generating economic growth and prosperity, securing the energy supply and preserving coastal livelihoods.[33] However, disputed SLOCs in the early twenty-first century may lead to conflicts between regional nations; they also are threatened by sovereignty disputes, terrorism, and international crime, usually falling under the rubric of "piracy." This last problem is one of the world's oldest professions and shows no sign of elimination, especially in Southeast Asian waters.[34]

These threat categories are addressed in the following chapters. Military threats to the Asian SLOCs are relatively slight. None of the regional states currently hold any apparent strategic objectives that would involve interdicting SLOCs, although China might do so, at least for a short period of time, should active military conflict develop over Taiwan's status. Similarly, the conflicting claims to sovereignty over the East and South China Seas land features could lead to a situation involving opposing military forces.

Finally, unintended escalation between two or more opposing naval and air force units might lead to an armed clash. This possibility gained some recent prominence when Beijing declared an air defense identification zone (ADIZ) over most of the East China Sea. Declaring an ADIZ was not in itself provocative, but the manner in which Beijing announced the zone and the lack of clarity in its requirements caused unnecessary international perturbation.[35]

The 2015 defense white paper also addressed other, essentially nonmilitary threats to the SLOCs; unsurprisingly, to a degree they are already happening. Natural disasters, international crime, and conflicting sovereignty claims are all facts of international maritime life. Examples include the 2004 tsunami in South and Southeast Asia; the incidents of maritime crime that characterize the waters in proximity to the Malacca and Singapore Straits, as well in the Bay of Bengal, western Arabian Sea, and Gulf of Aden; and the territorial claims held by the different states bordering on the South China Sea. It must also be noted, however, that most of these situations are currently being dealt with peacefully, on a multilateral basis.

While potential for major combat operations at sea remains, such potential has been slight since the end of the Cold War. Terrorism has been one form of conflict that increased the presence of "nonmilitary" and multinational threats in the maritime domain and present challenges difficult for maritime nations to counter. They present situations in which threats and adversaries are neither clearly defined nor perhaps of even readily identifiable origin. Additionally, defeating these threats usually requires more than purely military instruments and processes—hence Beijing's emphasis on improving the capabilities of its coast guard, maritime militia, and civilian assets. Similarly, defeat may well not be satisfactory: resolving causative bases will be necessary to ensure lasting peace at sea.

As is explored in chapter 2, Chinese president Xi Jinping has emphasized the need to deal with this variety of issues as part of strengthening the nation's defenses on land and sea, lest "the history of humiliation" be repeated.[36] Much discussion has been generated by Xi's sanctification of the idea of a "Chinese Dream," an ill-defined phrase that may significantly influence Beijing's policymaking. Xi has spoken of some tenets of his "dream," including the necessity of "long-term unity" to China's continued economic development, the "fundamental" importance of maintaining the CCP in power, ensurance that religious practice be "independent of foreign influence," and, in the realm of foreign concerns, the importance of "dealing well with affairs related to Taiwan, Hong Kong, Macao and overseas Chinese."[37]

Xi has directly tasked the PLA with a central role to play in the realization of the "China Dream":

> [It] is necessary to deeply understand the important status and role of national defense and armed forces building in the fulfillment of the China Dream, fully and clearly realize the opportunity and the challenges that our country's security and development [are] facing, keep a stronger sense of mission and responsibility for more quickly pushing forward the process of national defense and military modernization, provide strong power guarantee for the fulfillment of the China Dream by going down-to-earth work, stepping up efforts, and quickening progress. . . . the PLA must provide a powerful guarantee for realizing the Chinese dream, . . . [by opposing] hegemonism and power politics [and promoting] global peace and stability. . . . The China dream [is] a grand blueprint for armed forces building under the new historical conditions.[38]

Xi directly tasked the PLA with "being able to fight and win"—a common exhortation under Xi Jinping's regime—and with a "guarantee that the forces can take action instantly at the first call and are able to fight and win battles for sure."[39]

China naturally tries to use both "soft" and "hard" tools of statecraft to secure its national goals. This includes the "hard" sea power of the PLAN and other maritime security forces, recently demonstrated in the South China Sea in disputes with Vietnam and the Philippines, and "soft" power, comprising trade, maritime resources exploitation, humanitarian aid from the sea, fisheries conservation, and even tourism—all activities based on China's huge economic power in Asia.

Various SLOCs cross the Indian Ocean, but common sea lines pass through the One and a Half Degree, Six Degree, or the Nine Degree Channels, which take their names from the lines of latitude that they roughly follow and offer different passages between the Indian subcontinent and Indian Ocean archipelagoes. These and several other such channels in the vast Indian Ocean are not as vulnerable as either Bab-el-Mandeb or Hormuz as navigational chokepoints, and they pale in significance next to the primary access and egress to the eastern Indian Ocean at the Straits of Malacca and Singapore.

This book also examines the role of energy security in the formulation and execution of China's maritime strategy. Discussion focuses on three primary factors: first, the growth and modernization of the PLAN; second, Beijing's views of energy security; and, third, the effect of those factors on the interests of other nations. The issue of China's increasing demand and need for energy resources, much of which lie overseas, drives a perceived need for a naval capability to safeguard the SLOCs over which imported energy resources must flow.

Military Missions Other Than War

Terrorists are generally committed to and benefit from political instability in individual nations and even throughout a region, such as Southeast Asia. Such instability may be the result of large-scale environmental disasters; hence, intentionally causing such events can have far-reaching, negative effects on economic health and political stability, especially in a region already suffering from political unrest, economic deprivation, or religious conflict.

Additionally, recent and increasing competition for declining maritime resources has resulted in a number of violent incidents. These have occurred between nations, as in the East China Sea (China and Japan), and between national agents, such as those frequently occurring among the fishermen of almost all East Asian states. These incidents underscore the high stakes in diminishing resources such as fish stocks and increasingly valued resources such as petroleum.

China's ability to find, harvest, process, and distribute fish is an extremely important maritime interest. Fisheries production is estimated to provide between 13.8 and 16.5 percent of the Chinese population's daily protein requirements. More specifically, China's share of world fisheries production grew from 7 percent in 1961 to 34 percent in 2009, a trend that is continuing.[40]

Fisheries are a particularly fragile resource and a matter of vital importance to all the nations of East Asia, providing the single most important source of protein to the populations of the region. Overfishing is a relatively recent phenomenon in the East and South China Seas. A Chinese study claims that the total catch in the latter sea increased from 425,000 tons in 1955 to 3.34 million tons in 1999, while the total for the East and South China Seas was a stunning 12.2 million tons. Correspondingly, the "fish resources density" as of 1999 may have dropped to approximately one-quarter of its 1949 density.[41] A more recent study, completed in 2006, forecasts doom for the entire fisheries industry, warning, "If fishing around the world continues at its present pace, more and more species will vanish, marine ecosystems will unravel and there will be 'global collapse' of all species currently fished, possibly as soon as mid-century, fisheries experts and ecologists are predicting."[42]

Similarly, terrorists might cause deliberate, massive pollution of the oceans to damage ecosystems and undermine the national and economic security of the nations that depend on them. In the words of one scientist, the combination of sovereignty and ecological problems mean that the "whole ecological system in the areas is at the brink of collapse."[43]

Organization of the Book

This book is organized into seven chapters as well as the introduction and conclusion. Chapter 1 discusses the maritime geography with which Beijing is most concerned, with a focus on the Yellow, East China, and South China Seas. The broader Pacific and Indian Oceans supplement these regional seas in Beijing's concern. China's status as a global economic power further requires its attention to maritime issues worldwide.

Chapter 2 addresses China's maritime forces, including the PLAN, the coast guard (CCG) and associated "white hull" units, and its merchant marine and supporting shoreside infrastructure. Ship classes and numbers are noted, but the chapter's focus is on the capabilities China's maritime forces provide to execute national security missions and to support economic interests. These capabilities relate to securing maritime claims, both insular and seabed, as well as to guarding the SLOCs on which China is dependent. This also means maintaining the efficiency and reliability of the entire maritime transportation network.

The importance of maritime issues in China's energy and foreign policy organizations has for the first time resulted in a coherent maritime strategy being delineated by Beijing in 2015. That strategy is discussed in chapter 3. This discussion focuses on the interactions among, first, China's economic concerns and view of the importance of regional and global SLOCs and, second, the insular sovereignty disputes of central concern to Beijing.

Chapter 4 surveys China's economy, with a focus on the linkages with the nation's stake in the maritime element. It necessarily views the relationship from the national security perspective: the leadership's reliance on a growing economy to support the continued legitimacy of the CCP governance.

Chapter 5 discusses China's energy situation from a macro perspective. Indigenous supplies are surveyed and imports considered in detail. Beijing's attempts to rationalize the nation's energy requirements and resources lead off the chapter, while its dependence on the maritime importation of energy supplies form the core of this discussion. China's extensive pipeline infrastructure, both domestic and foreign in origin, is also addressed.

Chapters 6 and 7 pose a particularly challenging task as they attempt to describe the ins and outs—literally—of China's foreign policy process. Delineating and then describing any nation's policymaking process is difficult, given the unquantifiable role of policymaker personalities, but it is especially difficult with China, given the opaqueness and "stove-piping" of that nation's governmental processes. Nonetheless, reviewing the formal organization of China's State Council and Ministry of Foreign Affairs and the CCP's Politburo Standing Committee provide interesting indicators. A discrete number of foreign policy decisions made in Beijing concerning maritime issues are examined to flesh out these indicators.

Other governmental elements also influence foreign policy formulation and perhaps even more how that policy is implemented. The PLA, Ministry of National Defense, and other ministries have an input, as do the various "small working groups" that have been instituted to address specific issues such as Taiwan's status. The small working groups reflect Beijing's most serious foreign policy concerns; one category is the standard national concerns of homeland defense, counterterrorism, efforts against illegal drugs and other forms of international crime, and protection of citizens abroad.

China experienced a pivotal decade in the 1990s in terms of economic growth, maritime claims, and naval modernization. These all contributed to a maturing foreign policy as China began seizing upon its new position as a global power. During and since that decade, Beijing has repeatedly stated and followed, in practice, a strong preference for a bilateral rather than a multilateral approach to dealing with foreign policy issues. These issues have been led by the maritime and insular disputes to which China is a party, notably those in the East and South China Seas. Chapter 7 focuses on these disputes and Beijing's bilateral and multilateral approaches during the past decade or to their resolution.

The conclusion sums up the book's discussion of China's search for energy, its naval modernization, and its foreign policy formulation and implementation. The focus on the interaction among these three elements of domestic governance and international relations provides useful information about how China is governed, how foreign policy originates and is implemented, and how militaristic that policy may become in the future as Beijing seeks to maintain its economic growth and ensure its energy security.

A key question in the conclusion concerns China's reputed "assertiveness" in its foreign policy implementation since approximately 2009, particularly with respect to its insular claims in the East and South China Seas. Is this the pattern for the foreseeable future, or has it reflected Beijing's oft-stated belief that it is simply reacting to provocation by the other claimants?

Harvard professor Alastair Iain Johnston has concluded that claims of a new Chinese assertiveness are based on "problematic analysis" but that "the media-blogosphere interaction" may create a perception that is as important as "reality" in future security dilemmas involving China. Professor Aaron Friedberg of Princeton University concludes that Beijing has been assertive but has decided to "adjust the mix of and inducements" as the Chinese "pursue their long-term strategic objectives."[44]

The scope of Beijing's priorities is ensconced in the recently published national security law, described as "sweeping," addressing as it does "practically any aspect of social or economic life." The new law apparently follows

President Xi's definition of national security as "comprehensive, encompassing politics, the military, the economy, technology, the environment and culture." The draft law addresses the importance of ensuring that the political regime, sovereignty, national unification, territorial integrity, people's welfare and the "sustainable and healthy development" of the economy, society and other "major national interests" are "relatively free from danger and not under internal and external threats."[45]

What this means for future Chinese foreign policy choices as naval modernization and energy security concerns enable different courses of action lies at the center of this book's conclusions.

Chapter One

CHINA'S MARITIME WORLD

Although "Middle Kingdom" and "Central Kingdom" are not geographic terms, their common use in describing China makes them an interesting point of discussion. The term historically is best interpreted simply as meaning that China considers itself to be at the center of the world; however, it has acquired a sense of global superiority as well. One description of the culture more than the country was the "only civilization under heaven."[1] This description may well be a factor in the current Chinese self-image that influences the nation's foreign policies.

The "Indo-Pacific" defines the Western Pacific and Indian Oceans as a continuous maritime commons. This vast sweep of oceans, from the Aleutian Islands to the Persian Gulf, occupies half the globe and hosts an economy much larger than either that of the United States or of Europe. It accounts for approximately one-half of the world's manufacturing and is growing faster than any other major region.

The Indo-Pacific is increasingly influenced by China in economic and military capacity. In fact, China is already equipped and positioned to make any U.S. or other foreign military efforts problematic within Asian littoral waters, defined as those within two hundred to six hundred nautical miles (nm) of the coast.

Another important operational factor for China's military is that it holds interior lines of position, greatly enabling concentrating forces and focusing efforts against specific points of concern on the nation's periphery. The commander of China's navy, Admiral Wu Shengli, addressed this point in an April

21

2014 speech. "Our aim," he said, "should be to organically link up interior and exterior lines, making them mutually supportive and integrating offense and defense."[2]

This certainly affects political, social, economic, and military policy formulation for the other Asian nations. China is the region's most important country, with near-determinant geographical influence over nations anywhere in Asia—northeast, east, southeast, south, or central. Beijing cannot be ignored.

China's geographic domination of Asia means it also is a major influence on the Eurasian landmass, the largest "island" on a globe 70 percent of which is covered by water. Eurasia was a focus of Halford Mackinder, a British geographer who in 1904 wrote a seminal work in which he described the Eurasian continent as the world's "heartland" and the "pivot" of global power; the heartland was surrounded by the "maritime lands," which included the other continents and the seas.

Mackinder offered the following syllogism in 1919: "Who rules eastern Europe commands the Heartland; who rules the Heartland commands the World-Island, composed of the inter-connected continents of Asia, Europe, and Africa. Who rules the World-Island commands the world."[3] He averred that the world had evolved into a closed system, interpreting history as primarily a contest between continental and maritime powers. He further argued that the advent of rail networks (and presumably he would have included airplanes) had irrevocably shifted the strategic balance in favor of the continental nations. Nonetheless, Mackinder developed the view following the 1918–19 Paris Peace Conference that the maritime nations, chiefly Great Britain and the United States, could balance the power of the "Heartland."

Mackinder was writing in the years before and after World War I and was concerned about the threat of world domination posed by Germany and Russia (and the Soviet Union, after 1921). His views of the importance of the spread of railroads throughout Eurasia were based on their efficacy so dramatically demonstrated during World War I, particularly in the war's opening salvos, as the belligerents used rail transportation to conduct the massive mobilization process that made war almost inevitable during the summer of 1914.

Nicholas Spykman was a Dutch-born American geostrategist who followed Mackinder's line of thought but arrived at a very different conclusion.

Spykman was writing in 1942, when he speculated about power projection into and out of the Heartland. He argued that the key to controlling the world was the littoral areas of the Heartland, or what he called the "Rimland."

Whereas Mackinder assumed that land formations made for easiest access from the center, Spykman believed that the oceans offered the real strategic advantages to logistics and movement: "Who controls the Rimland rules Eurasia; who rules Eurasia controls the destinies of the world."[4] In terms of the classic maritime strategists, Mackinder was discrediting Alfred Thayer Mahan while Spykman was essentially endorsing him.

Their individual experiences and political environments no doubt influenced their different views. Mackinder had been affected by the Crimean War and the lesser wars of the second half of the nineteenth century, which were relatively localized conflicts and almost entirely continental in character. His most important work was published in 1919, while the Paris Peace Conference was still in session, and he must have considered the vast, tragic land battles of the Western Front as determinant, with the maritime campaigns of World War I as peripheral to the defeat of the Central Powers.

Spykman, however, lived from 1893 to 1943 and was too young to have experienced the wars that occurred during Mackinder's early adulthood. The American experienced the early years of World War II's global conflict. Both strategists were focused on control of the Eurasian supercontinent, home to many of the world's leading industrial and energy-consuming countries during the nineteenth and early twentieth centuries; Mackinder could be described as a Europeanist while Spykman could more accurately be described as a globalist.

Spykman was educated as a political scientist but believed geography was "the most fundamentally conditioning factor because of its relative permanence" and should be considered a prime motivator of a nation's national security strategy.[5] During the Cold War (1947–90), the United States led an anti-Communist strategy of containment against the Soviet Union; it was described by the leading American historian of that strategy as a Western attempt to use the Rimlands to control the Heartland, which was dominated by Russia and China.[6]

This Mackinder–Spykman construct may accurately be rephrased for the twenty-first century as using sea power to control land power. The Eurasian supercontinent today remains dominated by Russia and China, with India a rapidly rising force on that same gigantic landmass.

Maritime Theory

China's recent military strategy, released in May 2015, highlights "maritime military struggle and maritime PMS [preparation for military struggle]" while featuring the straightforward if historically inaccurate statement that "the traditional mentality that land outweighs sea must be abandoned, and great importance has to be attached to managing the seas and oceans and protecting maritime rights and interests." This statement may well reflect bureaucratic struggle within the PLA but ignores facts such as no major naval battle ever having been fought more than 200 nm from land, or that no seagoing force, naval or commercial, can operate without dependency on an extensive infrastructure ashore. Even more direct is the strategy's conclusion: "It is necessary for China to develop a modern maritime military force structure commensurate with its national security and development interests, safeguard its national sovereignty and maritime rights and interests, protect the security of strategic SLOCs and overseas interests, and participate in international maritime cooperation, so as to provide strategic support for building itself into a maritime power."[7]

Would either Mackinder or Spykman today consider China as a threat to dominate the great "world island" that the United States would oppose? This construct would view the United States and its allies in the Indo-Pacific as forming a modern "rimland," with the East Asian first and second island chains a primary feature. The staff of the U.S. Joint Chiefs of Staff initially defined the first island chain in the late 1940s in a study focused on delineating the boundaries of U.S. military interest and potential bases in the Pacific.[8]

Liu Huaqing, commander of the Chinese navy and later a member of the Central Military Commission, embraced and publicized the island chains in his strategic thinking during the 1980s. The first "chain" is usually described as beginning in the Kurile Islands, north of Japan, and then running south through Japan, the Ryukyu Islands, Taiwan, the Philippines, and then west through the Indonesian archipelago. The second island chain also begins in the Kuriles but, after running south through Japan, swings east to run through the Bonin Islands, the Mariana Islands, the Republic of Palau (at the western end of the Caroline Islands), and then southwest to and through the islands of Indonesia.[9]

Liu used the first two island chains as markers to establish goals for a three-phase modernization of the PLAN; his third marker was a navy able to exert global power, based on inclusion of aircraft carriers in the PLAN. Other Chinese strategists have identified a "third island chain," apparently defined by the Hawaiian Islands.[10]

The question of China aspiring to global domination cannot be answered with any finality but will be lurking throughout this book's chapters. The common element in the beliefs of the foregoing and other geopolitical theorists is that the world forms a single economic system.[11]

China has overtaken Japan as the leading maritime nation in Asia in terms of commercial ship numbers, shipbuilding capacity, and naval strength. Japan anchors the northern end of the island chains—the modern rimland surrounding the Chinese-dominated heartland—a heartland it shares with Russia and India.

China, Russia, and India are joined by the vibrant economies and formidable armed forces of the Republic of Korea (South Korea) and Japan, which mark the northern maritime end of the Pacific sweep of waters from the Arctic to the Antarctic. Japan remains one of the world's leading shipbuilders and deploys a powerful navy. All are located in the Asian heartland bordered by a maritime rimland. The Ryukyus are Japan's southernmost island group, stretching toward Taiwan. Their area of 2,200 square miles is concentrated on Okinawa, Miyako, and Ishigaki, as is the population of approximately 1,318,000. The Ryukyuan kingdom was a Chinese tributary state from 1372 to 1609, when it was seized by Japan and, in 1869, annexed by Tokyo. The Ryukyus' Japanese sovereignty has not formally been challenged by Beijing, despite this history.[12]

Further south lies Taiwan, an island approximately 245 miles north to south, 89 miles east to west, and just 105 miles off China's southeastern coast. Only twenty-two nations, all minor, recognize Taiwan as an independent state, the Republic of China. Beijing, of course, stridently insists that Taiwan is part of the People's Republic of China and is determined not to allow the "Republic of China" to gain further international status or diplomatic recognition. Reunifying Taiwan with the mainland is Beijing's number one "foreign" national security concern.

Taiwan's position under the presidency of Ma Ying-jeou, president from 2008 to 2016, was that of "no unification, no independence and no use of force." In other words, under Ma, Taipei worked simply to maintain the status quo while significantly increasing economic, social, and transportation links with the mainland.[13] Beijing has found this position acceptable during Ma's eight years in office but is very wary of the views of the president-elect, the Democratic Progressive Party's Tsai Ing-wen.

The Republic of the Philippines occupies an extensive archipelagic sweep of more than seven thousand islands extending approximately 1,150 miles, north to south, and forming the eastern border of the South China Sea. It is a primary contestant of China's for some of the land formations in the South China Sea. The Philippines is a weak military power, with a very small operational navy, but is troublesome to Beijing because Manila has brought suit in the International Tribunal for the Law of the Sea over their dispute in the South China Sea. Vietnam forms the western boundary of the South China Sea, as the Philippines forms the eastern. The two nations delineate the land boundaries exterior to China's nine-dash line and could pose a serious military challenge to the waters and land features lying within that line.[14]

The 3,300-mile long Indonesian archipelago extends from the southernmost Philippine islands to a point well west of the Malacca and Singapore Straits and forms the southern boundary of the South China Sea. Furthermore, Indonesia is the region's third-largest country, after China and India, and one of its wealthiest nations, after China, Japan, and South Korea.[15] Jakarta deploys a significant, modernizing navy and air force, acquiring submarines and fourth-generation tactical aircraft. Hence, despite not directly challenging China's territorial sovereignty claims, it is the most important nation posing a potential threat to China's strategic ambitions in Southeast Asia.

Lying north of Indonesia's western provinces, Malaysia contests other national claims to several South China Sea land features. It is also modernizing its armed forces with an emphasis on submarines and other naval combatants as well as with fourth-generation tactical aircraft. Malaysia has adopted a very nonconfrontational policy toward China's recently egregious actions in the South China Sea, to include June 2015 reports that China has been encroaching on Malaysian waters at the Luconia Shoals, which are known as Gugusan Beting Patinggi Ali, located just 84 nautical miles from the coast, but approximately 1,000 miles from the Chinese island of Hainan.[16]

The Malaysian government's refusal to publicly acknowledge instances of PLAN combatants marking as sovereign Chinese territory James Shoal, an underwater reef that never rises above the ocean surface and that lies at the southern extremity of the nine-dash line but well inside Kuala Lumpur's claimed exclusive economic zone (EEZ), indicates its reluctance to challenge Beijing's claims.[17]

Beijing thus faces a complex region rife with conflicting sovereignty claims, but one also to a significant degree subject to its huge economic weight, military force, and relatively unitary political direction. This region includes Japan and South Korea, together with the insular countries of Southeast Asia: Taiwan, the Philippines, Indonesia, Brunei, Singapore, Australia, New Zealand, and the small island states of the South and Southwest Pacific. Further afield but increasingly important to China's economic and political stature, the Indian Ocean states, including Myanmar, Bangladesh, Sri Lanka, India, and Pakistan, form an important consideration to any Chinese maritime strategy.

Modernization and the potential expansion of India's maritime presence, similar to that of China, may finally be reaching maturity. Japan is already a major sea power, while civilian and military leaders in Moscow have stated that Russia will reemerge as an Asian maritime power, but evidence of that has been slow to materialize.[18]

The Maritime Economy

Seaborne commerce dominates Asia's economic life, both in the bulk cargo now largely carried in containers and in the Southeast and Southwest Asian energy supplies so increasingly crucial to the region's economic powers. Asian SLOCs traverse a very complex geographical environment.[19] This includes many narrow transit points constraining the sea-lanes; despite the great distances involved, few areas of the Asian seas are remote from continental or insular landmasses.

Several straits provide entry and egress to the South China Sea. The Luzon Strait, lying between the northernmost large Philippine island of Luzon and Taiwan, and the Taiwan Strait serve as primary channels to and from the northern South China Sea. The San Bernardino and Surigao Straits through the Philippines are less frequented by large merchant ships but are significant.

Three primary north–south routes penetrate the Indonesian archipelago, on the southern rim of the South China Sea. The Sunda Strait is deeper than the Singapore and Malacca Straits, between Indonesia and Singapore-Malaysia, which form the primary strait to and from the southern South

China Sea. The more than 400-nm-long Malacca and Singapore Straits (commonly referred to as "Malacca") narrow to 1.5 nm near Singapore, creating one of the world's most significant navigation chokepoints.

This passage is the most important shipping lane in the world, more so than either the Suez or the Panama Canal in terms of both geopolitical significance and the number of ships and amount of tonnage that it carries. Malacca is the main ship route between the Indian and Pacific Oceans, directly linking Southwest, South, Southeast, and Northeast Asia, including India, Indonesia, Japan, Korea, and China.

The area is actively threatened by piracy and terrorism; its geopolitical importance means that it is potentially at risk in the event of major military conflict anywhere along the Asian rimland. Such narrow straits obviously increase the risk of ship collisions or groundings; as many as sixty such incidents occur annually.[20] This startling figure underlines the strait's importance with respect to security, economic, and environmental issues.

More than 79,000 transits by seagoing vessels were made through the strait in 2014, an average of 217 ships a day, carrying more than 33 percent of the world's maritime trade.[21] This includes 6 percent of the world's shipborne oil transiting global chokepoints, approximately 15.2 million barrels daily in 2013, an amount that will increase in direct proportion to increasing Asian energy consumption.[22]

Indian Ocean

The Malacca Strait empties to the west into the Andaman Sea, bounded by Thailand and Malaysia to the east and Burma to the north. It is guarded by the Andaman and the Nicobar Islands, two small Indian archipelagos that provide New Delhi with naval outposts close to the Malacca Strait.

The Andaman Sea serves as entry to the easternmost of the two great basins into which the northern Indian Ocean is divided. The first is the Bay of Bengal, lying north and west of the Andaman Sea and framed by India to the west, Bangladesh to the north, and Burma to the east. This is a tragic ocean basin, heavily trafficked by small merchant and fishing vessels that all too often fall victim to the massive cyclones that devastate the bay.

The Indian Ocean's other ocean basin is the North Arabian Sea, which lies to the west of the subcontinent. This sea leads to the Persian Gulf through the Strait of Hormuz and to the Red Sea (and through the Suez Canal to the Mediterranean) through the Bab-el-Mandeb Strait.

United Nations Convention on the Law of the Sea

The United Nations Convention on the Law of the Sea (UNCLOS) is an effort by most of the world's nations to rationalize and secure the maritime commons. It was opened for signing in 1982, after more than a decade of international negotiation, and came into force in 1994. The treaty has been signed and ratified by 162 nations.[23] The UNCLOS aims to further define the global commons and overcome obsolete definitions of national maritime sovereignty, particularly with respect to resource ownership. It accomplished this to a degree, primarily with establishment of the EEZ, but also has caused significant confusion and disputes. One important negative result of international acceptance of the UNCLOS regime is its impact on the concept of the oceans as "the common property of all," a concept implied in the traditional phrases "high seas" and "international waters." Hugo Grotius, an early seventeenth-century Dutch philosopher often described as the father of international law, probably originated the concept of the world's maritime areas as "a wide common."[24]

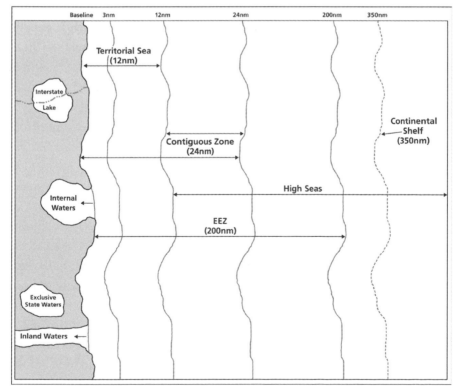

MAP 2. UNCLOS Zones

The treaty is integral to China's definition of its sovereignty. Beijing signed the UNCLOS and the National People's Congress ratified it in 1996 but stipulated some "declarations" (exceptions) when it ratified and then made another declaration in 2006. China now is attempting to change several of the treaty's meanings. Not only does the UNCLOS define areas of maritime interest and sovereignty, it also suggests conflict resolution venues.[25]

In terms of China's maritime strategy, the "declarations" published by Beijing when it ratified the UNCLOS and thereafter (as permitted by the treaty's Article 298) are more important than the treaty itself. Many nations issued such declarations, but China's are particularly relevant to our discussion. As mentioned earlier, four declarations accompanied China's initial adherence to the UNCLOS treaty on 7 June 1996 and another was made twenty years later on 25 August 2006.

The first declaration states that, in accordance with the UNCLOS, the PRC shall "enjoy sovereign rights and jurisdiction over an exclusive economic zone of 200 nautical miles and the continental shelf." This statement follows the UNCLOS delineation of the EEZ that a nation may claim but is counter to the UNCLOS definition of the rights that may be claimed for the EEZ. The UNCLOS, Article 2, states, "The sovereignty of a coastal State extends, beyond its land territory and internal waters and, in the case of an archipelagic State, its archipelagic waters, to an adjacent belt of sea, described as the territorial sea. This sovereignty extends to the air space over the territorial sea as well as to its bed and subsoil." The limits of the territorial sea are then defined in Article 3 as "up to a limit not exceeding 12 nautical miles, measured from baselines determined in accordance with this Convention," not the 200 nm that describes an EEZ, which the UNCLOS defines as an area "adjacent to the territorial sea [that] shall not extend beyond 200 nautical miles from the baselines from which the breadth of the territorial sea is measured."

Within this area, the coastal state possesses "sovereign rights for the purpose of exploring and exploiting, conserving and managing the natural resources, whether living or non-living, of the waters superjacent to the seabed and of the seabed and its subsoil, and with regard to other activities for the economic exploitation and exploration of the zone, such as the production of energy from the water, currents and winds." "Jurisdiction" in the EEZ is provided for "the establishment and use of artificial islands, installations and structures; marine scientific research, [and for] the protection and preservation of the marine environment."

Hence, the UNCLOS defines rights in the EEZ that are not "sovereign" to the same degree as defined for the territorial sea, which means that Beijing's first declaration upon signing the UNCLOS is problematic at best. Indeed, Article 310 of the Convention allows states and entities to make declarations or statements regarding this article's application at the time of signing, ratifying, or acceding to the Convention that do not purport to exclude or modify the legal effect of the provisions of the Convention—as does China's declaration.[26]

China's second statement when it signed the treaty was that, in case of conflicting claims, it would "effect, through consultations, the delimitation of the boundary of the maritime jurisdiction with the States with coasts opposite or adjacent to China respectively on the basis of international law and in accordance with the principle of equitability."[27] In other words, Beijing brazenly stated that it would deal bilaterally with jurisdictional claims, without recourse to international adjudication, which is counter to the treaty's spirit and intent. In practice, China is bullying and intimidating rather than negotiating.

Third, China stated that it "reaffirms its sovereignty over all its archipelagos and islands as listed in the [25 February 1992] Law of the PRC on the Territorial Sea and the Contiguous Zone."[28] This emphasized Beijing's claims to several disputed insular land features, notably the Diaoyu Islands in the East China Sea and in the South China Sea the Paracel and Spratly Islands, and the Pratas Islands and Macclesfield Bank features. This declaration restates Beijing's long-standing but highly controversial territorial claims to these land features. A second relevant statute is the 1998 Law of the PRC on the Exclusive Economic Zone and the Continental Shelf, which asserts a blanket EEZ claim from all Chinese territory. These two laws imply that China's EEZ includes nearly the entire South China Sea within Beijing's notorious nine-dash line.[29]

China's fourth statement when ratifying the treaty was to reaffirm "that the UNCLOS concerning innocent passage through the territorial sea shall not prejudice the right of a coastal State to request, in accordance with its laws and regulations, a foreign State to obtain advance approval from or give prior notification to the coastal State for the passage of its warships through the territorial sea of the coastal State."[30] This reflects Beijing's belief that its national laws will prevail over the stipulations of the UNCLOS treaty, a belief that appears even to the layman to be illogical and that is opposed by most international legal experts.

China's fifth declaration is linked to its second; it "does not accept any of the procedures provided for in Section 2 of Part XV of the Convention with respect to all the categories of disputes referred to in paragraph 1 (a) (b) and (c) of Article 298 of the Convention."[31] This supplements China's earlier declaration of intent to deal bilaterally with other nations in case of conflicting claims and underlies China's usual reaction to calls for multilateral resolution of sovereignty disputes, particularly in the South China Sea, where it consistently reacts negatively to discussion of possible multilateral resolution by the Association of Southeast Asian Nations (ASEAN). This recently occurred in April 2015, when Beijing said it was "extremely concerned" about ASEAN member nations' "worry about land reclamation and navigational freedom in the disputed South China Sea."[32]

Most basic to China's questionable interpretations of the UNCLOS provisions is its drawing excessive straight baselines, which form the originating point for measuring a nation's claimed territorial sea, contiguous zone, EEZ, and continental shelf limits. These baselines violate the UNCLOS, Part II, Section 2, Article 7, and constitute excessive claims by Beijing. Only archipelagic states, such as Indonesia and the Philippines, are entitled to draw such baselines; as a continental state, China is not so entitled. Nonetheless, Beijing in 1996 published straight baselines along its coast and the Paracel Islands, in the South China Sea.[33]

Rather, these interpretations are an example of Chinese "lawfare," the deliberate distortion and misuse of the law to justify a national position that violates international law and norms. The United States has also objected to similar excessive straight baseline claims by Vietnam and others.[34] In fact, approximately 25 of the 165 nations that signed the UNCLOS agree with China's citing domestic law as the basis for their right to control foreign military activities in their EEZ.[35]

The East and South China Seas contain a wide variety of land types that are best described as land features since they range from formations that remain beneath the water's surface at even low tide, to rocks, to low-tide elevations (LTE), to rocks that remain above the water's surface at even high tide, to islands capable of sustaining human life. Each of these land features is addressed in the UNCLOS, although not always with clarity. Even the precise geographical location of some land features remains uncertain, given relatively inconsistent geophysical charting and ongoing research in the areas.[36]

The UNCLOS attempts to categorize the various land features. Most obvious is an "island," defined in Article 121 of the treaty as "a naturally formed area of land above water at high tide." Although not specified in the UNCLOS, the definition of a "rock," quoted below, implies that an island is capable of sustaining human habitation or "economic life." That is hardly an unambiguous definition, however, given rapidly advancing desalinization technology, airlift, and modern communications capabilities. An island is entitled to the full range of UNCLOS-designated zones, including a 12-nm territorial sea, 24-nm contiguous zone, 200-nm EEZ, and a (maximum) 350-nm continental shelf. Connected to this description is Article 60(8) of the UNCLOS, which stipulates, "Artificial islands are entitled to no maritime zones, except for a 500 meter safety zone."

The next land feature addressed in the UNCLOS, Article 121, is a rock, "which cannot sustain human habitation or economic life of their own [and] shall have no exclusive economic zone or continental shelf." A rock is entitled only to a 12-nm territorial sea. The same definition uncertainty applies to a rock as it does to an island.

An LTE is even less entitled than a rock. An LTE is defined in Article 13 of the UNCLOS as "a naturally formed area of land which is surrounded by and above water at low tide but submerged at high tide. . . . [But] it may be used as the baseline for measuring the breadth of the territorial sea" if it lies within 12 nm from the mainland or an island. In other words, an LTE is not entitled to any UNCLOS-defined area but may serve as a point in a coastal baseline. The UNCLOS does not, for instance, clarify the possibility of physically linking an LTE to another LTE or to a recognized rock or island.

UNCLOS definitions are important. A state with sovereignty over an island enjoys 12-nm territorial waters around it and has the right to exploit living and nonliving resources within the island's EEZ. However, a state with sovereignty over an LTE or artificial island has no such rights.[37] Even if an artificial structure is built on an LTE, the state can claim no more than a five-hundred-meter-wide safety zone; no sovereignty over water or airspace beyond this is permitted. Even more disputable from the viewpoint of claiming sovereignty are permanently submerged features.

Such reefs as James Shoal (Zeng Anjiao in Chinese), located in the southern South China Sea, are submerged even at low tide, meaning they are classified by the UNCLOS as part of the seabed; yet China has traditionally claimed James Shoal as its sovereign territory, declaring in early 2013 and again in early 2014 that the permanently submerged feature, approximately 70 feet below the ocean's surface and 1,100 nm from China but 65 nm from Malaysia's coast—well within the latter's claimed EEZ—is the "southernmost point of [China's] territory."[38] Beijing has employed the navy to emphasize its claim to this submerged feature, which has no rights under the UNCLOS. In March 2013 an amphibious task group stopped near the shoal and mustered its crews on deck to "pledge to defend the South China Sea, maintain national sovereignty and strive towards the dream of a strong China."[39]

Articles 15, 74, and 83 of the UNCLOS provide for delineating the territorial sea, EEZ, and continental shelf zones at less than maximum distances, in view of the dictates of geography. The South China Sea is an example where various states are less than 700 or even 400 nm apart, thus preventing realization of full national continental shelf and EEZ claims.

Disputes over definition of land features have been subject to several court cases, but no definitive glossary of terms has emerged. Indeed, Beijing's fifth declaration, issued in 2006 following ratification of the UNCLOS, stated that it "does not accept any of the [dispute resolution] procedures provided for in Section 2 of Part XV of the Convention with respect to all the categories of disputes referred to in paragraph 1 (a) (b) and (c) of Article 298 of the Convention." China has instead cited domestic law and historic rights as a basis for its sovereignty claims, in addition to legal precedent.[40]

Many nations expressed declarations when signing the UNCLOS, and some agreed in large part with some of those put forth by Beijing. Brazil, for example, stated, "The Brazilian Government understands that the provisions of the Convention do not authorize other States to carry out military exercises or maneuvers, in particular those involving the use of weapons or explosives, in the exclusive economic zone without the consent of the coastal State." New Delhi similarly argued, "The Government of the Republic of India understands that the provisions of the Convention do not authorize other States to carry out in the exclusive economic zone and on the continental shelf military exercises or maneuvers, in particular those involving the use of weapons or explosives without the consent of the coastal State."

Many other nations expressed declarations assigning qualifications to the UNCLOS provisions. Argentina, for instance, stated that it "fully respects the right of free navigation as embodied in the Convention; however, it considers that the transit by sea of vessels carrying highly radioactive substances must be duly regulated."[41]

Air Defense Identification Zone

A different form of associated territorial "claim" is the declaration of an ADIZ. The United States was the first nation to declare an ADIZ, early in the Cold War, as a means of enhancing information and warning of possible Soviet-launched strategic air strikes against North America. Other nations have followed suit, including Japan in 1969, South Korea in 1950 (and expanded in 2013), and Taiwan (then the Republic of China) in 1950.

Three factors drew much international opprobrium against Beijing's declaration of an ADIZ over much of the East China Sea in November 2013. First was the lack of advance notice before issuing the declaration; second was the Chinese demand that it be notified of aircraft not just penetrating the ADIZ directly in the direction of China but also of aircraft passing through the ADIZ on oblique flight paths. Third was the new ADIZ overlapping already-declared ADIZs by South Korea, Japan, and Taiwan.

China's possible declaration of an ADIZ over the South China Sea is much discussed as a means of Beijing further solidifying its claim to the land features and unspecified water areas in that sea. A senior official in China's Ministry of Foreign Affairs justified the possible declaration of an ADIZ as a "right" that "has nothing to do with territorial or maritime disputes" based on "the long course of history."[42] A Chinese admiral commented during an appearance in Singapore that Beijing would declare such an ADIZ if justified by its threat assessment and the maritime security situation.[43]

Three Seas

The Chinese "Declaration on the Territorial Sea" in September 1958 declared straight baselines but failed to include their geographic points. This declaration claimed the Gulf of Bohai and the Hainan Strait as internal waters. It was succeeded in May 1996 by the "Declaration on the Baselines of the Territorial Sea," which claimed straight baselines for most of China's coastline and the Paracel Islands, in the South China Sea. Vietnam also claims the Paracels, and the United States refuses to recognize China's straight baselines because they are excessive.

China declared passage of its "Law on the Exclusive Economic Zone and the Continental Shelf" in 1998, in which it reaffirmed its previously expressed requirement for vessels that are nuclear powered or carrying nuclear, dangerous, or noxious substances to receive permission from Beijing before conducting innocent passage through these waters. Again, the United States has refused to recognize this stipulation.

China also issued the "EEZ and Continental Shelf Act" in 1998, in which it stated that "the PRC does not recognize the airspace above its EEZ to be 'international airspace,'" a statement counter to the UNCLOS and the basis of its continuing interference with U.S. reconnaissance flights in that airspace.

In 2002 Beijing passed a "Surveying and Mapping Law," in which it "criminalized 'survey' activities by foreign entities in any waters 'under the jurisdiction' of the PRC." This law also means the PRC does not distinguish between scientific research and military surveys, as the UNCLOS describes, which the United States has protested on several occasions. All of these laws and similar legislation declared by China are attempts to change accepted maritime law as expressed in the UNCLOS.[44]

The Yellow Sea, called the West Sea in Korea, forms the ocean basin across the Korean Peninsula from the Sea of Japan. It lies northwest of Tsushima and is bounded by the Korean Peninsula and the Chinese mainland. Although claimed in its entirety by Beijing, both North and South Korea dispute exact maritime boundaries with China. This relatively shallow sea, with an average depth of just 144 feet, or 24 fathoms, has important economic and military value for China; hence, any maritime disputes involving lines of demarcation or resources draw Beijing's immediate attention. One reason is the Yellow Sea's proximity to China's capital; another is its proximity to major seabed and shore-based energy reserves. A third reason is the major Chinese seaports that border the Yellow Sea. Perhaps most important is the sea's location between China and Japan as well as its border with the troublesome Korean Peninsula.

The Yellow Sea also continues to be the scene of significant disputes between North and South Korea. These include national boundaries, fisheries, and defense concerns that occasionally degenerate into naval clashes, most notably in 2010, when a North Korean submarine sank a South Korean corvette, the *Cheonan*.

East China Sea

The East China Sea is a maritime basin lying south of Korea, southwest of Japan, and west of the Ryukyus, between the Yellow and the Philippine Seas. The East China Sea stretches south from Tsushima to Taiwan, which is separated from the Asian mainland by the Taiwan Strait.

Perhaps more important for the international community is the question of China's position on the status of the Taiwan Strait as international waters. The UNCLOS not only states clearly that ships have the right of innocent passage through such straits (Article 45) but also tasks states bordering such straits with rights and responsibilities that provide rationale for controlling or limiting such free passage (Articles 37–44).

Beijing has intimated, however, that it views the Taiwan Strait as sovereign territorial water, or possibly even internal waters, as defined in Article 8 of the UNCLOS. China would presumably advocate this position by claiming a straight baseline from a point on its mainland to the northern end of Taiwan, and from the island's southern end back to the mainland, or perhaps directly to the island of Hainan, which lies at the northern end of the South China Sea. While such a claim would still require China to grant innocent passage (Article 17), it would empower Beijing to apply stricter measures of control, under the UNCLOS Article 19 qualifier that "passage is innocent so long as it is not prejudicial to the peace, good order or security of the coastal State."

The western Pacific Ocean south and east of the Ryukyus and Taiwan is the Philippine Sea, stretching eastward to a line approximately 2,000 nm from the Asian mainland and its important archipelagos. This sea thus includes the United States' Mariana Islands and the semi-independent island states of Micronesia, which are closely tied to the United States, defensively and politically.

South China Sea

The complexity of China's maritime environment is most graphically demonstrated in the South China Sea, where, despite agreeing to work toward implementing the 2002 Code of Conduct on peaceful resolution of disputes in the South China Sea, Beijing has carried on fortifying claimed land features and refusing to negotiate multilaterally about sovereignty issues. China continues to express cooperative intent about disputed South China Sea land features but then fails to acknowledge that sovereignty issues exist. China's efforts to resolve these disputes, although implied in the 2002 agreement, have accomplished little.

The South China Sea is marked by approximately 180 named land features as well as unnamed shoals and bits of land that remain submerged even

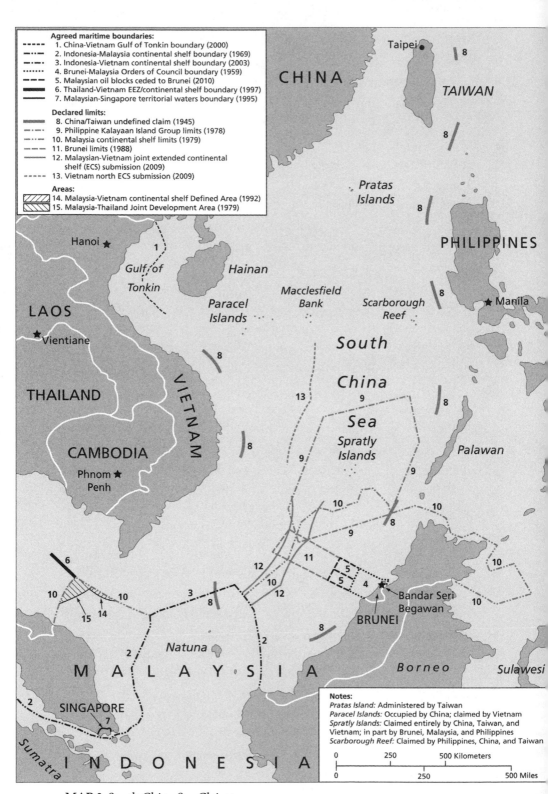

Agreed maritime boundaries:
- – – – – 1. China-Vietnam Gulf of Tonkin boundary (2000)
- –··–··– 2. Indonesia-Malaysia continental shelf boundary (1969)
- –·–·–· 3. Indonesia-Vietnam continental shelf boundary (2003)
- ········ 4. Brunei-Malaysia Orders of Council boundary (1959)
- – – – 5. Malaysian oil blocks ceded to Brunei (2010)
- ▬▬▬ 6. Thailand-Vietnam EEZ/continental shelf boundary (1997)
- ——— 7. Malaysian-Singapore territorial waters boundary (1995)

Declared limits:
- ▬▬▬ 8. China/Taiwan undefined claim (1945)
- –·–·–· 9. Philippine Kalayaan Island Group limits (1978)
- ——— 10. Malaysia continental shelf limits (1979)
- – – – 11. Brunei limits (1988)
- ——— 12. Malaysian-Vietnam joint extended continental
  shelf (ECS) submission (2009)
- – – – – 13. Vietnam north ECS submission (2009)

Areas:
- ▨ 14. Malaysia-Vietnam continental shelf Defined Area (1992)
- ▨ 15. Malaysia-Thailand Joint Development Area (1979)

CHINA

TAIWAN

Taipei

PHILIPPINES

Pratas
Islands

Hanoi

Gulf of
Tonkin

Hainan

Macclesfield
Bank

Scarborough
Reef

Manila

Paracel
Islands

LAOS

Vientiane

South

China

THAILAND

VIETNAM

Sea

Spratly
Islands

Palawan

CAMBODIA

Phnom
Penh

Natuna

MALAYSIA

Borneo

Sulawesi

SINGAPORE

Sumatra

INDONESIA

Bandar Seri
Begawan

BRUNEI

Notes:
Pratas Island: Administered by Taiwan
Paracel Islands: Occupied by China; claimed by Vietnam
Spratly Islands: Claimed entirely by China, Taiwan, and
Vietnam; in part by Brunei, Malaysia, and Philippines
Scarborough Reef: Claimed by Philippines, China, and Taiwan

0   250   500 Kilometers

0   250   500 Miles

MAP 3. South China Sea Claims

at low tide. These may be loosely grouped into five areas: Pratas Islands, Scarborough Reef, Macclesfield Bank, Paracel Islands, and the Spratly Islands. China and Taiwan claim all these land features; Vietnam claims the Paracel and Spratly Islands; the Philippines claims approximately 53 of the Spratly land features as well as Scarborough Reef; Malaysia claims some of the Spratly land features; and Brunei claims none but asserts that one is located in its EEZ.[45]

The South China Sea issue is particularly complicated by its geography. If the islands within the Pratas, Paracel, and Spratly groups are credited with the full range of UNCLOS-designated maritime zones, no area of the South China Sea will lie "outside of national jurisdiction," thus eliminating any area of "high seas" or "international waters" in that sea.[46]

The South China Sea disputes are especially complicated by the various cartographic and historical claims made by the disputants, although by signing the UNCLOS, the nations implicitly surrendered "historic rights." For instance, China's Wu Shicun, director of the Chinese Institute for the South China Sea, located in Haikou, Hainan, China, traces his nation's governmental awareness of that sea as far back as the Qin dynasty (220 BCE), while a Philippine expert cites maps of similar age as proving that China has no such ancient claims.[47]

In fact, China's modern claims in the South China Sea may be traced to Zhou Enlai's statement in August 1951 during the peace conference with Japan, when he "declared China's sovereignty over the Paracel and Spratly Islands."[48] Beijing repeated this claim in 1958 during that year's Taiwan Strait crisis. Next came the 1992 "Law on the Territorial Sea and the Contiguous Zone of the PRC," the 1998 "Law on the Exclusive Economic Zone and the Continental Shelf of the PRC," and the 2011 *note verbale* to the UN Commission on the Limits of the Continental Shelf.[49]

From Beijing's perspective, no South China Sea cartographic feature is as important as the nine-dash line. This U-shaped demarcation apparently first appeared on a Chinese map in 1922 as a solid line. It next showed on a 1936 map published by the Republic of China (ROC) government; then in 1948, a ROC map showed an eleven-dash line tracing the same U shape in the South China Sea but including a tenth line in the Tonkin Gulf (Beibu, in Chinese) and an eleventh east of Taiwan.

A nine-dash line accompanied the 1992 publication of the PRC's Law on the Territorial Sea and the Contiguous Zone. A final ten-dash line emerged in 2014, with reinstatement of a line east of Taiwan. The nine dashes represent the most constant delineation of China's unspecified claim in the South China Sea.[50]

Chinese and Taiwan government officials and academics recently described this line in a series of statements that range from legally defensible to propagandistic. First, Gao Zhiguo of the China Institute of Marine Affairs of the State Oceanic Administration described the nine-dash line as "a declaration of sovereignty over the islands in the South China Sea, which have belonged to China since ancient times," which was succeeded by the very troublesome statement that "moreover, the dashed-line has residual functions to be a future maritime boundary." Hu Dekun then claimed that the line "also denotes historic rights to engage in fishing, navigation, resource exploration/ extraction, and other maritime activities on the islands and in the waters adjacent to them." These analysts then continued conflating recognized maritime legal principals with "principles of historical title" and "historical basis." Hu further described the line as "China's maritime border in the South China Sea" and an "island/reef territorial boundary," and he claims the line delimits "historic fishing grounds." Zhu Feng concluded by claiming that this line involved "four issues: history, rights, rules, and the evolution of the future order."[51] Beijing is attempting to use "history" as a justification for its claims, but that factor features neither in the UNCLOS nor in maritime law generally.[52]

Most confusing about Beijing's continued use of the U-shaped line is its failure to define and publish the geographical coordinates of any of the dashes in latitude and longitude. The legal status of this line is very problematic; Indonesia, for example, described it as "clearly lack[ing] international legal basis and is tantamount to upset the UNCLOS 1982." The nine-dash line has appeared in several different forms, further blurring its precise location.[53]

U.S. analysts have made similar points.[54] Furthermore, China has never clarified whether it is making claims just to the land features and associated waters in the South China Sea or whether it is claiming sovereignty over all the maritime area inside the nine-dash line. However, in September 2011 a Ministry of Foreign Affairs spokesperson stated, "China enjoys indisputable sovereignty over the South China Sea and the islands. China's stand is based on historical facts and international law."[55] Even this relatively extreme statement fails to clarify Beijing's claim.

This conclusion is based not only on the two laws noted but also on Beijing's belief that most, if not all, of its claimed land features in the South China Sea are fully entitled to the UNCLOS zones. China's basic justification for its ownership of the land features and "adjacent waters" or "relevant waters" within the nine-dash line is that of "historic rights." In other words, since China is "one of the world's oldest civilizations, the South China Sea is part of the traditional Asian order and, hence, it would be inappropriate to comprehend the nine-dash line by relying solely on the Westphalian nation-state system," and "China's historic rights within the nine-dash line cannot be ignored."[56]

The Philippines is also taking legal action against China's activities in the South China Sea, bringing a case against Beijing in the United Nations under the UNCLOS provisions for dispute settlement. Vietnam also lodged a legal challenge to China's claims, with a submission to an arbitral tribunal at The Hague. China is refusing to participate in this legal action; Beijing immediately rejected Hanoi's challenge.[57]

China's foreign minister has proposed three more specific "initiatives to maintain peace [and] stability" in the South China Sea:

1. "South China Sea countries pledge to implement the Declaration on the Conduct of Parties in the South China Sea (DOC) in a comprehensive, effective, and complete way, accelerate consultations on formulating a Code of Conduct (COC) for the South China Sea; and actively discuss 'precautionary measures for maritime risk management and control.'"
2. "Countries outside the region pledge to support the above-mentioned efforts by countries in the region, and do not take actions that may cause tension and complexity in the region."
3. "Countries pledge to exercise and safeguard their freedom of navigation and overflight in the South China Sea in accordance with international law."[58]

These "proposals" and "initiatives" read well, but Beijing aims at isolating its disputes in the South China Sea with the much smaller and less powerful ASEAN states while preventing outside support by the United States or Japan.[59] When the Vietnamese head of ASEAN protested the legitimacy of

China's nine-dash line, Beijing accused him of making "biased comments . . . which were untrue."[60] This defensiveness exemplifies China's unwillingness to compromise on its South China Sea claims.

Beijing argues that "internationalizing" the issues reduces opportunities for resolving disputes, but given the inherently multilateral nature of the sovereignty issue in the South China Sea, the bilateral-only approach on which China insists equates simply to Beijing stonewalling the issue and delays any progress toward establishing a meaningful code of conduct.

China signed the 2002 DOC in which the signatories reaffirmed "that the adoption of a code of conduct in the South China Sea would further promote peace and stability in the region" and "agree to work, on the basis of consensus, towards the eventual attainment of this objective." The DOC was more aspirational than accomplished, however, and a "code of conduct" remains distant.[61]

In fact, the elements of this agreement have been honored in the breach, particularly by China, although ASEAN states are continuing to pursue implementation of the DOC as a precursor to trying to establish a code of conduct. China continues to support both goals in principle, but only to the extent it does not affect its own territorial claims.

Beijing has signed significant multilateral agreements pertaining to the search for energy reserves in the South China Sea. It signed a joint exploration project in the Gulf of Tonkin with Hanoi that remains in effect. The national oil companies from China (China National Offshore Oil Corporation, CNOOC), the Philippines (PNOC-Exploration Corporation), and Vietnam (PetroVietnam) agreed in 2004 to conduct seismic exploration west of the Philippine island of Palawan, and this Joint Marine Seismic Undertaking came into effect in July 2005. The three nations conducted some surveying, but the agreement was not renewed when its charter expired in 2008.[62]

Why does China care so much about the sovereignty of these remote, mostly uninhabitable land features, many of which never show above the ocean's surface? The first reason is national pride, with memories of the "century of humiliation." Second is the issue of natural resources in the features' surrounding waters, including fisheries, petroleum, and other minerals. Third is the strategic location of the disputed land features, especially those in the South China Sea, an area of crucial SLOCs. Finally, Beijing desires to prevent events from occurring in the three seas of which it does not approve.

China's construction of artificial "islands" in the South China Sea is the proximate cause of dissension between China and the Philippines, and between China and Vietnam. Beijing has employed massive dredging to turn land features not classified as "islands" into island-sized structures and is equipping them with airstrips capable of operating tactical jet aircraft, harbor facilities capable of berthing surface combatants, and other military installations. Despite the UNCLOS stating that such man-made structures are not entitled to the full panoply of coastal state entitled zones, there is little doubt that Beijing will claim such zones for its new "islands."

China has reacted to the criticism of the Philippines, Vietnam, Japan, the United States, and other nations of its land-feature-building program by claiming it is merely responding to similar programs by other South China Sea claimants. This Chinese reason is unconvincing, given the massive extent of its program, approximately three thousand acres as of October 2015, compared to the minor efforts of other nations.[63] Beijing's claims that these new features are intended for public benefit are not to be taken seriously.

China's new military airfields and facilities on the Fiery Cross, Subi, and Mischief Reefs in the Spratlys mean Beijing will be in a position to interfere with the vital commercial trade and naval movements through the sea. Beijing's current program of constructing fully armed artificial "islands" recommended by China's National Defense University as "strategic frontier islands" demonstrates precisely that danger.[64]

United Nations

The UNCLOS is just one facet of China's active role as a permanent UN Security Council member, possessing a permanent veto. China has assigned more personnel on UN peacekeeping missions than any other member of the Security Council. These have often included civilian administrators and police, as in Haiti, but in January 2015 the first Chinese infantry battalion was transported to South Sudan to serve as UN peacekeepers.[65] A PLA officer served as commander of a UN peacekeeping force for the first time in 2007, in Western Sahara.[66]

China has maintained its advocacy of noninterference in what it considers the domestic affairs of other countries. To this end, the nine vetoes it has cast since 1971 have with one exception all been against resolutions supporting UN attempts to rectify various situations in nations undergoing domestic conflict or gross humanitarian abuses. These have included, however, veto-ing Bangladesh's membership (1972) and vetoing a strong UN presence in Central America (1997), Macedonia (1999), Myanmar (2007), Zimbabwe (2008), and Syria (2011, 2012 (twice), and 2014).[67]

Asia-Pacific Economic Cooperation

China has become an active Asia-Pacific Economic Cooperation (APEC) member, with the Chinese president regularly attending the organization's meetings and hosting the 2014 gathering in Beijing. This meeting demon-strated China's linking economic and foreign policy objectives, as Xi Jinping called for all APEC members to support a free trade area of the Asia-Pacific. This signaled Beijing's opposition to the U.S.-sponsored Trans-Pacific Part-nership that currently omits China while linking China's proposal to the Asian Infrastructure Investment Bank as part of a Chinese-sponsored "Connectiv-ity Blueprint for 2015–2025."[68]

Association of Southeast Asian Nations

ASEAN was founded in 1967 by Indonesia, Malaysia, the Philippines, Sin-gapore, and Thailand; Brunei joined in 1984. The organization has proven a useful venue for regional economic, political, and military discussions. As an associate member, China is active in the association's full range of meetings, which include many annual sessions on political, economic, and military issues. Substantive accomplishments have been very slow in resulting from the organization's many meetings, however, and its status is very unlikely to approach that of, say, the North Atlantic Treaty Organization. Former Singa-pore prime minister Lee Kwan Yew explained this by comparing the geo-graphical propinquity of the European countries and the wide geographic spread of the Southeast Asian states.[69]

Nonetheless, the organization is important and China's participation in ASEAN is particularly significant, the member states of which now number all ten of Southeast Asia's major states: Brunei, Cambodia, Indonesia, Laos, Malaysia, Myanmar, the Philippines, Singapore, Thailand, and Vietnam. None of them approach China in economic, military, or political power, but all of them have very important economic relations with their giant neighbor to the north.

ASEAN member states' relations with China range from Laotian and Cambodian near-satellite status, to Thai accommodation, to Philippine near hostility. Each of the ASEAN members, however, recognize and are concerned about Chinese dominance; most seek some counterbalance, with Japan, India, and especially the United States most sought after for this role. Vietnam and the Philippines are taking notable steps in this direction, including seeking military—especially naval—assistance and diplomatic support.[70]

Beijing is concerned about ASEAN, both because it is a multilateral organization with which it must deal and because of the disputes it has with several of the organization's member nations. Senior officials, including Foreign Minister Wang Yi, have described China's relations with ASEAN as the "priority direction" for China's periphery diplomacy. Premier Li Keqiang offered a seven-point proposal in October 2013 for strengthening relations with ASEAN:

1. Discuss and sign a "treaty of good neighborliness, friendship and cooperation."
2. Strengthen exchanges and cooperation in the security field [to include] disaster prevention and relief, cyber security, cracking down on cross-border crime, and joint law enforcement.
3. "Launch negotiations on upgrading [the China-ASEAN] free trade area."
4. "Speed up the construction of inter-connectivity infrastructure."
5. Expand the scope of bilateral currency swaps and give good play to the role of the China-ASEAN interbank association.
6. Steadily "promote maritime cooperation." Build together "a 21st century maritime Silk Road."
7. Bring about closer "exchanges in culture, [science and] technology, and environmental protection."[71]

However, Li stipulated, any negotiations would have to be bilateral, reiterating China's historical reluctance to engage in meaningful multilateral dealings.

China's willingness to participate in multilateral forums is significantly more pronounced when issues of its sovereignty are not involved. The "one belt, one road" proposal is a prominent example. Beijing's National Development and Reform Commission noted that for the initiative to be successful, China "should enhance the role of multilateral cooperation mechanisms, make full use of existing mechanisms such at the SCO, ASEAN Plus China

(10+1), ASEAN Plus Three, APEC, Asia-Europe Meeting, Asia Cooperation Dialogue, Conference on Interaction and Confidence-Building Measures in Asia, China-Arab States Cooperation Forum, China-Gulf Cooperation Council Strategic Dialogue, Greater Mekong Sub-region Economic Cooperation, and Central Asia Regional Economic Cooperation," an impressive list of organizations in which China participates.[72]

In August 2015 Foreign Minister Wang Yi then put forward ten proposals for deepening cooperation with ASEAN:

1. Make full preparation for the twenty-fifth anniversary of China-ASEAN dialogue relations next year, and set 2016 as "Year of China-ASEAN Education Exchange."
2. Formulate the 2016–2020 Plan of Action to Implement Joint Declaration on the ASEAN-China Strategic Partnership for Peace and Prosperity, highlighting the sense of modern times, inclusiveness, and perspectiveness and exploring new fields of cooperation.
3. Set up a work group to negotiate the "Treaty on Good Neighborliness and Friendly Cooperation between China and ASEAN Countries."
4. Launch operation on international production capacity and realize complementary economic development of China and ASEAN as well as common prosperity.
5. Further advance in connectivity [between China and] ASEAN.
6. Ensure that "the Year of China-ASEAN Maritime Cooperation" [is] a success and brings new highlights to maritime cooperation between the two sides.
7. Jointly promote the development of subregions by establishing the Lancang-Mekong River Dialogue and Cooperation Mechanism.
8. Sign the protocol to the Treaty on the Southeast Asia Nuclear Weapon-Free Zone.
9. Strengthen cooperation with ASEAN on defense and security, welcome defense ministers of the ten ASEAN states and its secretary general to attend the China-ASEAN defense ministers' retreat, which will be held in China in October [2015] for the first time.
10. China and ASEAN should join hands to safeguard peace and stability in the South China Sea by properly handling disputes, maintaining peace, and boosting cooperation to create a win-win situation.[73]

Xi Jinping also linked ASEAN with his periphery diplomacy in October 2013, when he emphasized the need to "persist" in promoting a "new security concept," which would center on developing "mutual trust, mutual benefits, equality, and cooperation [and the ideas of] comprehensive security, common security, and cooperative security." Xi linked these to "regional and subregional security cooperation" while noting the need to maintain "the state's sovereignty."[74]

Beijing should be particularly concerned about antagonizing Indonesia, long the mainstay of ASEAN and other regional forums. Jakarta does not claim any of the land features lying within the nine-dash line, but the EEZs of Indonesia's Natuna Islands do extend inside that line. Indonesian president Joko Widodo explicitly asserted that the nine-dash line "lacks legal basis in international law."[75] The chief of Indonesia's armed forces, General Moeldoko, warned his PLA hosts in Beijing in February 2014 "we are a sovereign country, we will protect our territory, and we will do whatever is necessary to protect our sovereignty."[76] Jakarta is backing up this statement with a major naval modernization program. Hence, the assignment of warships by the PLAN in 2014 and 2015 to assert Chinese sovereignty over James Shoal, a subsurface reef located within Malaysia's claimed EEZ but not distant from the Indonesian Natuna Islands' EEZ, seems gratuitously risky on Beijing's part. Even Kuala Lumpur's cautious approach to sovereignty disputes is hardening because of China's assertive actions.[77]

China is reacting to ASEAN in several ways. Beijing primarily wants to approach each nation on a one-on-one basis but also approach ASEAN as an important multilateral venue. Second, Beijing is dual-tracking its diplomacy, applying a mix of soft and hard power. Finally, China is attempting to recreate a situation in which it dominates the region, as it has done historically. It is already positioned to do so economically and militarily. Political dominance can be established only with the de facto concurrence of the United States.

In a particularly egregious case of China's manipulation of ASEAN procedures, Beijing pressured Cambodia, host of the July 2012 meeting of the organization's foreign ministers, not to issue a postmeeting statement, the only time this has happened. Beijing's reason was its inability to have the attendees ignore Chinese actions in the South China Sea.[78] Less than two years later, however, "senior Chinese and ASEAN officials vowed to strengthen cooperation."[79] Beijing tried again to control any discussion of South China

Sea sovereignty issues at the most recent ASEAN meeting, in 2015. China succeeded in keeping the issue off the agenda of the ASEAN Defense Ministers
Meeting Plus session, but the topic nonetheless was discussed.[80]

Naval Diplomacy

The PLAN has established a robust schedule of ship port visits throughout
Southeast Asia, sometimes including exercises at sea with the host country's
navy. Beijing has also declared some degree of "strategic partnership" since
2005 with Australia, Pakistan, India, Indonesia, South Korea, Vietnam, Laos,
Cambodia, Mongolia, Myanmar, Thailand, Sri Lanka, Malaysia, and ASEAN.
China has added several Central Asian nations—Kazakhstan, Turkey, Uzbekistan, Afghanistan, Tajikistan, Turkmenistan, and Kyrgyzstan—to this list.[81]

PLAN activities increasingly link with these relationships, which range
from a substantial relationship with Cambodia, to a more ephemeral relationship with India, for example. Furthermore, the depth of the "partnership"
can change, as seen in the cooling of Beijing's relations with Myanmar following the replacement of that country's ruling military junta and opening
to the United States, and with Sri Lanka following the ouster of its pro-China
president.

The PLAN has played a positive role enhancing these relationships, making port calls in the region and conducting limited naval exercises with several
regional navies, although these all have been very rudimentary, consisting
almost entirely of communication drills, search-and-rescue exercises, and sea-
manship evolutions.

PLAN ship visits since 2008 have included Australia, Indonesia, Malaysia,
Myanmar, the Philippines, Singapore, Thailand, and Vietnam in Southeast
Asia; India, the Maldives, Pakistan, the Seychelles, and Sri Lanka in South
Asia; Cameroon, the Ivory Coast, Kenya, Mozambique, Namibia, Nigeria,
Senegal, South Africa, and Tanzania in sub-Saharan Africa; Algeria, Bahrain,
Egypt, Iran, Israel, Kuwait, Morocco, Oman, Qatar, Saudi Arabia, Tunisia, and
the United Arab Emirates in the Middle East; and Bulgaria, France, Greece,
Italy, Malta, Portugal, Romania, Turkey, and Ukraine in Europe. Additionally,
PLAN units have conducted exercises with maritime forces from many of the
participants in RIMPAC 2014, as well as with New Zealand, Pakistan, and
Russia.

Conclusion

Geography rarely if ever changes. The geopolitical importance of energy resource location, SLOCs and the straits, distances and depths, and coastal contours and ocean bottom gradients are all factors that contribute to defining Asia's maritime arena—and its foreign policies. Beijing is focused on its maritime geography, as evidenced in the frequent discussion by Chinese naval strategists about the three seas and the island chains.

Both civilian and naval strategists in Beijing think possessing Taiwan will yield significant strategic advantages with respect to controlling transits through the first island chain.[82] The PLAN's relatively new submarine base on the southern coast of Hainan, at Sanya, which may signal its intention to adopt a "bastion strategy" for its new Jin-class fleet ballistic missile submarines, is another indicator of the importance of geography in China's strategic thinking. The next two chapters survey the modernizing PLAN and the maritime strategy developing to employ it as a vital instrument of strategic statecraft.

Commercial sea power is even more important at the beginning of the twenty-first century than it was at the end of the nineteenth, when petroleum began gaining world prominence. China's rise as a global economic power has greatly increased the importance to Beijing of energy security.

The UNCLOS maritime zones are based on the concept that the land dominates the sea, a principle that has existed throughout history, as discussed earlier. It is clear that China plans or at least hopes to be able to change some of the rules of maritime law and usage embodied in the UNCLOS.[83] China also seems to claim that these zones, such as the EEZ, are not established by the coastal state concerned, when in fact the international community grants them—in this case, through the UNCLOS treaty.[84]

Beijing has moved significantly from insisting on only bilateral relations to embracing multilateral organizations, if cautiously and selectively. It still consistently emphasizes bilateral negotiations when addressing sovereignty disputes. China's strategy of straddling soft and hard power approaches in multilateral forums is exemplified in its relations with Southeast Asian nations, particularly Vietnam and the Philippines. Numerous violent and near-violent incidents between China and Vietnam have occurred over South China Sea issues, but most have been followed by agreements for peaceful resolution of the disputes and "friendly cooperation." These follow-ons have usually taken place between representatives of the two nations' communist parties and governing officials.[85] Despite the continuing clashes and disputes in the South China Sea, Beijing and Hanoi agreed to categorize their relationship as "a comprehensive strategic cooperative partnership."[86] Furthermore, a series of joint Chinese-Vietnamese patrols in the Gulf of Tonkin (Beibu Gulf, in Chinese) continued throughout 2014.[87]

China's refusal to participate in a multilateral effort to resolve the disputes in the South China Sea vitiates any settlement, other than the other disputants simply giving in to Chinese sovereignty over all the land features in that sea. Furthermore, if "any of the islands within the major groups of the Pratas, Paracel, and Spratly islands are recognized as generating a full set of maritime zones, there is no area of the South China Sea that is outside of national [e.g., Chinese] jurisdiction."[88] This result would be unacceptable to the United States and many other Indo-Pacific nations. In addition to territorial disputes in the South and East China Seas, China is involved in a dispute, particularly with the United States, over whether China has a right under international law to regulate the activities of foreign military forces operating within China's EEZ. The dispute appears to be at the heart of incidents between Chinese and U.S. ships and aircraft in international waters and airspace, with the most prominent examples having occurred in 2001, 2002, 2009, 2013, and 2014.

The South China Sea sovereignty issues could be resolved through bilateral negotiations if the disputants other than China would negotiate their differences and then present a pan-ASEAN position to Beijing. There seems little chance that will happen, however. The next two chapters address the core of China's maritime power, the PLAN, and the maritime strategy Beijing is developing to employ the navy.

Chapter Two

MARITIME FORCES

The earth's vast oceans and associated waters may not always be easily identified with specific nations. These maritime bodies invariably are bordered by several countries, each with its own priorities and concerns. Hence, sometimes poorly defined terms are applied, including "maritime commons," "high seas," or "international waters." They are often areas without legally acknowledged ownership or national sovereignty.

This state of affairs reflects the absolute dependence on the seas for national and international economic viability, a fact tempting to nations concerned about ensuring that reliance. The United States, Japan, India, and China are leaders both in dependence and concerns about maintaining the accessibility and security of the maritime commons. This is evidenced by China's development of a modern navy capable of conducting operations on twenty-first-century oceans, but that navy currently is being built and deployed at a moderate pace and with clearly prioritized strategic situations—Taiwan, the "three seas" that form China's eastern littoral, and the sea lines of communication (SLOC) reaching across the Indian Ocean to the energy-rich regions of the Middle East.

The 2015 white paper *China's Military Strategy* published by Beijing is most significant—the first Chinese white paper to focus on maritime concerns and issues. While bearing the title "military," it for the most part addresses the need for China to become and operate as a world-class maritime power, one able to defend national security interests globally.

The People's Liberation Army Navy

China is now deploying the results of its efforts to build a new navy, one capable of confronting modern maritime opponents, especially Taiwan, Japan, India, and the United States. The objective is not the ability to seize command of the sea in the face of opposition by any of these naval forces but to secure vital national maritime interests, despite the presence or active intervention of these foreign navies.

China's navy has been modernizing since its inception in 1949, of course, but the process intensified during the 1980s and received particular motivation from the 1995–96 Taiwan Strait crisis. It continued at a moderate but steady pace through 2015. China's 2008 defense white paper stated that "the goal of modernization of national defense and armed forces" is expected "by the mid-21st century," which also will mark the centennial of the founding of the People's Republic of China (PRC), in 1949. Senior U.S. Navy officials also cite this date.[1]

Progress toward this midcentury goal has been impressive, but the People's Liberation Army Navy (PLAN) still faces many challenges. First and foremost is attaining and then solidifying its position within the PLA to ensure receiving the share of China's military budget necessary to continue naval modernization and expansion. The army has always dominated China's military, as expected in a primarily continental nation. This in turn requires PLAN leadership to maintain an influential relationship with the government's civilian leaders. Second and more mundane but important challenges confronting China's navy include establishing the command-and-control mechanisms and, even more important, the command climate necessary to conduct joint operations.

The third challenge is absorbing likely organizational changes in China's defense infrastructure, consolidation of the current seven military regions (MR) into five operational theaters, while still retaining the navy's three fleets.[2] This in turn would include headquarters reorganizations and reductions. Finally, and most important, the PLAN is likely to benefit from increased emphasis, at the expense of the army, due to a shift in Beijing's security concerns from the traditional Chinese continental focus to the maritime sphere. This is evident in the 2015 military strategy white paper, as noted earlier.

Organizational reforms were included in China's May 2015 defense white paper, which for the first time focused on China's military strategy. The reforms will "optimize the size and structure of the army, adjust and improve the proportion between various troops, and reduce non-combat institutions and personnel." In addition, "joint operation command authority under the CMC [Central Military Commission] and theater joint operation command system will be improved."[3]

Xi Jinping announced an important element in this reform at the September 2015 ceremony celebrating the seventieth anniversary of the end of World War II, when he specifically mentioned a PLA downsizing of 300,000 personnel. The navy's "share" of this downsizing is unclear but is likely to be small, with almost all personnel cuts likely to come from the army.

The fourth challenge is the omniscient issue of personnel accession, training, retention, and probity. The PLAN faces an increasingly challenging environment. First, as the navy modernizes, it requires both enlisted and officer personnel with increased education and ability to master the operation and maintenance of technologically complex systems. This reduces the pool of suitable applicants.[4] The PLAN has launched a relatively sophisticated recruiting campaign; a 2015 video shows ships, submarines, and aircraft and is accompanied by a vocal that addresses "Our Dream," "The Call to Duty," "The Honor Gene," and "Seeking the Blue Dream." It concludes with

> Here the eyes of the entire world are upon us!
> This is the Chinese Navy!
> This is you with us—full of pride!
> A strong motherland needs a strong navy
> The Navy needs you.
> Let's together realize the dream of the great Chinese renaissance.
> Sail the four seas, brave and courageous
> We invite you to join the Chinese Navy.[5]

China's vibrant economy also offers that personnel pool opportunities of far greater financial benefit, without the exigencies of naval life. A fifth and related challenge is a natural reluctance of young men and women coming of age in an increasingly modern and free society to voluntarily subject themselves to the rigors and discipline of a military career.

The sixth challenge is the traditional Chinese culture that questions the value of the military profession; "one does not make nails from good iron; one does not make soldiers from good men" is a proverb perhaps originating in Confucian thought or during the thirteen century Song dynasty.[6] This reservation relates to China's past one-child policy and the traditional Chinese preference for sons; a family with a son as its only child is almost certainly going to look askance at that son choosing a military career, perhaps particularly in the navy, where simply going to sea poses inherent dangers.

In any event, the PLAN remains the smallest of China's military forces. It numbers no more than 235,000 personnel out of the PLA's total strength of approximately 2.3 million.[7] This number does not include naval reserve personnel, who are sometimes activated to participate in PLAN exercises.[8] Expected reforms are likely to increase the PLAN's percentage of PLA personnel.

The PLAN also must ensure it has access to the benefits of civilian research and development. This applies not just to scientific advances but also to technological improvements in shipbuilding and other production processes. This requirement is subsumed under the heading of improved military-civilian integration, another example of which includes the ability of naval forces to access civilian industrial infrastructure such as fuel systems, maintenance and repair facilities, information and communications systems, and civilian shipping.

Finally, the PLAN no doubt confronts operational and organizational challenges as Beijing adjusts its strategic guidance and develops China's force posture and operational plans. President Xi Jinping addressed several of these points in an August 2014 address to the CCP Politburo. After emphasizing the ritual mantra of the PLA upholding "the party's absolute leadership of the military," Xi emphasized the need to "prepare for military struggle," to take advantage of the "new military revolution" and its technological advances, and to "unswervingly take the path of innovation by merging the military with the civilian resources; incorporate the military innovation system into the state innovation system on a wider scope." He further asserted that China must become the "world's dominant power [and] a nation with a strong military."[9]

The PLAN is moving to meet these challenges, shown in its focus on developing the ability to operate in waters far from home base, the "far seas." As examined in the following, this is shown in the initiation of regular exercises beyond the first island chain, in the Philippine Sea, the Indian Ocean, and the Mediterranean Sea.

Multipurpose surface combatants and submarines capable of twenty-first-century combat operations are being deployed, as are modern large amphibious ships and China's first aircraft carrier. The PLAN's first seaborne nuclear deterrent is in the offing as the struggle continues to arm the new Jin-class fleet ballistic missile (FBM) submarines with Ju Lang (JL)-2 intercontinental ballistic missiles (ICBM). The navy has also embraced Special Forces (SOF) units, with a regiment stationed at Sanya, the primary South Sea Fleet base. SOF personnel have been deploying to the Gulf of Aden, and submarines have been deployed to serve as SOF operating vehicles.[10]

Personnel and organizational improvements are more important than these material accomplishments, as is the national government's willingness to use the navy as an instrument of statecraft. Recent events in the East and South China Seas include "regular rights defense patrols," which highlight this last fact, as do recent Chinese submarine deployments to the Indian Ocean.[11]

Defense Budgets

China's three decades or more of economic growth, the most remarkable in world history, have enabled PLAN modernization. The increase in national revenues resulting from the economic growth has allowed Beijing to increase the funding necessary for material improvements and increased personnel training and education. China today spends more on its defense than any nation in the world except the United States. Comparing defense budgets is not an easy process, however; for instance, a U.S. soldier costs approximately US$18,000 a year to put in the field, while his Chinese counterpart probably costs no more than US$2,000.[12]

China's defense budget first experienced a double-digit increase in 1989, but Beijing realized in 1996 not only that its modernization efforts had failed to close the gap with the U.S. military but that the gap had widened. U.S. forces continued to advance in terms of technology as well as in operational experience and expertise. Double-digit increases in defense spending have continued almost every year since the 1996 crisis, when apparently the PLA learned a significant lesson—combat operations at sea would require U.S. acquiescence. The military at that time was unable even to detect the presence of the U.S. carriers on its own; by any measure, the PLAN was a secondary force.

During the past two decades, the Chinese military has had much more money to spend on fewer troops than it did fifteen years ago. Almost all observers think Beijing's budget estimates are significantly underestimated, but Dennis Blasko has offered a reasonable conclusion to the different budget estimates: "Whatever the true numbers may be, the Chinese military has much more money to spend on fewer troops than it did 15 years ago. At the same time, personnel, equipment, and training costs for a more modern, technologically advanced military are significantly higher than in previous decades. . . . The growth of the defense budget in fact appears to be coordinated with the growth of the Chinese economy. . . . If need be, the government could increase spending even faster."[13]

Ascertaining details of China's defense spending, including that for the navy, is difficult for several reasons. First, there is a general lack of transparency to outside observers—and to Chinese analysts as well. Second, the nature of defense spending sources in China is diffuse; for instance, local governments provide some of the funds required for mobilization preparations, conscription, and demobilization. Third, China's "defense spending" categories do not aways match U.S. definitions. Research and development funding, for instance, draws on both the Ministry of National Defense and the defense industrial sector. Foreign military sales and purchases too may not be included in Beijing's figures. Hence, accurate computation of the PLAN's submarine- and ship-acquisition programs founders on the question of how to account for the purchase of Kilo submarines and Sovremenny-class destroyers from Russia, a question further complicated by the unknown but surely significant costs of the training, supply, and maintenance that accompanied those purchases.

China's more than two decades of double-digit defense spending increases continued in 2015, with a 10.1 percent increase. Between 2000 and 2014, China's announced defense budget increased from approximately 110 billion yuan to just over 800 billion yuan.[14] Most recently, Beijing announced a US$106.4 billion defense budget for 2012, an 11.2 percent increase over that authorized for 2010. These increases tracked with China's GDP increase for that year, evidence that the defense budget increases, while certainly significant, are being tightly controlled by the CCP to ensure that the nation's economic development remains the number one priority.

Beijing justified its 1994 defense budget increase, estimated to have been as high as 29 percent, as required to counter inflation and to increase PLA salaries, especially for officers.[15] Similarly, recent defense spending increases have been explained as responses to higher equipment and consumables costs, personnel pay and benefit increases, improvements in personnel living conditions, and compensation for the PLA ridding itself of commercial business investments 1998. These explanations are probably accurate. In 1993, for instance, inflation was a problem; officer salaries were doubled for 1994. More recently, in 2011, noncommissioned officer salaries and benefits were increased by as much as 40 percent.

The past two decades of double-digit increases in defense spending appear to be in line with the growth of the Chinese economy, as various defense white papers have claimed. Defense spending is not being allowed to increase at a pace that would conflict with China's primary objective of economic development. If a vital national security interest appeared threatened, the government could increase spending even faster.

Most significant, despite large annual defense budget increases, China appears to be adhering to a goal of achieving by 2049 a completely modern navy capable of defending the nation's maritime interests against even the United States. The PLAN probably sees itself at the halfway mark in its overall modernization program. However, this pace could be increased as the result of a crisis involving Taiwan or Japan scenarios, or if the PLAN gains significantly more influence within the PLA.

Fleet Organization

The PLAN is organized into three fleets, although the ship classes are not equally distributed. The North Sea Fleet (NSF), homeported in Qingdao, in Shandong Province and the Northern Theater Command, is the smallest of the fleets, numbering 81 vessels.[16] It includes the navy's oldest (two or three) Han-class nuclear-powered attack submarines (SSN) and 25 older conventional boats, including most of China's Ming-class submarines. The NSF's surface forces are led by approximately 10 of China's most modern warships, 2 Luzhou-class destroyers, 4 Jiangkai II–class frigates, and 4 Jiangdao-class corvettes.

The East Sea Fleet (ESF) is headquartered at Ningbo, in Zhejiang Province and the Eastern Theater Command, just south of Shanghai. It numbers 105 vessels, including 18 conventionally powered submarines, including modern Song- and Kilo-class boats. Its surface combatant force is led by 2 indigenously built Luyang II–class destroyers and 4 Sovremenny-class destroyers acquired from Russia. The Luyangs apparently are equipped with Aegis-like anti-air warfare (AAW) systems; the Sovremennys are relatively old ships with minimal AAW capability but are armed with potent SSN-22 "Sunburn" anti-ship cruise missiles (ASCM). Approximately 6 Jiangkai I– and II–class frigates and 6 Jiangdao-class corvettes also are assigned to the ESF. The PLAN's only modern hospital ship, the *Daishan Dao* (*Peace Ark*), is part of this fleet.

The South Sea Fleet (SSF) is headquartered at Zhanjiang, in Guangdong Province and the Southern Theater Command. The SSF is the largest and most capable of the navy's fleets, with more than 120 vessels assigned. These include China's largest amphibious flotilla, including its newest and most capable ships. The SSF also includes the navy's newest nuclear-powered submarines, both attack and ballistic missile boats, as well as more than a dozen of China's most capable conventionally powered submarines, including the new Yuan class, equipped with an air-independent propulsion (AIP) engineering plant.

The SSF also boasts China's most capable surface combatants, including the first Luyang III–class destroyer, 4 additional Luyang- and Lanzhou-class destroyers, at least 8 Jiangkai II–class frigates and 8 Jiangdao-class corvettes. As an example of this fleet's priority, it homeports more of China's most modern surface combatants than either of the other two fleets.[17] China's only aircraft carrier, the *Liaoning*, is also part of the SSF.

After decades of building successive small destroyer and frigate classes of one to four hulls, the PLAN apparently has decided on the Luyang-class of destroyers as its primary large combatant. Similarly, the navy seems to have seized upon the Jiangdao-class corvette as its primary surface combatant for operations in littoral waters. This class may still turn out to be China's primary warship for foreign sales; it may reflect the PLANs attempt to improve its antisubmarine warfare (ASW) capability, particularly in the three seas, in the waters inside the first island chain.[18]

The PLAN deploys no more than 7 to 9 replenishment-at-sea (RAS) ships. One of these, the *Nanyang*, is a large but old (ca. late 1970s) ship acquired from Russia; 2 are Fuqing-class oilers acquired in the early 1980s. The PLAN apparently has decided on the Fuchi class, capable of carrying ammunition as well as fuel, as its standard replenishment vessel; 4 are in service and at least 2 additional units are in production. The RAS ships are spread among the three fleets on a relatively equal basis.

Surface Forces

China's shipbuilding industry has repeatedly demonstrated its ability to build and equip a wide range of surface combatants, including patrol craft, corvettes, frigates, destroyers, small and large amphibious ships, and conventionally and nuclear-powered submarines, and has at least one additional aircraft carrier under construction. The industry has historically had difficulty building propulsion systems but may be overcoming that deficiency.

The Chinese navy currently numbers more than 300 ships, submarines, and advanced missile boats, including a 2000 to June 2014 increase from 284 to 290 front-line units (see table 2.1).

The U.S. Office of Naval Intelligence estimated in 2013 that by 2020, the PLAN would include the following ships of "modern design":[19]

Diesel attack submarines:	44 to 48
Nuclear-powered attack submarines:	6 to 9
Ballistic missile submarines:	4 to 5
Aircraft carriers:	1 to 2
Destroyers:	26 to 29
Frigates:	46 to 49
Corvettes:	24 to 30
Amphibious ships:	50 to 55
Missile-armed patrol boats:	85

TABLE 2.1 PLAN ORDERS OF BATTLE, 2000–2014

Type	2000	2010	2014	2020
SS	60	54	51	59–64
SSN	5	6	5	6–9
SSBN	0	3	4	4–6
CV	0	0	1	1–3
DDG	21	25	24	30–34
FFG/Corvette	37	49	63	83–97
Amphibs	60	55	57	50–55
PGM	100	85	85	85
TOTAL	283	277	290	318–353

Note: These numbers are my estimates, based on the Department of Defense annual *Report to Congress on Military and Security Developments Involving the PRC*, Washington, D.C.: OSD, 2015.

This force is the world's second-most-capable navy based on its approximately 60 warships capable of operating in a twenty-first-century naval environment. Although the PLAN is growing more in individual platform capability than it is in numbers and still lacks in world-class RAS vessels, by 2020 it will have become comparable in capability to any of the world's navies, including that of the United States.

While many of these ships (4 Sovremenny class, 1 Luhai class, 2 Luhu-class guided-missile destroyers (DDG), approximately 12 Jiangwei-class guided-missile frigates) are armed with limited AAW detection and weapons systems, the newer classes of destroyers (the Luyang I, II, and III and the Luzou I and II) have much more capable, perhaps state-of-the-art AAW systems. The Luyang II and III classes feature Aegis-like systems.

Other significant new surface combatants are the Jiangkai I- and II–class frigates and Jiangdao-class corvettes. Another forty or so Chinese warships are armed with ASCMs and in a non–air threat environment could perform SLOC defense duties in Chinese littoral waters. Approximately 60 Houbei-class missile boats are particularly notable among these vessels. This class is operationally limited by manning and sea state, but their stealthy construction and potent cruise missiles would form a serious presence in littoral waters. Indeed, the PLAN's formidable ASCMs are its most potent weapons, launched from submarines, surface combatants, aircraft, and shore batteries.[20]

The PLAN remains significantly limited in the crucial ASW mission, however; it is only since the 2005 commissioning of three new classes of destroyers that the PLAN has deployed ships capable of "area AAW." This important capability enables a single ship to provide antiaircraft defense not just for itself, but also for a formation of ships. Area AAW is crucial to fleet operations at sea, whether against a U.S. naval task force or for escorting an amphibious task force against Taiwan.

A larger surface combatant, tentatively described as a cruiser, reportedly is under construction. This ship, called the Type-055 by the United States, is estimated to displace approximately 10,000 tons, about the same as the latest version of a U.S. *Arleigh Burke*–class DDG. Since the U.S. *Elmo Zumwalt*–class combatants are called "destroyers," despite displacing 15,000 tons, the terminology for surface combatants obviously is evolving.[21]

Amphibious Forces

PLAN modernization also includes other naval warfare area improvements. Amphibious force growth since the mid-1990s has included significant ship-building programs, including almost 20 tank landing ships, each displacing approximately 3,500 tons, and several dock-landing ships (LSD) that displace more than 17,000 tons and strongly resemble the U.S. *San Antonio* class. Four of these ships have joined the fleet since 2007; a fifth is under construction, and a sixth reportedly is planned.[22]

Additionally, a larger helicopter carrier, given the U.S. designator Type 081, reportedly is under construction. It will probably resemble the 20,000-ton-plus helicopter assault ships long deployed by the U.S. and other navies.[23]

The PLAN's first mobile landing platform (MLP) is another recently developed and deployed ship, assigned the hull number 868. The MLP is apparently similar to the U.S. *Montford*-class platform and is intended to embark the PLAN's Zubr-class air-cushioned landing craft. While displacing just 3,200 tons, the MLP offers a modest offshore basing point when conducting amphibious operations.[24]

Submarine Force

The navy's most potent strength lies in its numerous, modernizing submarine force. It currently deploys an impressive force of conventionally powered submarines. China has built more than fifty-two submarines since 1995 and leads the world in numbers of modern boats, although their capabilities are not fully understood or proven. The new submarines are armed in accordance with the PLAN's emphasis on antiship cruise missiles as the first-choice weapons system, making the submarine China's capital ship.

China has deployed conventionally and nuclear-powered submarines to the Indian Ocean, most recently sending a Shang-class boat to the Gulf of Aden, as have the United States, the Netherlands, and India.[25] However, China's submarine force remains focused on the regional waters of the three seas. The twelve Kilo-class and seventeen Song-class conventionally powered attack boats are not well suited for long-range deployments (to the Indian Ocean, for example) but are formidable weapons systems within approximately 1,000 nm of China's coast. The PLAN's thirty or forty older Ming-class boats will be decommissioned.

The next likely steps in the development of China's submarine force will be, first, increased numbers of boats equipped with AIP systems, currently installed in the twelve-ship Yuan class. An AIP system enables a conventionally powered submarine to remain submerged for up to forty days (at slow speed) instead of the usual four days before snorkeling is required.[26]

The PLAN's remaining two or three nuclear-powered Han-class attack submarines are old and noisy, and difficult to maintain. The nuclear-powered submarine force now includes, however, two newer Shang-class SSNs. These boats became operational a decade ago, but China stopped building them, for unexplained reasons, but likely because of design/operational problems. A successor class, the Type 095 SSN, is now under construction, with an unknown number completed. Reports of this program are confused, with the most authoritative, that published annually by the U.S. Congressional Research Service, only identifying the Type 095 as likely armed with antiship and antishore target cruise missiles.[27] Almost all of China's submarines are armed with torpedoes and with ASCMs; only the Ming-class and the four older Kilo-class boats lack missiles. The most capable ASCMs are the SS-N-27, which has a 120-nm range, and the similarly capable YJ-18.

Four Jin-class FBMs have joined the fleet but still await arming with the JL-2 ICBM. These boats are all stationed at Yulin, Hainan Island, with the SSF. This submarine-missile combination is China's second attempt to deploy a maritime nuclear deterrent system. The JL-1 missile, with a theoretical range of just over 900 nm, was never successfully launched from its intended platform, the Xia-class (Type 092) FBM submarine. This boat entered service in 1986 and was reportedly modernized in 2005–6 but has never been considered operational. It remains based at Qingdao as a unit of the NSF but no doubt will soon be formally retired.

China's past failure to deploy an effective FBM submarine will soon change when the JL-2 ICBM becomes operational. U.S. intelligence sources have been predicting this missile's operational status for several years, but it was only in 2013 that the PLAN reportedly conducted a successful at-sea launch.[28] Two years later the JL-2 remains in development. When it reaches the fleet, the missile will arm the new Jin-class FBM boats based at Sanya, in Hainan Island. Four of these are reportedly operational, although the final number to be built is unknown.[29]

When it is deployed, the JL-2 will form China's first successful seaborne nuclear deterrent. A Jin-class submarine armed with twelve JL-2s will provide Beijing with a nuclear-tipped missile with a range of approximately 4,000 nm, capable of striking throughout East Asia and the Pacific, as far as Hawaii, Alaska, and the West Coast of the United States. The location of the submarine of course determines targeting ranges; if China stations the Jins in the South China Sea, under a bastion concept, then the U.S. West Coast is not within range.[30] The final number of Jins to be built is unknown, with various U.S. estimates since 2007, but former commander, U.S. Pacific Command, Adm. Samuel Locklear estimated in 2015 that China would build nine boats.[31]

More significant than the exact number of Jin-class boats joining the fleet is the total number of ballistic missile–armed submarines China builds. A follow-on class, the Type 096, may already be in design; China is likely developing a missile able to range most if not the entire continental United States. In addition to unresolved questions of range and numbers, open source material does not indicate how Beijing resolves very important doctrinal and operational issues.

First, China's practice of stationing conventionally and nuclear-armed missiles at the same bases raises dangerous targeting issues for an opponent. Second, no Chinese FBM submarine has ever conducted an operational deterrent patrol. China's centralized command-and-control philosophy constrains the independence of military commanders, especially when nuclear weapons are concerned. This centralization poses particular problems for employing a sea-based deterrent in submarines, whose effectiveness depends on their covertness and independent operations. Allowing individual submarine commanders custodianship and perhaps launching authority over nuclear-armed missiles would constitute a significant change of Chinese doctrine, which will have to be modified to include new command-and-control technologies and procedures.

Another unanswered question is why Beijing is even developing a sea-based nuclear deterrent. Submarines are very expensive to build and maintain, and they are susceptible to countermeasures at sea, whereas land-based missiles are easily hidden and even road-mobile as well as far less expensive than submarine-based weapons. The answer may lie in simple interservice rivalry within the PLA; the increased budget allocated to the navy is allowing it to spend on a system that is not required for China to maintain its traditional minimum-deterrence nuclear force. It may also result in part from Beijing wanting a sea-based nuclear deterrent because one is maintained by the United States and other world nuclear powers.

Beijing remains the world leader in building submarines, but that force's technological sophistication is problematic. According to the U.S. Office of Naval Intelligence, China's submarines are surprisingly noisy compared to other nations' submarines.[32] That means that the "self-noise" generated by Chinese submarines makes them easier to detect by passive sonar, the primary means of finding submerged submarines.

Submarine construction has been a marked exception to the general pace of modernization as the PLAN has continued focusing on possible Taiwan scenarios as its number one operational priority. Submarines are capable of launching mines as well as torpedoes and missiles, although usually on a one-for-one trade-off among these weapons. China's surface combatants are also capable of launching mines, of which China may have an inventory of as many as 50,000. Many of these are older contact mines, but the inventory is being steadily filled with the modern results of China's robust mine warfare research and development program.

Furthermore, during the 2014–15 search for the missing Malaysian airliner MH370, the PLAN has increased analysts' knowledge of its substantial program developing unmanned underwater craft.[33] These are effective platforms for conducting mine warfare, ASW, and other missions. Despite its obvious utility against Taiwan, however, mine warfare apparently is no more attractive to the PLAN than it is to the Taiwan or U.S. navies. The PLAN's mine laying capability is more formidable and could serve as an effective tool in a maritime campaign against Taiwan.[34]

Naval Aviation

Naval aviation remains the PLAN's least capable warfare community, but this is not a significant PLA weakness since many PLA Air Force (PLAAF) mainland bases are able to range Beijing's top concerns, Taiwan, and the East and South China Seas. The increasing integration of China's naval and air force aviation assets is also significant but remains rudimentary.

PLA aviation capabilities have benefited from the annual increases in the navy's budget. As is the case with amphibious warfare, more significant even than important equipment acquisitions—Su-27s, Su-30s, air-to-air refueling, and airborne warning and air control–type aircraft—has been increased training. The former category is made up for the most part of fighter and bomber aircraft, although it includes a force of longer-range aircraft capable of launching antiship cruise missiles.

Naval aviation is deficient in ASW and long-range search aircraft; its airborne electronic warfare capability is also weak. The PLAN obviously is aware of this shortfall and is working to overcome it, evidenced in the magnetic anomaly detection–equipped Y-9 aircraft, a Chinese-manufactured version of the Soviet-designed An-12 multipurpose airframe.

Most PLAN fixed-wing aircraft are shore based, although regiments flying the J-15 are training at sea to form the first carrier-based air wing. This aircraft was reported to have entered serial production in November 2014.[35] A vertical-takeoff-and-landing aircraft, designated the J-18, is reportedly under development.[36]

The PLAN continues exercising in and improving its performance in offshore air defense and strike operations. Increasing numbers of fourth-generation aircraft, both the Russian-designed Su-27s and Su-30s as well as the indigenously produced J-10A and J-11B, are participating in these missions. The PLAN also continues to fly the H-6, which is a copy of the old Soviet-designed Tu-16 Badger. Some H-6s have been configured to serve as aerial refuelers.[37] The PLAN may also be able in the future to employ ASCMs fired from unmanned aerial vehicles (UAV), China's J-20 stealth aircraft, and Soviet-designed Tu-22 Backfire bombers.[38] The 2014 Zhuhai Air Show emphasized the remarkable progress China has made in developing and operating UAVs, including models designed (and observed) to operate from surface combatants. Several Chinese models appear to be remarkably similar to U.S. UAVs and capable of a wide range of missions, including surveillance and strike.[39]

Helicopters are increasingly operating from shipboard, gaining valuable experience in regional and far sea missions. Their proficiency in logistics support, search and rescue (SAR), surveillance, electronic warfare, airborne early warning (AEW), strike, ASW, and special operations support has been demonstrated on numerous occasions during the navy's counterpiracy operations in the Gulf of Aden and in exercises in home waters. Beijing deployed its twentieth task group to the Gulf on 3 April 2015.[40]

The PLAN's helicopter force is remarkably small but growing in capability and numbers. It operates three primary models, all acquired or copied from foreign sources. The Z-8 and Z-9 are French in origin, while the HELIX is Russian. The PLAN's twenty Z-9s are licensed from the French Dauphin II helicopter, powered by Europcopter-designed engines. They include variants fitted with search radars, dipping sonars, and an ASW torpedo. The latest, the Z-9D, is armed with an ASCM. They are able to fly from any flight deck–equipped PLAN ship.

The Z-8 was reverse-engineered from the French-designed Super Frelon. It is a medium-lift helicopter employed for SAR, personnel transportation, and logistics support. It has been observed equipped with weapons pods normally associated with rockets and machine guns. These helicopters require larger flight decks; the Z-18, an AEW variant, has operated from the *Liaoning*. A medical evacuation variant, the Z-8JH, is assigned to China's large hospital ship, the *Peace Ark*.

The approximately seventeen HELIX variants currently flown by the PLAN include Ka-27PS birds largely dedicated to logistics and SAR operations. The Ka-28s are multimission capable but most often employed in ASW, equipped with dipping sonars, sonobuoys, and radar while armed with torpedoes, depth charges, or mines. China also purchased nine Ka-31 AEW helicopters, equipped with the E-801 radar system, in 2010.[41] Additional expansion of the PLAN's helicopter fleet is inevitable as its numbers of helicopter-capable ships increase.

Recent at-sea exercises demonstrating the navy's emphasis on operations between ships and aircraft, both fixed- and rotary-wing, have evidenced growing integration between the navy's surface and aviation forces. PLAN combatants also are capable of data linking with embarked helicopters.[42]

Aircraft Carriers

China has acquired four retired aircraft carriers for study since 1985, the Australian HMAS *Melbourne* and the ex-Soviet carriers *Minsk* and *Kiev*, and, in 2002, the ex-Soviet Kuznetsov-class carrier *Varyag*. This ship spent nearly a decade undergoing modernization, was renamed *Liaoning*, and became operational in 2012.[43] The carrier has been operating extensively on training missions; both ship's company personnel and embarked aircraft crews have been learning how to conduct operations that are new, complex, and very dangerous.

Future Chinese aircraft carrier acquisition plans have not been publicized, but Chinese officials have discussed building additional carriers.[44] Unanswered questions include the number (one per each of three fleets or more), propulsion systems (conventional or nuclear), and launching method (ski ramp or catapult). Additional carriers are a given; the most logical characteristics of China's future three or more indigenously constructed aircraft carriers are a final number of four to six nuclear-powered, catapult-equipped ships.

Lack of catapults limits the weight of aircraft that can be launched, which correspondingly limits their capability. Hence, future Chinese carriers are most likely to adopt either steam-driven or electronic catapults rather than continue the *Liaoning*'s ski ramp design.

Liaoning flight operations to date have relied on the J-15 "Flying Shark," a tactical fighter-bomber built by China with indigenously manufactured avionics but copied from the Soviet-designed Su-33. The ship is likely to deploy an air wing composed of twenty-four J-15s and twelve helicopters, six of the latter for ASW, four AEW, and two SAR.[45]

The J-15 launched from a ski ramp is weight constricted but extremely capable in terms of range and payload—if launched from a carrier equipped with steam-driven or electromagnetic catapults.[46] A full fuel load is required since the PLAN has no carrier-capable aircraft able to conduct in-flight refueling. However, given the navy's current operational focus on regional scenarios, shore-based refueling is a realistic option.

Marine Corps

China maintains a small marine corps composed of just two brigades, each numbering approximately six thousand personnel. Both units are stationed with the SSF, with an obvious mission of operating in and among the many islands and other land features that mark that sea. Its officer accession process has been regularized under PLAN aegis. Two PLA army divisions in the Nanjing and Guangzhou MRs form China's more numerous amphibious assault force. These divisions receive dedicated amphibious training, with a Taiwan assault their most probable mission.

Coast Guard

A significant addition to China's maritime capabilities is its ongoing effort to strengthen and regularize the many organizations performing missions typically categorized as "coast guard." These include customs enforcement, antismuggling of goods and human trafficking, safety of navigation and regulation of merchant traffic at sea and on China's riverine waters, homeland security, defense of the nation's insular claims and maritime economic infrastructure, and assisting the PLAN when called upon in time of need.

Under the reorganization, the coast guard is now under the State Oceanic Administration (SOA), headquartered in Beijing, although the Ministry of Public Security may also have a role in controlling the coast guard. The SOA includes the China Marine Surveillance; Maritime Police and Border Control, previously administered by the Ministry of Public Security; Fisheries Law Enforcement Command, previously administered by the Ministry of Agriculture; and the Maritime Antismuggling Police, previously administered by the General Administration of Customs. The SOA has also gained a new agency, the China Maritime Police Bureau.

The Maritime Safety Administration apparently has remained under the Ministry of Transportation, as have the various municipal and riparian agencies assigned coast guard–like missions. Additionally, the SOA apparently does not include the Ocean Mineral Resources Research and Development Association, the Polar Research Institute of China, the Chinese Academy of Sciences, or the China Geological Survey.

The issue of SOA authority is further clouded by lack of clarity of administrative control and operational control of the various agencies. The Ministry of Land and Resources supposedly administers the SOA, but the Ministry of Public Security reportedly retains operational control of the SOA. Also unspecified is the PLAN's attitude toward the new SOA, the operations of which the navy surely and naturally will want to influence.[47]

Recent events in the East and South China Seas show that Beijing is striving to coordinate and maximize the synergy gained from the activities of all of its maritime organizations, including the navy, coast guard, and maritime militia. This includes the linkage with China's state-owned enterprises and other major industries with these organizations, as demonstrated in the movements of HYSY-981 in and out of disputed South China Sea waters. The Central Maritime Rights Leading Small Group is the government's organization orchestrating the campaign to safeguard China's maritime claims and sovereignty.[48]

The SOA organizations have benefited from a dramatic increase in budget, personnel, aircraft, and surface ships. At least 52 patrol vessels have joined the SOA fleet since 2010. Many of these are extremely large for traditional coast guard duties, displacing as much as 5,000 tons, with one proposed ship reportedly weighing in at 12,000 tons. The SOA has also benefited from the PLAN transferring 11 old but still very serviceable warships, including Jiangwei-class frigates.[49]

Maritime Militia

A maritime militia has long been maintained by Beijing, but it is probably only since the middle of the past decade that it has received significant training, command-and-control capability, and assignment to support PLAN and coast guard operations, almost entirely in the South China Sea struggle over land features claimed by China and other nations but also in the East China Sea, where Japan is China's protagonist.[50]

The maritime militia may be employed in peacetime power projection and during wartime to "flood" an operational area, collect intelligence, support PLAN repairs and logistics, and provide training assistance. Many of the boats have been equipped with advanced communications and surveillance systems and have supported PLAN warships during exercises as well as carried materials for Beijing's "island" enlargement program. Military training afforded many of the fishing vessels in the maritime militia includes ship identification, use of light weapons, and fleet organization.[51]

Organization and employment of the maritime militia may be considered a modern form of "people's war" at sea, but this also poses real escalation dangers as half-trained militia personnel interact with foreign warships. China possesses approximately 200,000 fishing vessels, the world's largest fishing fleet, tens of thousands of which apparently have been assigned as unofficial constabulary and auxiliaries to support the PLAN and Chinese coast guard organizations.[52] China's fishing fleet does not hesitate to go where the fish are expected; they have even clashed with North Korean police.[53] He Jianbin, chief of the state-run fishing corporation in Hainan Province, sounded a particularly aggressive note in June 2012 when he urged the government to further militarize the fishing fleet: "If we put 5,000 Chinese fishing ships in the South China Sea, there will be 100,000 fishermen. . . . And if we make all of them militiamen, give them weapons, we will have a military force stronger than all the combined forces of all the countries in the South China Sea. . . . We should train these fishermen/militiamen [in] military operations, making them a reserve force on the sea and using them to solve our South Sea problems."[54] The employment of maritime militia units in company with coast guard vessels, almost certainly under command and control of PLAN personnel, was evident in the Haiyang Shiyou 981 incident in May 2014, when Beijing directed one of China's largest oil companies, the China National Overseas Oil Company, to move and operate its newest maritime drilling platform into waters claimed by Vietnam.[55]

Shipyards

The PLAN suffered a serious mishap in 2003, when a Ming-class submarine lost its entire crew, probably as a result of carbon monoxide poisoning. That accident was due either to personnel error or to shoddy maintenance performed at a ship repair facility where the submarine had recently been overhauled. As a result, the PLAN very significantly overhauled its maintenance and repair systems. While undocumented in open sources, the results of those changes have almost certainly resulted in dramatically improved reliability of PLAN ships.[56]

China's commercial shipbuilding sector is subject to state control, including requirements to build merchant ships compatible to certain military requirements. These apply particularly to relatively recent construction of roll-on/roll-off ships reportedly being constructed in accordance with national defense requirements.

China is the world's biggest shipbuilder, recently surpassing South Korea and Japan in ship production measured by volume. That ranking is being challenged, as is that of China's two nearest competitors, by a global slowdown in merchant ship orders. The majority of Chinese shipyards have been on a downward trend since 2012 in terms of new ship orders. A particularly distressing indicator of the slowdown was marked by Chinese premier Wen Jiabao's visit to Greece in 2010, when a reported US$5 billion "Sino-Greek shipping finance fund" failed significantly to increase Greek ship orders to Chinese yards.[57]

This downturn resulted in a 2012 decision by Beijing to consolidate its shipbuilding companies, with a goal of establishing ten "superyards" that would control approximately 70 percent of the nation's ship production. This likely places only the largest shipyards, such as China Shipbuilding Industry Corporation and China Rongsheng Heavy Industries, among the top leaders in global shipbuilding.[58]

Beijing has reacted aggressively to the global downturn in new construction, moving to modernize its shipyards and increase the technological level of the ships they build. These improvements have been concentrated in state-owned yards, many of which are also capable of building naval vessels. Furthermore, by the end of 2014, 80 percent of China's tankers were less than ten years old, as were 68 percent of its bulk carriers and 51 percent of its container ships.[59]

This extensive infrastructure exists in a gray area between state-owned enterprises and private-sector businesses, which makes it difficult to estimate the actual cost of new PLAN systems.[60] Nonetheless, China's world-leading shipbuilding capability likely will make the PLAN the world's second-largest navy by 2020. China's heavy international maritime trade complements its shipbuilding and shore-based infrastructure. While global traffic normally travels on SLOCs as clearly delineated as interstate highways, China's dependence on these SLOCs is both massive and high in Beijing's strategic consciousness.

A 2015 Naval War College conference on China's shipbuilding industry identified five "key" and seven additional findings:

1. China's shipbuilding industry is growing more rapidly than any other in modern history.
2. That rapid growth has allowed it to "leapfrog" some engineering, technology, and production steps, resulting in significant cost and time savings.
3. PLAN shipbuilding choices are driven by, first, a combination of technological and strategic research and, second, ship construction that is increasingly subject to detailed national and military standards.
4. At current pace, the PLAN will become the world's second-largest navy by 2020 and equal to the U.S. Navy in quality and quantity by 2030.
5. The PLAN in 2020 will deploy greater quantities of missiles with greater range than those in the U.S. Navy.

Additional Findings:

1. The CCP has assigned the shipbuilding industry a key role in China's development as a great power.
2. China's state-owned shipyards, China Shipbuilding Industry Corporation and China State Shipbuilding Corporation, possess great capacity and resources but are inefficient, and their monopoly position is a major impediment to improving efficiency and innovation. Propulsion and electronic systems seem particularly to suffer from these bureaucratic impedimenta.
3. Shipbuilding plans and military standards come from the Weapons and Armament Development Strategy, which is drafted by the General Armament Department and approved by the CMC.
4. The PLAN's two main research organizations, the Naval Armament Research Institute and the Naval Research Institute, are tasked with rationalizing ship and weapon system design with naval strategy.
5. Naval ship design and production advances are achieved almost entirely through "imitative innovation," an official technology transfer policy under a policy called Introduce/Digest/Absorb/Reinnovate.
6. China's defense industrial base is uneven but improving; poor labor efficiency is a particular problem.
7. China has particular limitations in propulsion systems, some electronics, and some advanced weapons systems; Russian assistance is key to nuclear power developments.[61]

Personnel and Training

The two most important areas of PLAN "modernization" during the past decade have relatively little to do with hardware. The first is the overhaul of the personnel education and training system that has occurred as the Chinese military strives to enlist and retain personnel capable of mastering the technological complexities of current-day warships. This extends to the second area, the PLAN's revised and seemingly improved training system. The old ship and unit training method was tied to the calendar year; the new system seems now far more flexible, which enhances the integration of maintenance and shore-based training requirements.

One key question about PLAN readiness concerns the success of the new noncommissioned officer (NCO) corps program. The effort to emulate the success of the U.S. NCO system was launched over a decade ago as part of an attempted overhaul of the PLA's personnel accession system and in the face of cultural difficulties.[62] The PLAN reportedly began a program to assign senior NCOs to billets previously filled by junior commissioned officers. This program would link with the PLAN system of political officers and representatives as well as with a program of selecting enlisted "leaders" to monitor the crew and offer solutions to perceived problems.[63]

Exercises at Sea

The PLAN is also continuing to increase its participation in joint training and exercise activities. PLA exercises since approximately 2013 have demonstrated the navy's capability to effectively deploy and operate twenty-first-century ships in regional waters and its significant progress establishing that capability in the far seas. Regional waters are defined as the area within the first island chain; far seas are less clearly delineated, but include operations out to the second island chains and beyond. In addition to improving its capabilities in antisurface warfare (ASUW), AAW, and ASW, the PLAN exercise regimen has been notable for its increased emphasis on expanding from its previous concentration on littoral operations to preparing to operate in the far seas of the Indian Ocean and beyond.

The PLAN also continues trying to increase the flexibility and realism of its exercises, as urged by Xi Jinping to cultivate "real combat" awareness.[64] The "new normal" for exercises has been defined as "upgrading the combat effectiveness of the PLA."[65]

Fleet preparedness has been improved by the recently changed exercise program "complex multi-discipline warfare training throughout the year."[66] The new training paradigm is based on a three-level system, from a maintenance status to fully ready. Traditional underway training has been supplemented with an increased number of shore-based trainers dedicated to providing a full range of education and training, from individual enlisted personnel to new or transiting commanding officers.

The training cycle reportedly aims to achieve the following:

- Increase training in accordance with real-war requirements,
- Strengthen command authority and relationships through realistic opposing force training,

- Deepen tactical innovation,
- Improve training in the actual use of weapons in an electromagnetic environment,
- Continue "far-seas" training,
- Rectify training methods by avoiding formalism and scripting in exercise, and
- Improve joint campaign-level training.

The 2011–15 training plan also outlines the following objectives:

- Organize and improve multibranch training,
- Strengthen integration of units and information-based systems,
- Focus training for "far-seas" operations,
- Modernize management of training and standardize training evaluation and assessment process, and
- Develop a strong base for simulation and network-based training.[67]

These goals are not just ambitious but result from recognized weaknesses in PLAN training and readiness, some due to inflated and possibly dishonest evaluation results, unrealistic performance standards, and outright falsification. For instance, the PLA reportedly is trying to close loopholes in its financial regulations resulting from more than two hundred senior officers being relieved for misappropriation of funds. Of these, at least thirty PLA generals have been relieved.[68] These officers have been accused of a range of offenses, from excess spending on entertainment to outright embezzlement. More serious are accusations of bribery for promotions and special assignments. China's leadership, notably President Xi Jinping, views corruption as a serious impediment to combat readiness.[69]

The emphasis on far-seas training is a strong indicator of the PLAN's desire to better prepare for and routinely conduct the long-distant deployments currently conducted by the small task groups assigned to Gulf of Aden counterpiracy patrols. PLAN participation in the U.S.-led Rim-of-the-Pacific (RIMPAC) exercise in the summer 2014 marked the first such event for China's navy. PLAN participation included two combatants, an oiler, and its hospital ship.[70] This is just one of an increasing number of exercises, almost all of them consisting of very basic drills, being conducted by the PLAN.[71]

Major PLAN exercises now include PLAAF participation as well as ensuring that logistics support from both afloat and shore units is addressed. For instance, the navy has reported successful accomplishment of perhaps the most difficult replenishment-at-sea evolution, transferring missiles.[72] Exercises are also being conducted with a focus on integrating naval efforts with the civilian infrastructure. This includes Beijing requiring civilian shipbuilders to ensure that new ships can be adapted to military use in an emergency.[73] This will greatly augment the PLAN's capability for logistics lift of both personnel and goods, including fuel.

A 2012 exercise, East China Sea Cooperation, was conducted between the ESF and Chinese coast guard units. Health Service Mission 2013 was a similar exercise, conducted that year by the *Peace Ark* and civilian medical units from several provinces.

Constant emphasis has been placed on training under "complex electromagnetic conditions" since 2006. Another frequently verbalized training goal is to develop "integrated joint operations." This objective has been emphasized in China's *Science of Campaigns*, in the 2004–14 defense white papers, and in the 2008 *Outline for Military Training and Evaluation* (OMTE), published on 1 January 2009.[74]

The interoperability featured in this OMTE was evidenced in 2009 exercises. Examples include Joint Operation 2009, which involved all three services, the People's Armed Police, and local government elements; this last element demonstrated civil-military cooperation.[75] Another joint exercise that year was Vanguard-2009, reportedly notable as the "first time" the PLAN engaged in joint operations planning, command and control, intelligence, and combat decision-making.[76]

Exercises in "blue-water" scenarios increased in frequency and difficulty during 2010–12. The PLAN demonstrated improved confidence in its ability to engage in more complex, concurrent operations at sea. This was also demonstrated in the increased number of times its ships deployed outside the first island chain on what became routine operations. These operations were also notable for the different routes into the Philippine Sea taken through the first island chain, including the Miyako, Osumi, and Yonaguni Channels.[77]

One of the most significant of these operations occurred in April 2010, when the ESF deployed eight surface ships and two submarines through the

Miyako Channel into the western Philippine Sea. This operation was significant for at least three reasons. First, it demonstrated the PLAN's ability to operate surface ships and submarines together. Second, navy helicopters played an increasing role, demonstrating ASUW, ASW, command and control, and logistics capabilities. Third, sending this significant task group through the Miyako Channel sent a strong signal to Japan about Chinese naval power. The navy stated at the end of 2012 that it had "normalized open-sea training."[78]

This pattern continued in 2013–14 as PLAN operations in the Philippine Sea increased in number and complexity. In fact, such operations became routine during this two-year period. Several deployments included surface ships and submarines, helicopter operations, and, most significantly, exercising in several mission areas, such as ASUW and ASW. Additionally, the transit channels were expanded to include the Bashi Channel south of Taiwan and the La Pérouse Strait north of Japan. A PLAN spokesman described these transits as "cutting the first island chain into little pieces."[79]

The most notable PLAN exercise during these two years took place in October 2013. Mobility-5 apparently was the first exercise to involve ships from all three fleets. Navy helicopters and fixed-wing aircraft also participated. Its purpose was to build "the capability of distant-sea combat systems under conditions of informatization. In this exercise, importance was attached to exploring major and challenging problems related to the building of distant-sea combat systems, reconnaissance and early warning target identification and guidance, long-distance defense penetration conducted by aviation forces, and vessel-aircraft coordination in carrying out anti-submarine operations."[80]

Since 2012 the PLAN has routinely conducted multiunit and even multifleet exercises in the Philippine Sea, beyond the first island chain, including seven in that year. Recent notable exercises included ships, submarines, and aircraft from all three fleets conducting in December 2014 an exercise in the western Pacific. These exercises demonstrate the PLAN's maturing ability to conduct operations that include and may integrate surface, subsurface, and aviation units, a vital step toward becoming proficient in joint warfare.[81]

A deployment through the Indonesian archipelago into the Indian Ocean in January 2014 was another significant operation. A three-ship task group steamed throughout the South China Sea and in transiting to and from the Indian Ocean made a point to pass through the Sunda, Lombok, and Makassar

Straits. During their deployment, the ships conducted "more than ten combat-realistic training tasks, including the anti-pirate, joint search and rescue, anti-nuclear and anti-chemical contamination, and damage control tasks."[82]

An abbreviated plan for 2015 was provided at a January news conference, when the Ministry of National Defense representative stated, "The PLA will firmly uphold the criteria of improving fighting capacity in these [2015] training activities, deepen strategic and campaign training, strengthen mission-oriented and subject-oriented joint training, conduct training among different services and arms, strengthen modern warfare training at night, in complex, electromagnetic environment, in special terrains and under extreme weather conditions, expand joint exercises, joint training and competition with foreign militaries, so as to improve the capability of winning local wars under informationized conditions."[83] The exercise program during the first eight months of 2015 continued emphasizing joint operations, with multi-service and multifleet participation. Three significant exercises were conducted during the summer, two with PLAAF participation, two with Second Artillery support, and one with army electronic countermeasures units in support. This lineup indicates that these exercises were focused on anti-access/area denial operations. Army and marine corps units have also conducted smaller scale amphibious training.

The first of these exercises was conducted in early July in the Yellow Sea by "several missile-launching battalions of the Second Artillery" supporting "almost 100 warships and tens of naval aviation planes [and army] electronic countermeasure forces." The exercise was described as "close to a real IT-based sea battle." Torpedoes and shells were expended against air, surface, and subsurface targets in drills described as "closest to real combat."[84]

The second important naval exercise was the PLAN's "largest ever live-ammunition drill" in the South China Sea in early August. Participating units included "more than 100 naval vessels, dozens of aircraft and a number of [army] electronic warfare units in a sophisticated electronic warfare scenario." The Second Artillery also took part. The exercise reportedly focused on the navy's "air defense and early warning system and . . . emergency response capability," including "against super-sonic anti-ship missiles."[85]

The third of these exercises was conducted in late August 2015, a PLAN "live fire" drill in the East China Sea, involving "more than 100 warships, dozens of aircraft, and several missile launch battalions [with] nearly 100 missiles and several hundred shells and bombs" fired. Units from all three PLAN fleets participated, including destroyers, frigates, submarines, fighters, and "onshore support forces."[86]

The location and frequency of PLAN exercises are tied directly to Chinese foreign policy objectives. Hence, the navy conducted a significant, multiphase exercise with PLAAF support in May–June 2015. The exercise objective clearly was Taiwan and involved integration of civilian shipping into amphibious operations.[87]

China is emphasizing exercises in disputed waters of the East and South China Seas and beginning to include the Indian Ocean. Beijing clearly is using its navy in a classic maritime mission of presence, including it as a vehicle for exerting diplomatic pressure and underlining Chinese territorial claims.[88] Russia has been an exercise partner on at least an annual basis. The most recent PLAN-Russian navy exercise occurred in August 2015, followed by an interesting foray when five of the Chinese participating ships steamed through U.S. territorial waters off Alaska.[89] A more intriguing relationship with Moscow may involve the two nations constructing a port on the Sea of Japan. It would be intended primarily for cargo and energy transportation but would also offer significant basing for naval vessels.[90]

Operations

The PLAN has been deploying three-ship task groups to the Gulf of Aden and beyond since December 2008. It has also conducted noncombatant evacuation operations (NEO) and other international missions as far as the Mediterranean Sea. Those operations have provided a textbook illustration of a regional navy transitioning to a near-global maritime force. While those distant deployments have been limited to China's most modern combatants and support ships, they have created an entire generation of PLAN officers and senior enlisted personnel with the expertise and experience to operate far from home for long periods.

The PLAN's increasing emphasis on preparing for far-seas operations remains a work in progress. Logistics is the most important warfare area in which the navy requires the most development. The post-2008 deployments to the Gulf of Aden and beyond have depended on just five underway replenishment ships; more will be needed for the three fleets to become routinely prepared for far-seas deployments. Personnel experience will have to continue to increase, as will the sophisticated command-and-control capability necessary for independent and distant small unit operations.

PLAN blue-water training, also called "combat readiness patrols," increased from six in 2007 to twenty-eight in 2013, and the navy now maintains almost constant presence throughout the three seas, even out to the second island chain.[91]

Strategy and Doctrine

The PRC emerged in 1949 with no more of a maritime strategy than it had a navy; its initial maritime force was imported from the Soviet Union, as was its initial maritime strategy, the "Young School" of the 1920s. This defined a naval role largely limited to supporting the army's operations ashore.

As described in detail in the next chapter, Beijing now embraces the concepts of "command of the sea," "sea denial," and "sea control," as well as having developed impressive naval and commercial maritime forces and infrastructure. Chinese strategists are concerned about threats from the sea, with the United States their primary concern. The PLAN's planning concerns are expressed in specific scenarios. Most important, of course, is defense of China's maritime borders. China is responding with both a modernized navy and reorganized coast guard. Next important is the status of Taiwan, with the PLAN's goal not necessarily to be prepared to conduct an amphibious invasion of the island but to be ready to deter, slow, and possibly defeat U.S. intervention.

Third in importance to PLAN planning are various scenarios in the East and South China Seas, again the subject of improved navy capability and a vastly improved coast guard. Fourth, and evidence of Beijing's maritime ambitions, is the drive to develop the maritime capability, both afloat and ashore, both domestically and internationally, to secure China's global economic interests.[92]

The 2013 defense white paper, for instance, describes the PLAN as endeavoring "to accelerate the modernization of its forces for comprehensive offshore operations [and] develop blue water capabilities."[93] This goal includes defense of distant SLOCs, as demonstrated in the Gulf of Aden counterpiracy deployments that began in December 2008 and continue in 2015, despite the almost complete cessation of the piracy problem in those distant seas.

The May 2015 defense white paper on military strategy is even more specific, describing the PLAN's transformation from "offshore waters defense" to "open seas protection."[94] The 2015 strategy also focuses on the relationship among national naval power, economic development, and international relations that underlies Chinese maritime strategy.

Mao Zedong wrote in 1953, "We must build a strong navy for the purpose of fighting against imperialist aggression." In 1979 Deng Xiaoping called for "a strong navy with modern combat capability," although emphasizing its role in coastal defense. Jiang Zemin urged the navy in 1997 to "build up the nation's Great Wall." Hu Jintao urged the CMC in 2004 to "accelerate the transformation and modernization of the Navy . . . and make extended preparations for warfare in order to make greater contributions to safeguarding national security and world peace."[95] He later noted the importance of maritime border issues, Taiwan's status, and "protection of China's expanding national interests."[96] Most recently, President Xi Jinping's enunciation of a "China Dream" has engendered articles calling for a strategy of "outward-oriented military power," to include "limited global military power . . . capable of protecting distant sea lanes."[97]

China is also employing its navy as a diplomatic instrument. Since 1983 the PLAN has periodically deployed two- or three-ship task forces on diplomatic missions to Southeast, South, and Southwest Asia and to the Western Hemisphere. In 2002 a Luhu-class DDG and an oiler completed a circumnavigation of the globe, a significant accomplishment. Another task force visited the United States in September 2006. Chinese ship visits around the world have become much more common since then. The PLAN has also embraced humanitarian missions, including deploying the *Peace Ark* to Northeast Asia, the Indian Ocean, and the Caribbean. The PLAN also participated in the removal of Libyan chemical weapons in 2014.[98]

NEOs are becoming a more common mission for the PLAN. NEOs have been conducted in Libya in 2011 and in Yemen in 2015, while between 2006 and 2010 approximately 6,000 Chinese citizens were evacuated from Chad, Haiti, Kyrgyzstan, Lebanon, Solomon Islands, Thailand, Timor-Leste, and Tonga, in addition to the more recent 48,000 evacuated from Egypt, Libya, Japan, and Yemen.[99]

This navy mission reflects Beijing's increased attention to the status of Chinese citizens abroad. The Ministry of Foreign Affairs, for instance, has improved its consular protection system and reportedly established an inter-agency coordination mechanism. Not clear is the coordination of such efforts among the Ministry of Foreign Affairs, the PLA, the coast guard, the Ministry of Public Security, and similar foreign organizations.[100]

Merchant Fleet

Merchant ships are the centerpieces of seaborne commerce, of course, but they in turn depend on the shore-based infrastructure of dockyards, cargo ports, personnel training and employment facilities, and governmental regulation and safeguarding. China has six of the top ten ports in the world in total cargo tonnage.

China is also among the world leaders in the national registration of merchant ships. Its 73,892,000 tons of Chinese-flagged vessels, in combination with Hong Kong's 6,597,000 tons, places it in third place worldwide. This ranking is even more impressive since the leading two fleets—Panama and Liberia—are flags of convenience (as are other leaders, such as the Marshall Islands and the Bahamas). In terms of number of flagged ships, however, China ranks fourth, with 1,999, trailing Japan, Greece, and Germany.[101]

China's merchant fleet calls at more than 600 ports in more than 150 countries. As of 2014, China (including Hong Kong) flagged almost twice as many merchant ship tons as the next-largest fleet in Asia. Chinese ports also led the world in container traffic, with a 2013 throughput of 174,080,330 20-foot equivalent units.

The maritime environment directly influences China's serious and increasing resource problems, especially energy and food. International trade goes by sea; only 25 percent is carried in Chinese bottoms.[102] This reflects the economic benefit of using maritime transportation; it is cheaper to ship a ton of coal five thousand miles by sea than three hundred miles by rail, for instance.[103] China's long coastline, thousands of islands, and important rivers make sea transport attractive.

Beijing has been particularly concerned about the low number of the tankers sailing under the Chinese flag, many of them too small for profitable employment on the long SLOCs to the Middle East. In 2006 Beijing ordered a shipbuilding program to raise the percentage of oil imported in Chinese-flagged tankers from 10 percent to 60–70 percent by 2020.[104] This apparently appeals to China's leadership from an economic perspective, but it makes little sense from a military view of energy security to increase the number of Chinese-flagged tankers because doing so very significantly eases the "identification-friend-or-foe" problem for intercepting naval vessels.

Ships are and will likely remain the most cost-effective means of transporting oil: the cost of transporting one barrel of oil over a distance of 1,000 km (540 nm) was estimated in 2007 to be US$0.163 by tanker, US$0.793 via pipeline, and US$7.190 by train.[105]

Conclusion

China's creation of a large, modern navy capable of operating in the twenty-first-century maritime arena has been marked by three milestones. First was the 1995–96 Taiwan Strait crisis. PLAN modernization received increased priority and funding after the early to mid-1990s, almost certainly receiving additional impetus following the Taiwan Strait crisis in March 1996. Beijing began acquiring Kilo-class submarines from Russia and began indigenous production of the Song-class submarines in the mid-1990s. The new nuclear submarine program also began during this period. It is unlikely that the modernization of China's submarine force began by coincidence with the PLA's realization of its shortcomings following U.S. naval intervention in the Taiwan imbroglio in 1996. The events of the mid-1990s no doubt spurred PLAN modernization of its surface combatant fleet, as well. In particular, the PLAN realized its weaknesses in specific naval warfare areas, and more generally in lack of standardization, interoperability, and joint operations.[106]

The second milestone was the successive deployments of Chinese naval task groups to the Gulf of Aden and, most important, the success of admirals Liu Huaqing, Shi Yunsheng and Wu Shengli in creating a modern Chinese navy in a military dominated by the army.

This last factor appears to have led to the third milestone: the shift in influence and emphasis in the PLA in favor of the navy. China's 2004 defense white paper stated, "The PLA will promote coordinated development of firepower, mobility and information capability, enhance the development of its operational strength with priority given to the Navy, Air Force and Second Artillery Force."[107] At the CCP's Eighteenth Party Congress in November 2012, President Hu Jintao emphasized that the other services would be playing a more important role in China's military, asserting, "We should attach great importance to maritime, space and cyberspace security." General Xu

Qiliang argued, "We should . . . lay stress on strengthening the building of the Navy, Air Force, and Second Artillery."[108] Then, in November 2013, a senior MR commander stated that the PLA was going to become more balanced, with the army being deemphasized in favor of the navy and air force.[109] Finally, in January 2014, Chinese military analysts described a "new joint command system" reflecting "naval prioritization."[110]

Admiral Wu has led the PLAN for the unprecedented period of eight years and has been an extremely effective commander, as evidenced in all measures of naval effectiveness. His as-yet unnamed successor will have a very tough act to follow. That officer's warfare specialty—surface, submarine, and aviation—may well provide a clue as to Beijing's future plans for the navy.

Recent PLAN operations demonstrate that it is capable of impressive regional operations and can deploy twenty-first-century ships on far deployments, although the strategic theory espoused in public by Chinese analysts is based on island chains, which does not fit with traditional naval strategic theory. However, the Chinese version of "defense" is an "active defense" concept that enhances the PLAN's ability to defend the near seas. The mission is "to do all we can to dominate the enemy by striking first . . . as far away as possible."[111]

Beijing's continued investment in a twenty-first-century navy does not appear to have been affected by China's 2014–15 economic slowdown, but domestic priorities are lurking in the wings.[112] Establishing a Chinese navy capable of global reach will depend on continued economic growth in China as well as global ambitions. The PLAN no doubt possesses such ambitions, but the government confronts serious domestic issues that argue against deploying a global navy. These include long-term, basic issues of food and water, energy, and environmental problems, all of which must be dealt with for the CCP to remain in power. Regardless of the degree of GDP growth, Beijing's focus will remain on domestic problems as long as no vital national security interest is threatened.

Admiral Wu Shengli assumed command of the navy in 2006 and has been a member of the Central Military Commission since 2007, but not since Admiral Liu Huaqing retired in 1997 has any PLA officer served on the important Politburo Standing Committee. The navy's increased stature within the PLA, discussed above, would be emphasized by the appointment of an admiral to the Politburo Standing Committee.

In the final analysis, the PLAN's future will be determined by Beijing's view of the navy's ability to contribute to continued economic growth and the maintenance of the CCP in power. The party has emphasized that the "unchanging foundation of PLA modernization" is "loyalty to the party" and supporting achievement of the "Chinese Dream."[113]

A regionally focused PLAN in the future will develop into a smaller but more professionally competent force. How effective it will be in combat is impossible to say with assurance, but the PLAN's increasing operational experience certainly indicates greater competence, as does the evolving personnel and unit education and training system. The question is not one of PLAN versus the U.S. Navy or the Japan Maritime Self-Defense Force but the degree to which Beijing believes its forces must be engaged—to win decisively or to "teach a lesson"—in a given scenario.

The PLAN likely will increase its share of budget and personnel resources; the coast guard and other ancillary forces likely will develop into coherent, increasingly competent forces. The strategic goal of controlling events within the three seas will be largely achieved, and the next goal of controlling events within the second island chain will have made impressive progress. In regional terms, China will have completed the nearly unprecedented development into both a continental and maritime military power.

One uncertain issue is the degree to which the PLAN influences doctrine and strategy within the PLA and to what degree the PLA influences national security policy in Beijing. This question is dealt with in more detail in chapters 5 and 6. Before that discussion, China's maritime strategy is examined.

Chapter Three

MARITIME STRATEGY

This chapter discusses China's maritime strategy, both formal and informal, both de jure and de facto. It begins with some historical background and a review of previous maritime strategic efforts by Beijing.

China undoubtedly has a distinct strategic culture, but is it so "distinct" that foreigners are unable to understand its goals? Strategic culture may be defined as "the way [China] thinks about the use of force for political ends . . . rooted in the 'early' or 'formative' military experiences of [China] and are influenced to some degree by the philosophical, political, cultural, and cognitive characteristics of [China and its elites] as these develop through time."[1]

China's strategic culture may have been influenced by Confucius and Sun Zi, and perhaps by Mao Zedong, but it also reflects Western thinkers. One Chinese view is that China has expanded through cultural rather than military means and that the nation's "unique strategic culture" is "more peaceful and non-violent than the realpolitik Western one."[2]

However, this view of a culture unique and difficult for others to understand is supported neither by history nor by the past decade's events in East Asian waters. Western observers, including Warren Cohen and Alastair Iain Johnston, have described China's foreign policy and willingness to employ military force as little different from that of any other nation.[3] However, if Chinese strategists believe their strategy has and continues to be one of "peaceful rise," then it must be considered as a factor in their formulations.

Descriptions of the current state of maritime strategy development in China must draw on national security goals as defined by Beijing, recognize

85

China's increased awareness of the importance of the maritime realm, and consider the views and reactions of the PLA. The current campaign to modernize and expand the PLA Navy will impose costs on the other services as well as on China's national security infrastructure writ large. However, an effective maritime strategy must be part of a larger national military strategy. In China, that has meant a historically continental strategic focus. The 2015 defense white paper indicates a shift in that focus as Beijing moves to seize its perceived place as a leading global power in a world dependent on maritime power for economic growth and for energy security, buttressed by a strong navy and effective foreign policies.

This chapter assumes—with certain caveats noted—that China's remarkable economic progress will continue, albeit at increasingly reduced rates, measured by annual gross domestic product (GDP) growth. A reduced rate of GDP growth will not, however, lessen in Beijing's view the drive to increase energy security.

Riparian issues are included in Beijing's maritime environment and pose significant security issues. The Amur River, forming part of China's border with Russia, is one example; the Mekong (the Lancang, in Chinese), with its headwaters in China but its primary impact on the nations of Southeast Asia, is a second case. This river originates in southwestern China, but its course through Southeast Asia gives the nations of the Indo-Chinese peninsula—Vietnam, Laos, Thailand, Cambodia—a direct and intense interest in Beijing's attempts to harness the upper reaches of the Mekong for generating hydroelectric power. Hence, these ambitious energy-development efforts are directly affecting China's foreign relations.

The Chinese concept of "core issues" is at the heart of maritime sovereignty issues. Government officials have listed as "core interests" only the sovereignty status of Taiwan, Tibet, and Xinjiang. Classifying the East and South China Sea disputes as "sovereignty issues," however, would suggest that under certain circumstances these also would be considered "core interests." If so classified, these disputes would rise significantly in Beijing's security interest priorities and pose greater dangers of military escalation.

Coastal waters, defined here as those lying within 200 nm of China's shore, are in part sovereign, in part international, and marked by the thousands of islands belonging to or claimed by China. Of particular note are the islands and land features disputed with Japan, Taiwan, and several nations bordering the South China Sea.

Historical Background

Although China has been primarily a continental power throughout its history, it has been and remains very much a maritime nation as well. First, China relies on its extensive river network for communication, commerce, and energy transportation. Riverine issues are in the main domestic, although international complications arise from rivers on international borders or whose management affects other nations.

The nineteenth-century Western onslaught brought home to many Chinese officials the need to modernize their country's military might, especially its navy. Beijing succeeded in organizing and equipping a modern navy, but it foundered in wars with France and Japan, failures resulting largely from the absence of adequate training, unified command, common doctrine, and a clear strategy.

Alfred Thayer Mahan and Julian Corbett are at the head of classical maritime strategists who influence current Chinese maritime strategic thought. Others include admirals John "Jacky" Fisher, Ernest King, Arleigh Burke, J. C. Wylie, Elmo Zumwalt, and Sergei Gorshkov. Liu Huaqing and former U.S. Navy secretary John Lehman must also be considered, perhaps as "organizational strategists." Not all of these offered a formal maritime strategy, but their organizational and leadership contributions made a strategic difference in their nation's maritime narrative.[4] Additionally, while they probably never saw an ocean, Sun Zi and Carl von Clausewitz are influential strategists who deserve consideration when discussing Chinese maritime strategy.

Sun Zi's focus on deception, for instance, is certainly germane to the twenty-first-century emphasis on electronic and information warfare, expressed in innumerable reports of People's Liberation Army Navy (PLAN) exercises. Sun Zi also may be credited, or blamed, for what might be a dangerous weakness in Chinese maritime strategic thought: an unrealistic belief in the ability to control unintended escalation during an incident at sea, as evidenced in various crises since 1950. Whereas Clausewitz ("friction") and Mahan certainly understood the uncertain nature of events at sea, Sun Zi argued that one can plan for almost any eventuality in war.[5] This characteristic may be bolstered by the PLAN's lack of significant operational conflict for more than three decades.

As for Clausewitz, Beijing's propensity for "teaching a lesson" when employing military force fits into Clausewitz's discussion of two types of war, limited and absolute, despite the German's lack of maritime experience. PLA involvement in Korea in the early 1950s was a disaster in terms of personnel losses but is considered a "victory" because of the continuation of the North Korean state, a point perhaps not well enough known by American policymakers; and the PLA's performance in Vietnam in 1979 was by Deng Xiaoping's own measure poor—but considered to have taught Hanoi a "lesson" about actively opposing Chinese policies.[6]

Sergei Gorshkov may have been particularly influential, as China's maritime strategy has developed from its minor role in the 1949 PLA to its prominence in the 2015 defense white paper. The Soviet Union's navy was subservient to the army from 1917 to at least 1953, a status similar to that of the PLAN until approximately the mid-1990s. The Soviet navy attained national strategic status during the next three decades, developing under Gorshkov's leadership to a global maritime force by 1985.

Liu Huaqing no doubt agreed with his Soviet mentor that his nation "could not become a great power without a strong navy," with a focus on the United States as the primary threat. Liu certainly would have accepted Gorshkov's belief that "Western navies [had] been the primary vehicle for interjecting Western power," since it fits with the general Chinese view today that the United States is trying to constrain and contain China.[7]

Beijing's focus on maritime issues also is understandable, given China's 10,250 nm of coastline and more than 6,500 claimed islands. China also has 8 of the world's 10 busiest international ports, while its shipping fleet is among the world's largest, and "ocean-related activities" constitute at least 10 percent of the nation's GDP, with that percentage rising to 16 percent in some coastal provinces.[8]

Coaling Stations

Beijing's foreign port-building efforts, long evident in Pakistan, Bangladesh, and Sri Lanka, have been extended to include facilities construction in Bagamoyo, Tanzania, and almost certainly Djibouti. The ambitious $10 billion Tanzanian project is scheduled for a 2017 or 2018 completion and will include significant inland infrastructure as well as the port facility itself.[9] These Chinese efforts are unlikely to result in Mahanian naval bases, however, but in ports from which visiting ships will be able to draw supplies, refuel, and perhaps receive and transfer personnel.[10]

Chinese strategists acknowledge Corbett's and Mahan's strategic views emphasizing the importance of economics and trade, lines of communication at sea, and the employment of naval power to attain national security aims, currently framed by the "near seas": the Yellow, East China, and South China Seas; the "middle sea," including much of the Philippine Sea; and the "far sea," the waters outside the second island chain, a line drawn through the Kuriles, Japan, and the Bonin Islands, the Mariana Islands, Palau, and the Indonesian archipelago. Wylie's comment that sea power's purpose is "the actual establishment of control on land" applies to China's determination to establish sovereignty over numerous land features in the East and South China Seas.[11]

Mahan's emphasis on the need for overseas naval support bases is appreciated by the PLAN as it conducts deployments to the Gulf of Aden. While the "string of pearls" is more verbiage than reality, China is solidifying its relations with Bangladesh, Sri Lanka, Pakistan, and other Southwest Asian nations and has negotiated with Djibouti, for instance, to join several other nations in establishing a logistics facility in that country.[12] Additionally, increasing PLAN activity in the Mediterranean, including port calls and exercises with the Russian navy, have led Beijing to purchase control of the port facility in Piraeus, Greece.[13] China and Russia have conducted several military exercises, including significant naval drills.[14] Beijing and Moscow have "vowed to strengthen bilateral military co-operation and hold joint naval exercise to counter U.S. influence in the Asia-Pacific region."[15]

The Energy Factor in Chinese Maritime Strategy

Energy security is an objective in the formulation and execution of China's maritime strategy. Two factors are most significant. First is the growth and modernization of the PLAN; second is Beijing's view of energy security. The latter factor involves increasing demand and the need for increasing supplies, much of which lies overseas, and for a naval capability to safeguard the SLOCs over which imported energy resources must flow.

Coastal waters are trafficked by oceangoing vessels making or leaving port, of course, but also serve hundreds of thousands of fishing boats, ferries, and coastal commercial craft, including energy carriers. Hence, an important facet of Beijing's apparent determination not to compromise on insular sovereignty issues, no matter how thorny an international issue, is due in significant part to concerns about energy security. This in turn is a driver in PLAN modernization.

Beijing's view that acquiring new secure energy sources is a constant and the need for a navy able to safeguard that energy's transport to China form important elements in the formulation of China's foreign policies. Those policies of course involve other nations, ranging from the United States to most of the world's oil-producing nations, from Brunei to Venezuela.

China has developed significant energy resources in national waters that are for the most part undisputed: coastal waters, the Bohai and Yellow Seas, parts of Beibu Bay, and the northern seas. Two potentially valuable areas, however, the East and South China Seas, are very much in dispute. China is the world's fifth-largest investor in offshore minerals recovery, and the China Association for Science and Technology describes the increasing requirement for energy as one of the "five challenges" for the twenty-first century.

The nation increasingly relies on imported oil and natural gas supplies. China became the world's largest oil importer in 2014, importing 57 percent of its oil from abroad that year and 61 percent in 2015. Reliance on imported energy resources will continue to grow; it is forecast to increase to 75 percent by 2030.[16] The bulk of this oil arrives by sea, over very long SLOCs. The value of offshore resources will continue to increase for China as its population—still the world's largest at approximately 1.3 billion—continues to grow and its economy continues to expand.

China's Maritime Strategy in 2015

China's regional maritime arena of the Yellow, East, and South China Seas comprises much of the maritime area from Japan and the Korean peninsula in the north to the Strait of Malacca in the south. Beijing views these waters as forming a vital national security interest. This in turn places China in potential direct confrontation not just with its Asian maritime neighbors but also with the United States, through its defense treaties and special relationships with Japan, South Korea, the Philippines, Singapore, and Taiwan.

China's "perimeter security" was assessed by a prominent Beijing think tank in 2015. Three major challenges were identified: "first is the U.S.-Japan alliance's strategic squeeze on China's rise; second is the control of maritime safety and the development of a new maritime order; third is the promotion of the 'One Belt and One Road' strategy and dealing with relevant external pressures."[17]

In the view of some Chinese analysts, "half of [China's maritime territory] is under [China's] actual control. These areas are in dispute with Japan,

South Korea, Philippines, Indonesia, Malaysia, and Brunei." Furthermore, they assert, "as the U.S. has shifted its strategic focus to the Asia-Pacific region, the situation of island and reef disputes, maritime boundary demarcation, ocean development, and the plundering of resources along China's maritime periphery continues to escalate and worsen."[18]

U.S. observers describe the most discussed Chinese maritime strategy as anti-access / area denial (A2/AD), intended to prevent an opponent—the United States—from intervening effectively in an armed Taiwan scenario or other military operations in East Asian waters. The PLA cannot prevent the U.S. military from intervening in the three seas, but it can try to frustrate that intervention.[19] China is more likely to view the weapons and surveillance systems developed for this purpose as improving surveillance of the littoral waters viewed by Beijing as an area of vital national security interest.

Presumably, China would rely primarily on submarines, aircraft, cruise missiles, and ballistic missiles such as antiship ballistic missiles (ASBM), likely between the coast and the second island chain. The most discussed Chinese weapon in this effort is the DF-21D ballistic missile, designed to be maneuverable after it reenters the atmosphere on its mission to attack moving U.S. aircraft carriers or other capital surface ships. The effort would be an element of "active defense," a construct that a U.S. analyst might well consider "offensive."[20]

In its 23 September 2015 military parade, China displayed sixteen units each of the DF-21D and the DF-26, a longer-range ASBM capable of reaching as far as Guam. It is PLA practice to only parade weapons that it has already deployed operationally. Many of the aforementioned weapons are part of a land-based "anti-navy" that China wields as part of a doctrine involving "using the land to control the sea."

The point here is that, as noted earlier, the PLAN will not be constrained by lines or Western defensive concepts in defending China's maritime interests. Its doctrine has been described as a "strategically defensive and active self-defense counterattack," one that could be triggered "as soon as the enemy splits and invades China's territory, severely harming China's interests, . . . equivalent to firing the first shot at China at the strategic level." Furthermore, the PLA's mission is "to do all we can to dominate the enemy by striking first . . . as far away as possible."[21] None of this points to a linear Chinese maritime strategy. PLAN campaign planning appears instead to focus on the nonlinear character of naval warfare.

In its 2006 book *Science of Military Strategy*, the PLA describes its vision of maritime operations as marked by shifting battle lines and the maneuverability and offensive power of naval forces. Battles at sea are characterized as asymmetric operations occurring on, above, and beneath the sea. The 2013 edition of this work also discussed naval strategy, but not in terms as specific as the May 2015 defense white paper.

Naval campaigns are specifically discussed at length, taking note of the sea's openness and lack of defensive lines, a fact that requires taking the initiative with offensive operations to neutralize enemy forces. Flexibility and the clever employment of tactics and forces are emphasized. Even defensive naval operations should, in the PLAN's view, be imbued with an offensive spirit, that of always taking the initiative and attacking the opponent's weak points.

These views reflect the PLAN's recognition of the inherent value of unconstrained, mobile naval power, limited as little as possible by geographic features or the capabilities of statically based weapons.

PLAN strategists are focused on mobile, noncontiguous, nonlinear operations that can bypass the island chains to "reach out and touch" foreign forces in order to achieve specific objectives for specific periods. This concept is distinctly not that of Alfred Thayer Mahan; attempts to identify twenty-first-century Chinese naval thinking closely with that maritime strategist are largely irrelevant.[22]

Strategic Intent

Despite the lack of a published maritime strategy, the PLAN plans and operates along the lines of guidance from China's civilian and military leadership, the CCP's Politburo Standing Committee, guidance that equates to a strategy. Separate but under the same category is guidance provided to the ministries responsible for the fisheries and coast guard–like functions. The fact that at least five and possibly twenty-one separate government organizations are responsible for these economic and quasi-naval sectors complicates all their associated missions.

Liu Huaqing's Vision

China's most influential flag officer, Liu Huaqing, played a role similar to that of Admiral Sergei Gorshkov in the Soviet Union. Liu's "sea daddy" instituted dramatic changes in maritime strategy during a long tenure as Soviet navy commander. Gorshkov no doubt influenced Liu, but he confronted significant obstacles in the 1980s, including a long-standing continental security perspective, internal PLA resource battles, and domestic politics; these had to be overcome through the nitty-gritty of implementing a maritime strategy addressed by Arleigh Burke and demonstrated by John Lehman.

Liu's 1980s plan for modernizing the navy is usually described as occurring in three stages:

1. By 2000, the PLAN would be capable of exerting sea control out to the first island chain, defined by the Kurile Islands, Japan and the Ryukyu Islands, the Philippines, and the Indonesian archipelago.
2. By 2020, sea control would be enforced out to the second island chain.
3. By 2050, the PLAN would operate globally, with aircraft carrier battle groups.[23]

Liu's most important achievement, however, was gaining civilian leadership support for the increased resources to develop a twenty-first-century navy. He was trying to alter China's historic continentalist strategic focus in a basic way, to bring to the fore the importance of the maritime environment on which China would have to depend to regain its position as a global economic and political power.

Defense White Papers

China's defense white papers are important indicators of Beijing's strategic thought in the maritime arena. The 2010 version, published in January 2011, describes the PLAN's role in a national defense focused on "safeguarding national sovereignty, security and interests of national development . . . tasked to guard against and resist aggression, defend the security of China's lands, inland waters, and territorial waters . . . [and] safeguard its maritime rights and interests." The PLAN was directed "to accelerate the modernization of its integrated combat forces, enhance its capabilities in strategic deterrence and counterattack, and develop its capabilities in conducting operations in distant waters and in countering non-traditional security." It is also to improve its "combat capabilities."[24]

To ensure the success of military operations other than war (MOOTW), the PLAN is continuing to develop and deploy "new types of submarines, frigates, aircraft and large support vessels." It is also trying to "build a shore-based support system which matches the deployment of forces and the development of weaponry and equipment." Particularly important is "the Navy [accelerating] the building of surface logistical platforms [and] working to improve its surface support capabilities," to include "new methods of logistics support for sustaining long-time maritime missions." Assisting the PLAN in these responsibilities are "organs of maritime surveillance, fisheries administration, marine affairs, inspection and quarantine, and customs" as well as a recently "improved . . . border and coastal defense force system."[25]

The growing out-of-area role for the PLAN in the Gulf of Aden is described as "in line with relevant UN resolutions," as "China takes a proactive and open attitude toward international escort cooperation . . . [joining] international regimes such as the UN liaison groups' meeting on Somali pirates, and the international conference on 'intelligence sharing and conflict prevention' escort cooperation."[26] The 2013 defense white paper was notable as the first to devote an entire subsection to "safeguarding China's maritime rights and interests," stating that "it is an essential national development strategy . . . to build China into a maritime power."[27]

Piracy has almost disappeared from the Gulf of Aden, with no successful attack on a large commercial vessel since 2012, but regular PLAN deployments continue to that region. This underscores Beijing's emphasis on the navy's increasing role in international efforts in general, striving "to maintain maritime security through multiple peaceful ways and means."[28] China has highlighted PLAN ship visits to foreign ports, with "more than forty naval ships" visiting "more than thirty countries."[29]

The PLAN first took prominent part in MOOTW in 2011, when the frigate *Xuzhou*, on antipiracy patrol in the Gulf of Aden, was dispatched into the Mediterranean to assist in evacuating Chinese citizens trapped by the civil war in Libya. The fact that this Jiangkai II–class frigate did not actually evacuate any Chinese citizens is less significant that the fact that Beijing had sufficient confidence in its navy to dispatch a warship on such a mission and that the navy was able to execute it successfully.

The PLAN also is engaging regularly in one traditional naval mission not specifically addressed in the earlier documents: presence, or naval support for diplomacy. This is rectified in the 2015 white paper, which addresses this and other noncombat roles in Section VI.

The defense white paper also addresses the need for improved "maritime surveillance, fisheries administration, marine affairs, inspection and quarantine, and customs enforcement" as well as coastal defense.[30] The PLAN's role in UN peacekeeping operations is touted, as are its exercises with foreign navies. These latter are described as occurring on a "regular basis." In fact, they have numbered no more than a dozen over the past decade; the white paper takes a positive slant and is worded for the public. Nevertheless, it remains an important document, reflecting China's national security concerns.

China began publishing defense white papers in 1998, nominally on a biannual basis. Various Chinese government bodies have also issued important documents addressing the maritime theater.[31] These include earlier defense white papers.[32] For instance, the 2004 white paper claimed "the Navy has expanded the space and extended the depth for offshore defensive operations." The 2006 version then stated "the Navy aims at gradual extension of the strategic depth for offshore defensive operations ... ," which was followed by the 2008 white paper's statement that "since the 1980s the Navy has realized a strategic transformation to offshore defensive operations." The PLAN's strategic aim was described in the 2010 version as "in line with the requirements of offshore defense strategy."[33]

The 2012 defense white paper described the navy's role in a national defense focused on "safeguarding national sovereignty, security and interests of national development . . . [and] tasked to guard against and resist aggression, defend the security of China's lands, inland waters, and territorial waters . . . [and] safeguard its maritime rights and interests," pressured by the ongoing sovereignty disputes in the East and South China Seas. Defending the security of territorial waters is repeated as integral to "National Defense Policy."

While Beijing has not published a formal maritime strategy, the most recent defense white paper, issued in May 2015, addresses China's military strategy, which subsumes a viable maritime strategy and is an authoritative, important signal of Beijing's intentions.[34]

The biannual defense white paper issued by Beijing in May 2015 was the first to directly present a Chinese military strategy. It is also a significant document of national intent since it marks the first time Beijing has addressed maritime issues in such a detailed fashion. It clarifies and sums up previous Chinese documents that contribute to gaining an understanding of Beijing's views and intentions for its modernizing navy and national strategic policy.

The 2015 defense white paper contains the most direct focus on maritime strategy issued by the Beijing government. This de facto strategy includes several telling points.

1. The plan identifies two key "centenary" dates; 2021, the one hundredth anniversary of the founding of the CCP, to "complete the building of a moderately prosperous society," and 2049, for "the building of a modern socialist country." The second date, marking the one hundredth anniversary of the founding of the PRC, is also the date by which PLAN modernization is supposed to achieve readiness to exercise sea control out to the second island chain and beyond.

2. While the tenor of the white paper's description of the world China faces is generally benign, an almost schizophrenic element is present in the claim that "some of [China's] offshore neighbors take provocative actions and reinforce their military presence on China's reefs and islands that they have illegally occupied. Some external countries are also busy meddling in South China Sea affairs; a tiny few maintain constant close-in air and sea surveillance and reconnaissance against China."

3. The PLAN's responsibility to maintain "the security of overseas interests concerning energy and resources, strategic SLOCs, as well as institutions, personnel and assets abroad" is mentioned on several occasions.

4. The PLAN's responsibility "to maintain strategic deterrence and carry out nuclear counterattack" is noted, as is, on more than one occasion, its responsibility to perform MOOTW, such as counterpiracy and humanitarian assistance and disaster relief.

5. The modernization and increased use of reserve forces are noted, which ties to the emphasis on increased "civil-military" integration, to include building "a national defense mobilization system."

6. "Preparation for military struggle" is emphasized throughout the paper, particularly to "protect the country's maritime rights and interests" with a goal to "improve its routine combat readiness" by conducting "combat training in realistic conditions [to include] live-setting training, IT-based simulated training, and face-on-face confrontation training in line with real-combat criteria." Honest evaluation of training is also emphasized.

7. The PLAN is directed to "optimize battlefield disposition and strengthen strategic prepositioning," while continuing "to perform regular combat readiness patrols and maintain a military presence in relevant sea areas."

8. Most significant is the strategic direction to the PLAN to "shift its focus from 'offshore waters defense' to the combination of 'offshore waters defense' with 'open seas protection.'" This is based on the inaccurate assertion that "the traditional mentality that land out-weighs sea must be abandoned," with "great importance" on "manag-ing the seas and oceans and protecting maritime rights and interests." The PLAN must be prepared to "safeguard [China's] national sover-eignty and maritime rights and interests, [and] protect the security of strategic SLOCs and overseas interests."

These points outline strategic direction to China's navy to transform itself from a regional to a global force, one that is constantly prepared to "fight and win" both in regional waters and wherever Chinese interests are present around the world.[35]

The May 2015 defense white paper provides strategic and operational direction to the navy. The PLAN was directed to transform from a force dedi-cated and limited to "offshore waters defense" to "open seas protection," phrases previously given by various analysts as "near seas" and "far seas" or, in U.S. phraseology, as "brown-green-blue waters" or "littoral waters" and "high seas." Whatever the terminology, this strategy announces the PLAN's status as a global navy, in effect second in power and influence only to the U.S. Navy.[36]

The transforming Chinese navy is specifically charged with developing the capability for effective "strategic deterrence and counterattack, maritime maneuvers, joint operations at sea, comprehensive defense and comprehen-sive support." These missions are justified by the fact "it is clear that China's development interests are on the ocean, China's development space is on the ocean, and the primary security threats come from the ocean."

Furthermore, the PLAN "must be able to shoulder the heavy burden of safeguarding national interests in more remote spaces." This formula-tion is also provided for the first time in the 2015 strategy document; it also addresses "areas crucially related to China's overseas interests." These words describe essentially unlimited global ambitions, given the strategy's discus-sion of China's increasing economic interests in "every corner of the globe."[37]

The PLA has performed noncombatant evacuation operations (NEO) in the Solomon Islands, Fiji, Libya, and—most notably for the navy—in Yemen in 2015. NEO is now officially a mission for the PLAN.

The white paper includes in the MOOTW category "convoy operations, medical care missions, joint counter-terrorism operations, and joint exercises" as "normalized mission[s] of the navy."[38] This has included planning the establishment of an offshore observation network by 2020. Its purpose is to observe events in "coastal waters, the high seas, and polar waters." Missions are given as coping with natural disaster and developing the "coastal economy," but its most important mission will be to "strengthen [China's] maritime power."[39]

Leadership Statements

Presidential statements on maritime issues have been key to maritime strategic thought. Deng Xiaoping introduced "offshore defense," clarifying it in 1985, which helped move the PLAN from coastal defense to offshore defense. Deng's successor, Jiang Zemin, refined and operationalized the concept, in 1992 supporting offshore defense. He also promulgated "active defense" guidelines as the "Military Guidelines for the New Period," aimed primarily at countering U.S. intervention in a Taiwan scenario, as part of the concept of a "local war under high-technology conditions."[40]

Jiang also discussed "strategic guidelines of the active defense," requiring the PLAN to develop the capabilities to exercise the sea control operations to enforce sovereignty and territorial claims in the East and South China Seas. This concept may now be labeled "fighting and winning a local war under informatized conditions."

President Hu Jintao talked about "Four Historic Missions" in 2004, which was key to continued PLAN modernization and increased importance as an instrument of national security. The newly emphasized missions were to (1) consolidate the ruling status of the Communist Party; (2) help ensure China's sovereignty, territorial integrity, and domestic security to continue national development; (3) safeguard China's expanding national interests, and (4) help maintain world peace.[41] The two latter missions give the PLAN rationale for expanding operations beyond the Chinese periphery; they point toward "far seas" operations" as an operational guideline.

Most recently, President Xi Jinping in July 2013 endorsed the concept of "strategic management of the sea," followed in August 2013 by calling for

China to "bolster its maritime forces." In December of that year, he called for sailors in the South Sea Fleet to "be better prepared for [military] struggle" and emphasized a nonnegotiable position where China's sovereignty claims are discussed.[42]

Premier Li Keqiang then described "China as a major maritime country: "We need to draw up and implement a strategic maritime plan, . . . improve coordinated maritime management, strengthen our law enforcement and defense capabilities at sea, resolutely safeguard China' s maritime rights and interests, . . . and move closer to achieving the goal of building China into a maritime power."[43]

Strategy Documents

Beijing promulgated a national security law shortly before the 2015 white paper on military strategy was published. The law addresses both domestic and international security, integrating the two in detail, and has a notable maritime flavor.

Article 2 of the law defines "national security" as including "sovereignty, unity, and territorial integrity," stating "China's sovereignty and territorial integrity brook no violation or division." Article 17 then notes, "The state will strengthen the construction of border defense, coastal defense, and air defense [and] defend the security of territorial waters and territorial seas, and territorial airspace, and safeguard China's territorial sovereignty and marine rights and interests." This focus on maritime defense is then buttressed by emphasizing "active defense." Article 33 notes the importance of protecting "the safety and legitimate rights and interests of overseas Chinese citizens, organization and agencies, and protect[ing] China's overseas interests."[44]

As noted, the 2015 defense white paper effectively contains a maritime strategy, and its importance is buttressed by documents previously issued by the national government and other Chinese organs. First are central government documents that address these issues. Perhaps the most important is the 1992 Law of the People's Republic of China [PRC] on Its Territorial Seas and Adjacent Zones.

Next of note is the 1998 maritime policy, which promised that "China will strengthen the comprehensive development and administration of its coastal zones . . . and protect the offshore areas," while it notes forming "coastal economic belts and marine economic zones," and emphasizes that

China will "reinforce oceanographic technology research and development." "Comprehensive marine management systems" will be established, while the PLAN will participate in "international cooperation in the field of marine development."[45] Beijing also reiterated in the 1998 document its "reaffirmation" of the reservations it expressed when signing the UNCLOS.

The 2013 *Science of Military Campaigns* discusses "blue water defense." The concept of "active defense" lies at its core, with an emphasis on striking first, or taking the "tactical offensive" while on the "strategic defensive." This edition of the *Science of Military Campaigns* replaces the 2001 edition, which, in describing maritime operations, noted their shifting battle lines, maneuverability of forces, and the offensive power of those forces since they are mobile, noncontiguous, and nonlinear, able to bypass the island chains. The 2013 edition also emphasized that future warfare would be "informatized" and would depend increasingly on jointness, especially with the air force and the 2nd Artillery. Finally, Beijing's strategic maritime goals are conventional, and the United States clearly is the opponent.

The National Ocean Policy is another official document with a strong maritime strategic character. This policy paper identified several maritime concerns that remain current. One is "safeguarding the new international marine order and [China's] marine rights and interests," outlined by the 1992 Law of the People's Republic of China on its Territorial Seas and Adjacent Zones. Another is the promise that "China will strengthen the comprehensive development and administration of its coastal zones . . . and protect the offshore areas" while participating in developing "international sea beds and oceans" in order to "form coastal economic belts and marine economic zones."

The National Ocean Policy's second goal is to simultaneously plan and implement "the development of marine resources and the protection of the marine environment" while improving the "monitoring, surveillance, law enforcement, and management" of that environment. The third goal is "reinforcing oceanographic technology research and development," and the fourth is "setting up a comprehensive marine management system." The final goal is to participate actively in "international cooperation in the field of marine development."[46]

One Chinese analyst has rephrased the National Ocean Policy as "four co-ordinations." The first is to "harmonize national and international maritime law," which is a crucial point since China has built a body of domestic legislation that diverges in basic ways from the UNCLOS. The second issue of coordination urges the integration of China's several agencies responsible for various aspects of maritime security. This is still very much a work in progress, and the "stove-piping" of the organizations dealing with security issues continues to cause confusion, both domestically and internationally.

The third issue is coordinating traditional and nontraditional maritime security concerns. The former is obvious; the latter refers to operations other than war, such as reacting to economic and environmental problems, natural disasters, and incidents involving safety at sea. The fourth coordination issue refers to traditional maritime issues, both national and international. Sovereignty disputes in the East and South China Seas, on one hand, and antipiracy deployments to the Gulf of Aden, on the other, mark the range of these issues.[47]

In addition to the National Ocean Policy, several provinces issued "Maritime Economic Development" documents. The Hainan, Guangdong, and Guangxi provincial governments have each directly addressed maritime economic objectives in formal documents. They each listed "Developing the Ocean Economy" as a key mission under the national development master plan, the Twelfth five-year plan (2011–15) issued by the State Council.[48]

None of these provincial goals is explicitly naval, but all require deployment of a modern navy to support China's overall maritime development. A prime example is improving oceanography: a civilian-manned research ship conducting bottom surveys is producing data that may indicate the presence of seabed minerals but will also facilitate submarine operations.

Operational Goals

China's goal is to have the capability to prevent events from occurring in the three seas of which it does not approve. It is closing in on that goal in 2016 for the waters inside the first island chain; it has good potential for achieving that capability for the waters inside the second island chain by 2049.

A particularly interesting aspect of China's maritime interests concerns the air space above the seas. Beijing's declaration in November 2013 of an air defense identification zone (ADIZ) over much of the East China Sea was a major declaration of intent. China certainly was not the first nation to declare an ADIZ, but the declaration came, first, without formal notice to other nations; second, it overlapped previously declared air defense zones by Japan, South Korea, and Taiwan; and, third, Beijing declared all aircraft entering the

ADIZ must request transit permission and comply with instructions or face unspecified "emergency defensive measures," while for all other such zones, aircraft are required to request permission only if inbound to the host nation. Hence, China's declaration was seen as an aggressive move.[49]

A pending, often discussed question in mid-2016 is whether Beijing will declare an ADIZ over the area within the nine-dash line it has delineated in the South China Sea. This seems a very likely occurrence and would seriously heighten tension in that disputed sea, particularly if, as indicated, the airspace over artificial "islands" being constructed by China are included by Beijing.[50]

To the Sea Lines of Communications

Asia's inherently maritime environment retains the characteristics addressed by the Western naval theorists of the late nineteenth century. At the same time, this environment is subject to the rapidly changing technology of the twenty-first century as well as the developments that succeeded, first, the end of the Cold War in 1990 and, second, the changes in the conduct of international relations imposed by the United States following the events of September 11, 2001.

These changes are characterized by complexity and ambiguity in the current maritime security environment. The SLOCs remain a focal point of maritime security concerns. Threats to the SLOCs in the early twenty-first century include military conflicts between regional nations, sovereignty disputes that threaten military conflict, terrorism, and international crime, usually falling under the rubric of "piracy."

Each of these threat categories are addressed below. Military threats to the Asian SLOCs are relatively slight. None of the regional states currently hold any apparent strategic objectives that would involve interdicting SLOCs, although China might do so, at least for a short period of time, should active military conflict develop over Taiwan's status. Similarly, the conflicting claims to sovereignty over the South China Sea land features might lead to a situation involving opposing military forces. Unintended escalation between two or more opposing naval and air force units might also lead to an armed clash.

The other essentially nonmilitary threats to the SLOCs are more likely to occur; in fact, to a degree they are already occurring. Natural disasters, international crime, and conflicting sovereignty claims are all facts of international maritime life. Examples include the 2004 tsunami in Southeast Asia; the incidents of maritime crime that characterize some of the waters in proximity to the Malacca and Singapore Straits as well as in the Bay of Bengal and western Arabian Sea; and the territorial claims held by the different states bordering on the South China Sea. It must also be noted, however, that most of these situations are currently being dealt with peacefully, on a multilateral basis.

While the potential for major combat operations at sea remains, terrorism has significantly increased the presence of "nonmilitary" and multinational threats in the maritime domain. These threats present challenges difficult for maritime nations to counter. They present situations in which threats and adversaries are neither clearly defined nor perhaps even readily identifiable by source. Additionally, defeating these threats will require more than purely military instruments and processes. Similarly, defeat may well not be satisfactory: resolving their causative bases will be necessary to ensure lasting peace at sea.

SLOCs crossing the Indian Ocean from west to east offer various routes, as noted earlier. These routes pass through areas of common water, however, and border the ocean's insular nations. Hence, while none of these trans-ocean SLOCs are as potentially vulnerable to blockage as either Bab-el-Mandeb or Hormuz, not to mention the Straits of Malacca and Singapore, they are still objects of maritime concern to China and to other regional nations. This is due to their critical location between those straits and rich energy basins in Southwest Asia, the Middle East, and sub-Saharan Africa.

Nonstate Threats at Sea

China is faced with terrorism, piracy and other crimes at sea, and environmental destruction, just as other maritime nations are. Terrorists are generally committed to and benefit from political instability in individual nations and even throughout a region, such as Southeast Asia. Such instability may be the result of large-scale environmental disasters; hence, intentionally causing such events can have far-reaching, negative effects on economic health and political stability, especially in a region already suffering from political unrest, economic deprivation, or religious conflict.

Terrorist threats remain a concern at sea in terms of both range and impact. This is due in part to the oceans' role as the world's commons, presenting opportunities for global movement and relative covertness: despite satellites and other modern detection systems, the vast oceans remain capable of hiding even large vessels and embarked terrorists.

The maritime commons also eases access to a broad array of potential targets suitable for terrorists to maximize the ability of their disruptive activities to cause mass casualties and catastrophic economic damage. The terrorist threat cannot be neatly described or enumerated and may grow in method and capability; however, sources can be broadly categorized as nation-states, religious extremists, transnational criminals, and pirates.

As is the case across the spectrum of man-made threats to maritime commerce, terrorist groups are most likely to target seaborne commerce at straits, where ships are constrained by slow speeds and restricted maneuvering in the face of geographical restrictions and navigational hazards. Most notable of these for the energy exporting and importing nations of Asia are the Southeast Asia chokepoints previously noted, including the Bab-el-Mandeb and the Straits of Hormuz, Malacca-Singapore, Sunda, Lombok, Makassar, Surigao, San Bernardino, Luzon, and Taiwan.

The Asian terrorist groups currently posing the most active maritime threat are located in the Philippines and Indonesia. These groups' ability to exploit inherently open maritime borders challenges the sovereignty of Southeast Asian nations and increasingly threatens regional peace and stability since successful maritime attacks may disrupt regional and global economies out of proportion to the attack itself as shippers and insurers react to the danger. Furthermore, maritime avenues serve terrorist groups admirably for personnel and logistics carriage and often offer a target-rich environment with escape routes readily at hand.

The presence of terrorist groups in maritime Asia is incontrovertible, as unfortunately is the continued presence of the social, economic, and political conditions that give rise to their existence. Weapons in the form of individual arms and vessels laden with dangerous cargo are also all too readily at hand. Financial support may be obtained from illegal activities at sea, including piracy, armed robbery, the international drug trade, and human trafficking.

These crimes have a recorded history in Asian waters dating at least to the fifth century. Chinese dynasties suffered from the problem, as did Western traders who entered the region. Portuguese, Spanish, Dutch, British, and other outsiders all tried to deal with the problem, but with inconsistent success. Today's pirates are different from the classic picture—except in the commonality of ferocity. They are often well organized and well equipped with advanced communications, weapons, and high-speed craft. The capabilities to board and commandeer large underway vessels, although difficult and occurring in only a few piracy incidents, could also be employed to facilitate terrorist acts.

Southeast Asia is one of the world's most frequent scenes of pirate attacks against seagoing vessels. Piracy attacks in Asia have been reduced by 75 percent since 1995; only twelve "armed-robbery and piracy incidents" were reported in the first quarter and no pirate attacks were reported in the Malacca area for the second quarter of 2007, but are still occurring. In fact, 41 percent of all the world's piracy incidents between 1997 and 2013 took place in Southeast Asian waters.[51] Incidents of piracy and armed robbery involving tankers, a particularly lucrative target, increased from forty-five in 2012 to sixty-eight in 2013 to eighty-three in 2014.[52]

The narrow waters of the Malacca Strait bounded by Indonesia, Singapore, and Malaysia certainly provide pirates with good opportunities, especially at the strait's eastern and northern ends, as ships have to slow down to maintain safe navigation. This lends a different definition to the "Malacca dilemma" that some Chinese analysts offer as a concern that the United States would prevent oil shipments from transiting the strait en route to China.

Regional stability may also be influenced by illegal international migration. This long-standing issue will increase in proportion to national instability. Illegal international movement of people is often a maritime issue; terrorists can easily take advantage of human smuggling networks to circumvent national border security measures.

Conventional Maritime Threats

More important than the number of advanced technology platforms joining the PLAN, however, is the strategic direction Beijing has adopted. Chinese strategists typically view their operational paradigm of defending vital maritime areas as a subset of "active defense" rather than "anti-access," but these are two sides of the same coin.

By whichever name, the concept is seen as a Chinese operational plan to prevent other military forces from entering a given area that Beijing believes is vital to its national security. This may be defined by the three seas or more simply as including all the waters within the first island chain.

The ASBM is a major new PLA weapon system for achieving A2/AD. The land-launched ASBM is seen as providing China with the means to attack moving, over-the-horizon targets, particularly U.S. aircraft carriers. China faces significant challenges in deploying and operating an ASBM system, apart from technical problems with the hardware itself. The broader problems include accurate targeting and, perhaps even more challenging, the joint issues attendant to the maritime employment of a system apparently assigned to and operated by the Second Artillery Force.

From China's perspective, the United States military is responding with a new strategy designed specifically against China and its maritime interests, especially those vital to its national security. The new U.S. development known as Joint Concept for Access and Maneuver in the Global Commons (JAM-GC), formerly called Air-Sea Battle, part of the Joint Operational Access Concept, is viewed with particular suspicion. It remains much more of a concept than a reality, but Chinese analysts are treating JAM-GC as a solid accomplishment.[53] They see it as a doctrinal descendent of the Air-Land Battle doctrine, which was designed to combat Soviet-bloc military superiority in Europe during the Cold War and employed against Iraq in the 1990–91 Gulf War.

Furthermore, Chinese strategists and policymakers often accuse Washington of trying to contain China, to prevent it from achieving its rightful place in the world. It is not difficult to see how Beijing might draw such a conclusion, given the U.S. defense treaties and special arrangements with Japan, South Korea, the Philippines, Australia, Singapore, Malaysia, Thailand, and Taiwan. That conclusion may be buttressed by the improving U.S. relationships with Vietnam, Myanmar, and India as well as by military facilities in various Central Asian nations.

There may be "pragmatists and free marketers" in China," however, who advocate a cooperative maritime strategy.[54] This school of thought might be described as fitting a more general Chinese concept of civil-military relations, one in which the PLA remains a party army and not a "national" army— devoted, that is, to ensuring that China's national security infrastructure remains firmly in the hands of the Communist Party leadership. This relates to the oft-repeated statements by Chinese leaders that their nation requires a peaceful world in which to continue growing its economy and overall development.

Developing the strategic vision as well as the doctrinal and operational capabilities to bring its new naval power to fruition requires naval leadership capable of succeeding in the contentious national and military resource allocation process. Admiral Wu Shengli appears to have fared well in that process, establishing the PLAN as a key element in China's status as a major power in the 2015 defense white paper.

A January 2012 assessment of "China's naval rivals" focused on the U.S. Navy as "a strategic opponent of the Chinese Navy." Japan was then highlighted as a more immediate concern based on "naval hatred stretching over 100 years; Diaoyu Island [Senkaku Islands] sovereignty, maritime boundaries in the East China Sea, and the possibility of Japanese military interference in the Taiwan issue and the South China Sea." Vietnam and the Philippines were listed as "local tactical opponents" and India as a "potential blue water opponent." The analysis concluded that the "Chinese Navy now faces a maritime competition structure that involve a broad maritime region, great depth, and multiple opponents."[55]

Beijing delineates defensive maritime security zones in which it aims to prohibit foreign surveillance and reconnaissance activities or any other actions it finds objectionable. This provides the basis for a maritime strategy with legal, national security, domestic political stability, and fleet composition components. For instance, during the 2010 discussion of possible (ultimately successful) U.S. aircraft carrier deployments to the Yellow Sea following the *Cheonan* incident, a Chinese Foreign Ministry spokesperson stated, "We resolutely oppose foreign military ships and aircraft coming to the Yellow Sea and other Chinese adjacent waters and engaging in activities that influence China's security interests."[56] This view, combined with the aggressive actions against foreign surveillance and fishing craft in the South China Sea during the past decade or more and with actions against U.S. surveillance aircraft and ships, points toward a view of "sovereign" waters far in excess of those delineated by the UNCLOS.[57]

These strategic maritime concerns must be addressed by Beijing in an environment potentially dominated by the U.S. Navy and heavily influenced by other powerful navies, especially those of South Korea, Japan, and India. Furthermore, despite its long coastline of over 14,000 kilometers, thousands of insular possessions, and an increasing awareness of maritime issues, China's view of national security has almost always focused on continental, not maritime, dangers.

The events of the mid-1990s no doubt spurred PLAN modernization of its surface combatant fleet. In particular, the PLAN realized its weaknesses in specific naval warfare areas, especially anti-air warfare (AAW). Hence, the new Luyang I–, II–, III–, and Luzhou-class destroyers appear to be equipped with significantly improved AAW defense systems. An area AAW capability, crucial for fleet operations in opposed scenarios, is apparently included.

PLAN modernization also includes other naval warfare area improvements. Amphibious force growth since the mid-1990s has included significant shipbuilding programs, including almost twenty tank landing ships displacing approximately 3,500 tons and possibly a landing platform dock that may displace more than 10,000 tons. Even more important, however, has been additional amphibious training, even mission specialization, assigned to at least two PLA divisions in the Nanjing and Guangzhou military regions. The marine corps remains at two-brigade strength, but its officer accession process has been regularized under PLAN aegis.

PLA aviation capabilities have also benefited. As is the case with amphibious warfare, more significant even than important equipment acquisitions—Su-27s, Su-30s, air-to-air refueling and airborne warning and air control–type aircraft—has been increased air force and naval aviation integration, and advances in operational capabilities, including overwater flights.

The two most important areas of PLAN modernization during the past decade have relatively little to do with hardware. The first is the overhaul of the personnel education and training system that has occurred as the Chinese military strives to enlist and retain personnel capable of mastering the technological complexities of current-day warships. This extends to the second area, the PLAN's revised and seemingly improved training paradigm. The old ship and unit training system, slaved to the calendar year, seems now far more flexible, which enhances the integration of maintenance and shore-based training requirements. The PLAN is also continuing to increase its participation in joint training and exercise activities.

China's mid-century goal for achieving a completely modern military means that the PLAN sees itself in 2015 at approximately the halfway mark in its overall modernization program.[58]

Conclusion

China's emergence as a global economic power has been accompanied by dramatically increasing energy demand. At the same time, Beijing is modernizing its military to carry out specific national security missions. These two major developments—economic and military—will determine to a large extent the degree of security that China will demand for nondomestic energy supplies.

In the near term, China's efforts to build a navy able to satisfy these maritime security concerns focus on Taiwan; in the midterm, they include the disputes with Japan over natural gas deposits in the East China seabed and with the claimants to South China Sea territories.

This maritime area is also the most sensitive from a naval viewpoint since its control is necessary for Beijing to maintain national sovereignty, economic autonomy, and security for both regime and people. Coastal waters also provide China with critical maritime highways, as do the regional waters of East Asia, the third category of maritime dependence.

Beijing today faces a region rife with economic competition, a wide range of governmental systems, historic enmities, and a nascent naval arms race. The Japanese and South Korean navies are already capable, twenty-first-century forces; Vietnam, Malaysia, Thailand, Indonesia, and the Philippines are all at least talking about modernizing their navies, while the first four countries are allocating the resources to achieve that status. These naval developments will be limited by individual national resources but will continue, in significant part due to China's military modernization and renewed affirmation of its place as the major power in East Asia.

Chinese strategists are caught in a bit of a strategic conundrum; Beijing clearly is determined to insist on its perceived maritime rights throughout the three seas. Ensuring those rights would be easier if the PLAN and other Chinese maritime units were unchallenged by opposing national forces, but Beijing's determination is in fact leading to development of that very opposition.

That problem of course is not publicly recognized in China; instead, the "other" is always at fault in a dispute with Beijing. As noted earlier, the United States is painted as the primary offender in opposing China. This strategic viewpoint has not usually led to operations against the United States, however, which is accused of "meddling," but to actions taken against Japan, Vietnam, and the Philippines as perceived U.S. acolytes.[59]

China's maritime strategic thought assumes that the United States is determined to contain and encircle China. One analyst at the influential PLA Academy of Military Science recently described the PLAN as "relatively weak," with "China's maritime security at the mercy of . . . the United States Navy."[60] Another concern often voiced by Chinese analysts is that the United States might intervene in navigational choke points to intercept seaborne energy supplies destined for Chinese ports. This "Malacca dilemma" is baseless from a naval operational perspective due to the availability of several alternative routes and the internationalization of the energy trade, but it is apparently real at least to some in Beijing.

In other words, to a Chinese maritime strategist in 2015, the region is not without risks, and most of those are attributable to U.S. containment. This accusation is verbalized in terms of U.S. defense treaties, agreements with China's neighbors, arms sales to Taiwan, surveillance flights and ship operations in China's exclusive economic zone, and congressional restrictions on Sino-American military relations.

Representatives at the early 2012 National People's Congress in Beijing vociferously criticized the lack of a maritime strategy, calling for the government to "formulate and promulgate a complete, comprehensive, and systematic maritime development strategy, with all the national political, economic, military factors being brought into consideration!"[61] The delegates demand should be satisfied by the 2015 military strategy, which calls for a "transformation" of the PLAN's overall mission, from one of "offshore waters defense" to "open seas protection." This remains more of a goal than a reality in mid-2016. Indeed, "China's maritime strategy is one of offshore defense or, translated more literally, "near-sea active defense," meaning that the PLAN will strive to "maintain control over the maritime traffic in the coastal waters of the mainland" and the resources in those waters.[62] Delineating the capability necessary to accomplish these goals is not easy, even when focused on the waters extending from the Chinese coast to approximately 100 nm east of Taiwan along a line from the Philippines to Japan and all of the Yellow Sea.

This in turn has led the PLAN to delineate specific defensive zones in China's regional waters, zones in concept not unlike those instituted by the Soviet Union during the Cold War in preparation for possible U.S. attacks. Beijing's version appears to describe three zones. For the first, from 540 to 1,000 nm from its coast, China would use ASBMs and submarines to attack an adversary; submarines and air assets would be employed in the second defensive zone, from 270 to 540 nm; while all available naval, air force, and coastal defense systems would be applied from the coast out to 270 nm.[63]

Continued constructive relations with the nations of Southeast Asia should ease Beijing's concern about commanding the seas bordering the narrow Malacca Strait. Defense of more distant SLOCs, from Malacca, between the South China Sea and the Indian Ocean, to the Hormuz Strait at the mouth of the Persian Gulf, would require a quantum leap in PLAN capabilities.

Vice Minister of Foreign Affairs Dai Bingguo argued in 2010 that China would always follow a policy of "peaceful development" rather than the "Western powers' practice of invasion, plunder, war and expansion." That is a very selective view, at best, overlooking Chinese history ranging from the Qin dynasty's use of military force to Beijing's 2013 seizure of Scarborough Reef in the South China Sea. As noted by a professor at China's National Defense University, "peaceful development . . . does not mean that military means are not employed."[64]

Beijing's decision-making process for using the PLAN to ensure maritime security is not clear. Furthermore, a PLAN presence in Southwest Asian waters would be based on the defense of SLOCs and energy reserves in that region, but China is already moving along alternate paths to enhance its energy security. These include developing alternate fuel sources within China and establishing shortened or nonmaritime lines of transportation for energy imports. The former effort is already bearing considerable fruit in the areas of hydropower, solar power, and wind power; the latter may be seen in the very considerable and rapid domestic pipeline construction that has occurred in China during the past decade.

In fact, even the U.S. military would be unable to interrupt China's SLOCs in any environment other than a global war, but these appear vulnerable to PLAN eyes. Should the United States attempt to physically interrupt either SLOCs or overland pipelines, it would almost certainly mean directly attacking China, directly attacking other nations (hosting pipelines and their pumping stations), interfering with the peacetime passage of third-country tankers at sea, or all of the above.

The SLOCs are most vulnerable not on the high seas but at transit points through narrow straits, including Hormuz, Malacca, Luzon, and Taiwan and the Nine Degree Channel. The most likely tactic for the United States to employ would be a blockade of Chinese oil port terminals or of these choke points. Such actions would be acts of war against China and other nations and would likely not succeed in significantly reducing China's overall energy supply.

The use of the military instrument of statecraft will confront five primary factors. First, how secure does the CCP leadership feel about their place in power in Beijing? Second, how willing is the Chinese leadership to rely on the world energy market to ensure the affordability, availability, and safe passage of imported supplies? Third, how confident is the leadership about U.S.

peaceful intentions, possibly in the face of contentious Chinese actions, such as increasing military pressure against Taiwan? Fourth, how much confidence does the leadership have in PLAN capabilities?

Fifth, and most important, what are the possible effects on China's relations with neighboring and more distant nations as it both increases its share of global energy supplies and modernizes a navy already seen as the most powerful in Asia after that of the United States? Ensuring an integrated energy-navy–foreign relations paradigm should be a matter of grave concern to Beijing, but accomplishing that state in the intensely stove-piped nature of China's government is problematic.

A Sino-American crisis (over Taiwan, for instance) might drive Beijing to decide that the PLAN has to defend the SLOCs over which its energy imports flow. China would have to make a major change in national budgeting priorities to build a navy and air force capable of protecting the extended SLOCs that carry much of its imported oil and natural gas. This degree of PLA growth is inhibited by several factors.

First, Beijing's national priorities continue to fall under the rubric of "rich country, strong army": developing China's economy and ensuring the welfare of its people remains top priority for the government and the CCP. Second, while Taiwan remains the most sensitive issue between Beijing and Washington, the present economic and political situation on the island, U.S. and Chinese interest in keeping the issue within peaceful bounds, and common interest in the campaign against terrorism all mitigate against the reunification issue deteriorating to the point of hostilities. Hence, Sino-American relations should remain peaceful, if often contentious.

Links between the island and the mainland continue to develop and deepen, a positive indicator of eventual peaceful resolution of Taiwan's status. The extensive trade, financial, and economic links established during the past decade have resulted in nearly 10 percent of Taiwan's population present in China on any given day, hundreds of daily flights to and from the mainland, cooperative oil-drilling efforts in the northern South China Sea, significant academic exchanges, and, most recently, taxation and flight safety agreements.[65]

Countering those developments is the potential retaking of the presidency by the historically pro-independence Democratic Progressive Party (DPP) in the January 2016 election. The party's only tenure in office, under President

Chen Shui-bian from 2000 to 2008, was a period of heightened tension across the Taiwan Strait. Since the DPP candidate, Tsai Ing-wen, won the presidency in the March 2016 election, Beijing has adopted a cautious attitude, but one that has not disguised a noncooperative, hostile policy toward furthering links with Taipei, as noted in President Xi Jinping's "stern" messaging.[66]

Third, the army's dominance in the PLA appears to be ending as current military reform begun with Xi Jinping's 2015 declaration of a personnel reduction is likely to hit the army the hardest.

Fourth, China's relations with the rest of Asia are already tenuous, given their concern about the region's largest nation—geographically, culturally, economically, and in terms of military power. Failure by Beijing to carefully balance its energy, sovereignty, and maritime interests in general would have seriously deleterious effects on its foreign relationships.

Future out-of-area PLAN operations are certain, especially following resolution of Taiwan's status. These future operations may be dedicated nominally to SLOC defense but simply will repeat maritime expansion by any nation with global economic and political interests.

China is attempting to become both a continental and a maritime power, a difficult transition and rare in history. France, Germany, and Russia all failed to do so. A former U.S. commander of Pacific forces, Adm. Robert Willard, has opined that China "aspires to become a 'global military (power)' by extending its influence beyond its regional waters."[67] Only the United States has achieved this level of strategic effectiveness, a level of global power made possible not just by remarkable industrialization, innovation, and immigration but accompanied by the world-rending event of two world wars.

China will not experience such an environment, nor does it enjoy the U.S. democratic social and political experience. If China succeeds in deploying an effective global navy while remaining a strong continental power, it truly will have beaten the historical odds and established a new paradigm of national power.

In 1999 I wrote that "the PLAN required to carry out Liu Huaqing's strategy would include task groups of missile-firing, power-projection capable ships supported by nuclear-powered submarines and tactical air power."[68] This force structure (Deng Xiaoping's statement that "without air cover, winning a naval battle is out of the question") is still nascent but appearing on the horizon.[69]

China's navy today exercises at classic naval missions: presence, protection of seaborne trade, counterpiracy, NEO, deterrence, and preparing for joint warfare at sea in defense of vital national security interests, including power projection ashore. These missions fall under the rubric of defending China's "core interests," which are defending "state sovereignty, national security, territorial integrity and national reunification, China's political system established by the Constitution, overall social stability, and the basic safeguards for ensuring sustainable economic and social development."[70] These strategic goals are also part and parcel to China's foreign policy objectives.

Chapter Four

ECONOMY

This chapter addresses the current and possible future state of China's economy, with a focus on maritime and energy relationships. A basic premise is that the CCP depends on popular support to remain in power and that support requires popular confidence that "tomorrow will be better than today" because the economy will continue to grow. The next chapter addresses the energy requirements on which continued economic well-being depends. An important element in China's economic health is its dependence on maritime trade and resources, with a reported 10 percent of the nation's gross domestic product (GDP) coming "from the sea."[1]

That concern is evidenced in the dual nature of China's economy. State-owned enterprises (SOE) remain the leading elements in the country's semi-capitalistic economy. SOEs include China's ten largest companies by revenue or profit. They are expected to earn profits, but their primary objective is to serve as the government's instruments. All SOE senior officers are members of the CCP, and they commonly go back and forth between government and SOE positions.[2]

Beijing sees both advantages and problems in the SOE structure, where economic motives are significantly impacted by political motives and interactions. The government issued new guidelines in 2015 to reform the SOEs; as currently reported, these reforms seem potentially contradictory. The following guidelines are to be implemented "in key areas" by 2020 to make the SOEs "more robust and influential and have greater ability to avoid risks":

- "SOEs will be divided into two categories, for-profit entities and those dedicated to public welfare. The former will be market-based . . . and should aim to increase state-owned assets and boost the economy, while the latter will exist to improve people's quality of life and provide public goods and services."
- "SOE boards of directors will have greater decision-making powers, managers will be more tightly supervised, and intervention by government agencies will be forbidden under the new guideline."
- "A flexible and market-based salary system will be established. . . . SOEs will hire more professional managers."
- "China will improve the supervision over state-owned assets to ensure the security of assets and increase capital returns."
- "Supervision will be intensified both from inside and outside SOEs to prevent abuse of power . . . and to track violations, including corruption and embezzlement."[3]

This seems a mixture of wanting better management for more independent, market-oriented SOE performance but with greater central government supervision to fight endemic corruption and inconsistent economic performance. The reforms also reflect President Xi Jinping's apparent dissatisfaction with SOE performance.[4]

Beijing has made efforts to build international economic structures with the potential to redefine the international economic system, particularly with the Shanghai Cooperation Organization (SCO), the Asian Infrastructure Investment Bank (AIIB), and the "one belt, one road" (OBOR) initiative. This truly national effort is occurring in the Asia-Pacific region, which likely will be the world's richest region by 2016, with private wealth of at least $57 trillion.[5] A notable feature of President Xi's international travel is his emphasis on trade and economic relations, all—with the exception of his 2014 trip to South Korea—in connection with a major international organization. These have included AIIB; Asia-Pacific Economic Cooperation (APEC); Association of Southeast Asian Nations (ASEAN); Brazil, Russia, India, China, South Africa (BRICS); SCO; and the United Nations.[6]

China's economic growth since the early 1980s has been so dramatic that it has become a truism to note its uniqueness in history. For instance, China's GDP averaged 9.06 percent from 1989 until 2015. More recently, it increased by 9.9 percent in 2005, 10.7 percent in 2006, 10.5 percent in 2007, 9.6 percent in 2008, 9.2 percent in 2009, 10.6 percent in 2010, 9.5 percent in 2011, 7.5 percent in 2012, just over 10 percent in 2013, and only 7.4 percent in 2014, the slowest pace since 1990. The International Monetary Fund (IMF) projects China's economy to grow just 6.3 percent in 2016. This hardly constitutes a significant problem since China continues to lead the world in economic expansion; only India came close in 2014, with 7 percent GDP growth.

However, China still today produces 13 percent of the world's GDP with 21 percent of the population; the United States produces 23 percent of global GDP with just 4 percent of the population. Of course, all data coming from China must be treated with caution, due to corruption, lack of reliable information, and CCP political priorities. Even the Chinese government has admitted the problem of "economic data fraud."[7] A government analyst described as a "striking phenomenon" the "inconsistency and weak correlation among statistics." For instance, the acceleration of GDP growth did not match that of the industrial consumption of electricity and railway cargo transport; employment also kept increasing even though the GDP growth was slowing down.[8]

Premier Li Keqiang acknowledged the economy is facing increased downward pressures when he delivered the "Government Work Report" at the 3rd Session of the 12th National People's Congress, in March 2015.[9] Li started on an upbeat note, saying "China's economic and social development was generally stable, and progress was made in a steady manner." That opening statement is most notable due to its linking of economic and social factors, evidencing the CCP's view that continued economic growth underlies the social peace and satisfaction necessary to support continued CCP power.

Li proceeded to address a long list of advances in China's economy and social safety network but then turned to the other side of the coin. He said, "We need to not only see our accomplishments but also see the difficulties and challenges on our way ahead." Li listed these as weak investment growth, sluggish consumption, a stagnant international marketplace for Chinese goods, falling industrial production prices and rising costs, and financing difficulties. He highlighted "a lack of innovative capacity." Concerns about agricultural production would seem to result in part from Beijing's deliberate urbanization policy, which led to 54.8 percent of the population living in cities or "new towns in 2014."[10]

China's huge fishing fleet has a direct role in national security. The central government subsidizes fishing vessel fuel by as much as $480 per day per 500 horsepower engine and has installed the BeiDou navigation satellite system in approximately 50,000 boats, facilitating both fishing and participation in maritime security activities.[11]

Li also addressed direct social concerns, such as "the masses" dissatisfied with "health care, care for the elderly, housing, transportation, education, income distribution, food security, law and order, and other areas." He referred to "serious environmental pollution," "major safety accidents, [and] deficiencies in the work of the government"—namely, corruption. Li echoed this negative perspective in at least two other speeches during the spring of 2015, noting on one instance that China "must prepare to face bigger economic difficulties and challenges."[12]

Li Keqiang emphasized in his conclusion the need to adhere to "the law in an all-round way," which, while demonstrating the central government's awareness of the weak rule of law in China's economic and political sectors, fails to address the core of the problem. The "rule of law" in China today is based not on governmental/legislative legal principles but equates to what is good for the CCP.

Meanwhile, China's State Council named ten sectors as "top priorities" for economic development:

- New information technology
- High-end and Numerical Control machines
- Aerospace equipment
- Ships with advanced technology
- High-speed railway equipment
- Energy saving and new energy vehicles
- Power equipment
- New materials
- Biotechnology (medicine and equipment)
- Agricultural production machines[13]

No matter how honest Beijing is in assessing its economy and making changes in the infrastructure, the number one priority for China will remain taking the steps deemed necessary to ensure the CCP remains in power; the preservation of the party's dominance will always take priority.

Banking and Currency

China's banking system is an issue of serious concern. Potential problems include the valuation of the yuan, China's currency unit; the rationality of the banking system loan policies, which is slaved to CCP priorities and reportedly particularly susceptible to corruption; and the country's total debt, which at the end of 2014 equaled 282 percent of China's GDP, a concerning figure.[14] The status of the yuan also demonstrates China's relatively recent, very major role in the world economy; the series of revaluations of the yuan during the summer of 2015 by the Chinese government had major global effects.[15]

China's economic growth has included a pronounced rise in the value and globally recognized status of its currency. In fact, by one measure the yuan currently is the second most popular currency in the world, trailing only the U.S. dollar.[16] The currency issue that often draws criticism, particularly from U.S. politicians and analysts, is Beijing deliberately undervaluing the yuan. It probably was in the last decade, but foreign analysts almost unanimously believe it now is not undervalued and the Chinese government is not guilty of currency manipulation.[17]

Corruption

Corruption, a weak intellectual property rights (IPR) regime, and lack of innovation all characterize China's economy. The lack of enforceable IPR is particularly notorious and perhaps linked to the issue of sluggish innovation. As noted earlier, in addition to Le Keqiang addressing this problem to the 12th People's Congress in March 2015, President Xi has repeatedly highlighted the importance of innovation as "the most important ingredient for the Chinese economy" and as "the primary force of productivity."[18] China did not establish patent and copyright laws until 1980 and 1991, respectively, but their weak enforcement still affects indigenous innovation and foreign investment.

An argument is sometimes made that China merely is experiencing the same "copycat" phase that boosted other developing economies, including the United States in the late nineteenth century. The weakness in this argument probably relates most importantly to the domestic sector, in Beijing's view, where it exacerbates societal inequality. China is one of the world's "most unequal societies" according to a Chinese university's study.[19] This is an important concern for the CCP's leadership, which, as noted earlier, strives for the societal satisfaction weakened by corruption and inequality. Beijing has gone so far as to appeal for international assistance in its anticorruption campaign.[20]

One of President Xi's core campaigns has been fighting corruption at all levels in Chinese society, to find, prosecute, and punish both "tigers and flies," by which he means the wealthy and influential "tigers" as well as lower-ranking officials and ordinary citizens, the "flies." Xi has described corruption as a threat to the continued existence of the nation, warning that it could lead to "the collapse of the Party and the downfall of the state." A reported 270,000 party cadres have been punished for corrupt activities, but China's rating on the international "Corruption Perceptions Index" was worse for 2014 than it was for 2013, indicating a lack of effectiveness in Xi's anticorruption campaign.

Corruption in the economic sector of course affects a very wide range of daily life and governance in China. The judiciary is certainly corrupt by Western standards, given the primacy of the CCP over an objective set of legal standards; this also applies to the law enforcement infrastructure. Foreign companies investing in China often find it helpful to pay "consulting fees" to government officials or their relatives, while even accessing elite educational and medical facilities may require "*guanxi*," or personal influence, if not outright bribes. Perhaps most extraordinary is corruption in the PLA, where, according to several sources, "if it is worth something, it is for sale," particularly promotions and certain duty assignments.[21]

Additionally, corruption in the civil sector is self-induced. Municipal and provincial officials are driven to promote growth; CCP cadres often have privileged access to resources; bribery and mutual interests among party, official, and business interests often are mutually beneficial and capable of bypassing standards and regulations.

A reported 414,000 officials of all ranks have been disciplined and 201,600 prosecuted in court since Xi assumed office in late 2012. Few headlines report the "flies," but the "tigers" are subject to extensive publicity by the government. These have included both rising and retired major figures in the CCP, such as Bo Xilai and Zhou Yongkang.[22]

The anticorruption drive is reported as primarily aimed at individuals, but these almost invariably also represent organizations, including—perhaps focusing primarily on—CCP and state units. One recent case evidenced that the party- and state-controlled, state-owned enterprises are a target of the anticorruption drive. China's State Audit Office reported "falsified revenues and profits in the accounts of [fourteen] of the country's biggest state-owned companies" amounting to approximately US$8 billion in 2013 alone. This investigation resulted in "more than 100 top company executives" being detained and "250 people penalized." The charges involved false reporting, unqualified loans, misappropriated funds, and embezzlement.[23]

The president no doubt is sincerely concerned about the deleterious effects of corruption, but he is also motivated by political aims to consolidate his leadership position and discredit rivals and deter possible rivals. He faces an uphill battle, however, given traditional Chinese reliance on *guanxi* and the concealing effects of China's one-party rule and strict state control of the economy.

The most powerful anticorruption government body is the CCP's Central Commission for Discipline Inspection. In June 2015 it identified "three key 'black holes'" in the way government-owned companies operated, saying the companies "are not following the correct procedures" in procurement bidding, mismanagement of overseas investments, and the "unlawful transfer of company wealth to relatives of those on the management teams."[24] These obviously amount to corruption throughout the management process.

Demographics

China confronts an aging population, significant gender imbalance, and a shrinking labor force. It enacted a one-child policy in 1980 that has been remarkably effective in curtailing population growth. This restriction was eased in 2015, but the results of allowing two children per family will take many years to take effect.[25] However, it has also constrained growth of the labor resources necessary to continue China's economic boom. There were several exceptions to the one-child policy, but it prevented hundreds of thousands of births. The government now has eased the policy in view of the prognostication that "China will grow old before it grows rich"; that is, the lack of labor will halt economic expansion before the country's relatively high level of economic inequality is reduced.[26]

China's population is predicted to peak during the middle of the next decade.[27] This is normally judged as a negative factor in the country's economic future, but the decreased cost of automation is resulting in a lack of unskilled employment options, so the two factors—reduced population and reduced labor demand—may partially offset.

A dramatic gender imbalance is another demographic problem plaguing China. Worldwide, male births exceed female births by 106:100. In China, the ratio is 124:100, with Hubei Province registering a stunning 176:100 ratio. This probably most affects the pool of military conscripts, but the long-term effects of a predominantly male population are also significant. The gender imbalance results directly from the one-child policy and the strong cultural preference for sons in a society where a woman literally joins her husband's family when she weds, leaving her own parents potentially adrift and without support in their old age.[28]

Strategy

China joined the World Trade Organization in 2001, and the Tenth Five-Year Plan (2001–5) adopted that year included a formal "going-out" strategy. This encouraged Chinese companies to invest overseas; embassies and consulates were directed to facilitate Chinese business activities in foreign nations. The flip side of this policy is a major reason for China's remarkable economic growth; the country has attracted more foreign direct investment (FDI) than any country except the United States.[29]

The going-out strategy remains in place as an active instrument of Chinese economic growth, although apparently suffering problems. China's FDI amounted to $1.1 trillion since 2005, but $250 billion of that reportedly "failed." Problems include lack of careful planning or a clear strategy, unfamiliarity with a market-driven economy, and political risks.[30]

Premier Li Keqiang specifically supported the strategy in a June 2015 speech in which he urged greater Chinese investment in Europe. He recommended completion of a China–EU investment treaty as a platform to expedite expanded economic activity between his nation and the European Union. He argued, "If a comprehensive, balanced and high standard investment treaty could be reached early, it will bring opportunity for both sides to combine their respective strengths and form a new pattern of co-operation."[31]

In fact, Chinese companies face rising costs and eroding competitiveness in a slowing domestic market and are seeking acquisition targets to obtain technology and boost profits. This reflects a post-2008 financial crisis move to accelerate China's overseas investments, particularly in the advanced markets of the European Union and the United States.

Decision-makers in Beijing must also consider the domestic picture, of course. While China has, remarkably, lifted the great majority of its people out of poverty during the past thirty-five years, its per capita GDP remains well below desired levels; poverty is still a serious problem in some rural areas.

Xi Jinping's "China Dream" focuses on a self-strengthening movement, which includes reinvigorating the CCP, reducing corruption, and increasing economic equality throughout the population.[32] His dream includes China becoming a "moderately well-off society"—defined as doubling the per capita GDP to approximately $10,000 per year and housing 60 percent of the population in cities—by 2021, the centennial of the Chinese Communist Party. By 2049, the centennial of the founding of the PRC, China, Jinping believes, will be a fully developed nation, having overcome poverty, pollution, corruption, and ethnic strife.[33]

Substantial investments are directed at countries rich in natural resources, a policy that is creating a degree of foreign concern that China is trying to monopolize valuable resources worldwide. In 2013, for instance, the governor of Nigeria's Central Bank accused China of "a new form of imperialism," with a neocolonial agenda of taking Africa's natural resources without adequate compensation. Beijing's rather violent response to this charge—which was levied immediately prior to President Xi Jinping's first visit to the continent—underlines China's sensitivity to such perhaps valid concerns.[34]

China continues to make vast investments in foreign resources, with target areas listed by the National Development and Reform Commission as part of the Eleventh Five-Year Plan (2006–10). China has become a major investor throughout the world, with major stakes in Latin America, Africa, Southwest Asia, Southeast Asia, North America, and Australia.

Beijing has learned that the going-out policy brings problems as well as benefits, particularly because of China's lack of interest in the domestic politics of its investment destinations. Libya, Yemen, Pakistan, and Venezuela are examples; Beijing has found its economic investments brought into question by domestic political and economic unrest.[35]

Arms sales are a special area of international trade. China is increasingly engaged in this trade, ranking during the 2010–14 period as the third largest arms exporter in the world.[36] One increasingly prominent international trade venue for China is the free trade agreement, both bilateral and multilateral. In the past few years, Beijing has signed such agreements with Australia, Canada, Chile, Costa Rica, New Zealand, Pakistan, Peru, Singapore, South Korea, Switzerland, Thailand, and ASEAN.

China's overseas investments are estimated to rise to US$1 trillion by 2020.[37] The going-out campaign also has obvious political overtones, as Beijing moves to increase investments in Europe, as noted earlier, and in India. One particularly extensive area of overseas Chinese investments is that devoted to securing energy supplies, a topic that is addressed in chapter 5.

Caution is called for, however, when reviewing Beijing's announcements of dramatic overseas investments, due to unfulfilled promises.[38] Almost all announced investment agreements must be treated cautiously since the grandiose initial announcements sometimes fall victim to economic and political realities. For instance, President Hu Jintao announced during his extensive visit to South American countries in 2004 that Beijing would invest $100 billion in the region; the following decade has seen Chinese investments at a far slower pace. Similarly, the recently announced investment of $46 billion in Pakistan's infrastructure by President Xi Jinping is already in some doubt.[39]

Indeed, Xi has described a "new normal" of economic growth in China that includes forging "a partnership of mutual trust" with foreign partners. He also said the new normal has three "notable features." First, the "economy has shifted gear from the previous high speed to a medium-to-high speed growth"; second, "the economic structure is constantly improved and upgraded"; and third, the economy is increasingly driven by innovation instead of input and investment."[40] This goal has not been supported for FDI entering China, however, amid what is described as a "souring business environment" for foreign concerns. A Chinese analyst described threats to China's going-out strategy as Western opposition, both ideological and military; terrorism, including "Islamic fundamentalism and Pan-Turkism"; international sovereignty disputes; political instability; and threats to freedom of navigation and sea-lane security.[41]

Domestically, the "new normal" subsumes the government adopting policies to stabilize the growth, promote reform, adjust the economic structure, and benefit the public. It also recognizes an apparently inevitable slowdown in China's remarkable annual GDP increases. Third quarter 2015 GDP growth was 6.9 percent, the lowest since 2009, when Beijing implemented a massive stimulus to China's economy to address the global recession.

This reflects continued pressures on economic expansion, including reduced foreign trade, less-than-expected investment growth, and a financial structure requiring very active government intervention.[42] Government policies also reflect continued concerns about inconsistent growth among China's regions and industries.

Asian Infrasructure Investment Bank

The latest and arguably the most important element in China's going-out strategy is the 2013 announcement of the AIIB. This venture is made possible by China's very large financial reserves; offers a means of better use of those reserves; recognizes the extensive Asian infrastructure needs, estimated by the Asian Development Bank (ADB) in 2009 at approximately $5 trillion; and may serve as a vehicle for Beijing to reorder the post–World War II international financial structure.[43]

The AIIB may also contribute to the internationalization of the Chinese currency, help secure contracts for Chinese firms, and expand Chinese investments in international infrastructure projects. A 2013 G-20 report included the Organization of Economic Cooperation and Development's estimate that "$70 trillion in additional infrastructure capacity will be needed globally" by 2030, with the greatest need for that enormous sum in Asia.[44] There obviously is more than enough "business" in Asia for the AIIB as well as for the ADB and other financial institutions.

China formally launched the AIIB in Beijing in June 2015 at a ceremony attended by representatives of the forty-nine nations that initially joined the bank. These include four permanent members of the UN Security Council (all but the United States), all ASEAN members, five of the six [Persian] Gulf Cooperation Council members, six of eight South Asian states, and eighteen of thirty-four members of the Organization of Economic Cooperation and Development.

Fifty-seven members had joined the AIIB by September 2015, a number forecast to reach at least seventy, a number greater than the membership of the U.S.- and Japan-led ADB.[45] The AIIB's potential strength is noteworthy in the face of U.S. opposition since close U.S. allies have joined the new bank, including South Korea, Australia, and the United Kingdom. Indeed, Japan and the United States are the most notable nonmembers.[46]

Beijing announced an initial $40 billion investment in the AIIB, with India, Russia, and Germany also contributing to the bank's initial capitalization. China apparently will control more than 25 percent of the bank's votes, but final voting procedures remain undetermined.

Beijing no doubt is frustrated at its lack of authority in the ADB and other international banking organizations despite its status as the world's second-largest economy, but Xi Jinping has stated "[for] the AIIB, its operation needs to follow multilateral rules and procedures. . . . We have also to learn from the World Bank and the Asian Development Bank and other existing multilateral development institutions in their good practices and useful experiences."[47]

Establishing the AIIB may also indicate that Beijing is downgrading its aims for the BRICS Bank, now called the New Development Bank, that it helped organize in 2014. Four of the five organizers, apparently frustrated by their lack of voting power in the World Bank, reportedly contributed $10 billion to fund the New Development Bank, with China eventually contributing $50 billion.[48]

The New Development Bank opened in Shanghai on 21 July 2015 as an alternative to other multilateral lenders, officials said. Its Web site described it as "alternative to the existing U.S.-dominated World Bank and International Monetary Fund," although Chinese minister of finance Lou Jiwei said the bank "will supplement the existing international financial system in a healthy way and explore innovations in governance models." The bank's head, K. V. Kamath of India, announced in June 2016 that the bank had made its first loans.[49]

The AIIB may also attest to a Chinese loss of faith in its ability to use the SCO as a venue for ensuring long-term domination of Central Asian nations in the face of Russian opposition.[50] The SCO's original members were China, Russia, Kazakhstan, Kyrgyzstan, and Tajikistan. It now also includes Uzbekistan and, most recently, India, Pakistan, Iran, Belarus, and Mongolia.[51]

Beijing's concerns about slowing domestic economic growth spurred its interests in establishing the AIIB and the OBOR initiative. These concerns include at least three underlying problems: first, slowing technological developments; second, "the marginal product of capital is dropping"—that is, more investment is producing less growth, resulting, for instance, in the rows of half-built and completed but unoccupied apartment buildings in Haikou, Qingdao, and many other cities in China; and third, low domestic consumption. Beijing may also be concerned about better securing sources of raw materials, such as the extensive trade with Brazil's "massive agricultural sector."[52]

These international measures are judged by at least one prominent analyst not to be significantly ameliorating domestic economic problems, however, which are best addressed by domestic reform. The November 2013 Third Plenum of the CCP listed many such reforms. Reform of the household registration system, intergovernmental fiscal reform, financial liberalization, and the opening of China's service sectors to competition may prove especially promising.[53]

One Belt, One Road

A second striking move by Beijing to strengthen its leadership role in international investment and trade came in 2013 with Xi Jinping's announcement of a "Silk Road Economic Belt" and a "Twenty-first Century Maritime Silk Road," referred to as "one belt, one road" (OBOR), which Xi envisions spanning "from the Pacific Ocean to the Baltic Sea."[54] The Silk Road scheme aims to establish closer economic ties between China and sixty-four nations in Central Asia, the Middle East, and Europe. Beijing has already announced a huge investment, $113 billion, into supporting the OBOR.[55] The two schemes seem to have a common objective: to create an integrated set of land- and sea-based corridors linking China with markets across the Eurasian continents.[56] In the words of the Ministries of Foreign Affairs and Commerce in March 2015:

> The Belt and Road run through the continents of Asia, Europe, and Africa, connecting the vibrant East Asia economic circle at one end and developed European economic circle at the other, and encompassing countries with huge potential for economic development. The Silk Road Economic Belt focuses on bringing together China, Central Asia, Russia and Europe (the Baltic); linking China with the Persian Gulf and the Mediterranean Sea through Central Asia and West Asia; and connecting China with Southeast Asia, South Asia and the Indian Ocean. The 21st-Century Maritime Silk Road is designed to go from China's coast to Europe through the South China Sea and the Indian Ocean in one route, and from China's coast through the South China Sea to the South Pacific in the other.[57]

Hence, the Maritime Silk Road plan would extend through Southeast Asia, the Indian Ocean, and into the Mediterranean. More than sixty nations could be included in these two initiatives, the second of which underlines Beijing's awareness of the importance of SLOC security, a PLAN mission.[58] It is a near-revolutionary proposal, with no less an objective than aiming "to bring into being a new economic order on the Eurasian landmass. Everything

This report identifies continuing concerns, including the fall of "the Shanghai Composite Index by 43% from June 12 to August 25, 2015, despite extensive intervention by the Chinese government to halt the slide." Concern about its currency led the government to announce on 11 August 2015 that "the daily reference rate of the renminbi (RMB) would become more market-oriented." The RMB then depreciated by 4.4 percent against the dollar. Finally, China's new-found economic gravitas is evidenced by "concerns over the state of the Chinese economy appear to have contributed to recent sharp volatility in global stock indexes." In sum, this report notes: Beijing's ability "to maintain a rapidly growing economy in the long run will likely depend largely on its ability . . . to implement comprehensive economic reforms that more quickly hasten China's transition to a free market economy; rebalance the Chinese economy by making consumer demand, rather than exporting and fixed investment, the main engine of economic growth; boost productivity and innovation; address growing income disparities; and enhance environmental protection."[70]

The most significant problem identified by the World Bank is China's transitioning from middle-income to high-income status. Beijing is well aware of these various issues, addressed in its Twelfth Five-Year Plan (2011–15). As noted by Premier Li Keqiang in March 2015, the issues include a multiplicity of extremely challenging concerns.[71] An unquantifiable but core issue is confidence in China's future, both domestically and internationally.

Despite its historic contributions, the role of FDI is now significantly less important in China's economy due to the growth of that economy, important sectors that are closed to foreign investment, IPR problems, corruption, and Xi Jinping's "China dream," which seems to emphasize indigenous wealth and control.[72]

Another basis for China's historic economic boom has been the country's unfettered access to the American market. Hence, today the trade relationship between the world's two largest economies is subject to countervailing trends that can lead to major disturbances in the global economy. A China-U.S. bilateral trade treaty has been on the table since 2008 but is caught in the current maelstrom of the two nations' proposed new international banking and trading structures. The Chinese AIIB and the American Trans-Pacific Partnership pose the potential to benefit the global economy but, as of mid-2015, remain far apart.

China's leadership obviously understands the need for continued reforms, but implementing them will not be easy. One Chinese analyst has suggested four alternative futures for his country. The first, no doubt favored by the CCP, is that China would be a Singapore on a continental scale—a strongly authoritarian government overseeing a flourishing economy overseeing a docile population. A second alternative would be a continuation of the status quo; a continuing, stronger "socialism with Chinese characteristics." A third alternative predicts that a major crisis would lead to democratization. In the fourth alternative, democratization would proceed at a slower, deliberate pace. Of these, the second seems the most likely, given the CCP's determination to remain at the helm.[73]

A number of broad observations can be made. First, the thrust in the new leadership's economic diplomacy can be generalized as an attempt to proactively shape the external environment. Second, strategic competition between China and the United States does not have to be mutually exclusive. Third, Beijing is demonstrating China's flexibility and originality in handling multilateral trade and investment initiatives. The AIIB and offers of deeper integration with economies along the OBOR are potentially very significant. The naval and diplomatic implications of the AIIB and OBOR are clear, although linkages have yet to be defined.[74]

Beijing's dramatic 2014–15 announcements of the AIIB and the OBOR initiatives have scored a diplomatic triumph as even the United States' closest friends and allies, less Japan, have joined the new bank. The second initiative promises to ameliorate potential Chinese-Russian competition in Central Asia, very much to Beijing's advantage. It also may be a huge step toward reducing China's dependence on the SLOCs, should it successfully turn the Eurasian hinterland into an area of Chinese economic benefit rather than one of military threat, as it has been for much of its history.[75]

Beijing's concerns about corruption, the international environment, currency volatility, maritime security, and economic health in general all tie to concerns about feeding the economic engine. This requires a secure, affordable, and reliable supply of energy. The next chapter addresses this concern.

Chapter Five

ENERGY SECURITY

This chapter examines Beijing's views of energy security, the possible influence on PLAN modernization, and the effect of those views on foreign policy formulation. China defines energy security by the availability of supplies, the reliability of those supplies, and the affordability of available, reliable energy resources. The energy sector's priority is demonstrated in the government's ownership of the major energy companies as a strategic industry.

China's energy consumption in 2012 exceeded that of the United States by 24 percent and of the European Union by 63 percent.[1] The U.S. Department of Energy's Energy Information Agency (EIA) estimates that China will use twice the amount of energy as the United States by 2040.[2] The issue of China's increasing demand and the need for energy resources, many of which lie overseas, drives a perceived need for a naval capability to safeguard the SLOCs over which imported energy resources must flow.

The global energy picture has shifted dramatically during the past decade, led by the dramatically increased exploitation of shale reserves, particularly in North America; the United States has become essentially energy independent. The possible large-scale, global exploitation of methyl hydrate reserves would, in addition to the dramatic development of shale fracking, amount to a revolution in energy resourcing.[3]

These changes already are affecting petroleum-dependent nations, including China, which, as the world's largest importer of oil, lies at the heart of the current and potential energy revolution.[4] China needs to maintain very robust energy importing while working to ensure it is in position to take maximum advantage of new developments in energy resourcing.

China's emergence as a global economic power has been accompanied by dramatically increasing energy demands. At the same time, Beijing is modernizing its military to carry out specific national security missions. These two major developments—economic and military—will to a large extent determine the degree of security China will demand for nondomestic energy supplies.

China was self-sufficient in energy until the early 1990s; its remarkable economic growth until that point was relatively independent of foreign policy concerns focused on overseas energy resources. That situation has changed dramatically; China's economy is continuing to grow toward world leadership while raising concern about securing SLOCs.

China's indigenous oil production is not likely to increase. The potential for increasing natural gas recovery from shale formations through fracking is more promising. The EIA estimated in 2013 that China had the world's second-largest shale oil reserves and the world's third-largest shale natural gas reserves, but Beijing has been slow to access these reserves due to location and technology limitations, particularly the large amounts of water, which is rapidly becoming a scare resource in China, required for the process.[5] In fact, despite a declared ambition to move massively from coal to natural gas as a major source of energy, China in 2013–14 consumed just 6 percent of the world's natural gas.[6]

Hence, China's post-peak indigenous energy situation, at least in terms of nonshale possibilities, is an important driver in the nation's economic development and political future. China's 2015 defense white paper emphasizes the need for a globally capable navy to support the country's reliance on "effectively using overseas resources . . . to sustain its economic development."[7] The white paper notes China's increasing reliance on imported oil, 308 million tons in 2014, 68 percent of which comes primarily from Saudi Arabia, Angola, Russia, Jordan, Iraq, and Iran, and almost all of it by sea.[8]

Energy and the Economy

China has risen to become the world's second-largest economy, and the assurance of a secure supply of energy is a primary ingredient in maintaining China's remarkable economic growth; imported petroleum products form an increasing share of that supply. This has played a central role in the "going-out" strategy originated by Jiang Zemin, formally pronounced in 2001, and continued by his successors. This policy has led to increased requirements for energy and mineral resources. China has established a major economic presence in Central Asia, Southeast Asia, the Middle East, sub-Saharan Africa, and South America, much of it dedicated to obtaining energy resources. Even Iceland and Greenland are in Chinese sights.[9]

President Xi Jinping has declared a "new normal" for Chinese economic progress, with particular attention to the energy sector.[10] The "new normal" includes significant goals for that sector, with attention to an Energy Action Plan, which includes the following goals:

1. Strive toward energy self-sufficiency by developing clean coal technologies, reducing coal consumption, and increasing oil, natural gas, and shale gas as well as alternative energy sources.
2. Reduce energy consumption by promoting energy efficiency.
3. Increase international cooperation; energy technology, focus on "going out," especially for Russia and Central Asia, Middle East, Africa, America, and Asian Pacific; develop land and sea transport.
4. Promote energy research and development.[11]

Xi's ambitious plans for ensuring China's continued economic well-being currently focus on his OBOR strategy. This initiative includes increasing access to Central Asian energy resources.[12]

China became the world's second-largest net petroleum importer in 2009, its second-largest consumer in 2011, and the world's leading net petroleum importer in 2014, due primarily to increasing energy requirements but also to limited available domestic resources. China's oil consumption accounted for approximately 43 percent of global consumption increases in 2014 alone and is forecast to constitute between 27 and 28 percent of that amount in 2016.[13]

Beijing is trying to increase the use of natural gas, currently providing just 4 percent of China's energy requirements, which is not promising for reaching the nation's goal of natural gas providing 10 percent by 2020.[14] China wants to reduce the deleterious environmental effect of coal and to reduce its dependence on the SLOCs, which are increasingly important with China's growing dependence on energy imports from abroad. Beijing is expanding both pipelines and liquefied natural gas (LNG) imports in this effort. Sixteen LNG terminals are operating or under construction, which will enable China to import five times the LNG imported in 2013.[15]

Coal

Coal remains the most commonly used fuel in China, providing from 64.3 to 79 percent of the country's energy needs, according to different sources. In fact, China consumes almost as much coal as the rest of the world combined.[16] China remains the world's largest producer, consumer, and importer of coal, however, consuming approximately one-half of the global total. It is also the world's largest power generator and environmentally the dirtiest country.

Beijing outlined economic reform steps at the CCP's Third Plenum, in November 2013. These included more market-based pricing, competition among energy firms, increased energy efficiency, and improved pollution prevention. President Xi then told President Barack Obama in November 2014 that China would obtain 20 percent of its energy from non-fossil fuels by 2030.[17]

Beijing is moving on several fronts to ensure that its burgeoning economy remains supplied with sufficient energy. First is a concern to take full advantage of the strategic "security blanket" provided by the world's third-largest coal reserves, which provide at least 70 percent of China's daily energy needs and the use of which has increased 129 percent since 2000. Coal, however, has troubling environmental and health effects, and the government has been struggling for more than a decade to gain firm control over the politically influential industry.[18] Furthermore, promising technologies, such as gasification and liquefaction at the mouth of coal mines, are proving difficult. Second is the availability of offshore petroleum supplies.

In addition to oil and gas, a future source of seabed energy may be methane hydrates, a semiliquid form of fossil fuel that is likely abundant in seabeds around the world, including those of the South and East China Seas. The technology to recover methane hydrate efficiently remains under development, however, primarily because of the depth (more than 600 m) at which it lies below the ocean floor, the pressure under which it is found, and the problem of liquefying it for extraction.[19] A third source of future energy is represented in the investigation and use of non–fossil fuel sources of energy, primarily nuclear power but also hydroelectric, wind, tidal, and biomass-fueled power. Oil imported from other nations is the fourth source, and the fifth is the large-scale campaign now under way to buy foreign oil fields, or at least their product.

Oil

China is the world's fifth-largest oil producer, with an annual output of 164 million tons. Approximately 85 percent of China's indigenously produced oil comes from onshore sources, with the Daqing fields in the northeastern provinces providing one-fourth of all indigenous production. These fields have peaked, however, and will decline in future years. One expected major source, the Tarim Basin in northwestern China, has been disappointing.

Faced with peaking domestic production and explosive growth of domestic demand, China now imports at least half of its oil, with 80 percent of imports arriving by sea. The demand for imported oil is increasing as industrialization continues and probably will grow by as much as tenfold in future years.

China has seized on offshore drilling as one way to make up for the shortages in its onshore energy sources. The process of exploration, discovery, and recovery of offshore petroleum reserves is lengthy and complex, however, as is getting the product to market economically. Those factors have resulted in extensive participation by foreign oil companies.

Exploiting maritime energy reserves is further complicated for China by disputes with the two Koreas and Japan over the territory China claims on the continental shelf in the Yellow and East China Seas. Taiwan does not dispute Beijing's maritime sovereignty claims, but its self-proclaimed independence poses de facto challenges. Vietnam, the Philippines, Brunei, Indonesia, and Malaysia also claim some of the potential reserves that Beijing claims in the South China Sea.

Recovery of offshore resources is controlled by the state. Beijing reorganized this sector in the mid-1990s, promoting three state oil companies to the ministerial level directly under the State Economic and Trade Commission. These national oil companies (NOC) are the China National Petroleum Corporation (CNPC), the China National Petrochemical Corporation (Sinopec), and the China National Offshore Oil Corporation (CNOOC). China's oil company officials were concerned about maintaining their strong international competitive position after China joined the World Trade Organization (WTO) since WTO membership should force Beijing to remove the protective fence it has built around its oil industry; this has not been a problem.

Natural gas is China's second-largest maritime source of fuel; Beijing claims 164 trillion cubic feet (tcf) of proved natural gas reserves in 2015. Natural gas provided just 3 percent of China's energy requirements in 2005, and the country became a net natural gas importer for the first time in 2007. Beijing aims to have natural gas provide 10 percent of energy requirements by 2020, which will require increasing imports primarily by purchasing LNG from foreign sources as well as continuing its ambitious program to bring in natural gas from Russia and the Central Asian states.[20]

Maritime fields provide 20 percent of China's crude oil production as of 2014. Offshore exploration and production have focused in the Bohai Sea, the Pearl River delta, and the East and South China Seas.[21] The East China Sea also contains significant petroleum reserves, with production dating from 1998. These fields are especially troublesome because Japan claims them as well and is drilling in the area. Farther south, the area off the Pearl River estuary (near Guangzhou) may produce almost thirty thousand barrels per day when it reaches full capacity.

National Policy

Despite efforts in the 1990s to significantly reduce the country's reliance on coal, China continues to depend on that and other fossil fuels for most of its energy needs. Concern about increasing imports has been periodically exacerbated by problems with domestic energy production, such as the 3.3 percent drop that occurred in 1998 and the 9.6 percent drop in November 2008. This goal was met, and by 2015 China's refining capacity had reached 15 million barrels (mbl) per day, which equaled approximately 40 percent of global refining capacity.[22]

Chen Geng, deputy director of the State Petroleum and Chemical Industries Bureau, listed several corrective steps with international and maritime implications that the government was inaugurating to increase China's energy security:

1. Exploit domestic and overseas natural gas reserves, including via pipelines with Russia.
2. Use "technical innovation" to increase recovery of China's petroleum assets, including a nationally directed program of "science and technology projects" to increase oil and gas development.

3. Expand the domestic pipeline network to speed up energy distribution, especially natural gas.
4. Continue building national strategic reserves.
5. Increase overseas petroleum resources, including in Central Asia, Russia, Africa, and Latin America, in addition to the Middle East.
6. Authorize the NOCs to increase their profit limits.
7. Allow the NOCs to attract more foreign investors.[23]

This plan has been effective since it was instituted, both in allowing China access to increased energy resources and in giving freer play to international market forces in the energy industry. It is accompanied by a program to increase refining capacity that has been so successful that only 75 percent of that capacity was used at the end of 2015.[24]

The relationship with Russia holds great potential, given China's geographical proximity to the Siberian proven natural gas reserves, the second largest in the world, after Iran. That potential is endangered by the nation's social and economic deterioration and by Western Europe's continued role as Russia's most important energy customer.[25]

Offshore Oilfields

Seven ocean basins are wholly or partially contained within China's continental shelf; from north to south they are the Bohai Sea, North Yellow Sea, South Yellow Sea, East China Sea, Pearl River Delta, Beibu Gulf (Gulf of Tonkin), and South China Sea basins. Petroleum fields have been found in all of these basins, and the nation's continental shelf has yet to be fully explored.

Hence, the early 1999 decision to increase state-directed exploration efforts in offshore areas, especially those thought to contain significant natural gas deposits, has been widely implemented, with CNOOC dominating the effort. Promising fields in the South and East China Seas and the Yellow Sea have been exploited, in several cases with the involvement of foreign companies. CNOOC, for instance, announced 8 major new discoveries in offshore reserves since 2000, increasing the company's proven oil reserves to 1.6 billion barrels (bbl), and announced plans to double oil production in the Bohai Sea alone, which became China's second-most-productive oil-producing source in 2014. The Bohai fields are China's most important offshore energy resource area, with daily production of 557,000 bbl/day of oil in 2014. The Bohai Bay Basin holds the bulk of proved offshore reserves in China.[26]

The East China Sea is another significant source of petroleum products, especially natural gas. Discoveries indicate reserves of approximately 150 billion cubic meters (bcm), which are already providing the primary energy source for Shanghai and major industrialized cities in Zhejiang Province.

Foreign companies continue to play a significant role in many, perhaps most, of China's efforts to recover offshore energy. Since 1979 Beijing has "cooperated" with more than 50 foreign companies in exploring for offshore petroleum and has signed more than 130 contracts with more than 70 oil companies from 18 countries in joint development efforts. China's large NOCs increasingly seek foreign funding and investments in new oil field development.[27]

China possessed an estimated 25.6 bbl of proved oil reserves as of 2013. An additional 32 bbl of shale oil reserves are estimated, as are 3 billion tons of oil sands (bitumen) and 16 billion tons of oil shale (kerogen). Approximately 85 percent of China's indigenous oil production capacity is located onshore. As noted, the Daqing field is no longer producing at its previous level. Production has been reduced by CNPC since 2004 in an effort to extend the life of the field. Daqing's reduced output has been a significant motivating factor in Beijing's going out strategy.

Many foreign companies have contracted to undertake oil exploration and production activities in China, but China's NOCs are legally entitled (required, in practice) to take a majority (51 percent) stake in any commercial discovery. The NOCs can also take over field operations once the contracted firm has recovered its development costs. In offshore zones, the CNOOC reserves the right to take over operations at any new discoveries, although certain shallow-water locations such as the Zhao Dong field in the Bohai Sea—actually a large bay that extends from the Yellow Sea—are exempt. The Chinese government typically mandates a royalty fee of 12.5 percent for foreign companies involved in the oil sector, although discounts have been offered for development and exploration in more remote onshore areas, such as the western province of Qinghai and the Xinjiang autonomous region.

Getting the Energy: Pipelines Ashore

One way to facilitate the undoubted economic benefits from the increasingly huge tankers that are discussed in the next chapter is to use them only on the high seas, with pipelines to transfer their cargoes across isthmuses and around navigational chokepoints. This also ameliorates the threats to the security of the SLOCs over which tankers travel. A widespread program of pipeline construction is under way in Asia on both a regional and a national basis. The transportation issue goes directly to a central question of energy security: ensuring reliable access to energy resources.

One valuable find is the Yacheng 13-1 field, China's largest offshore natural gas field and, since 2007, Hong Kong's primary source of energy. This field also exemplifies the role of foreign companies in China's energy sector. CNOOC, British Petroleum, and Kuwait Foreign Petroleum Exploration Company developed this field. The British company later sold its interest to CNOOC, who retains 51 percent ownership.[28]

Beijing's reliance on offshore petroleum and natural gas reserves makes their defense a national security issue, and clearly a concern for the PLAN. These energy sources are located throughout China's continental shelf, extending more than 2,160 nm from Korea to Vietnam. The shelf is legally delineated by the 110-fathom (200-meter) curve, which lies 68–243 nm from China's coastline. China thus claims a huge continental shelf of approximately 463,500 square miles—an extensive area for PLAN attention.

These pipelines are built both to improve the weak internal energy distribution system and to link up to pipelines of foreign origin. The most significant among these are the proposed line from Siberia, designed to take advantage of the huge reserves in Asiatic Russia, and, to China's west, the line already under construction from the rich fields in Kazakhstan. Additional projects are under consideration or in planning that would enable China to draw on Caspian Basin reserves, either directly or through a pipeline through Iran to the Pakistani port of Gwadar, expansion of which is being funded and supervised by Beijing. This would at least shorten the at-sea time for tankers en route to China, as does the pipeline built from Yunnan Province through Burma to the coast of the Andaman Sea.

South China Sea

The South China Sea is one of China's two contested areas of known energy reserves. The sea is surrounded by seven other nations, most of whom claim part or all of the sea's resources. Estimates of the petroleum reserves in the South China Sea range from Beijing's wildly optimistic 125 bbl to the United

States' estimate of 11 bbl, with an additional 5–22 bbl possible from unexplored areas. A similar range of estimates exists for natural gas reserves, about which the Chinese are also optimistic, offering an estimate of more than 500 tcf, while the U.S. estimate is a more modest 190 tcf, with an additional 70–290 tcf possible from unexplored areas.[29]

The difference between Chinese (CNOOC) and U.S. estimates may demonstrate the former's domestic political interests more than a difference in objective estimates. CNOOC's clear linkages with the Chinese government have significant political implications for the NOCs' motivations, especially in the South China Sea.

Natural gas is the most abundant proven hydrocarbon resource in that sea—60–70 percent, according to the U.S. Geological Survey—but the most abundant areas are already being exploited by China, Taiwan, Vietnam, Thailand, Malaysia, Indonesia, Brunei, and the Philippines.

The enormous Chinese estimates make the Spratly Islands and surrounding waters an enticing prize to Beijing, despite the fact that no significant oil or natural gas has been discovered in the area after decades of exploration dating to the mid-1930s. Chinese belief and specific institutional interests in the apparently exaggerated estimates is more important than their dubious accuracy since such high expectations might lead to the allocation of very significant national security resources to protect China's sovereignty claims. Beijing's ability to garner those resources rests to a degree on the ability of its navy to enforce its national claims.

Total oil production from the South China Sea in 2011 was more than 1.255 mbl per day; natural gas production was 3.9 billion cubic feet per day. Almost all of this production has come from the sea's uncontested northern and southern areas, not the disputed central region around the Paracel and Spratly Islands.[30] Despite several decades of exploration, there are no proven oil reserves in these island waters.

The South China Sea's energy reserves lie almost entirely in shallow-water basins near the coastlines. The total amount of reserves is very uncertain, with wildly varying estimates offered by different sources. The EIA admitted in 2013 that "it is difficult to determine the amount of oil and natural gas in the South China Sea," but estimates there are "approximately 11.2 bbl of oil reserves and 190 tcf of natural gas reserves" in the sea. For instance, prominent energy consultancy Wood Mackenzie estimates oil reserves at just 2.5 bbl of oil, while the U.S. Geological Survey's 2010 estimate is a wide-ranging 5–22 bbl of oil and 70–290 tcf of gas. The most radical, and probably exaggerated for domestic political gain, estimate is that of CNOOC, that the sea holds approximately 125 bbl of oil and 500 tcf of natural gas.[31]

Natural gas is likely to be the most abundant energy resource in the South China Sea, but its recovery poses technical problems, given the need for sea bottom pipelines to carry the gas to shore processing facilities. The storms and rough topographical conditions require state-of-the-art maritime drilling rigs and technology. Beijing did just that, in 2013, when it moved its most modern deep-sea drilling rig, HYSY-981, into waters claimed by Vietnam as well as by China. This is the first of two deep-sea drilling platforms CNOOC is purchasing, with the second scheduled for completion in 2016.[32] Placing HYSY-981 in Vietnam-claimed waters amounted to a strong political signal, no matter what the economic motive. Although the rig was in place for less than two months, which seems too short a period of time for it to have been productive, especially when set-up and break-down times are considered, CNOOC announced discovery of "a major natural gas field."[33] This claim has not been validated by an outside source, however, and CNOOC and the Chinese government had political reasons for announcing a "discovery." CNOOC's economic motivation derives from its lack of success in discovering the "second Saudi Arabia" that it claims exists in the South China Sea, described as "guesstimates" by some energy experts, and the huge investments the company has made in deep-sea drilling technology.[34]

China has adopted oil rig placement as a continuing tactic to demonstrate its sovereignty over seabed resources in the disputed waters within the nine-dash line. Four more rigs were moved into those waters in 2014 alone, underlining Beijing's linkage of energy security and foreign policy.[35]

Vietnam protested Beijing's placement of HYSY-981, both diplomatically and by harassing rig operations with civilian- and coast guard–manned cutters and fishing vessels. Neither tactic, which Beijing protested to the United Nations, was effective in deterring China's activities.[36] China's withdrawal of the drilling platform may have been due to mission completion but more likely was due to Vietnam's harassment, the approach of bad weather, or, most likely, Beijing's satisfaction that its political point had been made.[37]

Indonesia claims the natural gas–rich fields offshore of the Natuna Islands, which have an estimated 46 tcf of recoverable reserves. Despite its counterclaim to a large part of these waters, China has not objected to continued Indonesian exploitation of these fields, which may represent Beijing's preference for diplomacy over military force.

The most important Philippine energy fields are the Malampaya and Camago natural gas reserves, which lie in waters also claimed by China. These two fields may contain as much as 4.4 tcf of reserves and are in full production; the Malampaya field also contains an estimated 150 mbl of oil, but exploitation had not begun as of 2015. As with Indonesia, Beijing has not objected to continued Philippine development of the fields.

Malaysia depends heavily on natural gas fields located offshore of Sarawak in waters also claimed by China; Beijing had not objected publicly to their development as of mid-2015. Brunei has, however, and Malaysia and Brunei are currently disputing ownership of oil fields offshore of Sabah discovered in 2002 and 2004 (by Murphy Oil and Shell Malaysia, respectively).

Beijing's 1992 territorial law brings it into direct contention with the other claimants to South China Sea resources. PLAN forces have regularly deployed to the Paracel Islands since the early 1970s, and to the Spratly Islands since the early 1980s. A military presence had been established on six of the islands by 1989, and more disturbing has been China's expansion of insignificant land features into man-made "islands."

China's increasing dependence on oil imports has led its major energy companies to acquire interests in exploration and production abroad. Import dependence is estimated to reach 80 percent by 2030.[38] The CNPC has exploration and production interests in twenty-one countries spanning four continents and in 2005 announced its intentions to invest a further $18 billion in foreign oil and gas assets by 2020.[39]

Oil Imports

In addition to using foreign investment and technological know-how to extract energy from offshore reserves, Beijing is pursuing an active campaign to secure energy supplies from international sources. China took advantage of the economic downturn and lower asset values in 2009 to step up its global acquisitions and financing of energy resources in several countries.

Beijing reportedly held international assets in twenty-nine countries by the end of 2013, with oil production from Southeast Asia, Central Asia, Russia, the Middle East, Africa, and Latin America. The CNPC holds oil concessions or has invested in the petroleum production industries of Bangladesh,

Canada, Colombia, Ecuador, Indonesia, Iran, Iraq, Kazakhstan, Malaysia, Mexico, Mongolia, Myanmar, Nigeria, Pakistan, Papua New Guinea, Peru, Sudan, Thailand, and Venezuela, including a $4 billion investment in Iraq.[40] Between 2008 and 2013 China made oil investments in the United States, the Caribbean, Southeast Asia and Oceania, Europe, Canada, sub-Saharan Africa, Latin America, Russia, and Eurasia.[41]

Crude oil imports in 2014 came primarily from the Middle East and sub-Saharan Africa. These ratios held true for the first half of 2015; the three largest sources of imported oil are Saudi Arabia, Russia, and Angola, the latter two located at the end of very long SLOCs.

Despite Beijing's campaigns to secure energy supplies around the world, the Middle East remains China's primary source of overseas oil, in part simply because these countries contain the world's largest proven petroleum deposits, with 65 percent of the global total, and offer the world's lowest recovery cost, one-tenth of that in China.[42] A report by China's Strategy and Management Society emphasized the security aspects of this relationship, urging that China adjust its policies in "political, diplomatic, economic, and trade fields" to ensure that "Middle East oil will be provided to China for a long time to come." This forecast holds true in 2016.[43]

Extensive foreign investment in its energy sector exposes China to foreign influence, an important factor because energy resources are at the heart of continued economic growth, which in turn directly affects regime legitimacy. China's position as the world's largest oil importer has strengthened since 2014.[44]

Relying on foreign sources of energy also poses strategic problems for China. Russia is severely troubled by demographic and economic problems and corruption. Furthermore, recovery of the huge reserves of oil and natural gas in Siberia poses significant financial and technological difficulties. Central Asia is beset by political uncertainty, lack of infrastructure, and high costs of doing business. The Middle East and Africa are politically complex, to say the least, and present unreliable dictatorships, religious and ethnic fault lines, and political hotspots.

Alternative Energy Sources

China is pursuing non-fossil sources of energy—including hydropower, solar, wind, geothermal, tidal, and biomass sources—with some success. Commercial nuclear power was inaugurated in 1990, and its use is growing, although at a slow pace. Nuclear power has been particularly slow to develop as a non–fossil fuel alternative.

Eight new plants were under construction in 2009 and eight more were planned. Beijing's goal for nuclear power is 15 percent of China's daily energy requirements by 2020 and 20 percent by 2030, both extremely ambitious goals. China is self-sufficient in nuclear power plant technology, but its energy requirements have increased so dramatically and coal is still so readily available and inexpensive that nuclear power still provides no more than an estimated 1 percent of national energy requirements.[45]

Another weakness in China's nuclear power development is Beijing's difficulty establishing a successful nuclear reactor industry, especially for foreign sales. The international market is wary since China has yet to demonstrate the ability to build and operate the many nuclear reactors it proposes to construct.[46] Nuclear power provided only 2 percent of the nation's electricity in 2015. Xi Jinping has described the nuclear industry as "a strategic high tech industry and an important cornerstone of [China's] national security." That may speed up construction and operation of nuclear power plants.[47]

Hydroelectric power has been a more successful source of energy. China is the world's largest producer of hydroelectric power and the fifth-largest producer of wind power. Regardless of the energy's source, however, it must be distributed. China's economic imbalance, with energy consumers concentrated in the eastern region of the country and primary energy sources located in the northeast and northwest, exacerbates the power distribution problem for Beijing. Massive reorganizations of this sector instituted since 2002 have had decidedly mixed results.

Beijing's often ham-handed development of hydroelectric power systems has serious foreign relations implications. Development of the Three Gorges Dam system is the most well-known example of massive engineering projects having both intended and unintended social and economic consequences; damming rivers in Tibet includes ongoing projects on the Salween and Brahmaputra Rivers, which are vital waterways in the downstream countries of Vietnam, Cambodia, and Bangladesh. Even more problematic are the dams built and planned for the Mekong River, the heart of agriculture for much of the Indo-Chinese peninsula. Beijing did suffer one setback to its expansive dam-building program in 2011, when Myanmar halted construction of a dam at the confluence of the Mali and N'mai Rivers and the source of the country's iconic Irrawaddy River.[48]

Major Chinese energy investment efforts have also been made in Kazakh-stan, where in 2006 CNPC finalized the purchase of PetroKazakhstan, with assets including eleven oil fields and licenses to seven exploration blocks. This purchase was complemented in December 2005 by completion of the 600-mile Sino-Kazakh oil pipeline, with a design capacity of 10 million tons annu-ally in 2012 and 12 million tons in 2013, with a planned increase to 20 million tons by 2020.[49]

Sinopec also signed a memorandum of understanding with the Iranian government in 2004 to acquire a 51 percent stake in the large Yadavaran oil field, but the deal fell through because of pricing disagreements. However, in 2015 China is Iran's largest trade partner and oil client, while Iran was China's sixth-largest source of imported crude oil in 2014.[50]

CNOOC is also working to expand its international oil production and exploration assets, with a concentration on maritime resources. CNOOC pur-chased Repsol-YPF's oil field interests in Indonesia in 2005, making it the largest operator in that country's offshore oil sector. Then, in 2006, it acquired a 45 percent stake in an oil and gas field in Nigeria for $2.3 billion. The com-pany also has successfully negotiated smaller exploration and development contracts with Equatorial Guinea and Kenya. These activities are only a sam-pling of the patchwork of international partnerships and acquisitions that Chinese oil and gas firms have made in recent years.

Strategic Petroleum Reserve

Chinese officials raised the possibility of building a national strategic petro-leum reserve (SPR) in 1993 and codified the proposal in China's Tenth Five-Year Plan (2001–5). This program was in progress by 2004; the first of these facilities, located in Zhenhai, was completed in August 2006, with a capacity to store 32 mbl of oil.

The second, at Zhoushan (25 mbl), was completed in March 2007; the third and fourth, at Huangdao (25 mbl) and Dalian (25 mbl), were com-pleted ahead of schedule, in December 2007. The first two of these are in Zhejiang Province, south of Shanghai in east-central China, and the last two in Shandong and Liaoning Provinces, both farther north in eastern China, respectively. All four SPRs, however, are located relatively near China's coast, with ready access to and from the sea.

These form the first of the project's three phases, the final goal of which is to provide ninety days' oil supply by 2020. By November 2014, however, the first four SPR sites were credited with a capacity of 103 mbl, 87 percent of which was filled.[51]

LNG has increasingly been considered by Chinese companies because of continued uncertainties about future reliability of piped Russian natural gas. In a joint venture with British Petroleum and local firms, CNOOC built China's first LNG import terminal in Guangdong Province, which received its first 60,000-ton shipment of LNG in May 2006. China had 14 LNG terminals in operation and 6 under construction at the end of 2014.[52]

China used only half its available LNG import infrastructure in 2014, however, as slower economic growth, rising domestic gas prices, and cheaper competing fuel reduced gas demand growth, from 10.8 percent in 2013 to 8.9 percent in 2014. Only ten of China's twelve operational LNG import terminals were active for all of 2014, and they operated at 55 percent of capacity, down from 67 percent in 2013.[53]

This contributes to Beijing's drive to secure energy supplies at the source. The drive for foreign energy assets combined with a strong interpretation of the "Five Principles of Peaceful Coexistence" (notably not interfering in the internal affairs of another country) has led China to support some of the world's most abusive governments, such as those ruling Sudan and Zimbabwe, as Beijing places access to energy resources near the very top of its list of international priorities.

The Sino-Venezuelan relationship includes a similar energy element. At issue is the petroleum product called Orimulsion. This product is produced by mixing bitumen (found in large quantities in the Orinoco region of Venezuela) with fresh water and surfactant. Bitumen has too high a viscosity for easy shipment or burning as fuel. Hence, the bitumen must be mixed with water at a 70:30 ratio to make it a viable source of energy. This process liquefies the bitumen into a crude oil-like state that is easier to ship and to burn in power-generating plants.

That Venezuela has both the largest of the world's currently known reserves of bitumen—267 bbl—and a special relationship with China makes this fuel an issue of importance to the general Asian energy situation. As early as 2000 Beijing committed to the purchase of Orimulsion, although this decision may have been made as much for political as for economic reasons relating to energy requirements. In 2016, however, Beijing is very concerned about the political unrest and economic uncertainties in Venezuela.[54]

China has an extensive domestic pipeline system, and the NOCs are working to establish an even more integrated and complete network to better satisfy growing demand. CNPC's subsidiary, PetroChina, currently owns and operates more than 6,000 miles of crude oil pipelines and more than 1,200 miles of refined product pipelines, with plans to build several new systems in the coming years. In 2005 less than half of the crude oil transported domestically by CNPC traveled via pipeline while the rest typically traveled by rail.

PetroChina, Sinopec, and CNPC are all engaged in constructing trans-China pipelines to deliver either oil or natural gas to eastern China from Lanzhou, in northwest China's Gansu Province; Jinzhou, in the northeastern Liaoning Province; and from China's far western Xinjiang Uyghur Autonomous Region. Finally, Sinopec, China's largest oil refiner, is actively expanding its pipeline network to provide crude oil connections between the Tianjin port and its petrochemical complex in Beijing, between domestic fields and its refineries along the Yangtze River, and with its pipeline network in northeastern China.

Energy's Role in Naval Modernization

Energy security requires military assurance of China's ability to safely and confidently obtain and import required energy supplies. These elements are not completely discrete, of course, but are linked by common geographical, economic, political, and military threads.

Asia's vast continental and maritime sweep is commonly divided into Northeast, Southeast, East, and South regions, but the increasing globalization of energy producers and consumers, linked by transportation and the world marketplace, dictates that consideration of energy security cuts across and includes all of these regions.

This maritime area is also the most sensitive from a naval viewpoint since its control is necessary for Beijing to maintain national sovereignty, economic autonomy, and security for both regime and people. Coastal waters provide China with critical maritime highways, as do the regional waters of East Asia, another category of maritime dependence.

Furthermore, a PLAN presence in South Asian and Persian Gulf waters would be based on the defense of SLOCs and energy reserves in that region, but China is already moving to establish alternate paths to ensuring their security. These include developing alternate fuel sources within China and establishing shortened or nonmaritime lines of transportation for energy imports. The former effort is already bearing considerable fruit in the areas of hydropower, solar power, and wind power; the latter may be seen in the very considerable and rapid domestic pipeline construction that has occurred in China during the past decade.

Energy demands and interests are to a significant degree maritime in nature and form a PLAN mission. Well over one-half, 63 percent, of the world's petroleum production is transported over the SLOCs.[55] China's 2012 defense white paper, published in March 2013, describes the PLAN as endeavoring "to accelerate the modernization of its forces for comprehensive offshore operations, develop advanced submarines, destroyers and frigates, and improve integrated electronic and information systems. Furthermore, it develops blue water capabilities of conducting mobile operations, carrying out international cooperation, and countering non-traditional security, and enhances its capabilities of strategic deterrence and counterattack."[56]

In the near term, China's efforts to build a navy able to satisfy national maritime security concerns focus on Taiwan; in the midterm, they include the disputes with Japan over natural gas deposits in the East China seabed and with the claimants to South China Sea territories. The SLOCs so vital to energy imports occupy PLAN planners, particularly since China is forecast to import 75 percent of its oil from abroad by 2030.[57]

Central Asia

Two states in this amorphously described area offer Asian customers good pipeline possibilities: Turkmenistan and Kazakhstan. These former Soviet Socialist Republics are in a tenuous geopolitical situation: they are located in the midst of the energy interests of their former and now resurgent ruler, Moscow; the European nations and the United States, which hopes to export the area's oil directly to the West; and their would-be exploiter, Beijing.

Beijing's dealings with Kazakhstan's primary oil production company, PetroKazakhstan, represent a significant diplomatic and economic victory for Beijing over New Delhi, which had also been bidding for Kazakhstan's energy reserves. When CNPC concluded its purchase agreement with Petro-Kazakhstan, the competing Indian companies claimed that Kazakhstan had not afforded them a fair opportunity to compete.

China signed an agreement with Turkmenistan in 2006 to build a multi-stage pipeline to import natural gas. The "Central Asia–China Gas Pipeline" starts at the Turkmen-Uzbek border city of Gedaim and runs through central Uzbekistan and southern Kazakhstan before reaching China's Xinjiang Province. Construction of the pipeline began in July 2008, and it became operational in December 2009. Delivery capacity of 30 bcm per annum was reached by the end of 2011. The pipeline was expanded in 2014, and the Central Asia–China Gas Pipeline's capacity will reach 55 bcm annually by the end of 2015. This equals approximately 20 percent of China's annual natural gas consumption.[58]

In September 2013 China signed intergovernmental agreements with Uzbekistan, Tajikistan, and Kyrgyzstan on the Line D project. On March 4, 2014, CNPC's subsidiary Trans-Asia Gas Pipeline Company Limited signed an agreement with Tajiktransgaz to jointly establish a natural gas pipeline company to manage the construction of Line D. On August 19, CNPC and Uzbekneftegaz signed an agreement on Line D of the Central Asia–China Gas Pipeline in Uzbekistan. Under the agreement, CNPC and Uzbekneftegaz will establish a joint venture company to construct and operate the Uzbekistan section of Line D. On 13 September construction of the Tajikistan section of Line D started. Totaling 1,000 km with 840 km outside China, Line D has a designed annual deliverability of 30 bcm and is routed via Uzbekistan, Tajikistan, and Kyrgyzstan to China. Upon the operation of Line D, the Central Asia–China Gas Pipeline will have an annual deliverability of 85 bcm, the largest gas transmission system in Central Asia.

China wants to be a primary destination for the Caspian Basin energy reserves but is competing with a less expensive and easier route to the West for these reserves. That is, Beijing apparently wants nothing less than to shift the general flow of Central Asian energy resources from Russia and the West—toward Europe—to the East, a stunning ambition.

Beijing is fighting to take full advantage of Central Asia's energy reserves. China's new pipelines and its purchase of PetroKazakhstan have placed Beijing in a position to decrease reliance on the maritime importation of energy reserves.

Russian energy deliveries remain somewhat problematic, however, as Moscow continues to struggle with resolving production, environmental, and political problems associated with the reserves. These factors perpetuate the importance of energy supplies by sea. Moreover, even an ambitious pipeline network from Russia/Central Asia to China would be less volume-capable, more expensive, and more disruption-prone than seaborne alternatives.

Looking at the obverse of this issue, the common desire for energy security could become a unifying factor in bilateral and international relationships, particularly with respect to ensuring the security of the SLOCs. Thus, the common goal of achieving energy security might play a positive role rather than serving as a divisive factor.

While the Middle East and sub-Saharan Africa provide the majority of China's imported oil, most of its imported natural gas comes from Southeast Asia. Hence, these imports must undergo a long seaborne transit. The PLA is perhaps most directly involved in China's search for energy security through the maritime role of securing SLOCs and ocean-bed energy fields, and the United States is viewed as the likely force that will have to be countered.

It would be difficult for even the U.S. military to interrupt China's SLOCs over which international energy flows, but these appear vulnerable to PLAN eyes. Should the United States attempt physically to interrupt either SLOCs or overland pipelines, it would almost certainly mean directly attacking China, directly attacking other nations (hosting pipelines and their pumping stations), interfering with the peacetime passage of third-country tankers at sea, or all of the above.

The SLOCs are most vulnerable not on the high seas but at transit points through narrow straits, including Hormuz, Malacca, Luzon, and Taiwan and the Nine Degree Channel. The most likely tactic for the United States to employ would be a blockade of Chinese oil port terminals or of these choke points. Such actions would be acts of war against China and other nations and would likely not succeed in significantly reducing China's overall energy supply. This last point is important. Other nations, other than perhaps Australia and Japan, would be loath to join the United States is such an effort.

The movement of energy supplies throughout Asia, including shipments from Southwest and Central Asia, is a core issue of energy security. The primary method remains seaborne tankers sailing well-known SLOCs among ports and fueling stations throughout the region's great sweep, south, and then west from maritime Russia into the Persian Gulf. The frailties of reliance on shipborne transport are recognized, which has given rise to major efforts to construct domestic and international pipelines to reduce the dependence on tankers.

China is leading all Asian nations in the comprehensiveness and extent of its energy pipeline construction programs. Since the turn of the century, Beijing has already constructed impressively long domestic pipelines throughout the country, both north–south and east–west, many to bring the energy resources of the underpopulated western sections of the nation to the heavily populated and economically advanced eastern Chinese areas. China also is in the midst of an extensive program of transnational pipeline construction. In addition to the proposed Siberian pipeline, Beijing's pipelines with Kazakhstan promise to make a significant contribution to China's energy requirements.

Both maritime and continental pipelines offer relief from the costs and dangers of the seaborne delivery of energy reserves. Ships are able to transport crude oil, petroleum products, natural gas, and coal at very economical rates. They are, however, susceptible to considerable risks, including navigational hazards and bad weather as well as the dangers posed by maritime terrorism and piracy in peacetime and by targeting and attack during wartime.

From the perspective of military defense, pipelines ashore are significantly easier to protect than ships at sea. First, defense ashore is a relatively straightforward task: the locations of both pipeline and potential dangers are well known and that of the former does not move. At sea, on the other hand, the lines of communication are inherently indefinite, as is the seascape. Second, every nation in Asia fields ground forces, both army and police. These vary widely in size and capability, of course, but are designed to achieve each nation's national defense priorities, which in every case includes security required for energy resources.

Relatively few nations deploy significant maritime forces, however, navy or coast guard. While Japan, China, and India are well able to defend at least coastal SLOCs and offshore energy fields to an appreciable degree, almost none of the remaining Asian nations possess that capability. And building naval forces is far more expensive than building land forces, in terms of equipment, personnel, and even the energy resources necessary for those forces to operate.

U.S. naval dominance guarantees maritime security issues throughout Asia. While this causes some unease, especially in Beijing, it provides a significant element of maritime reassurance to the nations of Asia. Within these considerations, maritime transport remains the dominant method of transporting energy. Until a clearer security picture emerges between pipeline and sea-lane, the latter will maintain that position. A Sino-American crisis (over Taiwan, for instance) might drive Beijing to decide that the PLAN has to defend regional sea lanes. China would have to make a major change in national budgeting priorities to build a navy and air force capable of protecting the extended SLOCs that carry much of its imported oil and natural gas.

SLOC defense is the PLAN mission most directly tied to energy security, as it is to trade in general. The navy must safeguard sea-lanes in the territorial waters that China claims, which requires an effective naval force in the Yellow Sea, the East China Sea west of the Japan–Philippines line, and in the South China Sea. The PLAN may possess the assets to defend its coastal SLOCs—those within 200 nm of the mainland—but the next level of SLOC protection includes sea-lanes that extend throughout East Asia from the Sea of Japan to the Andaman Sea west of Malacca.

Long-range SLOCs include sea-lanes throughout the East China Sea and South Asian waters, including the Indian Ocean, the North Arabian Sea, and perhaps even the Persian Gulf and Red Sea. PLAN operations in the Indian Ocean may not be tasked to a specific fleet, but the South Sea Fleet's area of responsibility includes the eastern approaches to the Indonesian straits—Makassar, Sunda, Lombok, and Malacca—that control the SLOCs into the Indian Ocean.

China's primary maritime concern west of Malacca is maintenance of the Indian Ocean SLOCs vital to China's international trade, highlighted by oil imports from the Persian Gulf. Defending its SLOCs is a vital national interest for China in view of its increasing dependency on foreign trade and energy sources, and its rapidly growing merchant marine.

Chinese policy analysts often refer to the "Malacca dilemma" to indicate China's unacceptable reliance on energy imports that must transit that choke point since 80 percent of China's energy imports in 2013 originated in the Middle East and Africa and were shipped across the Indian Ocean and through the South China Sea via the Malacca Strait.

As early as 2004, for instance, an article in the government's *China Youth Daily* stated, "it is no exaggeration to say that whoever controls the Strait of Malacca will also have a stranglehold on the energy route of China."[59] Even more extreme is the statement by noted hardliner Zhang Wenmu of the Beijing University of Aeronautics and Astronautics, who argued that "China's dependence on international energy imports is rapidly changing from a relationship of relative dependence to one of absolute dependence. . . . China is almost helpless to protect its overseas oil import routes."[60] One PLAN officer argued in 2014 that "it is extremely risky for a major power such as China to become overly dependent on foreign imports without adequate protection."[61]

This in turn has given rise to various projects designed to reduce China's reliance on the Malacca Strait, most notably proposals to build a pipeline across the Kra Isthmus or from the Andaman Sea through Burma to Yunnan Province. The former is unlikely to occur because of natural and political problems; the latter has been built and is in operation.[62]

While straits between the Indian Ocean and South China Sea are the primary means for energy from Southwest Asia and Africa to reach Northeast Asia, the role of the Malacca Strait is exaggerated. In fact, as of 2009, China imports no more than 10 percent of its daily energy needs through the South China Sea straits.

Russia

Russia is the world's third-largest producer of petroleum, behind the United States and Saudi Arabia. It is also the world's third-largest energy producer, behind China and the United States, and a leading energy exporter in the global energy market. Russia also is the world's second-largest supplier of natural gas, behind the United States. Of note is Russia's current ranking in all three categories, which is lower than in 2006.

The vast majority of Russian energy exports go to Central and Western Europe, but Russian companies have been working to increase oil sales to Asia, particularly to China. The government is encouraging companies in northern Russia and Siberia to build pipelines and oil loading stations in ice-free ports to meet growing demand.

China is probably key to the future direction of Russia's energy exports, which implies a continuing close strategic relationship between the two Asian giants. Moscow's energy exports still largely face West, to Europe, but government and industry spokesmen in a series of announcements since 2005 have given weight to previously contradictory statements from Moscow and Beijing about fulfilling agreements for the sale of huge amounts of oil and natural gas to China. These agreements are still tenuous—due in part to Beijing's concern about Moscow's high prices, the availability of sufficient reserves to make some of the more grandiose pipeline projects profitable, concern about political stability, and Russian concern about Chinese commercial challenges.

Ten Chinese companies own production rights in forty-two countries, half in the Middle East and Africa.[63] The energy industry's overseas investments during the past five years have demonstrated increased sensitivity to problematic political situations in nations of interest, with economic concerns losing some priority in the investment decision-making process. The political unrest in much of the Middle East and Southwest Asia has spurred an increased focus on North American and Organization of Economic Cooperation and Development countries. Chinese policymakers increasingly find themselves having to balance between their nation's traditional policy of noninterference into the domestic situation of even the most despicably governed nations and securing the productivity of Chinese companies operating overseas and their employees. The unrest in Syria and Sudan / South Sudan and the economic sanctions on Iran are two of these situations.

However, the large Chinese NOCs have also expanded investments in the richest resource countries, particularly Russia and Saudi Arabia. Investments in the former reached a hallmark in 2013, when the NOCs struck a deal with Rosneft "to double Russia's crude oil supply to China to 600,000 barrels per day (600 kb/d) through pipelines," and in 2014, when Gazprom and the CNPC signed an agreement to supply 38 bcm of natural gas to China for 30 years.[64]

A significant effect of increasing participation in "going out" by China's NOCs is the influence on the country's foreign policy; large investments in problematic polities both depend on and affect the objectives pursued by Beijing in its relations with those countries. Chinese crude oil imports in 2014 reflect this factor: Middle East and Southwest Asia, 52 percent; Africa, 23 percent; Russia / Central Asia, 13 percent; Western Hemisphere, 10 percent; and the Asia Pacific, 2 percent.[65]

China's Twelfth Five-Year Plan (2011–15) includes a goal of capping energy imports at 61 percent of consumption, a goal within reach.[66] An important element in this objective is to expand and increase the efficiency of natural gas as an energy source. China's National Energy Administration addressed this issue in a January 2014 series of meetings, as it is particularly concerned about gas shortages throughout the country. These shortages are due primarily to the distances between the major consuming centers and the gas sources.

China's 2012 National Energy Administration goal for developing shale gas was 6.5 bcm/yr by 2015 and 60–100 bcm by 2020. The goal was not met, despite China's estimated 1.1 tcf of shale gas reserves, the largest in the world. In 2014 the latter goal was drastically cut by Beijing, to just over 30 bcm. The reason is simple: coal remains plentiful, easily accessible, and inexpensive; as noted earlier, drilling shale gas wells in China is expensive, technologically difficult, and water intensive.[67]

These problems of geography and resource shortages have led China to try to increase imported gas, both by building LNG terminals and in making a new agreement with Russia to import gas through new pipelines.[68] The China-Russia agreement was signed in November 2014 to great acclaim in Beijing and Moscow but as of July 2015 faces a problematic future, a development not atypical of energy supply agreements between the two nations.

Indeed, one analyst has stated, "Essentially, this is a dubious battle between Moscow's political ambition of blackmailing the Europeans with 'alternative' Chinese sales and elementary arithmetic that ridicules the weak arguments of Gazprom and the Russian government," while a senior Russian official explicitly threatened the European Union in April 2015 by noting Gazprom's new "Eurasian strategy," urging the European Union "to decide whether the European market needs Russia's resource base."[69]

Beijing is pursuing other gas resources as well, including from Turkmenistan, Uzbekistan, Tajikistan, and Kazakhstan. These resources would pass through the Central Asia–China Gas Pipeline, which passes from the source countries through Kyrgyzstan and Xinjiang Province. This is a route subject to possible terrorist attacks and political instability.[70]

An even more problematic part of China's planned gas import infrastructure is the pipeline project planned in 2009 to reach from the Andaman Sea through Myanmar to China's Yunnan Province. This project, consisting of oil and gas pipelines, has been completed, but the ongoing political upheaval in Myanmar, both nascent democratization and continued ethnic warfare, has placed the future of these pipelines in doubt.[71]

Nigeria is another rich but troubled source of energy resources being exploited by China's Sinopec and CNOOC. The problems in this case are domestic political instability; criminal gang violence, including kidnapping, piracy, and theft; and Islamic extremism. Chinese workers have been kidnapped, injured, and murdered. The country is described as "one of the most dangerous places for Chinese companies to operate."[72] Nigeria is an example where the "going-out" policy has required increasingly close cooperation among China's international economic activity, the Ministry of Foreign Affairs, and the PLAN.

Despite these and other troubling political situations in many oil- and gas-rich countries, China's NOCs continue their overseas efforts, driven by China's limited indigenous petroleum resources, delayed shale gas exploitation efforts, problematic agreements with Russia, and, most of all, the vital need to keep fueling China's growing economy.

China's NOCs' foreign investments in 2013 yielded 50 percent of the nation's domestic oil production. They also further strengthened China's position as a major player in the global energy market. In fact, the NOCs are rapidly attaining a position of challenging and becoming attractive partners with, if not yet equally competing with, the large international oil companies.

Conclusion

Barring some massive domestic petroleum discovery, China's dependence on imported oil and natural gas will continue to increase annually, and it will remain a net energy importer. This in turn will increase the importance of the SLOCs over which petroleum products flow. None are more important than those that cross the Indian Ocean, and none are longer or pose a more difficult problem for a maritime planner. China must also account for the increased energy requirement of almost all Asian nations, again linking its search for energy security with effective foreign policy.[73]

The PLAN has played a slight role in China's very significant efforts to garner offshore resources. The navy does have an active oceanographic research program in cooperation with the State Oceanographic Administration, with major implications for commercial application. It has conducted extensive surveying operations on China's continental shelf, for instance, albeit more likely for operational reasons such as preparing for submarine and antisubmarine warfare operations than for finding resources. Nonetheless, the PLAN's presence in China's claimed territorial waters underlies the sovereignty that allows China to benefit from the sea's resources.

China has developed a series of "marine high-technology" plans devoted to both military and civilian economic ends. A notable example is the 863

Program, instituted in 1996 for its "far-reaching strategic significance for protecting China's maritime rights and interests, developing a marine economy, furthering marine S&T development, and building a stronger China."[74] The project focused on technology-intensive maritime territorial investigations, marine petroleum exploration and development, bio resources development, and marine environmental surveillance and warning. Particularly highlighted was "marine detection technology," including navigation and positioning systems; shipborne radar and GPS; and various sensor technology, including satellite optical, electronic, acoustic, and bottom-array systems. Extensive foreign investment in its energy sector exposes China to foreign influence, an important factor because energy resources are at the heart of continued economic growth, which in turn directly affects regime legitimacy.

Relying on foreign sources of energy also poses strategic problems for China. Russia's reliability as a partner is problematic due to its many serious problems. Furthermore, recovery of the huge reserves of oil and natural gas in Siberia poses significant financial and technological difficulties. Central Asia is beset by political uncertainty, lack of infrastructure, and high costs of doing business. The Middle East and Africa are politically complex, to say the least, and present unreliable dictatorships, religious and ethnic fault lines, and political hotspots.

Corruption is a common problem not only in many foreign countries but in China as well. The second-ranking executive of Sinopec, one of China's largest energy companies, was placed under investigation in April 2015 for "serious violations of laws and discipline." This follows previous investigations and accusations of corrupt practices by senior officers of the China National Petroleum Corporation, another large energy company.[75]

President Xi called for a revolution in China's energy sector at a meeting of senior political and economic officials in June 2014. He called for reform and modernization in five areas: demand, production, technology, institutional governance, and China's role in global markets. Xi noted that China's continued economic well-being depended on effective energy security, which in turn requires an energy strategy that supports and is integrated with long-term economic policies.[76]

For China, energy security equates to global power. One very experienced energy industry analyst describes China as an "energy superpower," pointing out that any policies adopted by Beijing will affect not just China but also "global markets and prices." He further notes:

- "Almost all of China's incremental oil consumption will need to be imported. . . ."
- "China's growing dependence on maritime oil supplies will be an additional "multiplier" in animating Chinese leaders' determination regarding territorial claims in the East and South China Seas. . . ."
- "China is on target to raise domestic gas consumption enormously, but this will mean depending on imports for at roughly one-half of its gas needs."[77]

He projects oil consumption to increase by more than 50 percent between 2013 and 2035, which in turn means that by 2040 China will be importing 70 percent of its oil. This significantly increased need for imported oil will require the attendant diplomatic skill to secure the necessary international relationships and the navy capable of ensuring the security of the imports that come via SLOCs.

Energy security underlies China's economic growth and lies at the core of China's national security concerns; it will remain a primary goal of China's foreign policy. It is required for continued economic growth and hence for CCP legitimacy. The navy will use SLOC defense, noncombatant evacuation operation contingencies, and presence requirements in support of diplomacy to justify its modernization plans.

China's search for energy security is a staple underlying its foreign policy. The following two chapters and conclusion examine Beijing's foreign policy formulation and execution, both bilaterally and multilaterally.

Chapter Six

FOREIGN POLICY
IN THE MAKING

I n his keynote speech to the 2013 Boao Forum for Asia, President Xi Jinping presented an optimistic view of the world but shadowed that optimism with warning of dangers ahead. This conflicted view drives China's foreign policy today.

> The world today is experiencing profound and complex changes. . . . The trend of the times [is] peace, development, cooperation, and mutual benefit. . . . Asia is one of the most dynamic and promising regions in the world, . . . but we should also be keenly aware that Asia still faces many difficulties and challenges. . . . The road ahead remains a bumpy and twisted one. . . . Stability in Asia now faces new challenges, . . . and both traditional and non-traditional security exist. [Hence,] we should steadily advance the reform of the international economic and financial systems. . . . We should work together to uphold peace. . . . We should boost cooperation. . . . We should respect the right of a country to independently choose its social system and development path.[1]

Much has been written in English about China's foreign policy formulation, but little of it is authoritative due to several factors.[2] One is simply the lack of access to the policymaking process. The Chinese government's decision-making process is characterized by secrecy and lack of transparency and under Xi Jinping's leadership "has become even more cryptic."[3] The precise role played and influence wielded by various organizations, particularly the PLA, is not clear.

However, the most important governing elements in the Chinese governments are likely the "leading small groups." The Maritime Rights Protection Leading Small Group, for instance, established in 2012, apparently has three mandates: formulate strategies to advance China's maritime rights and interests, coordinate policy among numerous state bodies with maritime responsibilities, and manage growing conflict over disputed maritime territories.[4]

The second factor is the difficulty—not unique to China—of evaluating the role played by various personalities involved not just directly in foreign policy formulation but also peripherally, in other government offices or private sector organizations. Xi Jinping's strong leadership style and personal ties to individuals may exacerbate this factor.

Third is the extremely "stove-piped" nature of any Leninist bureaucracy, which can lead to "left hand / right hand" failures. Fourth is the dual nature of that bureaucracy in China, where the Communist Party has the decision-making authority; the professional foreign affairs office and officials are limited implementers of policy.

A prevailing feature in China's attitude toward the rest of world is one of Chinese foreign policymakers carrying a particular burden of the "hundred years of humiliation." This refers to the period when the Chinese government was too weak to defend the country against Western (and later Japanese) exploitation. The CCP's standard interpretation of China's recent history is its struggle against foreign imperialism that between 1839 and 1949 invaded and dominated China through military aggression, economic deprivation, and cultural assault. This may be called a "myth" or "mythic," but it remains a frequently expressed thread in Beijing's attitude in 2015.

The CCP center holds the power in policymaking; at its heart is China's leader. President Xi described his vision, avowing that "realizing the great renewal of the Chinese nation is the Chinese nation's greatest dream in modern history."[5] The combination of humiliation, paranoia, and a perhaps exaggerated sense of China's growing strength has led its leaders to distrust U.S. dominance, especially in Asian maritime affairs, and to a reluctance to compromise, lest it be seen as weakness by their domestic audience. The sense that China requires a peaceful international environment, one without major conflict, is prevalent, however, so that its economic modernization may continue.

While Xi Jinping may not yet be as powerful as Mao Zedong or Deng Xiaoping, he appears to have eclipsed his two immediate predecessors, Jiang

Zemin and Hu Jintao. He is indisputably the final "decider," both by force of personality and his official position as president, chairman of the Central Military Commission, and general-secretary of the CCP. Xi is also leader of the most important "leading small groups" (LSG), such as those dealing with Taiwan and other important foreign affair issues, including an LSG for the East and South China Seas sovereignty issues.

During Hu Jintao's presidency, 2002–12, either he or Premier Wen Jiabao led the important LSGs, including those dealing with finance and economy, politics and law, national security, foreign affairs, Hong Kong and Macao, Taiwan affairs, propaganda and ideology, and party building.[6] Xi Jinping reportedly has revised the LSG organization since succeeding Hu Jintao in 2012. Three types of LSGs have been identified. First are "permanent small groups," which deal with "broad policy sectors and issues of abiding strategic importance"; examples are groups dealing with foreign policy; Taiwan affairs; the economy; and state science, technology, and education.

Second are "term-oriented" LSGs, established "to coordinate a specific task." These include groups dealing with nuclear programs, Olympics preparation, and possibly LSGs organized to deal with "party-wide study activities," such as the "scientific development concept" in 2009–10 and currently the "intra-party campaign to study the mass line." Another current LSG may be one for "comprehensively deepening reform," probably responsible for coordinating implementation of the 2013 to 2020 reform program.

The third category of LSGs is "task-oriented small groups." Usually short-term, these are the most common types of LSGs. They are established for specific tasks, such as managing responses to natural disasters, "large-scale social eruptions," and other emergent situations.

"Permanent" LSGs are the most important small groups and, indeed, are at the core of the policymaking process for the most important issues.

The [CCP Central Committee]'s leading small groups serve the policymaking process in two ways—policy formulation and policy implementation. With regard to the former role, once the leadership initiates the policymaking process, the relevant leading small group and its general office manage the preparatory work of enlisting the collaboration among relevant [CCP Central Committee] departments, State Council ministries and agencies, components of the Chinese People's Political Consultative

Conference, and other institutions, organizing relevant inspection work, and soliciting expert recommendations. The group then drafts a report for the leadership and formulates policy proposals to prepare for a final decision by the leadership. The leading small group's role in this process is critical in ironing out a consensus on the policy issue among competing and clashing views among the collaborating institutions."[7]

The group's recommended policy will almost always become official policy.

Other permanent LSGs led by other senior officials include those on propaganda and ideology, party building, Hong Kong and Macao, Tibet affairs, and Xinjiang affairs.[8] East and South China Seas issues fall in the foreign affairs LSG purview, underlining the importance Beijing places on these and other sovereignty matters.

These LSGs are not equal; the more important their issue, the more senior their leader. Hence, Xi Jinping heads the LSGs for national security, comprehensive deepening reform, finance and economy, the State Security Committee, foreign affairs, Taiwan affairs, and Internet security and informatization. The state councilor responsible for the Foreign Affairs Office (FAO) heads the foreign affairs LSG.

Members of these important LSGs usually include representatives from the ministries of foreign affairs, public security, state security, commerce, Taiwan affairs, Hong Kong and Macau affairs, and overseas Chinese affairs. The Information Office is represented, as are two CCP departments, propaganda and international. The minister of defense and head of the General Staff Department represent the PLA.[9]

The LSGs are not independent actors; their coordination responsibilities mean that the Ministry of Foreign Affairs (MOFA), for instance, does have the opportunity to input the policy formulation process. However, the MOFA probably spends most of its time managing the mechanics of implementing foreign policies and diplomacy. Other cabinet-level ministries, such as those of agriculture, commerce, finance, and defense, handle specific aspects of policy implementation.[10]

The CCP clearly holds the leading role in national security decision-making. Ranking decision-makers within the party begins with the president, the "paramount leader," then to the Central Committee to the Politburo, and thence to the Politburo Standing Committee (PBSC). The PBSC nominally meets weekly; an emergency meeting of course may be convened, usually organized by the Central Committee's FAO.[11]

A state councilor, whose position is akin to that of the U.S. national security advisor, leads the FAO. The small number of officials involved in these organizations increases the importance of personalities and personal relations. The presence or lack of PLA representation may also attest to the importance of an LSG in policy formulation.

Furthermore, the dramatic changes in China's economy, military capability, and cosmopolitanism since Deng Xiaoping initiated what may accurately be called a "revolution" in the early 1980s has led to the emergence of "powerful new interest groups," many based on economic interests. In the maritime arena, much of the fishing industry has become privatized, or at least "provincialized" to an extent that places the Beijing government in a less influential position for instituting and following through on day-to-day policies.

Even more important is the increased influence in government decision-making of CNOOC, which is supporting increasingly assertive policies in its search for petroleum resources, particularly in the South China Sea. CNOOC thus finds itself empathetic with PLAN modernists, who work to increase naval capabilities and influence. As an example, when China's first deep-sea drilling platform, HYSY-981, first began operations, the observers included representatives from CNOOC; Central Military Commission; Shanghai Waiqiao Shipbuilding Corporation; State Oceanic Administration; State Administration of Work Safety; State Administration of Taxation; National Energy Administration; Ministries of Land Resources, Transport, Public Security, Finance; and the PLA. Indeed, CNOOC chairman Wang Jilin asserted that "large-scale deep-water rigs are our mobile national territory and a strategic weapon."[12]

David M. Lampton has described China as a "fractured society," with bureaucracy adapting "to the proliferation of interests by becoming more pluralized itself. Officials use forums called 'leading small groups' to resolve fights among squabbling organizations and localities, and vice premiers and state councilors spend much of their time settling such disputes. Meanwhile, provinces, big cities such as Shanghai, and industrial and commercial associations increasingly rely on representatives in Beijing to promote their interest by lobbying national decision-makers—a model that has been replicated at the provincial level as well."[13]

Accurate information is key to any decision-making process; in China, all the represented governmental organizations may be expected to provide that information. Perhaps unique to China, however, are the intelligence-gathering arm of the Ministry of State Security and the PLA General Staff Department's "Second Department."

The many think tanks formally or informally linked to the government also provide information. For instance, the China Institutes for Contemporary International Relations is under the Ministry of State Security and "a major source for foreign policy studies that go directly to China's top leaders."[14] The China Institute of International Studies conducts research for the MOFA; the Chinese Academy of Social Sciences does the same for the State Council.[15] These and other think tanks offer the advantage of frequent interaction with foreign counterparts and gathering information from them; this form of "Track II" diplomacy frequently provides information to China's national security decision-making process.

Yun Sun, in her description of China's national security decision-making process, identifies "challenges" in that system, including

- Diffused decision-making authority;
- Lack of a National Security Council–like central coordination team;
- Well-defined civil–military relations with regard to PBSC and Politburo membership; unclear extent of PLA influence in the decision-making process;
- Narrow agency interests, which yields selective provision of information and biased analyses;
- Struggle for objectivity in information analysis, particularly when the information appears to lead to conclusions that contradict CCP guidance or "accepted truth"; and
- Lack of constitutional/legal guidelines for the policy process.[16]

None of these problems seems unique to China. Indeed, a similar set of challenges could easily be laid against the U.S. national security decision-making apparatus.

A persistent theme in China's foreign policy since the end of the Cold War is the need for a stable, peaceful international environment to support the nation's continued economic growth. When Premier Wen Jiabao spoke in

New York in December 2003, he asserted that "the Chinese nation has always cherished peace and harmony. The rise of China is peaceful. . . . It calls for arduous endeavors of generations for China to catch up with developed countries. China will never seek hegemony and expansion, even when it becomes fully developed and stronger."[17] The following passage in the 2013 defense white paper summarizes Beijing's self-described foreign policy:

> It is China's unshakable national commitment and strategic choice to take the road of peaceful development.
>
> China unswervingly pursues an independent foreign policy of peace and a national defense policy that is defensive in nature. China opposes any form of hegemonism or power politics, and does not interfere in the internal affairs of other countries.
>
> China will never seek hegemony or behave in a hegemonic manner, nor will it engage in military expansion.
>
> China advocates a new security concept featuring mutual trust, mutual benefit, equality and coordination, and pursues comprehensive security, common security and cooperative security.[18]

Asian Infrastrucure Investment Bank and One Belt, One Road

Major foreign policy initiatives include the AIIB and OBOR, which demonstrate Beijing's linkage between economic interests and foreign policy. This is turn leads China's leaders to emphasize the need for its navy to be able to secure the sea lines of communication upon which the country's continued economic well-being depends.

The PLAN plays a significant role in furthering China's foreign policies. A recent example is the fifteenth deployment to the Gulf of Aden by a counterpiracy task group, in 2014. After conducting operations in the gulf with or in proximity to the navies of the European Union nations, the United States, and other nations, the three PLAN ships proceeded to port visits in Tanzania, Kenya, and Sri Lanka. The sixteenth task group went even further, conducting port visits in eight African countries for the first time; it also conducted at-sea exercises with maritime units from Cameroon, Namibia, and Nigeria.[19]

This is one example of the much greater use of the military for diplomatic purposes. Beijing reported in 2008 that it had established ties with more than

150 foreign militaries and had posted attachés to 109 countries.[20] These contacts, combined with China's vastly increased overseas economic interests and personnel, constitute elements in Beijing's expanded foreign policies and support diplomatic activity.

Xi Jinping has also spoken directly to the employment of military diplomacy. He listed three goals, in all of which the PLAN has a significant role: (1) deterrence, a navy mission both conventional, "presence," and nuclear, carried out by the new Jin-class ballistic missile submarines; (2) for the military to "become an ideological leader" and "set the agenda" for military discussions; and (3) to "eliminate the 'China threat' theory and dispel suspicions of the PLA's intentions and strategies." The navy also plays the leading role in operations with significant diplomatic benefits, such as humanitarian assistance / disaster relief operations, counterpiracy and counter–maritime terrorism operations, and port calls, the latter demonstrating Chinese power in a nonpermanent, "soft" manner.[21]

Additionally, of course, Xi receives military advice from his most senior commanders during the policy formulation process. These officers almost certainly seek to provide information in a less formal fashion to other government officials.[22]

Xi's major policy initiatives may well prove to be the AIIB and OBOR, which represent the ambition to establish a commanding Chinese presence across Central Asia into Europe, from the Pacific to the Mediterranean and the Atlantic. These initiatives are a breathtaking effort and have made remarkable progress, at least on paper and in announced programs, since they were declared in 2013. If successful, they will strengthen Beijing's political, economic, and military influence across Central Asia and increase its defensive depth. The AIIB and OBOR represent "grand strategy" rather than merely economic initiatives.[23]

Territorial Disputes

This grand strategy only peripherally addresses territorial disputes. China has achieved remarkable success in settling territorial disputes with the fourteen nations with which it shares land borders. Only the disputes with India and Bhutan remain unresolved. The latter is minor and rarely discussed.

Maritime disputes have proven far more intractable, however, due to the factors of domestic history noted earlier, the determination to reunite Taiwan with the PRC, historic enmity toward Japan, the potential material value of the disputed insular territories and associated waters, and concern about the effects of the internationalization of the disputes on China's long-term position in East Asia.

China's reluctance to compromise over offshore disputes—it has done so only once, in 1957—likely is tied to its character as a multiethnic state. While more than 90 percent of the population is Han, the country must account for the presence of potentially divisive presence of Tibetans, Uyghurs, and several other minority ethnic groups possessing widely varying degrees of ethnic self-awareness.[24]

Taiwan's status remains the most critical territorial and political issue for China. It is nonnegotiable for Beijing. The insular disputes in the Yellow, East China, and South China Seas should not be in that category for China (these disputes are addressed in detail in chapter 7).

Evan Medeiros authored a very perceptive evaluation of China's foreign policy objectives and assumptions in 2009, which remains valuable in 2015. He identifies three historic factors that filter China's international outlook. First, China currently is striving to reclaim its position of greatness as a world power. Second, China's fall from that position of greatness was due to the onslaught of Western and Japanese imperialism during the "century of humiliation." And, third, China's security outlook and actions remain defensive, still concerned about foreign powers' attempts to prevent it from reclaiming its position as a world leader.

Two primary dimensions define Beijing's security outlook. First is a belief that China's future is inextricably tied to the international community. Linked to that belief, however, is the second concern about that future by other participants in the international community. In sum, China's leaders today believe that the next fifteen to twenty years offer their nation the necessary "window of opportunity" to achieve full revitalization. That estimate in 2015 should be restated as "by 2050," given Xi Jinping's highlighting 2049 as the year in which the PRC will mark its centennial.

Supporting Beijing's basic optimism about the international community are six perceptions:

1. No major power war is likely before 2049.
2. Globalization bolsters China's global economic growth and political interactions.

3. The global power balance is shifting toward multipolarity, although the United States remains the world's leading power.
4. Nontraditional security dangers will continue challenging China; these include terrorism, piracy, narcotics and human trafficking, environmental degradation, natural disasters, weapons proliferation (both conventional and nuclear), and the spread of infectious diseases.
5. Energy security remains a goal which China must continue to pursue as a vital national priority.
6. Beijing is increasingly confident—perhaps overly so—in its status as a world power in economic and security affairs.[25]

Peripheral Strategy

These points form a background for foreign policy concerns expressed by senior Chinese officials. President Xi spoke in October 2013 about the importance of a concept being called "peripheral diplomacy."

Xi said China should "strive for obtaining an excellent peripheral environment for our country's development, bring even more benefits of our country's development to peripheral countries, and realize common development." This goal has been actively pursued; for instance, twelve of the first twenty-two countries first visited by Xi and Premier Li Keqiang were China's close neighbors.[26]

"Periphery diplomacy" has become a term of art in Xi's foreign policy addresses, sometimes included as part of his "China's dream." He reportedly defined his "policy guidance" as aiming to (1) enhance political good will; (2) deepen regional economic integration; (3) increase China's cultural influence; and (4) improve regional security cooperation. However, Xi also "directed efforts to socialize the region to accept China's view of its 'core interests'" and to "enforce PRC sovereignty and territorial claims against rival disputants."[27]

Substantive programs designed at least in part to achieve successful peripheral diplomacy include the AIIB, OROB, the China-Pakistan Economic Corridor, the Bangladesh-China-India-Myanmar Economic Corridor, and the China-ASEAN High-Speed Rail Golden Corridor. These largely economic and "soft power" programs are consistently balanced by senior officials' statements such as the May 2014 declaration by a Ministry of National Defense spokesman who said, "Our determination and will to defend national territorial sovereignty and maritime rights and interests are unswerving; on this issue there is absolutely no room for bargaining, and any provocative actions will not be tolerated. . . . At present, we have with certain periphery countries some disputed issues regarding territorial sovereignty and maritime rights and interests; these problems are all provoked by other countries, and the responsibility is not on China [to resolve them]."[28] This and similar statements attest to Beijing's apparent obtuseness about the unease and even hostility being generated by its sanctimonious rigidity where issues of sovereignty are involved, particularly in instances such as Scarborough Reef, HYSY-981, and other cases when military and paramilitary forces are employed. The United States is blamed, particularly by the PLA, for taking "advantage of contradictions between China and peripheral countries to sow discord in China's relations with [them] in an attempt to unsettle China's peripheral environment."[29]

Xi Jinping again addressed the theme of periphery diplomacy when he stated, "There have been great changes in our country's relations with peripheral countries, . . . our country's economy and trade ties with peripheral countries have become closer and closer, and our interactions with them have become close in an unprecedented way." The president returned to this theme when he noted that China would "make overall arrangements for economy, trade, science and technology, financial resources, build well the Silk Road Economic Belt and the 21st Century Maritime Silk Road . . . accelerate the pace of implementing the free trade zone strategy, expand trade and investment cooperation space, and establish a new setup for regional economic integration. . . . The pace of the opening-up of border regions should be accelerated, and the mutually beneficial cooperation between border regions and peripheral countries should be deepened."[30] Foreign Minister Wang Yi then stressed, "China's destiny is linked with those of peripheral countries." A few months later Wang held a high-profile press conference at which he announced that "'active' is the most salient feature of China's diplomacy in the past year. . . . In 2014, China will continue to pursue an active foreign policy."[31]

President Xi Jinping delivered "an important address" on foreign affairs in November 2014.[32] In the view of one experienced U.S. analyst, Michael Swaine, it was

the most comprehensive expression yet of the current Chinese leadership's more activist and security-oriented approach to PRC diplomacy.

Through this speech and others, Xi has . . . redefined and expanded the function of Chinese diplomacy [and] presents diplomacy as an instrument for the effective application of Chinese power in support of an ambitious, long-term, and more strategic foreign policy agenda. Ultimately, this suggests that Beijing will increasingly attempt to alter some of the foreign policy processes and power relationships that have defined the political, military, and economic environment in the Asia-Pacific region.[33]

Using the PLA for diplomatic purposes has risen to new prominence in Beijing's foreign affairs efforts. Over eighty visits by senior officers or military units have taken place to neighboring countries as part of the practice of periphery diplomacy since 2013. These have included visits to Afghanistan Brunei, India, Indonesia, Kyrgyzstan, Thailand, Myanmar, Nepal, North Korea, Pakistan, the Philippines, Singapore, and Sri Lanka. Senior PLA officers have also represented China at significant multilateral organization meetings, including the Association of Southeast Asian Nations (ASEAN), the SCO, and the Shangri-La Dialogue.[34] This evidences Beijing's understanding of the classic naval mission of "presence."

A more significant question is whether and to what degree active-duty PLA officers influence the formulation of China's national security policy, including foreign policies. "Influence" may be negative, of course. For instance, senior PLA officers likely were less than truthful with their civilian seniors during the 2001 EP-3 incident, when a Chinese fighter collided with a U.S. surveillance aircraft.[35] The point to remember with respect to this question is that the PLA is not a national military in the Western sense but is a "party army" specifically responsible and loyal to the CCP, not to the nation.

The PLAN may have some influence in setting national security policy in Beijing. The navy commander Admiral Wu Shengli first became a member of the Central Military Commission in 2007 but is not a member of the important Politburo Standing Committee. The navy has almost certainly gained influence within the PLA during the past two decades, and the PLAN certainly has become a more prominent force, but the extent of that influence is unknown.

The navy is not represented on the Maritime Rights Protection Leading Small Group, headed by Xi Jinping. However, that group has at least seventeen representatives, including those from the Ministry of Foreign Affairs, the State Oceanographic Administration, the Ministry of Public Security, the Ministry of State Security, and the Ministry of Agriculture (which controls fisheries).

Four trends have been identified that are reshaping civil-military relations in China, including the military's possible role in national security policy-making. First is the erosion of belief in Marxist ideology. "Socialism with Chinese characteristics" is a current phrase used in Beijing to describe the country's polity. Chinese nationalism has replaced Marxism in significant part as the national creed.[36]

Second is increasing emphasis on professionalism within the PLA, as it remains a "party" rather than a "national" military. Emphasis on professional expertise does not necessarily displace ideological reliability as an important criterion for personnel qualifications, but it does enhance performance and potential. This increasing emphasis recognizes the importance of science and technology in personnel qualifications and ability to perform. This shift enhances military professionalism and may well accentuate military members' feelings of separateness from their civilian counterparts in the policy-making process.

Third, and related to the foregoing, is a bifurcation of military and civilian elites. Mao Zedong and Deng Xiaoping had both impeccable civilian and military records and reputations not replicated by their successors, Jiang Zemin, Hu Jintao, or Xi Jinping. Xi Jinping's three years as a personal secretary to the defense minister is near-meaningless military service when compared to that of Mao and Deng, but nevertheless appears to have conferred familiarity and comfort with the PLA lacking in Jiang and Hu.

A fourth trend is "reduced PLA representation in core CCP decision-making bodies" during the past quarter-century. A leading U.S. expert on CCP decision-making, Alice Miller, writes, "The reduction in military representation on the Party's Politburo and its Standing Committee appears part of a deliberate effort engineered by Deng Xiaoping in the 1980s to establish an effective collective leadership system that builds in checks and balances among the leadership oligarchy against attempts by any individual member—and especially by the Party General-Secretary—from asserting dominating power over the other."[37]

One result of this policy is that the PLA has been "locked out" of the crucial PBSC since 1997. Admiral Liu Huaqing, who may fairly be called the "father" of the modern PLAN, was the last uniformed member of the PBSC. Currently, only Xi Jinping, also chairman of the Central Military Commission, directly represents the PLA. Hence, that body may be seen as the military LSG. Among the other permanent LSGs, the military has representatives on only the foreign affairs and Taiwan affairs groups. PLA leaders have direct access to China's president, however, and the PLA is the sole source of military advice and expertise for the civilian leadership to draw upon.

This trend in civil-military relations appears to have enhanced civilian control of the PLA. It also means that naval modernization is not a perquisite of the PLAN but is sponsored and permitted by the civilian leadership. It further indicates that the military reforms announced by Xi in September 2015 are his, not the military's. This does not mean that elements in the PLA do not support the reforms, but the cut of 300,000 troops, the majority of them almost certainly from the army, and the rumored increased roles and missions of the navy, air force, and Second Artillery indicate a loss of army influence, an event engendering interservice disagreement and rivalry apparently overcome by Xi.

One caveat in civilian CCP dominance over the PLA is the lack of any severe test since the 1989 Tiananmen Square incident. A future trial, perhaps a flare-up over Taiwan or a severe economic slowdown, may alter current trends in party-military relations.[38]

The navy functions within the national policymaking process as part of the PLA but also may effectively wield influence as part of a maritime lobby. In this latter role, active-duty and retired PLAN officers would combine with civilian maritime agency representatives; shore-based maritime industry concerns, especially shipbuilding companies; and maritime economic industries, including fisheries and energy industries, in an attempt to initiate and forward national-level policies favoring their definition of the national interest and, in some cases, private interests.

The effectiveness of such naval lobbying is unclear. Long-term pressure by PLAN officers and analysts in favor of China acquiring aircraft carriers probably played some role in the acquisition of the navy's first carrier, the *Liaoning*, but that acquisition—and future aircraft carrier acquisitions—more likely remains the result of the financial resources becoming available as a result of China's continued economic boom. If, for instance, China's economy were to emulate Japan's 1990 slowdown, then, given the geographical proximity to China of Taiwan and the East and South China Seas concerns, carrier construction no doubt would be among the first items of PLA budget programmatic postponements or even cuts. Xi emphasized the need for "holding high the banner of peace, development and win–win cooperation, pursuing China's overall domestic and international interests and its development and security priorities in a balanced way, focusing on the overriding goal of peaceful development and national renewal, upholding China's sovereignty, security and development interests, fostering a more enabling international environment for peaceful development and maintaining and sustaining the important period of strategic opportunity for China's development." He then made a very interesting point in setting goals for China's next half century of progress. These were expressed as ensuring realization of the "two centenaries" of achieving a "moderately well-off society" by 2021, the one hundredth anniversary of the Chinese Communist Party, and China becoming a fully developed nation by 2049, the one hundredth anniversary of the People's Republic.

Conclusion

National policymaking is a messy process, more like a scrum than precision marching. The "hundred years of humiliation" may engender a degree of caution by Chinese foreign policy makers and diplomats, or it may imbue them with unjustified confidence in their ability to control the "stability-instability paradox," the ability to prevent unintended escalation during a crisis.[39]

Beijing has adopted soft power as an important instrument of statecraft. Xi announced in 2014, "We should increase China's soft power, give a good Chinese narrative, and better communicate China's messages to the world."[40] Some observers have concluded that Beijing is shifting its foreign policy away from strict noninterference, a conclusion based on China's vastly increased foreign investments during the past half century and the concomitant spread of Chinese citizens overseas.[41] The noninterference ideology of the regional 1950s China hardly seems suitable to the global China of 2015.

Balancing the noninterference mantra, however, are Xi's remarks, which have been consistently qualified with statements about maintaining China's sovereignty and territorial claims. Those qualifications gain prominence when linked with China's impressive modernization of its navy and associated maritime forces, and in view of its actions since about 2009 in the East and South China Seas. In other words, Beijing's support for taking advantage of soft power is running aground on the reality of its actions at sea and in the multilateral forums it so vociferously supports. A key indicator is the remarks of Foreign Minister Yang Jiechi at the July 2010 ASEAN meeting in Hanoi, when he chastised the Singapore minister of foreign affairs with the comment that "China is a big country and other countries are small countries, and that's just a fact."[42]

In 2014 David Shambaugh gave a particularly harsh but intriguing description of China, saying that it is "a partial world power":

> Despite this integration into the international community and Beijing's active diplomacy, . . . it enjoys the symbols of being a major world power. It's a permanent member of the UN Security Council, a member of the G-20 and other key global bodies, and a participant in all major international summits. [But] Chinese officials still remain remarkably reactive and passive in these venues and on many global challenges. China does not lead. It does not shape international diplomacy, drive other nations' policies, forge global consensus, put together coalitions or solve problems. Beijing is not actively involved in trying to solve any major global problem; rather, it is a passive and often-reluctant participant in multilateral efforts organized by others (usually the United States).[43]

China's predicament is described by this same senior U.S. sinologist as an ongoing problem since, "for all its economic and military might, the country suffers from a severe shortage of soft power. . . . While China's economic prowess impresses much of the world, its repressive political system and mercantilist business practices tarnish its reputation. And so, in an attempt to improve perceptions, Beijing has mounted a major public relations offensive in recent years, investing billions of dollars around the world in a variety of efforts."[44] "Yet for all the billions of dollars China is spending on these efforts," Shambaugh concludes rather convincingly, "soft power cannot be bought. It must be earned," and that will not be possible "so long as its political system denies, rather than enables, free human development its propaganda efforts will face an uphill battle."[45]

This conclusion is more substantively supported by Beijing's post-2009 willingness to employ its growing and modernizing maritime forces to enforce Chinese sovereignty claims and to bully the weaker nations who dispute those claims, particularly in the South China Sea. That year marked Beijing's apparent decision to muster its various maritime forces in defense of its perceived rights within its claimed exclusive economic zone. One of the features of Xi Jinping's leadership is China spreading its wings diplomatically, especially in Asia. Nonetheless, the relationship with the United States remains paramount among Beijing's diplomatic priorities.

Potentially dangerous sovereignty disputes in maritime Asia challenge China's historic policy of noninterference. The most important of these are examined in the next chapter.

Chapter Seven

FOREIGN POLICY IN ACTION

China's most important national security priority, apart from maintaining the Chinese Communist Party in power, is defense of the homeland. That is unremarkable in itself but in China's case is embellished by insular sovereignty claims that are problematic and disputed and are a potential source of conflict.

The most important of these claims is Beijing's insistence that Taiwan is part of the PRC. Xi Jinping has waved something of an olive branch at the island, saying he believes that "the unification we advocate today is very different from the unification of the past. It has changed from 'conquest by force' to 'peaceful integration.'"[1] Second only to Taiwan in the maritime realm are China's disputed insular sovereignty claims in the East and South China Seas. These are particularly important to Beijing, which views these seas, as it does the Yellow Sea, as areas of vital national security concern, if not outright "core national interests."[2]

Beijing's foreign policy seems centered on accomplishing five priorities, in addition to those of Chinese Communist Party control and homeland defense. These have been identified as

- Maintaining a stable international environment, necessary to allow continued economic growth;
- Reassuring the international arena, particularly its neighboring states, that China's remarkable economic growth, military modernization, and increasing political influence do not pose a threat to their interests or international security in general;

- Using diplomacy, including naval presence, to dissuade other nations from any attempts to constrain or contain China, as it resumes its historically justified position of global power;
- Achieving energy security, which involves secure SLOCs and building solid political and economic relations with the national sources of energy and other natural resources, particularly in Africa, the Middle East, and Latin America; and
- Reducing Taiwan's international profile and limiting any international attempts to enhance the island's status.[3]

Recurrent Themes

Xi described China's foreign policy as characterized by "continuity and consistency," while taking "bold initiatives" and "achieving notable progress," and then sounded one of his most prominent themes since he became president, that of "building a new type of international relations underpinned by win–win cooperation," especially through "a new model of major-country relations [with the United States]." Xi spoke of six priorities in building this relationship, saying the two countries should "improve exchanges and communication between high-level officials . . . respect each other's sovereign and territorial integrity . . . deepen cooperation in all aspects including trade, military, counterterrorism, law enforcement, energy, health and infrastructure . . . manage disputes and sensitive issues in a constructive manner . . . improve collaboration in the Asia-Pacific . . . [and] jointly respond to regional and global challenges." He stated that the "trend toward a multi-polar world will not change" and conditions of "peace and development" would continue, although China had to be "mindful of various risks and challenges," particularly because the nation "has entered a crucial stage" of achieving its "great renewal." He stressed the importance of a "distinctive" Chinese diplomacy based on peace, but without relinquishing "our legitimate rights and interests," or allowing "China's core interests to be undermined."[4]

In a long January 2013 article, Xi also averred that "the era of one or two great powers dominating the world should be gone never to return . . . an irreversible great trend of history." He then described the "world development center of gravity" shifting "from West to East," with "economic globalization" continuing to prevail. Xi cautioned that "great nation contradiction, just as before, still exists," mentioning specific threats. These include Japan's "strategic adjustment to turn to the right," India "actively expanding its military influence toward the [Indian] ocean." Xi cautioned, "We must be vigilant," to "guard against the West's strategy of infiltration and subversion . . . through military disposition, political remolding, economic controls, [and] cultural infiltration." Furthermore, "we must be vigilant and guard against the [United States] sticking [its] hand into the South China Sea issue" and the "infestation of 'new interventionism,'" which is "actually a type of new colonialism."[5]

Xi later reiterated another truism of Chinese foreign policy, advocating the Five Principles of Peaceful Coexistence probably first propounded in the 1954 Panchsheel Treaty between Beijing and New Delhi. These principles were not to counter "China's sovereignty, security and development interests," however, but to "firmly uphold China's territorial sovereignty, maritime rights and interests and national unity, and properly handle territorial and island disputes." Xi followed this point by stressing promotion of China's soft power—"neighborhood diplomacy [based on] amity, sincerity, mutual benefit and inclusiveness." Xi then held up the AIIB and the OBOR initiatives as venues for achieving these goals but cautioned that "China's overseas interests" had to be protected by forces able to do so.[6]

Premier Li Keqiang and other senior officials then spoke in sycophantic praise of Xi Jinping's remarks, notable among which was the need to "give top priority to economic development, manage our own affairs well, continue to enhance China's economic competitiveness, cultural influence and overall strength and provide strong support for achieving the strategic goal of China's diplomacy."[7]

Xi's speech and comments by other senior officials repeated several tropes of Chinese foreign policy, but also clearly emphasized important points. These included an emphasis on China's status as a world power, its recognized need for a secure international environment to allow continued economic growth and well-being, its relatively new enthusiasm for participating in multilateral forums such as ASEAN, and its recognition of the desirability of projecting soft power.

In June 2015 Foreign Minister Wang Yi addressed the Fourth World Peace Forum in Beijing. In a talk titled "China's Role in the Global and Regional Order," Wang began by repeating the mantra that China is "always dedicated to world peace." He then listed China's foreign policy principles: First, China "consistently [stands] for peaceful settlement of international disputes," opposing the "willful use of force," and is dedicated to "fostering a new pattern of state-to-state relations with win–win cooperation as the core," based on equal partnerships rather than alliances.

> Second, China has taken an extensive part in the settlement of global hotspot issues . . . from the Iranian nuclear issue, Ukraine, to the Middle East and South Sudan. And we get deeply involved in international cooperation in counter-terrorism, anti-drug trafficking, cyber security and climate change. China has contributed the biggest number of peacekeeping personnel among the permanent members of the UN Security Council. . . . [Currently] over 3,000 Chinese peacekeepers are discharging their duties. . . . We deployed a total of 59 vessels to the Gulf of Aden and the waters off the Somali coast in 20 missions to ensure safety of close to 6,000 Chinese and foreign ships."
>
> Third, China has . . . concluded over 23,000 bilateral treaties and agreements, acceded to over 400 multilateral treaties and almost all intergovernmental organizations and honored our due obligations. Since its accession to the [World Trade Organization], China has worked to push forward multilateral trade talks and promote a range of bilateral and multilateral free trade arrangements in a devoted effort to advance international trade liberalization. This month, China signed free trade agreements [FTA] with the ROK and Australia, raising the total number of FTAs it has reached to 14. If we count in the seven ongoing FTA negotiations, the FTAs China has been involved in would cover more than 30 countries and regions.
>
> Fourth, China has actively advocated exchanges and mutual learning between civilizations. We have established people-to-people exchange mechanisms with the United States, Russia, the UK, France, the EU and Indonesia, among others.[8]

Wang then continued to explain China's "full-fledged, mature and multidimensional foreign policy towards our neighboring countries" based on "mutual understanding and trust." We should, he stated "embrace three basic principles in the evolution of international relations, namely, more multilateralism and less unilateralism; stronger rule of law, not the law of the jungle;

and greater democracy, not power politics."[9] Wang closed his lengthy speech by arguing that China was different, that it would not

> repeat the path of previous major powers and put the development space of others under constraint. Let me reaffirm here that as a participant of and contributor to the global and regional order, a growing China would only mean greater strength for peace and more positive energy in the world. We are determined to break the so-called law of history that draws a simplistic equation between power and attempts to seek hegemony. . . . As President Xi Jinping has emphasized, China is committed to working with all countries to foster a new type of international relations featuring win–win cooperation.[10]

Maritime Disputes

China is concerned with three types of maritime disputes. The first type bears on territorial sovereignty and resources in the surrounding water and sea bed. This exists in all "three seas," the Yellow, East China, and South China. The second type concerns the operations of foreign naval vessels in China's claimed exclusive economic zone (EEZ) and focuses on U.S. reconnaissance activities in those waters within 200 nm of China's coast. The third type of dispute "is more strategic, extending the entire space within the first island chain."[11]

The United States is involved in all of China's maritime disputes, for several reasons. First is the vital U.S. concern with maintaining freedom of the seas, particularly freedom of access for U.S. and other seaborne trading. Second are the U.S. defense treaties with South Korea, Japan, and the Philippines, all of which border on areas in dispute with China. Third is the strategic assumption that global U.S. access, presence, and influence are being challenged by China's modernizing navy, expanding economic influence, and assertive foreign policy.

Yellow Sea

China's reliance on a peaceful international environment begins with the necessity of a peaceful Northeast Asia. With an area of about 400,000 square kilometers, the Yellow Sea basin has been estimated to contain anywhere from 1 to 90 bbl of oil.[12] It is also one of the few bodies of water in the world offering profitable, year-round commercial fishing.

China has a relatively minor border dispute with North Korea, but more serious are disputes in the Yellow Sea arising from different demarcations of the continental shelf between China and North Korea, and between China and South Korea. The sea is shallow, with depths averaging just twenty-four fathoms and nowhere exceeding just over eighty-two fathoms.[13] This shallowness is probably a factor in the sea's good fisheries but also severely limits its utility as a naval operating area, especially for submarines. A rule of thumb is that safe submarine operations require at least one hundred fathoms depth of water.

China claims most of the Yellow Sea continental shelf based on the principle of "the natural prolongation of land territory."[14] This in turn is based on the huge amounts of silt deposited in the Bohai by China's Huang He (Yellow River). Beijing specifically claims a continental shelf in the Bohai based on the farthest "silt line" created by this runoff. Where this silt line cannot be demarcated, in the Bay of Korea in the northern part of the Yellow Sea, China agrees to a maritime boundary based on an equidistant line between the two countries.[15]

This is in accord with both North Korea's and South Korea's adoption of the median line principle for seabed demarcation between their claims. North Korea cited this principle in 1977 when it claimed a 200 nm EEZ, as delineated in the United Nations Convention on the Law of the Sea (UNCLOS). South Korea also cited the median line principle when unilaterally declaring its sovereignty over four oil fields in the Yellow Sea seabed.

Oil exploration is proceeding on both sides of the median line between China and North Korea in the Bohai, in which both nations have discovered oil and natural gas on their sides of the line. The North Korean discoveries are within approximately 26 nm of the western extension of the military demarcation line with South Korea—the Northern Limit Line—which makes recovery of the resources a military issue.

The Yellow Sea is producing oil in commercially profitable quantities, to China's benefit. From a legal point of view, the disputes in the Yellow Sea should be relatively easy to resolve. The geographical circumstances are straightforward, but Chinese–North Korean relations have deteriorated since Kim Jong-un assumed leadership in 2011. Beijing has decidedly mixed views about his rule. While extremely leery about losing the North Korean buffer and anxious to maintain stability on the peninsula, China's concerns include

Pyongyang's continued development of nuclear weapons, long-range ballistic missiles, refusal to follow Beijing's guidance on economic behavior, and gratuitously hostile attitude and acts.

The fishing dispute between China and South Korea also remains a sore spot, marked by a fatal clash between the former's fishermen and the latter's coast guard in October 2014. Beijing and Seoul resolved the crisis, however, and renewed an annual fisheries agreement.[16]

China's relations with South Korea, however, have improved significantly in the economic realm since the 1992 normalization of relations; political ties also have improved, although slowed by Beijing's refusal to condemn North Korea's notorious aggression in such cases as the sinking of the South Korean corvette *Cheonan* in 2010. China is also very concerned about a united peninsula under Seoul's control; hence, Beijing seems determined to keep the north afloat economically. China's trade with North Korea in 2014 was "close to record levels," but China's trade with South Korea is "approximately 45 times as much."[17]

The China–South Korea economic relationship continues to "make steady progress." Chinese investment in South Korea was $3.11 billion in the first nine months of 2014, making China South Korea's largest source of foreign investment. South Korea has also joined the AIIB, although Seoul did not appear at the October 2014 signing ceremony marking the bank's establishment.[18]

Beijing and Seoul agreed to become "comprehensive partners" in 2003, "comprehensive cooperative partners" in 2008, and "comprehensive strategic cooperative partners" in 2014, the highest of the five levels of "partnership" offered by China.[19] Thus, China's attitude toward the two Koreas is troubled. Beijing and Seoul have a substantial and expanding economic relationship beneficial to both countries while Beijing is frustrated by Pyongyang's political and economic intransigence. That said, China seems so concerned about maintaining a North Korean buffer that it insists on championing the North Korean regime even when Beijing dislikes its actions.

Taiwan

China's most important maritime issue lies just south of the Diaoyus, contested with Japan, where the Taipei government has established de facto independence for Taiwan and several outlying islands, including Kinmen, Matsu, and the Penghus in the Taiwan Strait, and Pratas and Itu Aba in the South

China Sea. Beijing insists that Taiwan remains a Chinese province while the current Taipei government insists it represents the Republic of China.

The issue is likely to become more acerbic and probably dangerous following the 2016 election of the historically pro-independence Democratic Progressive Party (DPP) candidate for president in the place of the cautious Kuomintang incumbent, Ma Ying-jeou. Ma became extremely unpopular with the Taiwan electorate over his eight years in office; Beijing is taking a very wary view of Tsai's presidency.[20]

East China Sea

The dispute over where mainland Asia's continental shelf ends is a core question in the dispute between China and Japan. The primary topographical feature affecting this issue is the very deep sea trench known as the Okinawa Trough. Tokyo, however, argues that the continental shelf stretches to the much deeper Nansei-Shotō Trench to the east, and that the Senkakus and the Ryukyus are on the same continental shelf.

The dispute over where the mainland Asian continental shelf ends also influences the Sino-Japanese dispute over seabed energy resources in the East China Sea. Beijing insists that its mineral rights extend to a continental shelf limit that includes the Okinawa Trough, which it claims is in accordance with the UNCLOS definition. It submitted a claim in 2009 to the UN Commission on the Limits of the Continental Shelf, providing data supporting this claim. Tokyo, however, also cites the UNCLOS (the provision for resolving such disputes), insisting on using a median line between the different continental shelf limits argued by the two nations, but has not published its geographic coordinates.[21]

A 1968 survey found oil fields in this area. The Republic of China government in Taipei then formally claimed sovereignty over the Diaoyutais in 1971, matching Beijing's claims, as it has in the South China Sea territorial disputes. This underlines the importance of the disputes over these areas—both islands and seabed—as nationalistic as well as economic in character.

Beijing and Tokyo had conducted eleven negotiation sessions by December 2007, attempting to reach an agreement over joint recovery of these reserves. The dispute remains unresolved, although recent discussions between senior government officials focused on some form of joint development. Xi Jinping and Japanese prime minister Shinzō Abe held their first face-to-face discussions in November 2014. The meeting produced little more than platitudes, but the fact that the two leaders met is significant.[22] A follow-on meeting between senior officials did occur, however, with both sides agreeing to "gradually resume political, diplomatic, and security dialogue through various multilateral and bilateral channels and to make efforts to build political mutual trust."[23]

Meanwhile, China continues recovering seabed energy reserves, despite Japanese protests. Although one of many sore points in Sino-Japanese relations, the energy resources in the disputed area are difficult to estimate. The East China Sea is underexplored because of the political conflict. The U.S. Department of Energy estimates that the sea has about 200 mbl of oil in proved and probable reserves. Chinese sources, probably CNOOC, claim that undiscovered resources can be as high as 70 to 160 bbl for the entire East China Sea, mostly in the Okinawa Trough.[24]

The two nations have a second dispute over sovereignty of the group of five rocks and three reefs called the Senkaku Islands by Japan, the Diaoyu Islands by Beijing, and the Diaoyutais by Taiwan.[25] The English name for this group, Pinnacle Islands, is rarely heard. Japan took ownership of the Senkakus following its 1895 victory over China. The United States assumed custodianship of them, with the Ryukyu Islands, when Japan surrendered in 1945, although China protested. When Tokyo ceded Taiwan back to the Republic of China in 1945, it did not specifically mention the Senkakus.

The group's status drew heightened attention following the 1968 discovery of potential undersea oil reserves in the area. The land features were included with the Ryukyus when those islands were returned to Japanese control by the United States under the 1972 Okinawa Reversion Agreement. Both Beijing and Taipei protested this transfer, basing their claim to sovereignty of fourteenth-century discovery. In 2012 both the Tokyo Metropolitan and Japanese central governments announced plans to purchase the three largest land features.

To prevent the mayor of Tokyo from making this purchase, Japan's government announced nationalization of the Senkakus. This did not have the desired calming effect on the dispute with China, however, as Beijing vociferously protested Tokyo's change of status of the disputed land features. Significantly, Japan refuses to admit that a dispute exists over the land features' sovereignty, an unhelpfully rigid view.[26]

This attitude is of course anathema to China, which makes a strong historical case for sovereignty over the rocks and reefs that constitute the Senkaku/Diaoyu Islands. Chinese officials and analysts seem unanimous in viewing the current dispute as solely Japan's responsibility, and that "Diaoyu Dao" is an "inherent territory of China."[27]

The U.S. position on these land features is important. First, the United States takes no position on whether the Senkaku/Diaoyu Islands fall under Japanese or Chinese sovereignty. However, since the United States "gave" the land features to Japan's administrative control in 1972, senior U.S. officials and officers have repeatedly emphasized to China that the land features fall under the U.S.-Japan defense treaty.[28] In response, Beijing has accused Washington of adhering to a military alliance that is "an outdated product," a relic "of the Cold War," and a "bilateral arrangement" that "should not harm" China's interests.[29]

China is not moving as aggressively in the East as it is in the South China Sea, but there are reports of Beijing building a new naval or coast guard base on the Fujian coast. This facility would be close enough to the disputed islands to ease the monitoring activities that currently form the core of China's campaign to disprove the efficacy of Japan's "administrative control" over the disputed territory.[30]

These incursions into Japan's claimed contiguous zone and territorial waters around the islands have achieved a degree of regularity since mid-2014.[31]

The maritime disputes discussed above are the most important in Northeast Asia. Southeast Asia is the scene of more complex but less serious maritime sovereignty disagreements. Most of the sovereignty disputes in this subregion concern the archipelagos that spot the South China Sea, a relatively small body of water measuring no more than 1,200 by 600 nm and almost completely enclosed by the landmasses of China, Vietnam, Malaysia, Indonesia, and the Philippine Islands, with Taiwan sitting like a cork at its top.

Territorial Claims in the South China Sea

Brunei   Implicit claim to Louisa Reef, which is in its claimed EEZ

China   Claims all land features within the ten-dash line, which includes Paracel and Spratly Islands, Pratas Reef, Macclesfield Bank, Scarborough Reef, and various rocks, low-tide elevations, and reefs that are always submerged, based on history and the UNCLOS

Indonesia Does not claim any of the Spratly Islands, but China's (and Taiwan's) claimed EEZ intrudes into the EEZ of Indonesia's Natuna Islands

Malaysia Claims in the Spratly Islands based on continental shelf principle

Philippines Claims eight Spratly Islands

Taiwan Claims are nearly identical to China's

Vietnam Claims all the Paracel and Spratly Islands, based on history and the continental shelf principle

The Gulf of Tonkin (called the Beibu Gulf by China) is a semi-enclosed bay embraced by the mainland of China and Vietnam as well as by China's Hainan Island. Except for the width of the territorial sea within which China and Vietnam have exercised their respective jurisdictions, the two sides have never fully delimited their maritime boundary. Since the continental shelf in the gulf is the natural land extension of both China and Vietnam, and since the gulf is only 170 nm wide at its widest, dispute resolution will require active negotiation and compromise by Beijing and Hanoi.

The Gulf of Tonkin contains rich resources, including petroleum and fish stocks. China has proposed establishing a rectangular "neutral zone" in the gulf's center, which would remain free from exploitation until the two countries could reach an agreement on the delimitation. Vietnam has never formally accepted this proposal but like China has halted exploration for oil in the proposed joint development zone.

Although Beijing and Hanoi reached agreement on settling their land boundary in 1993, their maritime boundary dispute in the South China Sea remains unresolved, although Vietnam is recovering significant energy reserves from some of the disputed fields. The dispute has been marked by several sometimes violent disputes, but Beijing and Hanoi seem determined to keep their actions within peaceful bounds.[32]

The other disputes in the South China Sea involve five countries: China, the Philippines, Malaysia, Indonesia, and Brunei. Taiwan agrees almost completely with Beijing's claims.[33] The disputes concern the sovereignty issue over the Paracel Islands, the Spratly Islands, and the delimitation of maritime boundaries in the sea areas adjacent in the southern part of the South China Sea. This sea is a deep basin with a steep gradient that leaves "virtually no continental shelf along the Philippine side. . . . Only on the side of the Chinese mainland, Taiwan, and, to a lesser extent, Vietnam, is there some breadth of continental shelf."[34] This topographical feature seriously complicates applying UNCLOS criteria to the disputes.

Since China seized all of the Paracel Islands, in the northern South China Sea, after a brief naval battle with Republic of (South) Vietnam forces in 1974, the most unresolved, contentious claims are those concerning the Spratlys, further to the south. China maintained occupation of several of these islands after a similar battle with Vietnamese naval units in 1988. The Spratlys include more than four hundred land features—islands, reefs, shoals, and atolls. Among them, only thirty-three rise above the sea, and only seven have an area exceeding 0.3 square miles. They are scattered over an area that is 400 nm from east to west and 500 nm from north to south.

The area is rich in fish and may contain significant oil and other energy resources. Chinese surveys indicate that about 25 bcm of gas and 105 bbl of oil exist in the continental shelf around the Spratly Islands, but U.S. surveys are not nearly so optimistic. In fact, unsuccessful oil prospecting in the South China Sea dates back at least to Japanese efforts in the mid-1930s. Reserves are uncertain, as discussed in chapter 5, but remain an issue of great contention between China and the other regional claimants.

There are no proven reserves for the Spratly or Paracel Islands in the sea's central area, as opposed to the rich "proven" areas closer to the South China Sea's littoral areas. No commercially recoverable oil or gas has been discovered there, although efforts continue. Geologists and analysts disagree on the presence (and recoverability) of petroleum reserves near these islands, with widely varying estimates.

The level of emotional rhetoric over these territorial disputes was initially lowered with the signing of the 2002 "Declaration on the Conduct of Parties in the South China Sea," but sovereignty disputes in the area have fully reemerged and intensified by 2015. Beijing supported the 2002 "declaration," a nonbinding agreement. It encouraged the claimants to peaceful resolution of disputes, but neither resolved any of the disputes nor included a provision banning future construction of facilities on occupied land features.

This was a key failing since the other Southeast Asian states were concerned about China's militarization of Mischief Reef after occupying it in 1995, a pattern Beijing has continued and has increased significantly by artificially enlarging the geographic footprint of various land features. Beijing is trying to change the definitions and privileges in the UNCLOS of land features, both permanently and periodically submerged, to include low-tide elevations, rocks, and islands.[35] China believes that other claimants have taken advantage of past Chinese inaction by strengthening their claims, including land reclamation and facilities construction. Therefore, Beijing must take strong action to reassert its own sovereignty claims and presence.[36]

The 2002 declaration was followed in September 2004 by the signing of a three-year agreement between Chinese and Philippine companies—CNOOC and the Philippine National Oil Company—to exchange seismic data developed while they surveyed for energy reserves in disputed areas of the South China Sea's. PetroVietnam joined the agreement just six months later, in March 2005. The three nations emphasize that this was a commercial agreement only and in no way affects their respective sovereignty claims. It was little more than a tentative move to exchange information and was allowed to expire in 2008.[37]

The Spratly Islands are also of strategic military significance because of their central position in the South China Sea astride vital SLOCs. These are the main transit routes from Southwest Asia and the Indian Ocean and Northeast Asia and the Pacific Ocean. Their strategic value has been significantly increased by China's transformation of three land features in the Spratly Islands into artificial "islands" equipped with runways and military installations.[38] China was not the first to alter insular topography in the South China Sea, but its more than 2,000 acres of reconstructed land dwarfs the combined total of land dredged by all the other claimants.[39]

Almost all of the various land features in the South China Sea are claimed by China and Vietnam, while the Philippines, Malaysia, Indonesia, and Brunei claim particular bits of land based on various historical, geographical, and legalistic grounds.[40] Except for the latter two countries, all the claimants have established a military presence on one or more of the disputed land features, increasing tension and the chances of military confrontation. As of 2015 Vietnam has occupied twenty-seven of the land features; the Philippines, eight; Malaysia, nine; China, seven; and Taiwan, one.

The next possible escalatory step over South China Sea issues will result if Beijing declares an air defense identification zone over the majority of the South China Sea included within China's claimed Nine-Dash Line. Beijing has not discounted that possibility, and a Foreign Ministry spokesperson has declared that China is entitled to do so.[41]

The Spratly Islands

Both Beijing and Hanoi cite extensive historical bases for their respective claims in the South China Sea. China's claims, in fact, approach the mystical as it cites unsubstantiated "historic rights" and pre–common era (BCE) "evidence." One U.S. maritime legal expert has opined that "Vietnam clearly has a superior claim to the South China Sea Islands," basing his opinion on Hanoi's "symbolic acts of sovereignty in the early nineteenth century, followed by peaceful, effective, and continuous administration of the islands" by Vietnamese and French colonial governments. However, the "first demonstration of Chinese sovereignty over the [islands]," he notes, "did not occur until 1909."[42] This view in favor of other claimants is supported by China's use of military force to occupy the Paracels, Mischief Reef, Scarborough Shoal, and some of the Spratlys.

More recently, Wu Shicun, head of China's National Institute for South China Sea Studies, described Beijing's position as "a natural line of defense for Chinese national security, an important strategic waterway, and a strategic must-have for it to become a maritime power. For the U.S., controlling the South China Sea and maintaining its presence there is indispensable for its dominance in the Asia-Pacific based on its bilateral alliances formulated in the post-war era. In this sense, China-U.S. competition and rivalry in the South China Sea is structural, strategic, and irreconcilable."[43] Wu is well connected to the Hainan provincial government and to the national government, both for financial support via the MOFA and in his policy advocacy.

China has described its island-building activities in both straightforward and disingenuous terms, calling it "maintenance and construction work . . . with the main purposes of optimizing their functions, improving the living and working conditions of personnel stationed there, better safeguarding territorial sovereignty and maritime rights and interests as well as better performing China's international responsibility and obligation in maritime search and rescue, disaster prevention and mitigation, marine science and research, meteorological observation, environmental protection, navigation safety, fishery production service and other areas."[44] This is disingenuous, at best, as the built-up features are turned into well-armed military installations.

Association of Southeast Asian Nations

Beijing increasingly focuses foreign policy efforts on multilateral organizations, especially ASEAN, which is composed of Vietnam, the Philippines,

Indonesia, Brunei, Malaysia, Singapore, Cambodia, Laos, Myanmar, and Thailand. All of its members have economic importance to China; Laos and Cambodia are particularly close to Beijing, while China remains Myanmar's largest trading partner. Thailand's most recent military coup has alienated Washington to Beijing's advantage in making economic and military offers to Bangkok.[45] Vietnam, the Philippines, Indonesia, Brunei, and Malaysia are directly concerned with China's South China Sea claims, with Vietnam and the Philippines particularly vociferous and active in opposition.

In addition to attempts to ensure that ASEAN policy and actions do not seriously threaten its claims in the South China Sea, China is moving on several fronts to increase its influence in the organization. First is the AIIB, discussed earlier, to which all the ASEAN members have signed up. Second is the Maritime Silk Road, which Beijing has offered as a vehicle for achieving "grand connectivity" between China and its neighbors.

Third is Premier Li Keqiang's offer of China's "rich experience in infrastructure construction" to assist regional nations improve their "ports, roads, and railways."[46] Beijing also hosted ASEAN defense ministers at a meeting in October 2015, at which Chinese defense minister Chang Wanquan stated, "China desires cooperation and dialogue with ASEAN defense bodies to together safeguard regional peace and stability and join hands to create a good security environment," but he did not mention the South China Sea sovereignty disputes.[47]

Fourth is a proposed free trade area of the Asia-Pacific, proposed by Xi Jinping, at least in part in opposition to the U.S.-proposed Trans-Pacific Partnership. China's fifth proposed program with ASEAN is the Treaty on Good Neighborliness, Friendship and Cooperation. Li Keqiang offered this treaty to promote "permanent peace" in East Asia. Li also offered a sixth proposal, to upgrade the China-ASEAN free trade agreement to "reach new advances" and as part of increased Chinese economic assistance to the ASEAN members. Seventh is the premier's highlighting China's Investment and Assistance to Greater Mekong Subregion, a proposal no doubt intended at least in part to ameliorate Southeast Asian nations' resentment and fear of China's upstream damming activities on the Mekong River.[48]

Finally, Xi emphasized China's efforts to increase economic cooperation with the countries of Oceania, including Australia and New Zealand. This included a China-Australia free trade agreement.

Indian Ocean

Future out-of-area PLAN operations are continuing to increase and to expand geographically, despite continued prioritization of the strategic issues concerning Taiwan and the three seas. Such operations are aimed at securing the SLOCs but more practically reflect the historically typical moves by a nation gaining global economic status, one of which is to deploy a global navy.

Seabed mineral reserves in the Indian Ocean are a China-India issue that concerns both nations' navies and maritime resources. The UN International Seabed Authority allotted a 3,900-square-mile exploration area on the Indian Ocean's Southwest Indian Ridge to Beijing in 2007, to search for polymetallic sulfides. New Delhi is concerned about China's explorations of the Indian Ocean seabed as an indicator of Beijing's ambitions in that ocean.[49] Two issues of particular concern to the PLAN are India's apparent maritime strategy of effectively controlling the Indian Ocean and the potential for the United States to control navigational choke points crucial to China's trade and, hence, to its economy.

Islamabad is moving to improve its capabilities to import and export seaborne energy supplies, relying on Chinese financial, engineering, and construction assistance and aid. The focus of these efforts has been the port of Gwadar, a small, isolated city on the North Arabian Sea coastline just 110 nm east of the Iranian border and close to the Strait of Hormuz. Effective use of this port facility may be hindered by its remote location in the unstable Baluchistan Province of Pakistan and by the questionable stability of the Pakistani government itself.

China's estimated $250 million investment in Gwadar's expansion—80 percent of the project's total funding—no doubt makes India uneasy at this potential extension of Chinese naval presence into the eastern Indian Ocean. In the event of heightened tension with India, the new port would offer Islamabad little more than an attractive target that would have to be defended against hostile naval action. That said, China continues to invest in the port, reportedly signing a "43-year lease of more than 2,000 acres of land to construct the first Free Economic Zone" at Gwadar, with another 500 acres to be leased in the future.[50]

Another New Delhi concern is China's increased activities with Sri Lanka and the Maldives. Xi Jinping visited both island nations in 2014 before visiting India's President Modi. Beijing's large financial investments in the former's maritime infrastructure were emphasized by his visit. China's increased

Indian Ocean presence was further emphasized in 2015 by the first PLAN submarine visits to Colombo, Sri Lanka. Despite New Delhi's unease, which is understandable, Sri Lanka's relationship with India certainly is "deeper and more entrenched" than that with China.[51] Additionally, former Sri Lankan president Mahinda Rajapaksa, who strongly favored increasing ties with Beijing, was voted out of office in January 2015.[52]

Sovereignty and Negotiation

China has given little indication of flexibility on maritime sovereignty issues, in part because of the energy resources at stake and military considerations, including SLOC security implications. Beijing refuses to participate in the legal case that Manila is pursuing against China over the ten-dash line and has dismissed Vietnam's claim for the Paracel and Spratly Islands as "illegal and invalid."[53] Foreign Minister Wang Yi told U.S. secretary of state John Kerry in May 2015 that China was "unshakeable" in its defense of sovereignty. He then announced that "China's sovereignty . . . will never shrink." Wang's statement also exhibited a tinge of paranoia with his claim that "we [could not] let our ancestors and predecessors down" and that China "actually has been the biggest victim in the South China Sea issue."[54]

Beijing's claim to the South China Sea's land features is at least as convincing, and perhaps more so, as any other claimant's. The real issue is not whether China possesses or even installs land garrisons on the disputed islands, reefs, and rocks but whether Beijing claims the surrounding waters—those within the infamous nine-dash line—as sovereign waters. The meaning of this line is not clear. It might simply delineate all of the land features claimed by China, or it might mean that Beijing claims all of the ocean areas of the South China Sea as sovereign Chinese territory.

China's 1992 law on the territorial sea indicates that the latter is the case, although Beijing has never stated that claim in a public forum. If it were to do so, its claim would immediately generate an international crisis with almost guaranteed naval intervention by the United States. Beijing's official statement on the issue is that "China has indisputable sovereignty over the islands in the South China Sea and their adjacent waters, and enjoys sovereign rights and jurisdiction over the relevant waters as well as the seabed and subsoil thereof." However, this statement fails to clarify "adjacent waters" and "relevant waters" and does not provide the cartographic coordinates for the nine-dash line.[55]

Delineation of EEZs is another important aspect of the sovereignty disputes in the East and South China Seas, a particularly knotty problem because of relatively constrained waters in both seas. This has led to China's disputants—Japan in the East China Sea, the Philippines, Malaysia, potentially Brunei and Indonesia, and most troubling of all, Vietnam—protesting and even actively contesting China's efforts to drill for mineral resources in disputed waters.

The most notable such incident occurred when in the summer of 2014 Beijing moved its HD-981 deep-sea oil drilling rig into western South China Sea waters, well within Vietnam's claimed EEZ. This incident included clashes between Chinese coast guard and maritime militia vessels and their Vietnamese counterparts. Collisions, water-cannoning, and personnel injuries were part of several clashes during the month or so the rig was in contested waters. In mid-2015 Beijing moved the rig back into an area where both Chinese and Vietnamese claimed EEZs almost completely overlap, but there were no reports of a repeat of the 2014 clashes.[56]

Dai Bingguo's 2010 statement about Chinese uniqueness in conducting foreign affairs and domestic development is not just a selective view of history, but a claim representing a significant school of thought in China. This belief in "win-win" foreign policies unmatched by any other world power demonstrates the strength of growing Chinese nationalism, a force probably more prevalent throughout the country than any form of Marxism, with or without "Chinese characteristics."

Beijing's mantra about future military growth, with a specific focus on its naval modernization, is that China has never been expansive or aggressive or has stationed military forces overseas. All of these claims are at least extremely debatable, given China's dynastic history of expansion and foreign expeditions, but it is too soon to know to what extent current PLAN modernization will take Chinese forces overseas.

Chinese civilian officials, military officers, and civilian analysts also consistently continue to insist that any disputes are the fault of the other nation. The onus is always on the other party, which severely limits opportunities for negotiation and compromise.

Beijing's foreign policy objectives and concerns are unremarkable and relatively clear, although influenced by historic attitudes and cultural factors perhaps uniquely Chinese. The "century of humiliation" consciousness, which contributes a degree of paranoia, is exaggerated but expresses China's awareness of historic precedent and concerns in the international community resulting from its precedent-shattering economic growth, increasing military power, geographic reach, and overall modernization.

China's "going-out" policy and expanding use of the navy as a diplomatic instrument both support an apparently phased policy of diplomatic expansion. The nation's periphery is clearly and logically the initial focus of Xi Jinping's foreign policy. He declared in November 2014, for instance, that while a "new model of major country relations" with the United States was important, China's primary foreign policy focus was on a "neighborhood policy featuring amity, sincerity, mutual benefit, and inclusiveness" in Asia.[57]

Foreign Economic and Personnel Issues

The April 2015 emergency evacuation of Chinese citizens from war-torn Yemen marked the rising importance of Beijing's capability to protect its citizens visiting and working overseas. This has obvious implications for China's use of its navy to protect overseas economic and trade investments as well as its citizens. Most recently, the PLAN rescue mission in Yemen demonstrated the nation's capability to execute emergent evacuations of its citizens.[58]

The AIIB and other international financial initiatives and the OBOR effort represent an important linkage among economic, energy security, and national security concerns. Beijing and Moscow declared in 1992 they would be "constructive partners"; this became a "strategic partnership" in 1996, and they signed a treaty of "friendship and cooperation" in 2001. Presidents Xi Jinping and Vladimir Putin both were declaring their nations "strategic partners" by 2015.

This may well be a somewhat ephemeral partnership, however, given that China's economy, population, and social health dwarfs Russia's. The sanctions imposed on Moscow by the Western nations concerned about Russian aggression in Ukraine have further impacted the already damaged Russian economy. Moscow may have hoped that China would ameliorate that economic damage, but that has not happened. Presidents Dmitry Medvedev and Hu Jintao announced in 2011 trade goals of $100 billion by 2015 and $200 billion by 2020. These goals now seem unrealistic, given the uncertain future of the huge energy sales to China on which Russia was counting, the 20 percent decline in Chinese investment in Russia, and the 31.4 percent plunge in trade with China during the first seven months of 2015.[59]

Furthermore, the two are locked in a generally unspoken but real competition for power in Central Asia. The Shanghai Cooperation Organization was founded in 1998, initially to address regional economic issues; it soon became focused on cross-border terrorism and criminal activities, nominally resting on member cooperation, with Beijing and Moscow in the lead.

The Shanghai Cooperation Organization's fourteenth summit was held in Tajikistan in September 2014. It reflected security and economic concerns, with Xi Jinping's speech focused on economic issues. "We need to take common development and prosperity as our goal," he said, noting that China would increase its contribution to the China-Eurasia Economic Cooperation Fund, launched in 2013 with $1 billion.[60] Russia's President Putin echoed this economic emphasis, but the two nations face significant areas of potential conflict.

One area of potential conflict is over Central Asian energy resources, long a mainstay of Russia's economic well-being but now a primary focus of China's interest in the region. Another is the status of Mongolia, a part of China arguably for centuries, then a Soviet satellite, now an independent if uneasy country between the two. Finally, Moscow's military action against Georgia and Ukraine, effectively launching military invasions of independent nations, must be extremely disquieting to many in Beijing, which is so concerned about the "splittism" and "separatism" that underlie its "core interests" of Taiwan, Tibet, and Xinjiang.[61]

Beijing understands the importance of helping to maintain a secure and peaceful international environment necessary for its progress to continue, but this also raises expectations that China will behave as a world power across the spectrum of global concerns. Beijing seems to be having difficulty grasping these expectations.

Another major problem faced by China's government is the inevitable linkage between international and domestic issues. Former U.S. Speaker of the House of Representatives Tip O'Neill reportedly once declared that "all politics is local," meaning that a politician had first to satisfy his local constituents before dealing with larger, more impersonal issues. China certainly is not a U.S.-style democracy, but O'Neill's universal maxim nonetheless applies to China's rulers. They must be sensitive to popular sentiment and possible reaction to any significant foreign policy.

The problems in China's decision-making processes noted earlier are significant factors in formulating, gaining approval of, and executing foreign policy. Furthermore, the more important the policy objective, the more difficult the process becomes.

Conclusion

Beijing views the United States as the primary threat to its national security interests, especially in view of the 1979 Taiwan Relations Act and the 1996 Taiwan Strait crisis as well as the updating of American defense treaties with Japan, South Korea, the Philippines, and Australia and a policy of strengthening relations with Vietnam, Singapore, and India. That also means that relations with the United States are at the top of China's foreign policy concerns.

Taiwan retains pride of place, however; while Beijing remains patient, it also remains very concerned about the DPP's victory in Taiwan's 2016 presidential election, especially in view of the unexpected, very strong showing by that party in Taiwan's 2015 local elections. At a meeting with a pro-unification delegation from Taiwan, Xi Jinping warned that independence activities threatened peace.[62]

Beijing's primary national security concerns are in the domestic arena, one in which the nation's new and growing navy plays only a very marginal role. Historically, global ambitions demand a leadership eye on the international arena, and in Asia that means maritime. Hence, China continues to modernize and expand its navy as its economic and political maritime interests increase. However, domestic concerns will continue to take priority, and China's leader will continue to treat foreign policy as a secondary concern, although one driven significantly by nationalism, popular pressure, and Xi's "China Dream."[63]

Threats to those interests are mostly nontraditional, but PLAN planners, like those of all navies, look at the most likely opponents at sea. That selection is easy for Beijing—the United States is arguably the only maritime power capable of frustrating China's national security interests. Japan, however, is the historical enemy, very much a maritime nation, and, hence, a primary concern to PLAN planners and strategists.

All that said, Beijing is for the great part working within the established rules and procedures of the international community as it strives to attain its foreign policy objectives. Simply put, China "wants a seat at the table"; it wants to be treated as the world power status it historically possessed and is now regaining.[64]

A significant problem confronting Beijing is reconciling the goals of a successful peripheral strategy, which includes central economic and "soft power" instruments, while also seeking to defend sovereignty interests. This latter goal is pursued with "a fervent level of self-righteousness."[65] One American analyst has accurately described this two-sided foreign policy as having "a schizophrenic quality," which certainly complicates accurate analysis and foreign responses to the world's second most powerful nation's policies.[66]

This attitude contributes to China's emerging maritime strategy, provided in Beijing's 2015 defense white paper. Both soft and hard power policies are forwarded without any seeming sense of conflict between the two. Yet there is conflict in the eyes of China's neighbors.

CONCLUSION

China's new national security law presents a summation of ideas expressed by President Xi Jinping since he took power in late 2012 as well as the most expansive definition of the party's footprint across the world. The new law and Xi's anticorruption drive and renewed emphasis on China "standing up" indicate that his priority is reinforcing CCP authority and legitimacy, which he apparently believes necessary to maintain China's progress toward global power.[1]

The new law defines national security as a "condition in which a country's government, sovereignty, unification, territorial integrity, well-being of its people, sustainable development of its economy and society, and other major interests are relatively safe and not subject to internal and external threats."[2] It also included the capacity to sustain such a secure condition.

One U.S. analyst explained the law's references to safeguarding national security in space, on seabeds, and at the poles were meant to give China adequate "legal support" for its projects in those realms. However, the inclusion of seabeds is almost certainly due to the growing tensions over disputes involving China, the United States, and Southeast Asian nations in the South China Sea. *Xinhua*, the state news agency, recently described April 15 as "national security education day," when propaganda and education would be carried out "to enhance everyone's awareness of national security. . . . Any government will stand firm and not leave any room for disputes, compromises and interferences when it comes to protecting its core interests," the spokesperson said. "China is no exception."[3]

Strategy and the Sea

Many Chinese naval officers and analysts think the United States is determined to contain China and prevent it from achieving the dominant historical position to which it is entitled. This view has been strengthened by Washington's shift to Asia, its transfer of naval units to the Pacific, and the March 2015 Maritime Strategy released by the U.S. Navy, Marine Corps, and Coast Guard.

Several of this strategy's elements are particularly troublesome for China. These include the use of "Indo-Pacific" as the theater of most strategic concern to the United States and the strategy's goal of achieving "all domain access," with its emphasis on "electromagnetic maneuver warfare" as naval priorities. These objectives are widely interpreted in the United States, China, and elsewhere as in fact directed against China.[4]

Indeed, Beijing's 2015 military strategy clearly refers to the United States as China's most threatening security concern; one analyst stated that "as a result of American involvement, China's maritime rights protection will face more challenges and uncertainty." Hence, the country must "build a powerful navy," which must "maintain a state of unremitting combat readiness" while "continuously improving [its] ability to carry out open seas protection and far-seas military operations other than war."[5]

Another notable Chinese discussion of strategy was presented at the U.S. Army War College in 1997 but remains germane. The vice president of China's important military think tank, the Academy of Military Science, characterized his "civilization's" strategic thought based on "the pursuit of peace, the high priority accorded national unity, and [an] emphasis on defense rather than offense." He then qualified this by noting that "over the last 150 years, however, China has been the victim of repeated aggression and pillages." Hence, he concluded, "the people of China show such strong emotions in matters concerning our national independence, unity, integrity of territory and sovereignty."[6]

Notwithstanding concerns about foreign interference, China's most important problems remain domestic concerns about its economy, internal security, and social harmony. Naval modernization will continue, but under the nineteenth-century but still-applicable rubric of "rich country, strong army," which underlines Beijing's number one priority of economic growth, including reducing corruption and establishing greater income equality.

China has moved to consolidate and maximize operational benefits from both its navy and its other maritime forces. These include the reorganized coast guard, maritime militia, commercial fleet and shore-based infrastructure, and fisheries industry. Additionally, the national government clearly is coordinating the activities of its maritime forces with the state-owned enterprises in the energy industry.

People's Liberation Army Navy

Beijing is approximately halfway toward its midcentury goal of deploying a navy capable of defending China's perceived maritime interests. The drive for maritime power is common to almost every expanding world power in history. It is also driven, in China's case, by memories of nineteenth- and early twentieth-century humiliation, exemplified in the abject defeat inflicted on its new navy by France in 1884 and by Japan in 1895.[7]

China's maritime interests, in addition to defense of the homeland, are defined as, first, being able to prevent from occurring within the second island chain events of which it does not approve. This is not "command of the sea" in a Mahanian sense but simply means that China will deploy the most powerful navy in Asian waters, on a day-to-day basis, of any nation. Paramilitary maritime forces, including the coast guard and maritime militia, will support this effort.

Second, the PLAN must be able to protect China's overseas investments and personnel, to include conducting noncombatant evacuation operations (NEO) when necessary. Third, the navy and supporting maritime forces must be able to safeguard the global SLOCs on which the health of China's economy depends, both for trade and energy imports.

Fourth, the PLAN must be able to safeguard China's regional maritime interests, including fisheries and mineral resources, but especially the sovereignty disputes involving Taiwan and the Yellow, East China, and South China Seas. This objective is enabled by the first.

To accomplish these goals by midcentury, China is deploying a navy centered on submarines. Modern corvettes, frigates, and destroyers are slowly joining the navy. All of these escorts are armed with formidable, state-of-the-art antiship cruise missiles; an increasing number are armed with modern, Aegis-like, antiair warfare systems. Most important, the PLAN finally is beginning to expand and modernize its replenishment-at-sea ship numbers, which will expand its power-projection capability.

The PLAN in 2015 is finally fulfilling its decades-old recognition of the value of the fleet providing its own airpower. One aircraft carrier is operational; two to three others are likely to join the fleet by 2025, at the latest. The PLAN's amphibious force is also modernizing and expanding greatly in capability. The relatively new landing platform docks have proven themselves as long-distance deployers, operating hull-in-water and air-cushion landing craft, helicopters, and special operating force teams. They are likely soon to be joined by large, flat-deck amphibious assault ships, similar to the U.S. landing helicopter assault or landing helicopter dock vessels.

The navy is also benefiting from a renewed emphasis on "civil-military integration," emphasized in the 2015 defense white paper. This policy aims to strengthen PLAN capabilities by accessing civilian capabilities.

The PLAN is making remarkable progress but continues to suffer serious shortfalls.[8] First, it lacks operational experience, although the past eight years of deployments to the Gulf of Aden and beyond have taught the navy much about conducting distant deployments.

Second is the still nascent employment of airpower at sea, particularly the employment of ship-based helicopters. Related to this is, third, the evolving role of the navy in the PLA. Increasing the navy's role is one of the objectives of the ongoing military reorganization being directed by President Xi Jinping, beginning with his announcement of a 300,000-personnel reduction in the PLA. A reduction of the number of military regions from seven to perhaps four is expected, as is an increased role in the PLA's command structure for navy, air force, and Second Artillery officers, with a concomitant reduction for army officers in those billets.[9]

The fourth shortfall is the reported prevalence of corruption in the PLA, including in the PLAN. The PLA is a target of Xi Jinping's extensive, continuing campaign against corruption and may be at least partly the result of the CCP's apparent continuing unease about the military's loyalty. The May 2015 defense white paper, for instance, asserts the PLA's loyalty to the CCP on no less than eleven occasions in a six-page document.[10]

Fifth is the problematic nature of the PLAN as a "Leninist" force, one subject to a dual-command system of operational and political commanders. Sixth is an overabundance of noncombatant headquarters, a problem that may be addressed in ongoing military reorganization. Seventh is the unknown quality of the noncommissioned officer corps still under development.

Eighth is the training shortfalls repeatedly addressed by senior officers and civilian officials in recent years, most recently in the May 2015 defense white paper. Ninth is the nascent nature of joint warfare, particularly the integration of air power with land and naval forces. Tenth is the unclear role of the PLAN in national strategy formulation, including in the maritime transformation called for by Xi Jinping from regional to global capability.

A New Maritime Strategy

Preparing for potential Taiwan scenarios remains the PLAN's number one priority, followed by contingency operations in the East and South China Seas. These priorities are evidenced in the increasingly complex exercises conducted by the PLAN during the past five years.[11]

The 2015 military strategy envisions four possible military scenarios, all of them maritime:

1. A large-scale, high-intensity defensive war [against the United States];
2. A large-scale, high-intensity "anti-secession" conflict over Taiwan;
3. A medium- to small-scale conflict over islands, maritime boundaries, or "large-scale plundering" of offshore energy resources; and
4. Small-scale, low-intensity conflicts, including NEOs.[12]

These contingencies lead directly to the 2015 military strategy's direction to the PLAN to transform from a regional to a global navy. The navy's missions are described as SLOC security, counterpiracy, NEO operations, and humanitarian assistance / disaster relief operations.

China's new maritime strategy ties in nicely with the nation's domestic priorities, particularly CCP rule and economic progress, as it does with current foreign policy objectives summed up in Xi Jinping's periphery diplomacy. This latter role places the PLAN at the forefront of Beijing's hot and cold policies of conflicting soft and hard power initiative. For instance, while the navy is the primary military service for enforcing China's maritime sovereignty claims in the South China Sea, supporting Beijing's unspoken strategy of "Finlandizing" the other claimants, it is also tasked with supporting diplomacy with those claimants through port visits, joint exercises, NEO, and humanitarian assistance / disaster relief missions.

Beijing's maritime focus in 2015 still begins with a regional view on the Yellow, East China, and South China Seas, but also extends into much of the Philippine Sea. The Indian Ocean is an increasing PLAN concern, however, as China continues expanding its economic and political presence into that theater. Beijing is intent on eventually deploying a two-ocean navy, with the PLAN tasked with missions in the "Indo-Pacific" ocean, in support of the more far-ranging tasks of a global navy.[13]

Threats to the Chinese interests represented in the periphery strategy begin with perceived U.S. containment, both by American forces and through friends and allies. Specific threats seen by Chinese analysts include U.S. support of Taiwan and alliances with Australia, Japan, the Philippines, and South Korea; naval exercises between and among the United States, Australia, India, and Japan and others; India's "Look East" policy, which implies an increased naval presence east of Malacca; and the policies and actions of the many international organizations founded by Western nations and difficult to influence by China.[14]

The PLAN is emerging from the until now army-dominated military. It is benefiting from Xi's military reorganization plans, Beijing's 2015 declaration of a mainstream maritime strategy, and the increasing budget to deploy a twenty-first-century navy on global missions. Operational and organizational issues remain, but the future looks bright for China's navy as an instrument of the military and diplomatic statecraft supporting economic and energy requirements.

Foreign Policy

China's periphery diplomacy is more than just a formulation; it demonstrates how firmly Xi Jinping, just three years into his leadership of China, has formulated and imposed a new foreign policy. Periphery diplomacy, the modernizing and reorganizing navy, and the dramatic economic initiative of one belt, one road are ingredients in Xi's changing the nation's international course. This may be described as a "new grand strategy" for China, based on "peaceful coexistence and win–win cooperation," with a particular focus on "building a 'new type of power relationship.'"[15]

Deng Xiaoping, China's leader from the late 1970s to the mid-1990s, reportedly established a paradigm of "tao guang yang hui," which may be interpreted as "keep a low profile and work hard," for the China he so strikingly set on the path to economic modernization. This "sixteen-character slogan" has been interpreted in many ways and as indicating many objectives, from nefarious intentions to the more likely caution of allowing time for economic modernization to develop. That posture clearly seems to have changed, perhaps since the Western economic downturn in 2008, now that Xi and other Chinese leaders apparently think China has attained the economic, military, and political stature to regain its rightful place as a global power.[16]

Xi Jinping's more active strategy has been demonstrated in post-2009 actions in the East and South China Sea disputes and global economic initiatives. This new activity may be termed "assertive" or even "aggressive" by some observers, but it simply reflects China's undeniably powerful economic and military status. What is not clear, however, is whether Beijing's foreign policies are effectively using those two elements of national power to forward Chinese strategic objectives.

The maritime strategy embedded in the May 2015 military strategy reflects the absence of a significant military threat from China's northern and western borders and facilitates Beijing's focus on its eastern, maritime border. Except for Japan and, by extension, the United States, foreign concerns in that direction mostly involve smaller nations, posing little economic, political, or even military threats to China.

Russia, India, and Japan are the only potential competitors in close proximity to China. The first suffers from severe demographic and economic problems, and its military is trying, again, to regain some of its storied effectiveness. India remains something of an adversary, but geography makes it a maritime concern only insofar as China wants its navy to operate in the Indian Ocean. Only Japan approaches China in naval power, although the growing PLAN appears soon to negate the proven effectiveness of Japan's Maritime Self-Defense Force. Japan's economy remains among the world's strongest, despite the past quarter-century of problems.[17]

No regional concerns alter the fact, however, that the United States is Beijing's number one strategic concern. A senior PLA officer, General Liu Yazhou, who is a member of the CCP Central Committee, provided an extreme view of uncertain commonality in China when he blamed the United States for "curbing China's rise." He then accused the United States of trying "to disintegrate the ASEAN" and wanting "a conflict between Japan and China."[18]

Here too, Xi Jinping is trying to change the accepted foreign policy model, advocating a "new type of major power relations." The phrase has repeatedly been invoked by Xi and senior Chinese and military officials but seems to have had little impact on China's relations with the United States.[19] That said, the Obama administration clearly does not narrow the U.S. relationship with China down to sovereignty issues over small land features but, as does the Xi administration, understands a much more comprehensive picture of relations between the two global economic, political, and military leaders.

China is not a revolutionary state. It participates regularly in established international institutions, from the United Nations to various regional and subregional organizations. Its participation may not—in fact, frequently does not—support Western initiatives, but that reflects national priorities.

Speaking in March 2015, Chinese foreign minister Wang Yi described China's foreign policy as "building a new type of international relations with win–win cooperation at the core."[20] He noted China's continued active participation in the United Nations and international climate change cooperation, the increased number of Chinese citizens and enterprises overseas, with a concomitant increase in the quality of consular services to be made available.[21] Wang's address repeated familiar China-centric truisms but did nothing to contradict Xi Jinping's periphery diplomacy or determination to participate fully in and take full advantage of global institutions, if possible altering them to China's advantage.

However, domestic problems will continue to overshadow foreign concerns for China's leaders. Regime legitimacy rests more on societal satisfaction than on foreign issues, no matter the correlations between the two.[22]

Beijing's rigid position on maritime sovereignty issues is notable; Foreign Minister Wang Yi has stated that flexibility on the maritime sovereignty issues "would shame its ancestors . . . and would shame its children."[23] There is also, as noted earlier, an element of paranoia in Beijing's public positions; for instance, a recent *People's Daily* editorial claimed that "China is the real victim of the South China Sea disputes."[24] Officials have not, however, termed these issues, including those in the East and South China Seas, as "core" issues; that is, as issues that likely would serve as a casus belli for military action.[25]

Nonetheless, China's activities in the three seas since approximately 2009 demonstrate a strategy of creating a maritime frontier defining its economic and political sovereignty and forming a solid defensive border. These activities may be described as "strategic" but are more tactical in the sense of "salami slicing" or "cabbage peeling," of pushing as far as it can without drawing the United States into conflict. It is a perilous strategy, risking escalation into military conflict.

Beijing has not been willing to negotiate over any of the current inland disputes but has been willing to employ armed force to secure its claims. It has done so in the Paracels, Spratlys, and Scarborough Reef and is turning its newly constructed "islands" into armed facilities.

China's continued expansion of these land features has continued heightening regional nations' concerns, increased U.S. attention to the situation, and raised tension between Beijing and Washington. The PLAN commander's claim that the artificial islands could be used for "joint rescue and disaster relief operations" is not reassuring.[26] In fact, Beijing is constructing artificial islands to be used as naval and air bases. It "directly subverts UNCLOS. . . . China is already challenging the freedom of navigation and over flight of naval vessels and aircraft as well as fishermen in the area."[27]

While the South China Sea dispute is extremely complicated because of the several disputants and their inflexibility, the dispute in the East China Sea is the most dangerous because of China's historic and enduring antipathy toward Japan. Recent statements by senior Chinese officials have included calling Tokyo's foreign policy "two-faced," keeping "a wary eye" on Prime Minister Abe, and expressing concern over Japan's security bills as a "challenge to [the] postwar order of peace," while Japan has reciprocated. Tokyo's new defense strategy highlights potential Chinese military incursions, particularly from its modernizing navy, and criticizes Beijing's "growing assertiveness."[28]

China is, by most measures, already a major maritime power in 2016. It leads or is close to leading the world in fisheries, size of merchant fleet, shipbuilding and other shore infrastructures, and deploys the world's second-largest navy. Beijing seems intent on enlarging and improving in all those measures of maritime power. That power is being employed to enhance the nation's energy security and to ensure the security of insular claims.

Economy and National Strength

A veteran U.S. policymaker linked China's economic growth and diplomatic efforts with a sharply analytic warning:

China's amazing growth is also altering China's view of its external interests, regionally and globally. Last year, President Xi stated that the security of Asia should be handled by the people of Asia. . . . If China pursues a new Asian security order that seeks to exclude the United States, China will face resistance and could reawaken old geopolitical rivalries. If China's concept of world order is based on tributary relations—as Henry Kissinger suggests is China's traditional practice—there will be tensions with the American-led security framework in the Asia-Pacific.

As one Chinese scholar told me, some Chinese feel that they cannot just accept the international architecture designed by the Americans— but the Chinese also are not confident that they know what a successor system should look like.[29]

This Chinese attitude reflects a view commonly held in that country that its international problems, particularly those relating to Taiwan and maritime disputes, are due to U.S. policy and interference. This belief may simply reflect the growing nationalism to be expected of a nation that has risen from domestic turmoil to a position of world economic and military status in just four decades but, unless successfully controlled by Beijing, may significantly weaken progress toward solidification of that status and further progress.

Seven conditions that in Beijing's view would justify the use of military force against Taiwan were recently reported:

1. Taiwan declares independence,
2. Taiwan is clearly inclined toward independence,
3. Taiwan gets nuclear weapons,
4. Taiwan experiences internal disorder,
5. Dialogue on cross-strait peaceful unification is delayed,
6. Foreign forces intervene in Taiwan's internal affairs; or
7. Foreign military forces are deployed on Taiwan.[30]

Some of these are repeats from previous such lists emanating from Beijing, but this list is particularly troublesome, given the lack of clarity of the conditions, other than the first and third points.

For instance, China is reserving to itself how to define "clearly inclined toward independence." Does that mean merely that a DPP candidate is elected to the presidency in 2016? Beijing would not employ military force against Taiwan except as a last resort, but this list provides remarkably wide-ranging scope of casus belli.

The state of the economy will also affect the pace of naval modernization and the extent of PLAN global deployments. China's huge overseas direct investments, $60 billion in 2011; overseas property investment, estimated to exceed $10 billion in 2015; and investments of $7.6 billion in overseas property in 2013 all underline increasing naval responsibilities for protecting Chinese overseas investments.[31]

Rearming in Reaction

A result of Beijing's attitude toward the maritime disputes in the South China Sea including "island" construction and increased use of military and associated forces is an increased, if perhaps nascent, arms race, prominently demonstrated in the acquisition and modernization of submarine forces by Australia, Indonesia, Japan, Malaysia, Singapore, South Korea, and Vietnam.[32] China has employed its military, PLAN, coast guard, and maritime militia in the construction of artificial "islands" in the South China Sea, which has alarmed its neighbors and heightened U.S. concern.[33]

Vietnam has acquired from Russia the first two of six modern Kilo-class submarines, with land-attack cruise missiles; perhaps more significantly, its crews are receiving training assistance from the Indian navy.[34] Additionally, the United States in June 2016 lessened its arms sales limitations on Vietnam.[35]

The U.S.-Philippine defense relationship is defined by a mutual defense treaty; U.S. counterinsurgency personnel and equipment aid continues, and Manila's dispute with Beijing over South China Sea land feature sovereignty has evoked increased U.S. assistance. Amphibious exercises are conducted at least annually, usually with an amphibious emphasis, and in April 2015 the two nations signed an agreement that might bring U.S. troops and ships back to Philippine bases. The United States has not committed to supporting Manila's sovereignty claims in the South China Sea, but in May 2015 Secretary of Defense Ashton Carter pledged Washington's "ironclad" commitment "to defend the Philippines."[36]

Malaysia is moving to upgrade the air defenses on the Spratly Islands that it claims, Indonesia and Singapore are modernizing their navies and air forces in reaction to China's heavy hand, and Australia is considering a significant military modernization program, but Japan is carrying out the region's most extensive defense policy and equipment modernization program, "since power balances are changing with China's rise."[37]

Prime Minister Abe has been given new powers by the legislature to deploy and employ Japan's formidable defense forces. The Diet has approved the largest defense budget since the end of World War II, which will provide additional coast guard assets, maritime patrol aircraft, small aircraft carriers, advancing Japan's new marine corps, and a "special unit" for the disputed Senkaku Islands.[38]

More significant, Tokyo and Washington are expanding their defense ties, with Tokyo pointing explicitly to China's naval modernization as a new threat.[39] This last point was brought home by discussions about possible Japanese Self-Defense Forces patrols in the South China Sea. Tokyo also has announced that it will "permanently" join U.S.-India naval exercises.[40]

The most interesting and substantive result of China's recent assertiveness in the East and South China Seas has been the multinational military responses. Of particular note is a common feeling in Japan and South Korea that China poses a "threat," and they are going to "resume defense exchanges."[41] In addition, Vietnam and Australia have called on China to exert "self-constraint" in the South China Sea, and Hanoi and Manila have announced a plan to conclude a "strategic partnership." Recently conducted multinational naval exercises have included participation by Cambodia, India, Indonesia, Japan, Malaysia, New Zealand, Singapore, South Korea, and the United States.[42] This recent, increasingly multilateral defense cooperation is unlikely to lead to the formation of an "Asian NATO," but it has gotten Beijing's attention. Chinese analysts interpret this cooperation as spurred by the United States to buttress its anti-Chinese hegemony in the Asia-Pacific.[43]

On the positive side for Beijing is the relationship with Moscow. While Russia's leadership has few other friendly avenues to pursue, the Russo-Chinese relationship may develop into an alignment in Asia in which their continental bloc balances a U.S.–Japanese maritime bloc.[44] Hence, Beijing's attempt to follow a dual-track periphery strategy has established a very mixed record, raising concerns among its diplomatic partners, from North Korea to the United States.

China–United States Relations

China's relationship with the United States is vital to both countries and to the world. The relationship is based on both common and divergent interests in economics, military operations, and political goals and methods. The United States does not take a formal position on South China Sea sovereignty issues, but the commander, U.S. Pacific Command, described Beijing's claims there as "outrageous" and "preposterous," while China's ambassador to the United States accused Washington of having a "Cold War mentality" and "no right whatsoever to intervene in the legitimate activities conducted by China in the South China Sea."[45]

Many Chinese officials and analysts blame the United States for the opposition to its sovereignty claims in the East and South China Seas. They view former secretary of state Hillary Clinton's speech in Hanoi in July 2010 as the beginning of U.S. interference in the South China Sea. U.S. actions are interpreted as part of the rebalance to Asia and a policy of containing China, thus preventing the nation from regaining its rightful place as a leading world power. Washington is viewed as determined to maintain global hegemony.[46]

U.S. views of China are not consistently condemnatory but are at least cautious. This is due in large part to the lack of clarity in Beijing's policy formulation process and a habit of secrecy much in excess of that encountered in the Western nations. The overall China-U.S. relationship is led by the two nations' closely linked economies, with a huge trade account, and by a military-to-military relationship of some constancy. Additionally, Beijing and Washington have reached agreement on two measures that should reduce the risk of inadvertent military confrontations; the Code for Unplanned Encounters at Sea has proven an effective instrument; a September 2015 aviation supplement also has been concluded.[47]

Many global problems offer possible collaborative platforms for the two nations, including North Korea, Iran, the Islamic State, Afghanistan, counterterrorism, antipiracy, climate change and other environmental concerns, maritime security, economic stability, energy security, and rules for cyber and space activities. However, progress toward effective mutual action against global problems has been slow to develop.

China's maritime sovereignty claims in the East and South China Seas are not opposed by the United States, although Beijing's ongoing "island" construction has been strongly condemned as destabilizing and posing dangerous points of possible armed conflict. The United States and other nations are very concerned, however, about the freedom of navigation through this vital sea posed by China's activities.

Beijing understandably views the littoral waters of these two seas and the Yellow Sea as areas of vital national security interest. The United States has defense treaties with South Korea, Japan, and the Philippines, and has what might be termed "special defense relationships" with Taiwan and Singapore, all states bordering on the three seas. Neither China nor the United States is likely to yield in this confrontation, which positions Beijing and Washington in opposite corners of a sensitive ring.

Final Thoughts

China's naval modernization, increasing economic activities in Indian Ocean littoral nations, and especially its close political relationship with Pakistan are alarming to India, particularly to the Indian navy.[48] The increased PLAN presence in the Indian Ocean has been a factor in New Delhi moving closer to Washington to "preserve regional peace and stability." Prime Minister Modi and President Obama "expressed concern" at an October 2014 meeting "about rising tensions over maritime territorial disputes, and affirmed the importance of safeguarding maritime security and ensuring freedom of navigation and over flight throughout the region, especially in the South China Sea."[49] The prime minister and president then agreed to a "strategic partnership" in January 2015, saying that "a closer partnership between the United States and India is indispensable to promoting peace, prosperity, and stability in those regions." They supported this agreement by repeating the October 2014 mantra about maritime security and freedom of navigation. The two leaders also noted their "common commitment to the Universal Declaration of Human Rights."[50] All of these points were probably correctly interpreted in Beijing as U.S. and Indian interference in China's national security interests, especially the South China Sea.

Furthermore, almost all of these states are leaning heavily toward the United States as a balance against Chinese dominance. Is China pursuing unitary foreign and national security policies without allies? Is Xi's assertion that "the people of Asia" would "run the affairs of Asia" a viable policy? A long-time

U.S. analyst has provided a very sobering evaluation of China's foreign and national security policies since 2010, described as "a qualitative change in Chinese regional policy" as Beijing attempts "to peel back the maritime *status quo ante* in the East and South China Seas, one thin layer at a time, without making a move dramatic enough to justify a major response by others." This assertiveness has caused China's "relations with its periphery" to suffer "a net decline over the last five years: Beijing's 'box score' for bilateral relations shows overall losses with minuses in Myanmar, Vietnam, Indonesia, Philippines, Australia, Malaysia, India, Singapore and of course Japan, with South Korea being a complex case but not a plus for Beijing. China's relations with ASEAN as a whole would have to be counted as weaker."[51]

The trifecta of national security elements confronting Beijing—navy, energy, and diplomacy—were highlighted by Xi Jinping in his November 2014 "Address to the Central Conference on Work Relating to Foreign Affairs: Assessing and Advancing Major-Power Diplomacy with Chinese Characteristics." Xi argued for "the importance of holding high the banner of peace, development, and win–win cooperation, pursuing China's overall domestic and international interests and its development and security priorities in a balanced way, focusing on the overriding goal of peaceful development and national renewal, upholding China's sovereignty, security, and development interests, fostering a more enabling international environment for peaceful development and maintaining and sustaining the important period of strategic opportunity for China's development."[52]

Beijing has published a collection of eighty speeches by Xi, the majority of them dealing with domestic issues, Asia-centric, and rarely referring to the West, except for noting the "century of humiliation." He emphasizes the need to retain the CCP in power to continue China's economic progress.[53] China's national strategy focus under Xi Jinping may be summed up as demanding the status earned by the nation's remarkable economic progress, military modernization, and global diplomatic presence.

The United States remains a very powerful Asian nation in economic, political, and military terms. Beijing must deal with that status but maintains its primary foreign policy focus on its regional neighbors. Chinese strengths are formidable in all these areas, but Beijing must also deal from a hand weakened by a "bad rap" for assertiveness, mediocre international accomplishments, and the U.S. presence noted earlier.[54]

Beijing believes its continued legitimacy depends on the support of the CCP, the legitimacy of which in turn depends on the support of the Chinese people. That support requires a healthy, improving economy, which in turn requires ever-increasing energy supplies. China's economy is international and maritime; China believes that a strong, globally capable navy is required to secure that international economy and the foreign-origin resources required to support continued economic growth.

The success of Beijing's pursuit of these three paradigms is yet to be determined. The PLAN is modernizing; the economy remains healthy, if growing at a slower pace—the "new normal"—but the success of China's foreign policies to build on those two success stories seems problematic.[55] Many of the Asian nations with whom China's trade is growing are now building their own navies in reaction to the modernizing PLAN and Beijing's willingness to employ it in sovereignty disputes. Potential problems in its relations with Indonesia reflect Beijing's diplomatic issues. The lack of clarity in Beijing's sovereignty claims in the South China Sea leads to Jakarta fearing Chinese intrusion and demands on Indonesia's vital Natuna gas fields.[56]

China's foreign policy addresses both bilateral relations and participation in multilateral organizations. Beijing's view that "domestic law trumps, even creates, international law" is a problem for resolving the sovereignty issues that affect both of these facets of Chinese foreign policy.[57] Both the international trading economy and world-class navy require effective foreign diplomacy and participation in global affairs. This policy trifecta in large part defines China's posture to the world.

Notes

Introduction

1. The members of the "gang" were Jiang Qing, Mao's widow, and three close supporters: Wang Hongwen, Yao Wenyuan, and Zhang Chunqiao. They received a show trial in 1981. Jiang Qing was defiant throughout the trial and subsequent imprisonment. Zhang Chunqiao refused to admit any wrong. Yao Wenyuan and Wang Hongwen expressed repentance and confessed their alleged crimes. Jiang and Zhang received death sentences that were later commuted to life imprisonment while Wang Hongwen and Yao Wenyuan were given life and twenty years in prison in 1996 and 1998, respectively.

2. China was already declared in 2014 to have surpassed the United States in economic strength as measured by purchasing power parity, but that measure is not always supported as determinative. See Dornbusch, "Purchasing Power Parity."

3. See, for instance, Osborne, "Report: China's Navy Fleet Will Outnumber U.S. by 2020"; and O'Brian, "The Navy's Hidden Crisis."

4. Mearsheimer, *The Tragedy of Great Power Politics*; also see Mearsheimer, "The Rise of China; and Zhao, "Managing Crises in Sino-US Relations." Kenneth Allen has described Zhao as a lieutenant colonel in 2013, with a doctorate in "military studies," and an assistant professor at China's National Defense University (Allen correspondence with me, October 2015).

5. Zhao, "Managing Crises in Sino-US Relations," 42.

6. Liff and Ikenberry, "Racing Toward Tragedy?" The United States peacefully surpassed the United Kingdom in naval and economic power, for instance.

7. See, for instance, Shen, "Will China Replace U.S. as Global Superpower?," which criticizes Michael Pillsbury's view that China has and is pursuing a deliberate policy to do exactly that; see Pillsbury, *Hundred-Year Marathon*. Pillsbury's conclusion obviously touched a nerve in China, but Shen's criticism is manifestly biased. A more convincing view of China's historic behavior as a typical empire was provided by Warren Cohen, in a conversation with me in March 2004 in

Washington, D.C. Cohen pointed out, for instance, that the China of the relatively small Qin Dynasty of ca. 220 BCE grew to the continentally dominant Qing Dynasty of the early twentieth century through military, economic, and political expansion.

8. Matthew, "China Working to Dominate Sea Routes."

9. My discussions with senior PLA officers, 2015. The defense white papers, including the 2015 version, have consistently tasked the PLA with forwarding China's economic well-being and continued growth.

10. *China's Military Strategy*, sections I, II, at Ministry of National Defense of the People's Republic of China Web site, http://eng.mod.gov.cn/Database/White Papers/2014.htm.

11. Yang, "Xi Jinping: China to Cut Troops by 300,000."

12. Zheng Shuna, quoted in "China Adopts New Law on National Security," *Xinhua*, 1 July 2015, http://news.xinhuanet.com/english/2015-07/01/c_134372198.htm.

13. For the full text of China's 2015 defense white paper on military strategy, see *China's Military Strategy*, http://eng.mod.gov.cn/Database/WhitePapers/2014.htm.

14. See Zhang and Cao, "Promote the Transformation of Naval Strategy"; and Li and Ma, "The Complexity of the Maritime Military Struggle." The 2002 defense white paper describes the "armed forces" of China as including three elements: the PLA, the militia and reserves, and the People's Armed Police. See *China's National Defense in 2002*, http://eng.mod.gov.cn/Database/WhitePapers/2002 .htm.

15. Zhang and Cao, "Promote the Transformation of Naval Strategy."

16. Buckley, "Communist Leadership Approves Security Goals." This report also cautioned, "There must be unwavering adherence to the Chinese Communist Party's absolute leadership of national security work."

17. This concept emerged from the 1648 Treaty of Westphalia, which ended Europe's Thirty Years' War. The treaty's goal was to end religious wars by emphasizing the nation-state as the primary actor in international relations. It established a system of coexisting states, with each respecting the others' sovereignty.

18. "Responsibility to protect" is the view that the United States, as the world's most powerful nation, has a responsibility to prevent and stop genocides, war crimes, ethnic cleansing, and crimes against humanity. It was spurred by the delayed response to the Rwandan genocide but is weakened by the interventions in Libya and Syria. See, for instance, Western and Goldstein, "R2P."

19. Perlez, "Xi Jinping of China Calls for Cooperation."

20. Jonathan Greenert, quoted in Garamone, "Greenert Discusses U.S. Maritime Strategy Shift."

21. Mahan, *Influence of Sea Power upon History*; and Kennedy, *Rise and Fall of the Great Powers*.

22. Discussed in Parry, *Super Highway*, 42–45.

23. Osnos, "Born Red."

24. Yuan Guiren, quoted in ibid.

25. Mary Clabaugh Wright concluded that the Tongzhi Restoration failed because "the requirements of modernization ran counter to the requirements of Confucian

stability." Wright, *Last Stand of Chinese Conservatism*, cited in Cohen, *Discovering History in China*.

26. See Magnier, Wei, and Talley, "Economy Expanded 7.4% in 2014"; and "China to Deepen Economic Reforms," Reuters, 5 December 2014, http://www.reuters.com/article/2014/12/05/us-china-economy-politburo-idUSKCN0JJ0RX20141205.

27. Osnos, "Born Red."

28. See the Asian Infrastructure Investment Bank Web site, http://www.aiib.org/; and Bird, "China's New Development Bank."

29. Wu and Zhang, "Xi in Call for Building New 'Maritime Silk Road.'"

30. See Stephens, "Now China Starts to Make the Rules."

31. Calamur, "China's President Promises Pakistan."

32. Discussed in Zhang and Guschin, "China's Silk Road Economic Belt."

33. "G7 Foreign Ministers' Declaration on Maritime Security," Lübeck, Germany, 15 April 2015, www.auswaertiges-amt.de/EN/Infoservice/Presse/Meldungen/2015/150415_G7_Maritime_Security.html.

34. Several piracy attacks were reported to be on just 21 and 22 August 2015; see "Six Pirate Attacks Off Singapore," *Maritime Executive*, 23 August 2015, http://www.maritime-executive.com/article/six-pirate-attacks-off-singapore. This report also stated, "Southeast Asia reclaimed the dubious honor of global piracy hotspot, with at least 134 attacks reported in the first six months of this year."

35. The East China Sea ADIZ is examined in Swaine, "Chinese Views and Commentary on the East China Sea Air Defense Identification Zone (ECS ADIZ)." Also see Wood, "China's 'Eternal Prosperity.'"

36. Cited in "China's Xi Calls for Stronger Frontier Defenses," *Xinhua*, 29 June 2014, http://news.xinhuanet.com/english/china/2014-06/28/c_133444528.htm.

37. Quoted in "Xi Urges Solidarity for National Rejuvenation," *Xinhua*, 20 May 2015, http://news.xinhuanet.com/english/2015 05/20/c_134255527.htm. Of course, Beijing considers Taiwan, Hong Kong, and Macao to be very much "domestic" and not "foreign" issues.

38. Ibid.

39. General Political Department circular, quoted in Mulvenon, "Military Themes from the 2013 National People's Congress."

40. The World Health Organization also notes the increasing importance and share of "seafood" provided by aquiculture, in which China leads the world by a factor of more than three; "Availability and Consumption of Fish," World Health Organization, http://www.who.int/nutrition/topics/3_foodconsumption/en/index5.html. See also "Inland Captures Fisheries," Figure 8, *Green Facts*, http://www.greenfacts.org/en/fisheries/figtableboxes/figure-08.htm, which reports that in 2006 China produced 25.7 percent of the world's "inland" production, with Bangladesh the next largest producer, at 9.5 percent. The global production data may be found at "FAO State of World Fisheries, Aquaculture Report—Fish Consumption," *The Fish Site*, 10 September 2012, http://www.thefishsite.com/articles/1447/fao-state-of-world-fisheries-aquaculture-report-fish-consumption/.

41. "Marine Fisheries Development in China," UN Fisheries and Aquiculture Department, http://www.fao.org/docrep/005/y2257e/y2257e04.htm.

42. Dean, "Report Warns of 'Global Collapse' of Fishing."
43. Butler, "Oceans on the Brink of Ecological Collapse."
44. See Johnston, "How New and Assertive Is China's New Assertiveness?"; and Friedberg, "The Sources of Chinese Conduct."
45. See Lu, "China Offers First Glimpse."

Chapter 1. China's Maritime World

1. Alain Peyrefitte, cited in Brendon, *The Decline and Fall of the British Empire, 1781–1997*, 103.
2. Wu Shengli, "Learn Profound Historical Lessons," 1–4.
3. Mackinder first published his views in "The Geographic Pivot of History," a paper of the Royal Geographic Society. He followed this with *Democratic Ideals and Reality* (first published in 1919; a paperback edition was published by Forgotten Books, 2012). Mackinder's syllogism is on page 194 of the latter publication.
4. See Spykman, *America's Strategy in World Politics*, 41.
5. Ibid.
6. See Owens, "In Defense of Classical Geopolitics."
7. The 2015 military strategy may be found at "Full Text: China's Military Strategy," *Xinhua*, 26 May 2015, http://www.chinadaily.com.cn/china/2015-05/26/content _20820628.htm.
8. See discussion in Dobbins et al., *America's Role in Nation Building*, 35; and Leffler, *A Preponderance of Power*, 436.
9. Many charts erroneously depict the first island chain swinging north to join the U-shaped line that delineates China's South China Sea claims.
10. See, for instance, Qi, "Article on International Security Affairs," 7.
11. Other theorists of note include the British James Fairgrieve (1870–1953) and the contemporary John M. Collins, best known for his *Military Geography*. These writers are discussed in Sempa, "Geography and World Power at 100."
12. McCurry, "China Lays Claim to Okinawa."
13. Ma is quoted in "President Ma Attends 2015 East Asian Maritime Peace Forum," Office of the President of the Republic of China (ROC), 17 August 2015, http:// article.wn.com/view/2015/08/17/President_Ma_attends_2015_East_Asian_ Maritime_Peace_Forum_Of/.
14. This U-shaped line probably first appeared in a 1922 map; it was later replicated in a 1947 map published by the Republic of China government and in 1992 by the PRC government. It has sometimes been drawn with ten or eleven lines; the lines themselves have been inconsistently placed and never precisely located by latitude and longitude. Furthermore, no Chinese government has ever clarified exactly what the dashed line means in terms of sovereignty.
15. "Wealthiest" is admittedly a relative, even amorphous, term, but Indonesia qualifies by several measures.
16. A compilation of reports of this and similar Chinese incursions is at https:// johnib.wordpress.com/tag/encroaching-on-the-waters-surrounding-the -luconia-shoals/.

17. This is drawn from my conversations with senior U.S. military and civilian officials in 2014 and from Laeng, "China Coast Guard Vessel Found." Also see Grudgings and Blanchard, "Malaysia Navy Chief Denies Chinese Incursion."

18. See, for instance, Vladimir Putin, quoted in Bender, "Putin"; "Russia's Naval Might Will Only Grow," *Famagusta Gazette*, 27 July 2014, http://famagusta -gazette.com/president-putin-russias-navy-might-will-only-grow-p24520-69 .htm; and Fedyszen, "Renaissance of the Russian Navy."

19. "Southwest Asia" is defined as including Pakistan, Iran, and the nations of the Arabian Peninsula.

20. This approximate number is due to underreporting and different data recorded in different databases. See Xu, Meng, and Li, "Analysis and Implications of the Accidents in the Singapore Strait."

21. Hand, "Malacca Strait Traffic."

22. "World Oil Transit Chokepoints," Energy Information Agency (EIA), 10 November 2014, http://www.eia.gov/beta/international/regions-topics.cfm?RegionTopic ID=WOTC.

23. The United States has not signed or ratified the UNCLOS, despite the positive recommendation of every president and other senior officials since Ronald Reagan, but has stated repeatedly that it will adhere to all UNCLOS provisions.

24. Grotius's "Mare Liberum" was published in 1609 and is cited in Till, "Close Encounters of the Maritime Kind," 179. The "wide common" phrase is from Mahan, *Influence of Sea Power upon History, 1660–1783*, 25, also quoted by Till.

25. The UNCLOS may be investigated through its Web site, http://www.un.org/ depts/los/convention_agreements/texts/unclos/closindx.htm. Since the 1982 Convention came into force in 1994, twelve cases have been arbitrated under Annex VII of UNCLOS. The Permanent Court of Arbitration (PCA) is acting, or has acted, as registry in eleven of those cases. The cases arbitrated under the auspices of the PCA include the following:

- The Duzgit Integrity Arbitration (*Malta v. Sao Tome and Principe*), instituted in October 2013 and still pending;
- The Arctic Sunrise Arbitration (*Netherlands v. Russian Federation*), instituted in October 2013 and still pending;
- The Atlanto-Scandian Herring Arbitration (*Denmark re Faroe Islands v. European Union*), instituted in August 2013 and terminated through a tribunal order in September 2014, following agreement between the parties;
- *Philippines v. China*, instituted in January 2013 and still pending;
- *Mauritius v. United Kingdom* ("Chagos Marine Protected Area Arbitration"), instituted in December 2010 and decided (declared illegal) on 18 March 2015;
- *Bangladesh v. India* (Bay of Bengal Maritime Boundary Arbitration), instituted in October 2009 and decided on 7 July 2014;
- *Argentina v. Ghana* (the "ARA Libertad Arbitration"), instituted in October 2012 and terminated in November 2013 following agreement between the parties;
- *Barbados v. Trinidad and Tobago*, instituted in February 2004 and decided by a final award in April 2006;

- *Guyana v. Suriname*, instituted in February 2004 and decided by a final award in September 2007;
- *Malaysia v. Singapore*, instituted in July 2003 and terminated by an award on agreed terms in September 2005; and
- *Ireland v. United Kingdom* ("MOX Plant Case"), instituted in November 2001 and terminated through a tribunal order in June 2008.

26. China's declarations when it signed the UNCLOS are at http://www.un.org/depts/los/convention_agreements/convention_declarations.htm#China%20Upon%20ratification.
27. Ibid.
28. Ibid.
29. See Dutton, "An Analysis of China's Claim," 57.
30. China's declarations when it signed the UNCLOS.
31. Ibid.
32. Reported in "China 'Extremely Concerned' by ASEAN Statement on Disputed Sea," Reuters, 28 April 2015, http://uk.reuters.com/article/2015/04/28/uk-china-southchinasea-idUKKBN0NJ0W220150428.
33. U.S. Department of State, "Limits in the Seas."
34. China's deliberate misinterpretation of recognized international law is examined in detail in Pedrozo, "Responding to Ms. Zhang's Talking Points." His article is in rebuttal to Zhang, "Is It Safeguarding the Freedom." Also see Beckman, "China, UNCLOS and the South China Sea."
35. Peter Dutton, conversation with the author, Oslo, June 2011.
36. Andrew Browne points out that navigational charts mark the large area of the South China Sea containing the Spratly Islands as "Dangerous Ground," due to less than perfect geophysical knowledge, even in the twenty-first century. Browne, "Tiny Reef Poses a Big Hazard."
37. Beckman, "China, UNCLOS and the South China Sea," 7.
38. Page, "Chinese Ships Approach Malaysia"; Grudgings, "Insight"; and Zheng, "The Nine-Dashed Line."
39. Torode, "PLA Navy Amphibious Task Force."
40. Beckman points out that China "gave up whatever historic rights it had to natural resources" when it signed the UNCLOS in 1996. Beckman, "China, UNCLOS and the South China Sea," 12.
41. All UNCLOS signatories' declarations are at http://www.un.org/depts/los/convention_agreements/convention_declarations.htm.
42. See Osawa, "China' ADIZ over the East China Sea"; and Clover, "China Raises Prospect." The Ministry of Foreign Affairs position was articulated by Ouyang Yujing, director-general of the Department of Boundary and Ocean Affairs, in Zhang, "Nansha Islands Construction."
43. Wong, "China Says It Could Add Defense Zone."
44. These and other pertinent Chinese laws and declarations are neatly summarized in DoD 2005.1-M, "China, People's Republic of, Summary of Claims," n.d., http://www.jag.navy.mil/organization/documents/mcrm/China2015.pdf.
45. Beckman, "The UN Convention on the Law of the Sea," 143–45. Also see McDevitt, "South China Sea," 2–3.

46. Elferink, "Islands in the South China Sea," 169, cited in Bateman, "Maritime Boundary Delimitation," 124.
47. Two current, if both problematic, claims are represented in my discussion with Wu Shicun, 7 May 2014, Haikou, Hainan, China; and Wu, *Solving Disputes for Regional Cooperation*; and Bondoc, "China's Own Ancient Maps." The clearest explanation of the background of China's claim is in Chung, "Drawing the U-Shaped Line."
48. Zhou is quoted in Dzurek, "The Spratly Islands," 16.
49. China's rationale for its South China Sea claims is clearly and succinctly explained in Fravel, "China's Strategy in the South China Sea."
50. My discussion with former senior U.S. government official, Washington, D.C., 2014; also see Kazianis, "China's Ten Red Lines in the South China Sea."
51. Gao Zhiguo, Song Yann-Huei, Hu Dekun, and Zhu Feng, statements in "Highlights of a Cross-Strait Conference." Taiwan's near-full agreement with Beijing over the sovereignty disputes in the East and South China Seas is in "President Ma Attends 2015 East Asian Maritime Peace Forum."
52. Peter Dutton's response to Chinese Foreign Ministry spokesperson Hua Chunying's "Remarks on US Defense Secretary Carter's Speech Relating to the Issue of the South China Sea at the Shangri La Dialogue," 30 May 2015, http://jm.china-embassy.org/eng/wjbfyrth/t1268781.htm, in which Dutton also accuses China's legal view as "designed to perpetuate obfuscation." He also points out that "there is no right under international law to claim sovereignty over a fully submerged feature," as Beijing is claiming over the James Shoal.
53. These are discussed and depicted in Franckx, "Chinese Claims in the East China Sea and South China Sea: A Legal Assessment of Cartographic Evidence."
54. Permanent Mission of the Republic of Indonesia to the United Nations, Note no. 480/POL-703/VII/10, 8 July 2010, http://www.un.org/depts/los/clcs_new/submissions_files/mysvnm33_09/idn_2010re_mys_vnm_e.pdf. U.S. views are in Bader, "The U.S. and China's Nine Dash Line"; and Rosen, "U.S. Slams Chinese 9 Dashed Line Claim."
55. Quoted in Dutton, "An Analysis of China's Claim," 59. The most complete explanation of the nine-dash line and China's South China Sea claims is Chung, "Drawing the U-Shaped Line."
56. Zheng, "Why Does China's Maritime Claim Remain Ambiguous?" This position has no validity in recognized international law, as explained by Beckman, "UN Convention on the Law of the Sea," 142.
57. See the extensive analysis by Beckman, "The Philippines v. China Case"; and Parameswaran, "Vietnam Lodges a Submission."
58. "Chinese FM Proposes Three Initiatives to Maintain Peace, Stability of South China Sea," *Xinhua*, 5 August 2015, http://news.xinhuanet.com/english/2015 –08/05/c_134484814.htm.
59. "Chinese FM Puts Forward 10 New Proposals on China-ASEAN Cooperation," *Xinhua*, 6 August 2015, http://news.xinhuanet.com/english/2015-08/06/c_134484881.htm.
60. Parameswaran, "China Blasts ASEAN Head."

61. "Declaration on the Conduct of Parties in the South China Sea," ASEAN, 4 November 2002, quoted in http://www.asean.org/?static_post=declaration-on -the-conduct-of-parties-in-the-south-china-sea-2.

62. Thayer, "South China Sea."

63. Alexander, "China Land Reclamation"; "Philippines Hits Back at Beijing Over South China Sea," Agence France-Presse (AFP), 28 March 2015, http://sports .yahoo.com/news/philippines-hits-back-beijing-over-south-china-sea -084114750—spt.html; Sun, "South China Sea Disputes"; and Rosenberg, "Building of Islands Is Debated."

64. China's ambassador to the United States, Cui Tiankai, stated in March 2015 that "of course" China would arm the artificial islands. The NDU description is in "Chinese Military and Civilian Integration Development Report 2014," National Defense University (Beijing), 25 July 2014, http://ccasindia.org/newsdetails.php ?nid=434 discusses this report.

65. "Details of China's First Peacekeeping Infantry Battalion," PRC Ministry of National Defense, 23 December 2014, http://eng.mod.gov.cn/DefenseNews/2014 -12/23/content_4560107.htm.

66. "First Chinese UN Peacekeeping Force Commander Takes Office," *Xinhua*, 17 September 2007, http://news.xinhuanet.com/english/2007-09/17/content _6742592.htm.

67. The United States, by contrast, has cast more than seventy vetoes during the same period. See United Nations, Dag Hammarskjöld Library Research Guides, http://research.un.org/en/docs/sc/quick.

68. Zhu, "Beijing's Successful Agenda-Setting"; and Solis, "China Flexes Its Muscles."

69. See Alagappa, "Community Building"; and Desker, "ASEAN Integration." Lee is quoted in "Prime Minister Meets Foreign Correspondents at Television Singpura, Sunday, 5th November, 1967," http://www.nas.gov.sg/archivesonline/ data/pdfdoc/lky19671105a.pdf.

70. See, for instance, Boudreau, "Japan to Give Vietnam Boats"; Ko, "Mekong States Aim to Maintain Balance"; Mehta, "US Providing Vietnam $18M"; Alexander, "Vietnam, U.S. Discuss Military Cooperation"; Mogato, "Philippines, Vietnam Upgrade Ties"; and Press Trust of India, "India, Vietnam Ink Seven Pacts."

71. Li is quoted in "Li Raises Seven-Pronged Proposal on Promoting China-ASEAN Cooperation," *Xinhua*, 10 October 2015, http://news.xinhuanet.com/english /china/2013-10/10/c_125503874_3.htm. While Li's talk was titled "Seven Proposals," only six were reported (my discussion with Michael Swaine, September 2015, Washington, D.C.).

72. "Vision and Actions on Jointly Building Silk Road Economic Belt and 21st Century Maritime Silk Road," National Development and Reform Commission (Beijing: March 2015), http://en.ndrc.gov.cn/newsrelease/201503/t20150330 _669367.html.

73. Wang Yi (China's foreign minister), cited in "ASEAN: China Makes 10 New Proposals."

74. Quotes are in Swaine, "Chinese Views and Commentary on Periphery Diplomacy," 11–13.

75. Ibid.
76. Quoted in Kapoor and Sieg, "Indonesian President Says." Also see Chang, "Even Indonesia."
77. Gindarsah, "Indonesia and the South China Sea." Also see Parameswaran, "Playing It Safe"; and Ng and Moss, "Malaysia Toughens Stance."
78. Bower, "China Reveals Its Hand."
79. "Senior Chinese, ASEAN Officials Vow to Enhance Maritime, Security Cooperation," *Xinhua*, 22 April 2014, http://news.xinhuanet.com/english/china/2014-04/22/c_133281958.htm.
80. Tiezzi, "China Nixes South China Sea Discussions."
81. Allen, "PLA Foreign Relations under Xi Jinping."
82. This argument is made in Wachman, *Why Taiwan?*
83. My conversation with Wu Shicun, director of the Chinese Institute for the Study of the South China Sea, 7 May 2013, Haikou, Hainan, China; and Wu, quoted in Renz and Heidemann, "China's Coming 'Lawfare.'"
84. Kraska, "Confidence Building Regimes."
85. Examples are reported in "Friendly Cooperation in Fundamental Interest of Vietnam, China: Ambassador," Vietnamnet, 19 January 2015, http://en.vietnamplus.vn/friendly-cooperation-in-fundamental-interest-of-vietnam-china-ambassador/70856.vnp; Vu and Trung, "Deference or Balancing Act"; "Vietnam-China Economic and Trade Cooperation Discussed," TalkVietnam, 18 December 2014, http://www.talkvietnam.com/2014/12/vietnam-china-economic-and-trade-cooperation-discussed/; and "President Xi Jinping Holds Talks with President Truong Tan Sang of Vietnam, Stressing China and Vietnam Should Unswervingly March along Path of Friendly Cooperation," Embassy of the PRC in the U.S., 19 June 2013, http://www.china-embassy.org/eng/zgyw/t1052303.htm. Also see Bartel, "Report: Chinese Ship Sinks Another Vietnamese Fishing Vessel."
86. Thayer, "Vietnam's East Sea Strategy," 12.
87. "China, Vietnam Hold 17th Joint Patrol in Beibu Gulf," *China Military Online*, 29 December 2014, http://english.chinamil.com.cn/news-channels/china-military-news/2014-12/29/content_6288326.htm.
88. Elferink, "Islands in the South China Sea," 169, cited in Bateman, "Maritime Boundary Delimitation," 124.

Chapter 2. Maritime Forces

1. "China's National Defense in 2008," http://www.china.org.cn/government/white paper/node_7060059.htm; also see Lai, Introduction to *The PLA at Home and Abroad*, 15. Jesse L. Karotkin, of the Office of Naval Intelligence, stated the PLAN's goal was to win "informationized wars by the mid-21st century," quoted in O'Rourke, "China Naval Modernization," 85.
2. My discussion with a senior MR commander, fall 2012. Also see Johnson, "Sweeping Reforms Announced at Third Plenum."

3. First announced in "China to Optimize Army Size, Structure: CPC Decision," *Xinhua*, 15 November 2014, http://news.xinhuanet.com/english/china/2013–11 /16/c_132892304.htm.

4. Reportedly less than 20 percent of the PLAN's 235,000 total personnel are privates or privates first class (the two most junior enlisted ranks), while the number for the entire PLA is 33–34 percent, which is evidence of the navy's requirement to enlist and retain more qualified personnel. "Naval Male JNCO to Put on Sailor Uniform," *China Military Online*, 24 December 2014, http://english.chinamil .com.cn/news-channels/china-military-news/2014-12/24/content_6283095 .htm.

5. Cole, "Watch: China's Shocking New Military Recruitment Video."

6. See discussion in Ch'en and Tarling, *Studies in the Social History of China*, 324.

7. Hackett, *Military Balance 2016*, 241. This number includes conscripts serving two-year enlistments but not reserves or militia.

8. For a recent example, see "South China Sea Fleet Called Reserves for Exercise," *Global Times*, 20 June 2015, http://chinascope.org/main/content/view/7227/40/.

9. This discussion leans heavily on Finkelstein, "2015 Should Be an Exciting Year." Xi Jinping is quoted in "Xi Jinping Addresses CPC Central Committee Political Bureau 17th Collective Study Session," *Xinhua*, OSC-CHR2014083042078686 (30 August 2014); also cited in Wang, "Si Jinping Urges China's Military"; Xi's argument is also discussed in "What Does Xi Jinping's China Dream Mean?" BBC, 5 June 2013, http://www.bbc.com/news/world-asia-china-22726375.

10. Gulf deployments have included stationing SOF units on ships deploying on antipiracy operations. Blasko, "PLA Special Operations Forces"; also see LaGrone, "New Chinese Nuclear Sub Design."

11. Chubb, "China's Expansion of 'Regular Rights Defense Patrols.'"

12. Chipman, *Military Balance 2015*, 4. The cost comparison is in "China's Military Gets More for Less," *Korea JoongAng Daily*, 10 September 2014, http://korea joongangdaily.joins.com/news/article/Article.aspx?aid=2994639.

13. Blasko makes his point in "An Analysis of China's 2011 Defense Budget."

14. These numbers come from various sources in the "2014 Report to Congress of the U.S.-China Economic and Security Review Commission" (Washington, D.C.: U.S. GPO, November 2014), Figure 3: "China's Announced Defense Spending 1989–2014," 287, http://origin.www.uscc.gov/sites/default/files/annual_reports/ Complete%20Report.PDF.

15. My discussion with Dennis J. Blasko, August 2015, via Internet. Also see Blasko's "An Analysis of China's 2011 Defense Budget and Total Military Spending."

16. Ship numbers are from "The PLA Navy: New Capabilities and Missions for the 21st Century," Office of Naval Intelligence (Washington, D.C., 2015), 14, http:// www.oni.navy.mil/Portals/12/Intel%20agencies/China_Media/2015_PLA_ NAVY_PUB_Print_Low_Res.pdf?ver=2015-12-02-081233-733 (hereafter ONI Report). The PLAN attaché to the United States told me in 2009 that at least five Type 071 ships would be built.

17. "Intensive Commissioning of PLAN Warships," *China Military Online*, 1 January 2014, http://eng.mod.gov.cn/Opinion/2014-01/09/content_4483443.htm.

18. Fang Bing, cited in "Military Expert Foresees PLAN's Largest Surface Ship Family," *China Military Online*, 4 December 2014, http://eng.mod.gov.cn/Top News/2014-12/04/content_4555507.htm.
19. O'Rourke, "China Naval Modernization," 39–41, explains the sources and rationale for these numbers.
20. Goldstein, "Real Military Threat from China."
21. Lin and Singer, "China's Getting Ready"; and O'Rourke, "China Naval Modernization," 25.
22. O'Rourke, "China Naval Modernization," 34.
23. The Type 081 may displace 35,000 tons; the U.S. landing helicopter dock class displace 45,000 tons, but the most significant feature of China's new ship is its flat deck design. Ibid., 35.
24. "Wenchong Shipyard Delivers Mobile Landing Platform to PLA Navy," *Defense World*, 30 June 2015, http://www.defenseworld.net/news/13316/ Wenchong_Shipyard_Delivers_Mobile_Landing_Platform_To_PLA_Navy# .VZMIouu4k0p. Andrew Tate also reports construction of a roll-on/roll-off logistics ship for the PLAN: Tate, "China Building Mobile Landing Platform."
25. A conventionally powered Song class deployed to the Gulf of Aden in 2014, making a port visit to Sri Lanka en route, where it rendezvoused with the *Changxing Island*, a submarine support ship. See "PLA Navy Submarine Visits Sri Lanka," *ChinaMil*, 29 September 2015, http://eng.chinamil.com.cn/news-channels/china -military-news/2014-09/24/content_6152669.htm. A Shang-class SSN then deployed to the gulf in December 2014. See Page, "Deep Threat"; Page's report is accurate, although the headline is an exaggeration.
26. The Defense Department estimates that China may build up to twenty Yuan-class submarines. U.S. Department of Defense, *Annual Report to Congress*, 7.
27. O'Rourke, "China Naval Modernization."
28. The JL-2 was successfully tested in 2012; ONI Report.
29. The latest forecast is found in Capaccio and Tweed, "U.S. Says Chinese Sub."
30. The "bastion concept" is one of two methods for stationing FBM submarines developed during the Cold War. The United States kept its FBMs on patrol, but after realizing U.S. intelligence successes, the Soviet Union stationed its FBMs in "bastions" in the White Sea and other locations, where the missile submarines were defended by series of attack submarines and minefields.
31. The most complete compilation of various estimates, including Locklear's, about China's current and future submarine numbers is in Kristensen and Norris, "Chinese Nuclear Forces, 2015."
32. Hans M. Kristensen reproduces a table from an unclassified publication by the U.S. Office of Naval Intelligence. Kristensen, "China's Noisy Nuclear Submarines."
33. See Innismay, "Search for Missing Malaysia Airlines Jet"; and Keck, "China Tests New Unmanned Mini-Sub."
34. The best single work on China's mine warfare capabilities remains Erickson, Goldstein, and Murray, *Chinese Mine Warfare*. Also see ONI Report, 23–24.
35. Yeo, "Chinese Carrier Fighter Now in Serial Production."
36. Tiezzi, "China to Showcase". Interesting pictures are at "Jane's: It's beyond All Doubt China Is Developing J-18 VTOL Stealth Fighter," *Errymath* (blog) (2014),

http://errymath.blogspot.com/2014/07/janes-its-beyond-all-doubt-china-is
.html#.VdsHLHi4kXo.

37. ONI Report, 21.
38. O'Rourke, "China Naval Modernization," 35. Chinese acquisition of the Tu-22 has been rumored/reported for several years, without result.
39. China's UAV programs were investigated at the 2014 Zhuhai air show by Col. Stephen Jones, USAF, an experienced UAV operator and unit commander. His observations are in the very sobering report "Red Swarm Rising: The Strategic Threat of Chinese Drones," which Jones wrote while he was a student at the U.S. National Defense University. Also see Arthur, "China Confirms CH-4 UCAV."
40. The best work on China's counterpiracy operations is being written by Erickson; in particular, see Erickson and Strange, *No Substitute for Experience*. A PLAN frigate commanding officer noted in a discussion with me in 2008 that his ship and embarked helicopter could data link; that capability is more generally noted in a Renmin Haijun article in July 2013. Also see Wood, "China Plays Helo Card"; and "New Navy Escort Fleet Leave for Gulf of Aden," *Xinhua*, 3 April 2015, http:// english.chinamil.com.cn/news-channels/china-military-news/2015–04/03/ content_6429098.htm.
41. ONI Report, 20–21.
42. My conversation with a PLAN frigate commanding officer.
43. Cole, "China's Carrier."
44. Construction of at least one additional carrier was announced in April 2015 in Clover, "Chinese Media Confirm Second Aircraft Carrier"; also see Tiezzi, "Chinese Admirals Spill the Beans." A report from the always interesting but not always reliable Kanwa, concludes that China will build ten carriers; see Blanchard, "China's First Aircraft Carrier."
45. Report in *Shanghai Morning Post*, 28 August 2014, cited in Minnick, "Chinese Carrier's Purported Air Wing."
46. A derogatory report of J-15 capabilities is reported in iMan, "Chinese Media Takes Aim." A more balanced view is in Reed, "How Effective Will China's Carrier-Based Fighters Be?" *Defensetech*, 25 April 2012, http://defensetech.org /2012/04/25/how-effective-will-chinas-carrier-based-fighters-be/. Film clips of J-15 operations from the *Liaoning* are at "J-15 Naval Multirole Fighter," *Errymath* (blog), February 2014, https://errymath.wordpress.com/2014/02/06/j-15-naval -multirole-fighter/.
47. My discussions at SOA headquarters, 5 May 2014; and Morris, "Taming the Five Dragons?" The uncertainties and unknowns pertaining to the SOA are addressed thoroughly in Jakobson, "China's Unpredictable Maritime Security Actors."
48. Glaser, "China's Maritime Actors."
49. The most prolific U.S. authority on China's new coast guard organizations is Ryan D. Martinson. For instance, see his "Here Comes China's Great White Fleet"; and "China's Second Navy." The 12,000-ton-displacement ship is reported in Yifei, "China to Launch 'World's Largest' Coastguard Patrol Vessel." Both Jianghu- and Jiangwei-class frigates, the latter armed with rapid-fire guns and ASW suites and able to hangar and operate helicopters, have been transferred; see Tate, "China Converting Old Frigates."

50. See the brief but comprehensive article by Erickson and Kennedy, "Tanmen Militia." Also see "Less Government Ships, More Fishing Boats Intruding into Japanese Waters Near Senkakus," *Sankei*, 10 September 2014, 30; and "Trends in Chinese Government and Other Vessels in the Waters Surrounding the Senkaku Islands, and Japan's Response," Ministry of Foreign Affairs of Japan, 7 August 2015, http://www.mofa.go.jp/region/page23e_000021.html.

51. Ruwitch, "Satellites and Seafood."

52. "Your Rules or Mine," *Economist*, 15 November 2014, http://www.economist.com/news/special-report/21631792-trade-depends-order-sea-keeping-it-far-straightforward-your-rules-or.

53. "Chinese Captain Forced by N. Korea to Admit Illegal Fishing," *Yonhap*, 24 September 2014, http://english.yonhapnews.co.kr/northkorea/2014/09/24/31/0401000000AEN20140924008700315F.html.

54. Quoted in Miles Yu, "Inside China: Armed Fishermen," *Washington Times*, 18 July 2012, cited in Kraska and Monti, "The Law of Naval Warfare," an excellent analysis on which my discussion is based.

55. Vu and Nguyen, "Vietnam, China Trade Accusations of Vessel-Ramming Near Oil Rig"; and van der Kley, "The China-Vietnam Standoff: Three Key Factors."

56. My 2008 conversation with a senior PLAN flag officer; my 2005 conversations with North Sea Fleet deputy chiefs of staff; but the best evidence of these improvements is the twenty successful PLAN deployments to the Gulf of Aden and beyond.

57. Badkar, "Country with the Largest Maritime Fleet."

58. Merrigan, "Chinese Ministry Plans to Consolidate Its Shipyards."

59. Scott, "China-Owned Ships."

60. See Gabe Collins' very interesting, if admittedly tentative, estimates in "How Much Do China's Warships Actually Cost?"

61. Erickson, "CMSI Conference."

62. Forsythe, "As China Prospers." Until this change in the personnel system, the longest an enlisted person could serve in the PLA was, nominally, seventeen years. The new system allows a decade longer than that. The cultural issue was explained to me by a senior U.S. Army officer who served two attaché tours in China: the problem would be a junior officer from a well-to-do urban family with a college degree accepting advice from a senior NCO from a rural village with no more than an eighth-grade education.

63. Erickson and Strange, *No Substitute for Experience*, n2.

64. Quoted in ONI Report, 27.

65. "PLA Made Great Changes in 2014: Part 1," *Ta Kung Pao* (Hong Kong), 29 December 2014, quoted in *China Military Online*, 30 December 2014, http://english.chinamil.com.cn/news-channels/china-military-news/2014-12/30/content_6289824_3.htm.

66. Ibid.

67. Ibid., 28.

68. Page and Wei, "Takedown of Generals"; and Gan, "Retired Generals."

69. A senior U.S. intelligence official once told me "if it is valuable in the PLA, it is for sale." Also see the report "CCP Military Brigades Fraud in Exercise," 4 October 2013, https://www.youtube.com/watch?v=S6w3hzwUfb0, which notes Xi Jinping's concern; "PLA to Regularize Management of Grass-Roots Units," *China Military Online*, 3 July 2015, http://eng.mod.gov.cn/TopNews/2015-07/03/content_4592869.htm; as well as McCauley, "President Xi Clears the Way"; "PLA Issues Regulation to Close Loopholes, End Regularities," *China Daily*, 6 July 2015, http://en.people.cn/n/2015/0706/c90786-8916020.html; and Chase et al., *China's Incomplete Military Transformation*. Especially damning is Clover, "China's Military Goes to War on Corruption"; and Blasko, "Corruption in China's Military."

70. Page, "In Pacific Drills, Navies Adjust;" "Chinese Navy Near Hawaii: First Time Participation in US Led RIMPAC Drills," RT News, 27 June 2015, reported PLAN participants as "missile destroyer Haikou, the missile frigate *Yueyang*, the supply ship *Qiandaohu* and the hospital ship *Daishan Dao*) with two helicopters on board, a commando and diving units—altogether 1,100 servicemen."

71. For instance, see "Singapore Navy Participates in Multilateral Maritime Exercise and Western Pacific Naval Symposium in China," *Channel News Asia*, 25 May 2015, http://www.channelnewsasia.com/news/singapore/singapore-china-complete/1871162.html; "China-US Task Forces Conduct Joint Anti-Piracy Drill in Gulf of Aden," *Xinhua*, 12 December 2014, http://en.people.cn/n/2014/1212/c90786-8822093.html; "Chinese, Russian Navies Will Further Cooperation and Partnership," *Jiefangjun Bao*, 26 May 2014; Parfitt, "Russia-China Clinch Tightens; Erdbrink and Buckley, "China and Iran to Conduct Joint Naval Exercises"; and "Chinese and Nigerian Navies Conduct First Anti-Piracy Joint Drill," *Jiefangjun Bao*, 29 May 2014, http://eng.mod.gov.cn/DefenseNews/2014–05/29/content_4512775.htm.

72. Successful completion of an evolution that the U.S. Navy has been unable to conduct routinely is reported in "China Navy Holds First Missile Combat Resupply Drill," Reuters, 2 July 2015, http://www.reuters.com/article/us-china-defence-drill-idUSKCN0PC19H20150702.

73. Chen and Du, "Advanced Passenger Ro-Ro Ship"; "China Launches Passenger RoRo Ship with Military Capability," *PLA Daily*, 10 August 2012, http://www.marinelink.com/news/passenger-military-launch346881.aspx; and "China Approves Plan for Civilian Ships to be Used by Military," Reuters, 17 June 2015, http://in.reuters.com/article/2015/06/18/china-defence-shipping-idINKBN0OY08U20150618.

74. The 2013 edition of *Science of Campaigns* is not available in English; it is available at Zhang Yuian, et al., eds., *Science of Campaigns* (Beijing: National Defense University Press, 2016); the defense white papers are at http://eng.mod.gov.cn/Database/WhitePapers/index.htm, and a discussion of the OMTE is in Blasko, *Chinese Army Today*, 2nd ed., 176 ff.

75. "Learn How to Fight Battles in Exercise Analysis of PLA's Training Reform from Military Exercises in 2009 (II)," *Jiefangjun Bao*, 15 December 2009, translated at http://news.everychina.com/wz40086c/learn_how_to_fight_battles_in _exercise_analysis_of_pla_s_training_reform_from_military_exercises_in _2009_ii.html. Also see a version of this report (same title) in *People's Daily*, 14 December 2009, http://eng.chinamil.com.cn/news-channels/china-military -news/2009-12/14/content_4095381.htm.

76. Cole, "China's Navy Prepares," 24–27. Also see Blasko, *Chinese Army Today*, 266n31.

77. Takahashi, "Japan Mulling Plans," 5.

78. This deployment is described in Sharman, "Closing the Information Deficit," n64–69. A version of this paper was published as "China Moves Out: Stepping Stones Toward a New Maritime Strategy," *China Strategic Perspectives* 9 (Washington, D.C.: NDU Press, 2015), http://www.andrewerickson.com/2015/04/ china-moves-out-stepping-stones-toward-a-new-maritime-strategy/ (accessed 18 July 2015)." The PLAN announcement is in "Chinese Navy Normalizes Open-Sea Training," *China Military Online*, 12 December 2014, http://www.ecns.cn /military/2012/12-13/40350.shtml.

79. "China Sails through First Island Chain," *China Daily*, 2 August 2013, http:// en.people.cn/90786/8350100.html.

80. "PRC Weekly Interviews PLA South Sea Fleet Commander on 'Jidong-5,'" *Laowang Dongfang Zhoukan*, 7 November 2013, discussed in Berglund, "'Maneuver-5' Exercise"; this report is described in Berglund, "'Maneuver-5' Exercise."

81. "Why PLA Organizes Free Air-Combat Confrontation Drill," *China Military Online*, 15 September 2014, http://english.chinamil.com.cn/news-channels/ china-military-news/2014-09/15/content_6138320.htm, and "Three Fleets of PLAN Sail to Western Pacific for Drill," *China Military Online*, 5 December 2014, http://eng.chinamil.com.cn/news-channels/china-military-news/2014-12/05 /content_6257336.htm.

82. Sharman, "China Moves Out," 30, notes that the PLAN categorizes the Indian Ocean as the "far seas." The deployment is described in "China's Navy Extends Its Combat Reach to the Indian Ocean," U.S.-China Economic and Security Review Commission Staff Report, 14 March 2014, http://origin.www.uscc.gov/sites/ default/files/Research/Staff%20Report_China's%20Navy%20Extends%20 its%20Combat%20Reach%20to%20the%20Indian%20Ocean.pdf.

83. Yang Yujun, quoted in "Defense Ministry's Regular Press Conference on Jan. 29, 2015," http://english.chinamil.com.cn/news-channels/china-military-news /2015-01/29/content_6332211.htm.

84. I am grateful to Dennis J. Blasko for bringing these exercise reports to my attention: "PLA's ECM and SAF Troops Join Naval Drill in Yellow Sea," China. mil, 3 July 2015, http://english.chinamil.com.cn/news-channels/china-military -news/2015-07/03/content_6570397.htm.

85. Zhao, "Navy Stages Live-Ammo Drill."

86. I am grateful to Dennis J. Blasko for bringing these exercise reports to my attention: "PLA's ECM and SAF Troops Join Naval Drill in Yellow Sea," China .mil, 03 July 2015, http://english.chinamil.com.cn/news-channels/china -military-news/2015–07/03/content_6570397.htm; Zhao, "Navy Stages Live -Ammo Drill"; "Navy Tests Armaments in East China Sea," *Xinhua*, 27 August 2015, http://news.xinhuanet.com/english/2015-08/27/c_134562379.htm.

87. Fisher and Hardy, "China Practices Taiwan Invasion."

88. For instance, see "China Conducts Air, Sea Drills in South China Sea," Reuters, 28 July 2015, http://www.reuters.com/article/2015/07/28/us-southchinasea -china-military-idUSKCN0Q218S20150728.

89. "Chinese, Russian Navies Complete 9-Day Joint Exercise, Hold Parade," *China Daily*, 29 August 2015, http://eng.mod.gov.cn/MilitaryExercises/2015-08/29/ content_4616513.htm; and Page and Lubold, "Chinese Navy Ships Come to within 12 Nautical Miles of U.S. Coast."

90. "China, Russia Reported to Build Huge Seaport in North Asia," RT.com, 11 November 2014, http://www.rt.com/business/186900-russia-china-huge-port/. A port on the Sea of Japan has long been discussed between Russia and Japan.

91. Various sources for these numbers are given in "2014 Report to Congress of the U.S.-China Economic and Security Review Commission."

92. *China's Military Strategy*, at Ministry of National Defense of the People's Republic of China Web site, http://eng.mod.gov.cn/Database/WhitePapers/2014.htm; Peng and Yao, *Science of Military Strategy* (2013).

93. China's defense white papers, 1995–2014, are available at http://eng.mod.gov.cn/ Database/WhitePapers/index.htm.

94. This white paper will be discussed at length in chapter 3; see CCTV, http:// www.cctv-america.com/2015/05/26/full-text-chinas-military-strategy-white -paper.

95. Mao Zedong and Deng Xiaoping are quoted in Cole, *Great Wall at Sea*, 172, 14; Jiang Zemin is quoted in Cha Chun-ming, "Chinese Navy Heads toward Modernization." Hu Jintao is quoted in "Chinese President Meets Deputies for Military Meetings," *Xinhua*, 7 December 2011, http://news.xinhuanet.com /english/china/2011-12/06/c_131291648.htm.

96. Discussed in Mulvenon, "Chairman Hu and the PLA's 'New Historic Missions.'"

97. "The China Dream on the Threshold of the Dream of a Strong Military," quoted in Cohen, "China Examines Military Strategy."

98. The Libyan NEO is described in Collins and Erickson, "Implications of China's Military Evacuation"; the Libyan operation is discussed in Koh, "Westward Ho"; the Yemen operation is discussed in Areddy, "China Evacuates Citizens"; and Panda, "Implications of China's Military Evacuation."

99. Duchâtel and Gill, "Overseas Citizen Protection." This report also notes that an estimated 60 million Chinese citizens were expected to travel abroad in 2012.

100. Discussed in Duchâtel, Brauner, and Zhou, "Protecting China's Overseas Interests," iv.
101. See "Top Ten Largest Merchant Shipping Fleets," Maps of the World, http://www.mapsofworld.com/world-top-ten/largest-merchant-shipping-fleets.html. No matter what the source and categorization, China ranks near the top in the size of its merchant fleet.
102. Data in these two paragraphs are from "Review of Maritime Transport, 2014," UN Conference on Trade and Development, Geneva, 2015, http://unctadstat.unctad.org/CountryProfile/MaritimeProfile/en-GB/156/index.html; and Zhao, "FTZ to Allow Foreign Private Players in Shipping Industry."
103. My discussion with U.S. transportation analyst, Beijing, May 2014.
104. Erickson and Collins, "Beijing's Energy Security Strategy," 665.
105. "Oil Transportation," PetroStrategies Inc., 16 June 2015, http://www.petrostrategies.org/Learning_Center/oil_transportation.htm. No longer online; accessed 20 July 2015.
106. Objective exercise reports are difficult to find in the open literature, but one instance is in Xia Hongping, Wei Bing, and Shi Binxin, "Standardization, an Urgent Issue for 'System of Systems' Operations," 2. A U.S. view of PLAN weaknesses is at Cavas, "China's Navy Makes Strides."
107. "China's National Defense in 2004," at Ministry of National Defense of the People's Republic of China Web site, http://eng.mod.gov.cn/Database/White Papers/2004.htm.
108. Hu and Xu are quoted in Cole, "Reflections on China's Maritime Strategy," 2 (Hu) and n12 (Xu).
109. The author participated in the meeting with the MR commander.
110. Cole, "Reflections on China's Maritime Strategy," n12.
111. Anti-access / area denial apparently is not discussed, per se, in Chinese literature, although Shi Xiaoqin advocates the PLAN developing "the capacity to deny access to the [U.S.] navy to China's sea territory"; Shi, "Boundaries and Directions of China's Sea Power," 137. The PLA's "active strategic counterattacks on exterior lines"—or "counterintervention"—approximates that operational policy and is discussed in Wishik, "An Anti-Access Approximation." Major General Peng Guangqian, quoted in Wishik, "An Anti-Access Approximation," 3; and in McDevitt, "The PLA Navy Anti-Access Role," 3.
112. See Erickson and Liff, "China's Military Spending Swells."
113. Quoted in Mattis, "Army Day Coverage Stresses Continuity."

Chapter 3. Maritime Strategy

1. Quoted in Steinberg and O'Hanlon, *Strategic Reassurance and Resolve*, 38.
2. Huiyun Feng, quoted in ibid., 38–39.
3. My conversations with Cohen and Johnston, Washington, D.C., April 2004.
4. Much of this discussion appeared in Cole, "Island Chains and Naval Classics."

5. Discussed in Fitzsimmons, "Evaluating the Masters of Strategy." In addition, of course, Admiral Horatio Nelson reportedly said, "nothing is sure in a sea fight."

6. See Shu, *Mao's Military Romanticism*; Ryan, Finkelstein, and McDevitt, *Chinese Warfighting*; Peng and Yao, *Science of Military Strategy*; and O'Dowd, *China's Military Strategy*.

7. Quoted in Watson, "Evolution of Soviet Naval Strategy," 113–17.

8. Takeda, "China's Rise as a Maritime Power;" and Zhao, Hynes, and He, "Blue Growth in the Middle Kingdom."

9. See Balile, "Tanzania and China Sign Port Development Package"; and "Bagamoyo Sez Master Plan," https://mpoverello.files.wordpress.com/2014/07/bagamoyosez_zps9cd0561d.png. Several reports indicate that the initial 2014 start date was delayed; see, for instance, "Tanzania Says Construction of China-Funded Port to Start in 2015," Reuters, 27 October 2014, http://www.reuters.com/article/2014/10/27/tanzania-port-idUSL5N0SM1QT20141027. There is an even more problematic report of China building a "base" in Namibia; "Are the Chinese Seeking a Second Africa 'Military Base' in Namibia? Influential Paper Reports Top Level Talks," *Mail & Guardian Africa*, 13 December 2014, http://mgafrica.com/article/2015-12-09-are-the-chinese-seeking-a-second-military-base-in-africa/.

10. The subject of PLAN bases is examined in Yung and Rustici, "'Not an Idea We Have to Shun.'" However, China's primary port-expansion project in Sri Lanka has been suspended, due in part to cost underestimates and in part to the ouster of the pro-China president, Mahinda Rajapaksa.

11. Wylie, *Military Strategy*, 33.

12. "Djibouti Wants to Reinforce Military Cooperation with China," *Shabelle Media Network* (Mogadishu), 28 February 2014, http://allafrica.com/stories/201403010068.html.

13. "Greece Sells Largest Port, Piraeus, to Chinese Company" (8 April 2016), at: https://www.rt.com/business/338949-greece-china-port-sale/. This is a lease, not a sale, and took several years of negotiation.

14. Zhou, "Scientist Outlines Five Challenges."

15. Anderlini, "China and Russia Vow to Build Naval Cooperation."

16. U.S. Energy Information Administration, "China"; and Durden, "Where Does China Import Its Energy From?"

17. ZYH and AEF, "Chinese Think Tank."

18. Su, Wu, and Zhu, "China's Maritime Security Challenges and Opportunities."

19. Discussed in detail in Fravel and Twomey, "Projecting Strategy."

20. See the excellent, thorough work by Erickson, *Chinese Anti-Ship Ballistic Missile*.

21. Quoted in Cole, *Asian Maritime Strategies*, 106.

22. The obsolescence of Mahan's logic is addressed in Rubel, "Navies and Economic Prosperity," 2–6.

23. Hartnett, "Father of the Modern Chinese Navy."

24. *China's National Defense in 2010*, at Ministry of National Defense of the People's Republic of China Web site, http://eng.mod.gov.cn/Database/WhitePapers/2010.htm.

25. Ibid.
26. "China Takes a Proactive and Open Attitude Toward International Escort Cooperation," *Xinhua*, 31 March 2011, http://news.xinhuanet.com/english2010/china /2011-03/31/c_13806943.htm.
27. Quoted in Jakobson, "PLA and Maritime Security Actors," 300.
28. "Report of the Secretary-General on the Situation with Respect to Piracy and Armed Robbery at Sea Off the Coast of Somalia," UN Security Council Report S/2015/776, 12 October 2015, http://www.un.org/en/ga/search/view_doc.asp ?symbol=S/2015/776. Also see Erickson and Strange, "China's Global Maritime Presence."
29. "China's Navy Sails onto the World Stage," *Xinhua*, 21 April 2009.
30. 2015 defense white paper, Section VII, http://www.china.org.cn/english/features /book/194476.htm.
31. See, for instance, Fei Shiting and Chen Xiaojing, "Enrich and Strengthen the Nation through Maritime Development—PLA Deputies to the NPC Call for Introducing a Maritime Strategy," *Jiefangjun Bao*, 9 March 2012, 7, cited in Cole, "Reflections on China's Maritime Strategy"; Rear Admiral Yin Zhou's statement is in "China's Maritime Strategy Being Tested Amid South China Sea Disputes," *Beijing Caijing*, 24 October 2011, http://english.caijing.com.cn/2011-10-24/ 110914257.html; and Major General Luo Yuan is quoted in Hsiao, "Military Delegates Call for National Maritime Strategy." The degree of policymaking incoherence in Beijing was indicated in a July 2011 speech by Major General Zhu Chenghu, reported at huanqui.com (no longer available online), who called for a South China Sea strategy "where the lead agency is the State Oceanic Administration with input from the PLA, MFA, PSB, Ministries of Agriculture, Transportation, Defense, Customs, and coastal provincial governments."
32. The white papers are found at the Ministry of National Defense of the People's Republic of China Web site, http://eng.mod.gov.cn/Database/WhitePapers/ index.htm.
33. I am indebted to Dr. Nan Li, of the U.S. Naval War College's China Maritime Studies Institute, and to Dr. Thomas Bickford, of the Center for Naval Analyses, for this discussion.
34. See Fravel, "China's New Military Strategy."
35. The repeated direction about "preparation for military struggle" and training for "real combat" will strongly remind Cold War–era U.S. naval officers about that time's mantra to prepare for a "come-as-you-are war" that would begin with a Soviet surprise attack.
36. See Michael A. McDevitt, quoted in Parameswaran, "Will China Have a Mini-US Navy by 2020?"
37. This discussion (and quotes) are from China's 2015 military strategy; also see Zhang and Cao, "Promote the Transformation of Naval Strategy."
38. Ibid. Also see Li and Ma, "The Complexity of the Maritime Military Struggle."
39. Wang and Zhang, "Network Planned to Cope with Sea Disasters."
40. Finkelstein, "China's National Military Strategy," http://www.strategicstudies institute.army.mil/pdffiles/PUB784.pdf, 87–89.

41. Discussed in Mulvenon, "Chairman Hu."
42. Martinson, "A Salt Water Perspective."
43. Li's comment are in his March 2015 "Report on the Work of the Government," *Xinhua*, 16 March 2015, http://news.xinhuanet.com/english/2015-03/16/c_134071415.htm.
44. The "Full Text of PRC National Security Law" is at *Xinhua*, 1 July 2015, http://chinalawtranslate.com/nsld2/?lang=en.
45. "National Ocean Policy of China," in Cole, "Reflections on China's Maritime Strategy."
46. "White Paper on National Ocean Policy," Information Office of the State Council, 77–78, http://ioc-unesco.org/images/stories/LawoftheSea/Documents/National OceanPolicy/nop.china.pdf.
47. This discussion is based on Cole, *Asian Maritime Strategies*, 92–94.
48. Ibid., 93–94; and Zhao, Hynes, and He, "Blue Growth in the Middle Kingdom."
49. See "Announcement of the Aircraft Identification Rules for the East China Sea Air Defense Identification Zone of the PRC," *Xinhua*, 23 November 2013, http://news.xinhuanet.com/english/china/2013-11/23/c_132911634.htm. Also see Rinehart and Elias, "China's Air Defense Identification Zone." The United States declared the first ADIZ, in 1950, as a defensive move against possible USSR attack.
50. Philipp, "China Claims Airspace"; and McCurry, "China Warns U.S. Plane."
51. See, for instance, Steve Herman, "Malaysian Tanker Hijacked on South China Sea," Voice of America, 16 July 2014, http://www.voanews.com/content/malaysia-oil-tanker-latest-target-of-south-china-sea-pirates/1958584.html; and McCauley, "Most Dangerous Waters in the World." The decrease in piracy incidents in Asia is documented in "UNOSAT Report on Global Piracy," 25, https://unosat.web.cern.ch/unosat/unitar/publications/UNITAR_UNOSAT_Piracy_1995-2013.pdf.
52. "SE Asia Tanker Hijacks Rose in 2014 Despite Global Drop in Sea Piracy, IMB Report Reveals," *ICC Commercial Crime Services*, 14 January 2015, http://www.iccwbo.org/News/Articles/2015/SE-Asia-tanker-hijacks-rose-in-2014-despite-global-drop-in-sea-piracy,-IMB-report-reveals/; and Graham, "Maritime Security and Threats to Energy Transportation," 25.
53. My discussions with senior PLA officers and U.S. analysts, Beijing and Shanghai, May and October 2014.
54. Tunsjo, *Security and Profit in China's Energy Sector*, 122.
55. Hai Tao, "The Chinese Navy Has a Long Way to Go to Get to the Far Seas," *Guoji Xianqu Daobao* (Beijing), quoted in Givens, "Fleshing Out the Third Plenum," 13.
56. Statement is found at the Ministry of Foreign Affairs Web site, "Foreign Ministry Spokesperson Hua Chunying's Regular Press Conference on April 27, 2016," http://www.fmprc.gov.cn/mfa_eng/xwfw_665399/s2510_665401/t1358994.shtml.
57. Only six other nations share China's excessive maritime claims: Bangladesh, India, Iran, Myanmar, North Korea, and Pakistan. See Odom, "Freedom of the 'Far Seas,'" n23.
58. My discussion with Dennis J. Blasko, Internet, September 2015. Also see Blasko's "An Analysis of China's 2011 Defense Budget."

59. The applicable section of the 2015 military strategy white paper is at http://eng .mod.gov.cn/Database/WhitePapers/2015-05/26/content_4586708.htm; also see Zhao and Zhang, "China Pledges to Protect Maritime Sovereignty"; and Wong, "China to Expand Naval Operations."

60. Shi, "Boundaries and Directions of China's Seapower."

61. My discussions at SOA headquarters, Beijing, May 2013; my conversations with Capt. Bernard Moreland, USCGR (Ret.), former USCG representative in Beijing, January 2013; and my conversation with the director of MOFA's Bureau of Boundary and Maritime Affairs, Beijing, December 2012. For a useful explanation of China's pre-reorganization coast guard organizations, see Goldstein, *Five Dragons Stirring up the Sea*. Nine such organizations are noted in Fei and Chen, "Enrich and Strengthen the Nation."

62. The best work on the geographical elements in China's maritime strategy remains that by Nan Li of the U.S. Naval War College's China Maritime Studies Institute. See his "The Evolution of China's Naval Strategy and Capabilities."

63. "The PLA Navy: New Capabilities and Missions for the 21st Century," U.S. Office of Naval Intelligence (2015), cited in Erickson, "Revelations on China's Maritime Modernization."

64. Quoted in Cole, *Asian Maritime Strategies*, 12.

65. I was told in an interview with a senior Taiwan government official in 2004 that approximately 2 million Taiwanese were on the mainland as tourists or business people on any given day; Hu and Lo, "Taiwan, China Sign Taxation, Flight Safety Pacts."

66. Xi is cited in Glaser and Vitello, "Xi Jinping's Great Game"; also see Xi's statement warning against "independence forces" in Zhao, "Stay Vigilant over Taiwan Separatists"; and Tiezzi, "Taiwan Will Have a Female President in 2016."

67. Quoted in Kato, "U.S. Commander Says China Aims."

68. Cole, "China's Maritime Strategy," 296.

69. Deng is quoted in Lewis and Xue, "China's Search for a Modern Air Force," 10.

70. "Core interests" are explained in Feng, "What Are China's Core Interests?"

Chapter 4. Economy

1. "The Outlook for Energy: A View to 2040," ExxonMobile, 2015, http://cdn .exxonmobil.com/~/media/global/files/outlook-for-energy/em-2015-energy -outlook-chinese.pdf.

2. Lee, "China's Geostrategic Search for Oil," 80–82. At least twenty-seven senior officials who served both in the civilian government and one of the energy SOEs are in the China Vitae Database, http://www.chinavitae.com/research/.

3. "China Issues Guideline to Deepen SOE Reforms," *Xinhua*, 13 September 2015, http://news.xinhuanet.com/english/2015-09/13/c_134620039.htm.

4. "Xi Eyes Future of NE China, Stresses Role of SOEs," *Xinhua*, 18 July 2015, http:// news.xinhuanet.com/english/2015-07/19/c_134424759.htm; and "SOE Profits Nosedive," *Xinhua*, 19 August 2015, http://news.xinhuanet.com/english/2015 -08/19/c_134534699.htm.

5. Paul Welizkin, "With China in the Lead, Asia Pacific Poised to be Richest Region."
6. Xi's visits are listed on the Chinese Ministry of Foreign Affairs Web site, http://www.fmprc.gov.cn/mfa_eng/.
7. LLD and AEF, "Chinese Official Acknowledges the Economic Data Fraud." In China's defense, the mutability of economic data in general is discussed in Pettis, "What Multiple Should We Give China's GDP Growth?"
8. Data are from "China GDP Annual Growth Rate," *Trading Economics*, 1 July 2015, http://www.tradingeconomics.com/china/gdp-growth-annual. On data reliability: my discussions with Lucian Pye and a senior Chinese official, Washington, D.C., April 1994. Also see Schurtenberger, "Reassessing China's Economic Growth Potential"; and Johnson, "Capital Economics Claims." Also see Kuo, "Shortcomings of Electricity; and Xu, "'New Normal' and the Future of China's Economy."
9. Li, *Report on the Work of the Government.*
10. Xu, "'New Normal' and the Future of China's Economy."
11. "Fishing Competition in the South China Sea," Center for Strategic and International Studies, *cogitAsia* (blog), 22 August 2014, http://cogitasia.com/fishing-competition-in-the-south-china-sea/.
12. Quoted in TGS and AEF, "Downward Pressure Continues and Greater Difficulties Lie Ahead."
13. Schurtenberger, "Reassessing China's Economic Growth Potential," 10.
14. Chen, "China's Dangerous Debt."
15. Wei, "China Moves to Devalue Yuan."
16. Yu, "China Yuan Moving up the World Currency Ranks"; and Aitken, "Chinese RMB Consolidates."
17. For instance, see Li, "IMF Official Says Yuan No Longer Undervalued"; Frankel, "Chinese Currency Manipulation Not a Problem"; and especially Chin, "China in a Changing Global Monetary System" (cited with author's permission).
18. Quoted in Schurtenberger, "Reassessing China's Economic Growth Potential," 9.
19. China's "Gini coefficient," which measures a nation's economic inequality, is .61, with 0.0 indicating practically no inequality and 1.0 indicating the most inequality. This discussion draws on Raustiala and Sprigman, "Fake It till You Make It," who make an interesting but ultimately unconvincing argument that lack of innovation in China is not a problem.
20. Hornby, "Wanted List Reveals Nature of Chinese Corruption."
21. Quoted in Leung, "Xi's Corruption Crackdown." Senior U.S. officers and civilian officials have described PLA corruption to me in graphic detail.
22. Keliher and Wu, "How to Discipline 90 Million People."
23. Waldmeir and Wildau, "China Graft Probe Uncovers Falsified Revenues."
24. RWZ and AEF, "CCDI Identified Three Key 'Black Holes.'"
25. Demick, "Judging China's One-Child Policy."
26. Different estimates of prevented births range from 200,000 to 400,000, as discussed in Oleson, "Experts Challenge China's 1-Child Policy Claim." Also see Denyer, "One Child Is Enough." The new policy is explained in Qing, "Relaxing

China's One-Child Policy." The "old before rich" theory is examined in Shobert, "China Will Get Old"; the counter argument is in Luo, "China Will Get Rich."

27. Kuhn, "One County Provides Preview," gives 2025 as the date of peak population; also see U.S. Census Bureau, "China's Population to Peak."

28. These numbers are from Beardson, *Stumbling Giant*, 201. Also see "China Says Its Gender Imbalance 'Most Serious' in the World," Reuters, 21 January 2015, http://uk.reuters.com/article/2015/01/21/uk-china-onechild-idUKKBN0KU 0V720150121.

29. "Going Out," *Economist*, 8 November 2014, http://www.economist.com/news /china/21631114-more-outflows-going-out.

30. Phoenix Weekly, "Chinese Overseas Investment Hindered by Lack of Experience, Political Opposition in Host Countries."

31. Quoted in Kynge and Oliver, "Li Keqiang Pushes for China-Europe Investment Treaty."

32. Discussed in Stout, "Is Xi Jinping's 'Chinese Dream' a Fantasy?"

33. Discussed in Carlson, "The World According to Xi Jinping"; and Kuhn, "Xi Jinping's Dream."

34. Sanusi, "Africa Must Get Real about Chinese Ties"; also see Okeowo, "China in Africa."

35. Bello, "The Dragon and the Gringo."

36. Wezeman and Wezeman, "Trends in International Arms Transfers, 2014."

37. The Eleventh Five-Year Plan, http://www.gov.cn/english/special/115y_index .htm; the 2020 estimate is at KPMG, *China Outlook 2015*, http://www.kpmg .com/ES/es/Internacionalizacion-KPMG/Documents/China-Outlook-2015.pdf. Also see Zhang, "China's Global Resources Drive." See Zhong, "Key Pact Sealed with Australia"; Pearson, "China Breaks India Monopoly; and Mitchell, "China Rail Group."

38. Burke, "India and China Announce Trade Deals"; Hornby and Schipani, "China Tilts towards Liberal Latin American Economies"; Bran, "China Pledges $46 Billion for Pakistan"; and especially Berthelsen, "Trouble Could Be Brewing."

39. See Watson, Mohr, and Roett, "Enter the Dragon?" regarding China's announced Latin American investments, which fell victim to the extreme deterioration of Venezuela's economy but even more so to the geographical proximity of the United States. Chinese concerns about Pakistan's financial and political stability and the technical difficulties of some of the proposed projects are discussed in Kiani, "6,600MW Put on Back Burner."

40. "Xi: A New Normal for China's Economy Emerges," *Xinhua*, 9 November 2014, http://news.xinhuanet.com/english/china/2014-11/09/c_133776047.htm.

41. Freeman, "Fear and Loathing in China's New Economic Normal." Some of the threats confronting Xi's "new normal" are addressed in Cai, "China's Evolving Overseas Interests."

42. The National Development and Reform Commission announced: "More Reform Measures to be Introduced," *China Youth Daily*, 18 May 2015, http://finance .youth.cn/finance_gdxw/201505/t20150518_6640811.htm.

43. Nachemson expresses this view in "China Seen as Launching Plan." The Asia Development Bank estimate is in Ding, Lam, and Peiris, "Future of Asia's Finance."
44. Wyne, "American World Order."
45. Kato, "AIIB on Track."
46. Sun, "China and the Changing Asian Infrastructure Bank." The number of AIIB members was "nearly sixty" as of August 2015, according to Dollar, "China's Rise as a Regional and Global Power." The bank's president, Jin Liqun, announced in September 2015 that "up to twenty additional countries" wanted to join the AIIB"; quoted in Watts, "Up to 20 Countries Waiting."
47. Quoted in "Three Nations Absent as China Launches W. Bank Rival in Asia," Reuters, 24 October 2014, http://finance.yahoo.com/news/three-major-nations-absent-china-040036987.html; and Ashraf, "AIIB."
48. Desai and Vreeland, "What the New Bank of BRICS Is All About."
49. "AIIB Announces First Loans in Xi Push for Influence," Bloomberg, 24 June 2016, http://www.bloomberg.com/news/articles/2016-06-24/china-led-aiib-announces-first-loans-in-xi-push-for-influence.
50. Gabuev, "Another BRIC(S) in the Great Wall."
51. Liang, "India's Accession."
52. Horta, "Brazil-China Relations."
53. See Dollar, "China's Rise as a Regional and Global Power."
54. Quoted in Zenn, "Future Scenarios on the New Silk Road."
55. This announcement has yet to be fulfilled; see Knowler, "Investment Floods into China's One Belt, One Road Strategy."
56. This mammoth project is clearly described in Swaine, "Chinese Views and Commentary on the 'One Belt, One Road' initiative."
57. "Vision and Actions on Jointly Building Silk Road Economic Belt and 21st Century Maritime Silk Road," National Development Reform Commission (Beijing, March 2015), http://en.ndrc.gov.cn/newsrelease/201503/t20150330_669367.html.
58. See "Prospects and Challenges on China's 'One Belt, One Road': A Risk Assessment Report," *Economist* (2015), http://www.eiu.com/public/topical_report.aspx?campaignid=OneBeltOneRoad.
59. Freeman, "China and the Economic Integration of Europe and Asia."
60. Wang, "Rethinking the 'Strategic Crossroads.'"
61. See "Chinese President Proposes Asia-Pacific Dream," *Xinhua*, 10 November 2014, http://www.2014apecceosummit.com/apec/news1/1721.jhtml.
62. Samaranayake, "The Long Littoral Project," 1–3.
63. *China's Military Strategy*, at Ministry of National Defense of the People's Republic of China Web site, http://eng.mod.gov.cn/Database/WhitePapers/2014.htm.
64. Gowen, "Troops Face Off at India-China Border."
65. The quotes in this paragraph are from Zhang and Cao, "Promote the Transformation of Naval Strategy"; also see Li and Ma, "The Complexity of the Maritime Military Struggle."
66. Ansari, "Pakistan to Buy 8 Submarines." According to SIPRI, China ranks among the world's top ten arms exporters, with 5 percent of total arms sales, but this

does not compare with the United States' 31 percent share. "Recent Trends in Arms Sales," SIPRI (Stockholm, 2015), http://www.sipri.org/research/armaments /transfers/measuring/copy_of_at-images/top-10-arms-exporters_2010-14 /image.

67. Li, "Major Challenges Facing China's Economy in 2015." Also see Johnson et al., *Decoding China's Emerging 'Great Power' Strategy*.

68. Wong, "China Sees Long Road."

69. Morrison, *China's Economic Rise*.

70. Ibid.

71. World Bank, "China Overview," in Wang, et al., "Wage Growth, Landholding, and Mechanization in Chinese Agriculture."

72. James Zimmerman presents an American Chamber of Commerce in China view; see Zimmerman, "Beijing's Negative Stance on Investment."

73. Youwei, "The End of Reform in China."

74. Former Chinese vice minister of finance Jin Liqun has been appointed as first AIIB president, as reported in Li, "AIIB Appoints Jin Liqun as Its First President." Jin claimed that the bank will not be a "Chinese diplomatic vehicle" but will be independent of the government's influence. This statement is problematic at best, given the AIIB's location in Beijing's financial district and the inevitable diplomatic weight accruing to such a potentially powerful global financial institution. See "China Nominates Jin Liqun AIIB's President-Designate," *China Daily*, 6 July 2015, http://www.chinadaily.com.cn/business/2015-07/06/content_2119 2038.htm. Also see Clemens, "Maritime Silk Road and the PLA."

75. Just as Mahan's theories of historically climactic sea battles came to naught, so the economic basis of his 1890 arguments, vitiated by the rapid spread of rail networks throughout much of the Western world, would be further invalidated by Chinese economic dominance over the vast Eurasian island. Interestingly, railroad construction continues to play a major role in OBOR continental economic development plans; see, for instance, Beauchamp, "Rolling Out the New Silk Road"; Kuo and Timmins, "China Is Building a $46 Billion Railroad"; and Liu, "Xi Jinping and Recep Tayyip Erdoğan."

Chapter 5. Energy Security

1. Noel, "Asia's Energy Supply," 203.

2. "International Energy Outlook 2014," U.S. Energy Information Administration, http://www.eia.gov/forecasts/ieo/.

3. Fracking is the process of drilling down into the earth and directing a high-pressure water mixture of water, sand, and chemicals at the rock to release the gas inside, which flows out to the head of the well. See Shukman, "What Is Fracking?" The revolutionary possibilities of mining methane hydrates are discussed in Parry, *Super Highway*, who also examines some little-discussed energy sources, such as sea bottom electrical grids and sea surface solar power generation, 158–65.

4. Collins and Erickson, "China Peak Oil."

5. Street, "China's National Effort in Oil," may be an extreme view; the U.S. Energy Information Agency (EIA) estimates are at "EIA/ARI World Shale Gas and Shale Oil Resource Assessment," Advanced Resources International, June 2013, http://www.adv-res.com/pdf/A_EIA_ARI_2013%20World%20Shale%20Gas%20and%20Shale%20Oil%20Resource%20Assessment.pdf, 6. Another very valuable source of global energy information is the Paris-based International Energy Agency.

6. Burman, "Giant Appetite," citing "World Bureau of Metal Statistics," provides a chart of China's share of global resources, which is startling for a wide range of minerals and other products, from aluminum (54 percent of the world total) to barley (5 percent).

7. *China's Military Strategy*, at Ministry of National Defense of the People's Republic of China Web site, http://eng.mod.gov.cn/Database/WhitePapers/2014.htm.

8. The data in this paragraph comes from Zhang and Cao, "Promote the Transformation of Naval Strategy."

9. Boersama and Foley, *The Greenland Gold Rush*; and Wang, "China Going out 2.0."

10. The best work on the energy aspects of this policy is Tunsjo, *Security and Profit in China's Energy Policy*; and Nash, "China's 'Going Out' Strategy." Xi is quoted in "How China Plans to Clean up Its Energy Act," *World Review*, 9 February 2015, http://www.worldreview.info/content/how-china-plans-clean-its-energy-act.

11. "How China Plans to Clean up Its Energy Act." Also see Tiezzi, "In New Plan."

12. Discussed in Downs, "Mission Mostly Accomplished."

13. "China Overview," EIA Beta, last updated 14 May 2015, http://www.eia.gov/beta/international/analysis.cfm?iso=CHN.

14. Ibid. The EIA reported other energy sources: Hydroelectric, 8 percent; Natural Gas, 5 percent; Nuclear, 1 percent; and "Other Renewables," 1 percent; "China Overview," "International Energy Statistics," *EIA: International Energy Statistics*. Another usually reliable source, the World Nuclear Association, estimated, also in 2014, that coal provided 79 percent of China's energy; see "Nuclear Power in China," World Nuclear Association, October 2014, http://www.world-nuclear.org/info/Country-Profiles/Countries-A-F/China—Nuclear-Power/. The 10 percent for natural gas in 2020 is in Huang, "Closer Look."

15. "Gas Infrastructure of China," Map 5.3.2 in *Energy Supply Security 2014*, Part 3, Ch. 5, IEA (2014), 530, https://www.iea.org/media/freepublications/security/EnergySupplySecurity2014_China.pdf.

16. "China Consumes Nearly as Much Coal as the Rest of the World Combined," EIA (29 January 2013), http://www.eia.gov/todayinenergy/detail.cfm?id=9751. Beijing claimed that coal usage had been reduced to 64.5 percent of total energy consumption; see U.S. Energy Information Administration, "China," 2.

17. Ibid.; Gardiner, "Asia Pushes Hard for Clean Energy"; and Currier, "China and the Global Surge for Resources," 165–166.

18. Discussed in Cole, *Sea Lanes and Pipelines*, 36.

19. Discussed in Cole, *Great Wall at Sea*, 45.
20. U.S. Energy Information Administration, "China," 15.
21. Ibid., 6.
22. Gordon, Sautin, and Tao, "China's Oil Future."
23. Cole, *Great Wall at Sea*, 47.
24. U.S. Energy Information Administration, "China."
25. Sabonis-Helf, "Russia and Energy Markets," 18, as of 2013; energy sales' limitations as a strategic linkage between Russia and China are addressed in Jaffe, Medlock, and O'Sullivan, "China's Energy Hedging Strategy."
26. U.S. Energy Information Administration, "China."
27. See, for instance, ibid.; and Wei, "Chinese Firms Turn to Foreign Investors to Borrow."
28. "Yacheng 13-1 Gas Field," *A Barrel Full*, accessed 26 September 2015, http://abarrelfull.wikidot.com/yacheng-13-1-gas-field.
29. U.S. Energy Information Administration, "South China Sea." The considerable range of "possible" reserves from the EIA demonstrates how uncertain the energy reserves in the South China Sea are and hence how uncertain national interests may actually be.
30. Ibid.
31. These figures are in ibid.
32. Graham, "Energy Competition in the South China Sea."
33. Peng, "China Discovers Major Natural Gas Field"; and "China Finds Sizable Natural Gas Field in South China Sea," AP, 10 February 2015, https://www.yahoo.com/news/china-finds-sizable-natural-gas-field-south-china-083147368.html.
34. See, for instance, Lannin, "South China Sea Tensions"; and Voigt and Robehmed, "Explainer: South China Sea."
35. See Ian Storey interview in Dominguez, "Beijing 'Setting Precedent'"; and Rajagopalan, "China Sends Four Oil Rigs."
36. Wang, "Letter Dated 22 May 2014."
37. From Vietnam's perspective, the platform's withdrawal may have reflected Hanoi buckling under Chinese pressure; Abuza, "Vietnam Buckles under Chinese Pressure." Or it may have reflected that Hanoi forced Beijing to "blink"; Vuving, "Did China Blink?"
38. "China," Country Analysis Briefs, EIA, July 2006.
39. "China Unveils Energy Strategy, Targets for 2020," *Xinhua*, 19 November 2014, http://news.xinhuanet.com/english/china/2014-11/19/c_133801014.htm.
40. Feng and Wong, "Iraq Keeps a Close Eye."
41. Gordon, Sautin, and Tao, "China's Oil Future."
42. Huber and Mills, "Oil, Oil, Everywhere."
43. Qin Anmin made this prediction in 1999; China's continued reliance on Middle East oil is documented at the EIA Web site on its "Today in Energy" page, http://www.eia.gov/todayinenergy/detail.cfm?id=15531.
44. EIA's "Today in Energy."

45. Yap and Spegele, "China's First Advanced Nuclear Reactor"; the IEA estimates, however, that by 2050 China could be producing 25 percent of its electricity requirements from nuclear power plants; IEA, "Nuclear Energy Roadmap," (2010), https://www.iea.org/media/freepublications/technologyroadmaps/nuclear_foldout.pdf. The 2020 estimate is in Ma, "Rebalancing China's Energy Strategy."
46. Zhu and Stanway, "'Made in China' Nuclear Reactors"; and my conversations with U.S. nuclear power experts, Beijing, October 2004.
47. TGS and AEF, "Xi Jinping"; production goals are from Dunn, "China Will Soon Surpass."
48. Recent articles on this issue are Buckley, "The Price of Damming Tibet's Rivers"; and "Myanmar Halts Chinese Dam," *Wall Street Journal*, 1 October 2011, http://www.wsj.com/articles/SB10001424405297020413820457660198026421892.
49. Wu, "Deal Signed to Expand Sino-Kazakh Pipeline."
50. Rose and Aizhu, "Iran Oil Officials in Beijing to Discuss Oil Supplies, Projects."
51. Collins and Erickson, "Tank Watch."
52. U.S. Energy Information Administration, "China," 24–25.
53. O'Sullivan, "LNG Import Infrastructure."
54. Bello, "Dragon and the Gringo."
55. "World Oil Transit Chokepoints," EIA, 10 November 2014, http://www.eia.gov/beta/international/regions-topics.cfm?RegionTopicID=WOTC.
56. *The Diversified Employment of China's Armed Forces*, at Ministry of National Defense of the People's Republic of China Web site, http://eng.mod.gov.cn/Database/WhitePapers/2012.htm.
57. "China Increasingly Reliant on Oil Imports—IEA," *China Daily*, 19 November 2008, http://www.china.org.cn/environment/news/2008-11/19/content_16790574.htm.
58. "Flow of Natural Gas from Central Asia," China National Petroleum Company (n.d.), http://www.cnpc.com.cn/en/FlowofnaturalgasfromCentralAsia/Flowof naturalgasfromCentralAsia2.shtml. Also see "Fourth Link of Central Asia-China Gas Pipeline to Start Construction This Year," *Platts*, 10 March2014, http://www.platts.com/latest-news/natural-gas/beijing/fourth-link-of-central-asia-china-gas-pipeline-26749048.
59. Quoted in Storey, "China's Malacca Dilemma."
60. Zhang, "Sea Power and China's Strategic Choices."
61. Erickson and Collins, "Beijing's Energy Security Strategy," 670.
62. Meyer, "With Oil and Gas Pipelines."
63. Jiang and Ding, "Update on Overseas Investments."
64. Ibid.
65. Ibid., 10.
66. "Chinese Imports," EIA (June 2015), "China Overview," http://www.eia.gov/beta/international/analysis.cfm?iso=CHN.
67. See Feng, "China Backpedals on Shale Gas," 22–23; and especially Wang, "China's Elusive Shale Gas Boom," 1.
68. Paton and Guo, "Russia, China Add to $400 Billion Gas Deal"; and O'Sullivan, "China-Russia Gas Pact." This agreement's problematic future is addressed in Lelyveld, "Doubts Rise on Russia-China Gas Deal."

69. See, for instance, Pinchuk, Burmistrova, and Golubkova, "Russia Could Postpone Gas Pipe." Quotes are from Krutikhin, "East or West, Home Is Best"; and Gabuev, "Smiles and Waves." Also see Hille, "Putin Aims to Cement China Links."
70. Jiang and Ding, "Update on Overseas Investments," 26.
71. See Myer, "With Oil and Gas Pipelines."
72. Jiang and Ding, "Update on Overseas Investments," 27.
73. See Eberling, *Future Oil Demands of China*.
74. Cole, *Great Wall at Sea*, 56–57.
75. Wong, "China Opens Corruption Inquiry."
76. Ma, "Rebalancing China's Energy Strategy," 1.
77. Herberg, "China's Search for Oil and Gas Security."

Chapter 6. Foreign Policy in the Making

1. Xi, "Working Together toward a Better Future."
2. See, for instance, books by Garver (*Foreign Relations of the People's Republic of China*); Nathan and Ross (*Great Wall and the Empty Fortress*); Johnston and Ross (*Engaging China*); Medeiros (*China's International Behavior*); Sutter (*China's Rise in Asia*); Fravel (*Strong Borders, Secure Nation*); Steinberg and O'Hanlon (*Strategic Reassurance and Resolve*); and an article by Lampton, "How China Is Ruled."
3. Glaser provides the best explanation of this important small leading group but notes that the group's routine and proceedings remain largely unknown. Glaser, "China's Maritime Rights Protection."
4. Ibid.
5. See Garver, *Foreign Relations of the People's Republic of China*, 4–7. Xi is quoted in Steinberg and O'Hanlon, *Strategic Reassurance and Resolve*, 22.
6. LSGs are explained and identified in Miller, "CCP Central Committee Leading Small Groups."
7. This discussion comes from Miller, "More Already," 4–5.
8. Ibid., 7.
9. These organizational remarks draw heavily on Miller, "More Already."
10. See the analyses by Sun, "Chinese National Security Decision-Making." On policymaking mechanics, see Nathan and Ross, *Great Wall and the Empty Fortress*, 123–33.
11. Sun, "Chinese National Security Decision-Making," 5.
12. Wang is quoted in Murphy, "Deepwater Oil Rigs as Strategic Weapons." See also Downs, "Business and Politics in the South China Sea."
13. Lampton, "How China Is Ruled," 80–81.
14. A classic and still useful work is Barnett, *Making of Foreign Policy in China*, 123–24.
15. Glaser and Saunders, "Chinese Civilian Foreign Policy Research Institutes," 599.
16. Sun, "Chinese National Security Decision-Making," 17–24.
17. Quoted in Sutter, *China's Rise in Asia*, 265.
18. Quoted in Steinberg and O'Hanlon, *Strategic Reassurance and Resolve*, 29–30; the 2013 defense white paper is *The Diversified Employment of China's Armed*

Forces, at Ministry of National Defense of the People's Republic of China Web site http://eng.mod.gov.cn/Database/WhitePapers/2012.htm.

19. Discussed in Erickson and Strange, "China's Blue Soft Power," 79.

20. Tanner and Mackenzie, *China's Emerging National Security Interests*, 115.

21. Cited in Tiezzi, "Three Goals of Beijing's Military Diplomacy." Also see Allen, "Top Trends in China's Military Diplomacy."

22. Willy Lam identifies this as one of two ways military personnel influence "foreign and national security policies"; Lam, "Generals' Growing Clout in Diplomacy." The other is military-to-military activities and participation in international conferences and peacekeeping missions. Lam goes further in "White Paper Expounds Civil-Military Relations in Xi Era," in which he argues that "the generals are spearheading Chinese foreign policy."

23. Swaine, "Chinese Views and Commentary on the 'One Belt, One Road' Initiative," 1. Also see Wheatley, "China Applies to Join EBRD."

24. M. Taylor Fravel addresses this point in *Strong Borders, Secure Nation*, 6. Beijing identifies fifty-six ethnic groups, including the vastly majority Han; see Information Office of the State Council of the PRC, "China's Ethnic Policy." It must be noted that none of the other nations disputing sovereignty issues in the East and South China seas are showing any flexibility in their positions.

25. Medeiros, *China's International Behavior*, xvii.

26. Xi is quoted in "Xi Jinping's Speech at Meeting on the 60th Anniversary of Publication of the Five Principles of Peaceful Coexistence," *Xinhua*, 28 June 2014, http://www.china.org.cn/world/2014-07/07/content_32876905.htm. Also see Glaser and Pal, "China's Periphery Diplomacy Initiative." The visits are analyzed in Szczudlik-Tatar, "China's New Silk Road Diplomacy," 1.

27. Heath, "Diplomacy Work Forum."

28. Quoted in Swaine, "Chinese Views and Commentary on Periphery Diplomacy," 6. This source is the primary source of this discussion on peripheral diplomacy.

29. Quoted in Deal, "PLA Strategy and Doctrine," 15.

30. Quoted in Swaine, "Chinese Views and Commentary on Periphery Diplomacy."

31. Wang's 8 March 2014 speech is at the Ministry of Foreign Affairs of the People's Republic of China Web site, http://www.fmprc.gov.cn/mfa_eng/wjb_663304/wjbz_663308/2461_663310/t1135385.shtml.

32. Xi's speech, on 29 November 2014, is at the Ministry of Foreign Affairs of the People's Republic of China Web site, http://www.fmprc.gov.cn/mfa_eng/zxxx_662805/t1215680.shtml.

33. Swaine, "Xi Jinping's Address to the Central Conference."

34. Swaine, "Chinese Views and Commentary on Peripheral Diplomacy," 15n60.

35. My discussions with senior U.S. officials involved in the associated negotiations, Washington, D.C., 2001, 2002.

36. This discussion draws heavily on the introduction to Saunders and Scobell, *PLA Influence on China's National Security Policymaking*. It is doubtful that Karl Marx would recognize the concept.

37. Miller, "The PLA in the Party Leadership Decisionmaking System," 58.

38. Discussed in ibid., 74–75, 79–82.

39. The so-called stability-instability paradox is discussed in terms of nuclear escalation in Schreer, "China's Development of a More Secure Second-Strike Capability," 16.
40. Quoted in Shambaugh, "China's Soft Power Push," 99.
41. See, for instance, Duchâtel, Brauner, and Hang, "Protecting China's Overseas Interests."
42. Pomfret, "U.S. Takes a Tougher Tone with China."
43. Shambaugh, "The Illusion of Chinese Power."
44. Shambaugh, "China's Soft Power Push," 100.
45. Ibid.,107.

Chapter 7. Foreign Policy in Action

1. Quoted in Chung, "One Country, Two Systems."
2. Beijing's views of China's "core national interests," with history and possible definitions, are examined in Swaine, "China's Assertive Behavior, Part One."
3. Medeiros, *China's International Behavior*, xviii.
4. Quoted in "China Marks Six Priorities for New Type of Major Country Relations with US," *Xinhua*, 12 November 2014, http://news.xinhuanet.com/english/china/2014-11/12/c_133785087.htm.
5. Quoted in Qi, "Pondering and Understanding the Impact."
6. Ma, "Xi Eyes More Enabling Int'l Environment."
7. Li is quoted in ibid., 5.
8. Wang's speech is at the Embassy of the People's Republic of China in the Republic of Indonesia Web site, http://id.china-embassy.org/eng/jrzg/t1277090.htm.
9. Ibid.
10. Ibid.
11. Glaser, "People's Republic of China Maritime Disputes."
12. The 90 bbl estimate is from CNOOC and is probably politically driven; see "Another Unfathomable in North Korea Is Oil Reserves," *JoongAng Daily*, 24 March 2015, http://koreajoongangdaily.joins.com/news/article/Article.aspx?aid=3002247. Oil deposits in the Bohai part of the Yellow Sea, however, have long been a source of petroleum; see "China's Bohai Bay May Hold 146 Bil Barrels Oil Reserves," *Platts*, 10 May 2007, http://www.petroleumworld.com/story0705 1011.htm (both accessed 28 September 2015).
13. One fathom equals six feet.
14. UNCLOS, Part VI, Continental Shelf, Art. 76, Definition of the Continental Shelf, http://www.un.org/depts/los/convention_agreements/texts/unclos/closindx .htm.
15. The Chinese–North Korean dispute is discussed in Zou, "China and Maritime Boundary Delimitation," 157–60.
16. Scott Snyder and See-won Byun note that "in 2012, 467 Chinese were arrested for illegal fishing in ROK waters," and that China's illegal catch "amounted to 21 percent of South Korea's total fisheries output." Snyder and Byun, "China-Korea Relations," 3–4.
17. Pollack, "Is Xi Jinping Rethinking Korean Unification?"

18. Ibid., 5.
19. Hwang, "The ROK'S China Policy under Park Geun-Hye."
20. Blanchard and Gold, "Beijing Warns Taiwan Opposition."
21. James Manicom provides a still-relevant explanation of this dispute in an interview with Acheson, "Disputed Claims in the East China Sea."
22. Kaiman, "Japan's Abe and China's Xi Hold Ice-breaking Meeting."
23. "Yang Jiechi Meets National Security Advisor of Japan Shotaro Yachi," MOFA of the PRC, 7 November 2014, http://www.fmprc.gov.cn/mfa_eng/zxxx_662805/t1208360.shtml.
24. "East China Sea Analysis," EIA, 17 September 2014, http://www.eia.gov/beta/international/regions-topics.cfm?RegionTopicID=ECS. Other sources have not corroborated these reports. Moreover, undiscovered resources do not take into account economic factors relevant to bring them into production, unlike proved and probable reserves.
25. This dispute is described in Smith, "The Senkaku/Diaoyu Island Controversy."
26. Evidence of this attitude, which is anchored in domestic political concerns, is provided in "Cabinet Approves Ordinance to Expand Japan's Continental Shelf," *Japan Times*, 9 September 2014, http://www.japantimes.co.jp/news/2014/09/09/national/cabinet-approves-ordinance-to-expand-japans-continental-shelf/#.Ve8_mLS4nUo.
27. An analysis of these views is in Swaine, "Chinese Views Regarding the Senkaku/Diaoyu Islands Dispute." Beijing has published a white paper "Claiming 'Diaoyu Dao' Inherent Territory of China," full text available at *Xinhuanet*, http://news.xinhuanet.com/english/china/2012-09/25/c_131872152.htm.
28. The president, secretaries of state and defense, the national security advisor, and chairman of the Joint Chiefs of Staff have all made this point with Chinese counterparts. See "Kerry Renews U.S. Pledge to Japan Security, Including East China Sea Islets," Reuters, 28 April 2015, http://www.reuters.com/article/2015/04/28/us-usa-japan-defense-kerry-idUSKBN0NI1SI20150428.
29. Geng, "Defense Ministry's Regular Press Conference on 30 April 2015."
30. Suzuki, "China Plans to Build a New Base."
31. A record of these incursions is in Przystup, "Japan-China Relations."
32. "Vietnam, China Negotiate Sea Area off Tonkin Gulf," *Tuoitre News*, 1 June 2013, http://tuoitrenews.vn/politics/10236/vietnam-china-negotiate-sea-area-off-tonkin-gulf.
33. My discussion with senior Taiwan officials, Taipei, 2005–12; also see "Taiwan Rejects Advice to Drop South China Sea Claims," *Want China Times* (Taipei) 13 September 2014, http://focustaiwan.tw/news/aipl/201409130019.aspx.
34. Ji, "Maritime Jurisdiction in the Three China Seas."
35. J. Ashley Roach provides a discussion of the legal aspects of Beijing's actions. Roach, "China's Shifting Sands in the Spratlys."
36. Sun, "China's New Calculations"; and Jakobson, "China's Unpredictable Maritime Security Actors."

37. "China, Philippines, Vietnam Sign Joint South China Sea Oil Search Accord," Radio Free Asia, 14 March 2005; http://www.rfa.org/english/news/business/china_vietnam_spratlys-20050314.html; and Storey, "Conflict in the South China Sea."

38. Perlez, "Images Show China Building Aircraft Runway in Disputed Spratly Islands"; and Glaser, "A Big Deal."

39. Shear, "Statement of David Shear"; Brunnstrom, "Images Show Vietnam Reclaiming Land"; and Lubold and Entous, "U.S. Says Beijing Is Building Up South China Sea Islands."

40. An excellent explanation of the varying territorial South China Sea claims is Poling, "South China Sea in Focus."

41. Tweed and Blake, "China Reserves Right to Declare Air Zone."

42. Pedrozo, "China versus Vietnam."

43. Wu Shicun, "Gains and Losses."

44. "Foreign Ministry Spokesperson Hua Chunying's Regular Press Conference on April 9, 2015," MOFA of the PRC, 9 April 2015, http://www.fmprc.gov.cn/mfa_eng/xwfw_665399/s2510_665401/t1253488.shtml. Also see "Q&A: China's Ambassador to the U.S. on the South China Sea, Trade, and Security," *Wall Street Journal*, 29 May 2015, http://www.wsj.com/articles/chinas-ambassador-to-the-u-s-on-the-south-china-sea-trade-and-security-1432935890.

45. Crispin, "Thai Coup Alienates U.S."

46. Quoted in Sutter and Huang, "China–Southeast Asia Relations."

47. Quoted in Bodeen, "China Hosts 10-Nation ASEAN."

48. Ibid., including quotes.

49. Cole, *Asian Maritime Strategies*, 133. Also see "India Goes Deep Sea to Mine Gold," *Pakistan Defense*, 30 June 2015, http://defence.pk/threads/india-goes-deep-sea-to-mine-gold.383484/.

50. "2,000 Acres at Pakistan's Gwadar Port Leased to China for 43 Years," *India Defence News*, 11 September 2015, http://www.indiandefensenews.in/2015/09/2000-acres-at-pakistans-gwadar-port.html.

51. See Bastians and Harris, "Chinese Leader Visits Sri Lanka"; but especially Samaranayake, "After the Visit."

52. Aneez and Chalmers, "Sri Lanka's Strongman President Voted Out."

53. For Beijing's position on Manila's law case, see "China Dismisses Vietnam's Sovereignty Claim for South China Sea Islands," *Xinhua*, 11 December 2014, http://news.xinhuanet.com/english/china/2014-12/12/c_133848818.htm; and "Foreign Experts: The Philippines Seeking Int'l Arbitration Is a One-Man Show Doomed to Fail," *Xinhua*, 3 April 2014, http://news.xinhuanet.com/english/indepth/2014-04/03/c_133236090.htm. Of course, none of the other claimants have exhibited much more willingness to negotiate sovereignty.

54. Quoted in Haas, "Beijing Rebukes U.S."; and Zhang Yunbi, "FM: China Will Watch over Waters." A good summary of China's land reclamation projects is in Dolven et al., "Chinese Land Reclamation in the South China Sea."

55. Quoted in "China's Nine-Dotted Line: A Vague Claim," *Voice of Vietnam*, 22 May 2014, http://english.vov.vn/Politics/World/Chinas-ninedotted-line-a-vague -claim/256735.vov; also see Ikeshima, "China's Dashed Line."

56. Panda, "China's HD-981 Oil Rig Returns." Also see "China Flares up East China Sea Dispute with Japan," Reuters, 24 July 2015, http://indianexpress.com/article /world/asia/china-flares-up-east-china-sea-dispute-with-japan-says-has-every -right-to-drill-for-oil-gas/.

57. Quoted in Perlez, "Leader Asserts China's Importance on Global Stage."

58. Perlez, "Rescue Mission in Yemen."

59. Gabuev, "Sino-Russian Trade after a Year of Sanctions." Chen Weidong, a senior CNOOC official, notes the problematic nature of Sino-Russian energy plans. See Chen, "Is There Trouble in Sino-Russian Paradise?"

60. Quoted in "Xi Urges Closer Asia-Pacific Cooperation," *Xinhua*, 20 November 2015, http://news.xinhuanet.com/english/2015-11/20/c_134834807.htm.

61. Yu, "China–Russia Relations." Also see Ting, "Li's Silk Road Trip." Also see Trenin, "From Greater Europe to Greater Asia?"

62. Brown and Scott, "China-Taiwan Relations," 3.

63. Jakobson, "China's Foreign Policy Dilemma." Also see Kaufman and Hemphill, "PRC Foreign Policy under Xi Jinping."

64. Medeiros, *China's International Behavior*, xx–xxi.

65. Quoted in Swaine, "Chinese Views and Commentary on Periphery Diplomacy," 24.

66. Saunders, "China's Juggling Act."

Conclusion

1. "Standing up" is a phrase reportedly uttered by Mao Zedong on 1 October 1949 when he announced the founding of the PRC; see Jones, "The Day the Chinese People Stood Up."

2. National Security Law of the PRC, 1 July 2015, http://www.cfr.org/homeland -security/national-security-law-peoples-republic-china/p36775.

3. The new law is discussed in "China Observes First National Security Education Day," *Xinhua*, 15 April 2016, http://news.xinhuanet.com/english/2016-04/15 /c_135283197.htm.

4. Zhang, "The New U.S. Maritime Strategy"; and my conversations with senior PLA officers, 2014.

5. Li and Ma, "The Complexity of the Maritime Military Struggle."

6. Li, "Traditional Military Thinking and the Defensive Strategy of China."

7. Liebenberg, "How a 120-Year-Old War." The naval battle that began the Franco-Chinese war was a disaster for the new Chinese fleet; see Wortzel, *Dictionary of Contemporary Chinese Military History*, 94.

8. The following list draws on Blasko, "Ten Reasons Why China Will Have Trouble."

9. Chase, "Xi in Command"; and my discussion with a senior MR commander, 2013.

10. Ellis Joffe correctly pointed out that a military could be both professionally competent and politically loyal, but the frequency and passion with which China's political leaders remind the PLA of its subservient role to the CCP is remarkable.
11. Sharman, "China Moves Out."
12. Peng and Yao, *Science of Military Strategy* (2013), 99–100.
13. I first heard this designation of the Pacific and Indian Oceans from a Canadian maritime strategist in May 2005. "Indo-Asia-Pacific" is a variation; one of the two has found favor in the U.S. and the Chinese navies, but not the Indian navy (my discussions with senior U.S., Chinese, and Indian naval officers in Washington, Beijing, Shanghai, New Delhi, and Goa, 2011–15).
14. Peng and Yao, *Science of Military Strategy* (2013).
15. Wang, "How to Implement China's Foreign Strategy in 2015," 97.
16. Ezra Vogel addresses this thought in "Xi Jinping Compared to Deng Xiaoping."
17. The United States is number one today, China two, and Japan three, according to GDP per capita; Japan is passed by India and slips to fourth if a Purchasing Power Parity method is used. See "India Displaces Japan," *Economic Times*, 30 April 2014, http://articles.economictimes.indiatimes.com/2014-04-30/news /49523310_1_capita-income-third-largest-economy-world-gdp.
18. Quoted in "Chinese General Liu Yazhou: Diaoyu Islands and Sino-Japanese Relations," *China Military Online*, 14 October 2015, http://english.chinamil.com .cn/news-channels/china-military-news/2015-10/14/content_6722812.htm.
19. Chen, "Defining a 'New Type of Major Power Relations.'"
20. "Foreign Minister Wang Yi Meets the Press," Ministry of Foreign Affairs of the PRC, 9 March 2016, http://www.fmprc.gov.cn/mfa_eng/zxxx_662805/t1346238. shtml.
21. See "Toward a New Type of International Relations of Win-Win Cooperation: Speech by Foreign Minister Wang Yi at Luncheon of the China Development Forum," Ministry of Foreign Affairs of the PRC, 25 March 2015, http://www .fmprc.gov.cn/mfa_eng/wjb_663304/wjbz_663308/2461_663310/t1248487.shtml.
22. Linda Jakobson addresses this point in "China's Foreign Policy Dilemma."
23. Quoted in Blanchard, "China Says Changing Position."
24. "Commentary: Time for Manila to End Farce of Arbitration on South China Sea," *People's Daily*, 17 July 2015, http://news.xinhuanet.com/english/2015-07/17 /c_134421924.htm.
25. Yuan expresses the rigid view in "Philippines' Illegal Occupation of Ren'ai Reef Must Be Ended With Determination." On the other hand, Qiao Liang, a PLA analyst, described the maritime disputes as "not China's current core interest" and of secondary priority to Beijing, which should continue focusing on economic development; TGS, NNL, AEF, "PLA Strategist."
26. Admiral Wu Shengli is quoted in Page, "China Puts Conciliatory Slant on Land Reclamation." The same claim is in Zhao, "Maritime Efforts 'to Help Others.'"
27. Thayer, "No, China Is Not Reclaiming Land."

28. Alistair Iain Johnston concludes it is not very "new" in his examination of Chinese "assertiveness"; Johnston, "How New and Assertive Is China's New Assertiveness?" Also see "Chinese DM Expresses Concern over Japan's Security Bills," *Xinhua*, 17 July 2015, http://news.xinhuanet.com/english/2015-07/17/c_134422144.htm; "China: We Are Preparing for 'High-Level' Talks with Japan," Reuters, 16 July 2015, http://www.businessinsider.com/r-china-says-japan-china-preparing-for-high-level-talks-2015-7; "China Calls Japan Foreign Policy 'Two-Faced,'" Reuters, 22 July 2015, http://www.reuters.com/article/2015/07/22/us-china-japan-idUSKCN0PW02520150722; and Slavin, "Japan Defense Report Criticizes China."

29. Zoellick, "Remarks on AUSFTA." Also see Blanchard and Mogato, "China Says U.S. 'Militarizing' South China Sea."

30. This list apparently sums up previous "red lines" listed by senior Chinese officials since President Jiang Zemin was in office, 1992–2000. It was reported in August 2015 from Taiwan's Ministry of Foreign Affairs, but the precise source is unknown.

31. Data is in Mastro, "China's Military Is about to Go Global!"

32. Franz-Stefan Gady reports the commissioning of the fourth of six Kilo-class submarines Hanoi has purchased from Moscow, the crews of which are being trained by Indian submariners; Gady, "Vietnam Commissions Two Subs." Also see Kallender-Umezu, "Tokyo to Challenge China on Fiery Cross Reef"; "The Submarine Choice," *Strategy*, Australian Strategic Policy Institute, September 2014, https://www.aspi.org.au/publications/the-submarine-choice-perspectives-on-australias-most-complex-defence-project/Strategy_submarine_choice.pdf; and Keck, "Submarine Race in the Malaccan Strait."

33. "Small Reefs, Big Problems," *Economist*, 25 July 2015, http://www.economist.com/news/asia/21659771-asian-coastguards-are-front-line-struggle-check-china-small-reefs-big-problems; and Cheng and Lubold, "South Korea Calls for South China Sea Rights."

34. Thayer, "Can Vietnam's Maritime Strategy Counter China?"; and Torode, "Vietnam Buys Submarine-Launched Land Attack Missiles to Deter China."

35. Gordon, "U.S. Eases Embargo on Arms to Vietnam."

36. "Philippines, U.S. Marines Conduct Exercises Near China-Held Reef," AFP, 5 October 2014, http://www.spacewar.com/reports/Philippines_US_marines_conduct_exercises_near_China-held_reef_999.html. Carter is quoted in "U.S. Affirms 'Ironclad' Vow to Defend Philippines," AFP, 27 May 2015, http://www.spacewar.com/reports/US_affirms_ironclad_promise_to_defend_Philippines_999.html.

37. Medcalf and Brown, "Defense Challenges 2035"; and "SECNAC Completes Partnership-Building Visit to Indonesia," *Navy News*, 27 October 2014, http://www.navy.mil/submit/display.asp?story_id=86207.

38. Ozawa, "Japan Approves Biggest Defense Budget Ever."

39. Slavin, "US, Japan Announce Expansion of Defense Ties"; and Davis and Gordon, "Japan and U.S. Set New Rules for Military Cooperation."

40. My discussion with a senior U.S. Navy officer, Washington, D.C., 2015; ZYH and AEF, "U.S. Invites Japan to Patrol the South China Sea"; and Gady, "Japan Will Permanently Join U.S.-India Naval Exercises."

41. "Future-Oriented Efforts" at over 80% in Japan, S Korea," Nikkei, 1 June 2015, 1; and Tajima, "Japan, South Korea to Resume Defense Exchanges."

42. Hammond, "Malabar 2014 Kicks Off"; Thayer, "Philippines and Vietnam Forge a Strategic Partnership"; "Vietnam Calls for 'Self-Restraint' in Disputed South China Sea," Reuters, 18 March 2015, http://www.reuters.com/article/2015/03/18/us-southchinasea-vietnam-australia-idUSKBN0ME07220150318; Karsten, "U.S. 7th Fleet, Singaporean, Malaysian, and Indonesian Navies Meet"; Robson, "Japan, New Zealand Joining Talisman Saber for First Time"; and Dempsey, "7th Fleet Commander Kicks Off CARAT Cambodia 2014." Also see "Joint Statement: Third India-Philippines Joint Commission on Bilateral Cooperation," Ministry of External Affairs, Government of India, 14 October 2015, http://mea.gov.in /bilateral-documents.htm?dtl/25930/Joint_Statement__Third-India Philippines_Joint_Commission_on_Bilateral_Cooperation.

43. See, for instance, Wang, "Cooperation between the Maritime Forces"; and Parameswaran, "Why the 'New' U.S. Trilateral Dialogue with Japan and India Matters."

44. Discussed in Garver, "Sino-Russian Relations," 131.

45. Adm. Harry Harris, quoted in Spitzer, "New Head of the U.S. Pacific Command"; Cui Tiankai, quoted in "U.S. Has No Right to Intervene in China's Legitimate Activities in the South China Sea," Xinhua, 13 May 2015, http://news.xinhuanet .com/english/2015-05/14/c_134238737.htm; Lynch, "Carter Warns China"; and "Japan Pledges More Vessels to Vietnam Amid South China Sea Tensions," Nation, 20 September 2015, http://www.nationmultimedia.com/breakingnews /Japan-pledges-more-vessels-to-Vietnam-amid-South-C-30269168.html.

46. Chu, "China's View on U.S. Policy," 13–15; and Deng, "Origins of Misperceptions."

47. Dempsey, "USS Fort Worth Conducts CUES"; and "China, U.S. Agree on Code of Conduct for Military Aircraft," Taipei Times, 16 June 2015, http://www.taipei times.com/News/front/archives/2015/06/16/2003620807.

48. My discussions with senior Indian naval officers, 2012, New Delhi; Agnihotri, Strategic Direction of the Chinese Navy; and Singh, "A 'PLA-N' for Chinese Maritime Bases."

49. Quoted in "Indian, U.S. Leaders Vow to Enhance Bilateral Ties," Times of India, 1 October 2014, http://timesofindia.indiatimes.com/india/Modi-Obama-vow-to -take-ties-to-new-levels-discuss-WTO-climate-ISIS/articleshow/43921128.cms.

50. "U.S.-India Joint Strategic Vision for the Asia-Pacific and Indian Ocean Region," White House Office of the Press Secretary, 25 January 2015, https://www.white house.gov/the-press-office/2015/01/25/us-india-joint-strategic-vision-asia -pacific-and-indian-ocean-region.

51. Lampton, "The U.S. and China."

52. China's president considers the international situation favorable to China; hence the reports in "Xi Eyes More Enabling International Environment," China.org, 30, November 2014, http://www.china.org.cn/china/Off_the_Wire/2014-11/30 /content_34187877.htm.

53. Discussed in Noor, "How China Sees Itself."
54. Sutter, "Asia's Importance, China's Expansion and U.S. Strategy."
55. A former State Department official and long-time China expert described Beijing's move in 2010 as "ham-fisted." See Christensen, "Obama and Asia," 30. Also see Mastro, "Why Chinese Assertiveness Is Here to Stay."
56. Supriyanto, "Indonesia's Natuna Islands."
57. Observation of a senior U.S. international law expert, 2 November 2015.

BIBLIOGRAPHY

Abuza, Zachary. "Vietnam Buckles under Chinese Pressure." *Asia Times*, 29 July 2014, http://www.atimes.com/atimes/Southeast_Asia/SEA-01-290714.html.

Acheson, Chris. "Disputed Claims in the East China Sea: An Interview with James Manicom." National Bureau of Asian Research (NBR), 25 July 2011, http://www.nbr.org/research/activity.aspx?id=159.

Agnihotri, Kamlesh K. *Strategic Direction of the Chinese Navy: Capability and Intent Assessment*. New Delhi: Bloomsbury India, 2015.

Aitken, Roger. "Chinese RMB Consolidates Second Most Used Currency Ranking for DC Trade Transactions." *Forbes*, 28 February 2015, http://www.forbes.com/sites/rogeraitken/2015/02/28/chinese-rmb-consolidates-second-most-used-currency-ranking-for-dc-trade-transactions/.

Alagappa, Muthiah. "Community Building: ASEAN's Millstone?" RSIS Commentary no. 063/2015 (24 March 2015), http://www.rsis.edu.sg/rsis-publication/rsis/co15063-community-building-aseans-millstone/#.VvIBMEd_e4M.

Alexander, David. "China Land Reclamation in South China Sea Creates 'New Facts'—U.S." Reuters, 28 May 2015, http://uk.reuters.com/article/2015/05/29/uk-asia-usa-carter-idUKKBN0OD1G620150529.

———. "Vietnam, U.S. Discuss Military Cooperation, South China Sea Islands." Reuters, 1 June 2015, http://www.reuters.com/article/2015/06/01/vietnam-usa-defense-idUSL3N0YN27T20150601.

Allen, Kenneth. "PLA Foreign Relations under Xi Jinping: Continuity and/or Change?" Washington, D.C.: National Defense University Press, 2017.

———. "The Top Trends in China's Military Diplomacy." *China Brief* 15, no. 9 (1 May 2015), http://www.jamestown.org/single/?tx_ttnews%5Btt_news%5D=43866&tx_ttnews%5BbackPid%5D=7&cHash=752f59005db39a815c5d947cb86f9b7a#.Ve3LsbS4mgQ.

Anderlini, Jamil. "China and Russia Vow to Build Naval Cooperation." *Financial Times*, 19 November 2014, http://www.ft.com/intl/cms/s/0/16364ade-6fb2-11e4-90af-00144feabdc0.html.

Aneez, Shihar, and John Chalmers. "Sri Lanka's Strongman President Voted out after a Decade." *Reuters*, 10 January 2015, http://in.reuters.com/article/2015/01/09 /sri-lanka-election-rajapaksa-idINKBN0KI04F20150109.

Ansari, Usman. "Pakistan to Buy 8 Submarines from China," *Defense News*, 3 April 2015, http://www.defensenews.com/story/defense/naval/submarines/2015/04/ 03/pakistan-to-buy-8-submarines-from-china/25233481/.

Areddy, James T. "China Evacuates Citizens from Yemen." *Wall Street Journal*, 30 March 2015, http://www.wsj.com/articles/china-evacuating-citizens-from-yemen -1427689845.

Arthur, Gordon. "China Confirms CH-4 UCAV in PLA Service in 'Peace Mission 2014' Drill." *IHS Jane's Defence Weekly*, 1 September 2014, http://defence.pk/ threads/china-confirms-ch-4-ucav-in-pla-service.331981/.

Ashraf, Sajjad. "AIIB: The Beginning of Economic Challenge to the U.S." *China-US Focus Digest*, 14 July 2015, http://defence.pk/threads/china-confirms-ch-4-ucav- in-pla-service.331981/.

Bader, Jeffrey A. "The U.S. and China's Nine Dash Line: End the Ambiguity." Brook- ings, 6 February 2014, http://www.brookings.edu/research/opinions/2014/02/06 -us-china-nine-dash-line-bader.

Badkar, Mamta. "The Country with the Largest Maritime Fleet Says No Thanks to Chinese Ships." *Business Insider*, 8 June 2012, http://www.businessinsider.com/ greece-does-not-want-chinese-ships-2012-6.

Balile, Deodatus. "Tanzania and China Sign Port Development Package." *Sabahi*, 27 March 2013, http://allafrica.com/stories/201303280126.html.

Barnett, A. Doak. *The Making of Foreign Policy in China: Structure and Process.* Boulder, Colo.: Westview Press, 1985.

Bartel, Francis. "Report: Chinese Ship Sinks Another Vietnamese Fishing Vessel in South China Sea." *Breitbart*, 16 October 2015. http://www.breitbart.com/national -security/2015/10/16/chinese-ship-sinks-another-vietnamese-fishing-vessel-in -south-china-sea/.

Bastians, Dharisha, and Gardiner Harris. "Chinese Leader Visits Sri Lanka, Chal- lenging India's Sway." *New York Times*, 16 September 2014, http://www.nytimes .com/2014/09/17/world/asia/chinese-leader-visits-sri-lanka-chipping-away-at -indias-sway.html?_r=0.

Bateman, Sam. "Maritime Boundary Delimitation, Excessive Claims and Effective Regime Building in the South China Sea." In *Major Law and Policy Issues in the South China Sea: European and American Perspectives*, edited by Y. Song and K. Zou, 119–36. Surrey, U.K.: Ashgate, 2014.

Beardson, Timothy. *Stumbling Giant: The Threats to China's Future.* New Haven, Conn.: Yale University Press, 2009.

Beauchamp, Nathan. "Rolling out the New Silk Road: Railroads Undergird Beijing's Strategy." *China Brief* 15, no. 8 (16 April 2015), http://www.jamestown.org/ single/?tx_ttnews%5Bswords%5D=8fd5893941d69d0be3f378576261ae3e&tx _ttnews%5Bany_of_the_words%5D=PKK&tx_ttnews%5Bpointer%5D=3&tx _ttnews%5Btt_news%5D=43799&tx_ttnews%5BbackPid%5D=7&cHash=e7c7 be19da6c47df91b2b16101a5e4b4#.VeH5qLS4nUo.

Beckman, Robert. "China, UNCLOS and the South China Sea." Paper presented at the Asian Society of International Law: Third Biennial Conference, Beijing, 27–28 August 2011, http://cil.nus.edu.sg/wp/wp-content/uploads/2009/09/AsianSIL -Beckman-China-UNCLOS-and-the-South-China-Sea-26-July-2011.pdf.

———. "The Philippines v. China Case and Maritime Disputes in the South China Sea." Paper presented at the ILA-ASIL Asia-Pacific Research Forum, 25–26 May 2015, http://www.cil.nus.edu.sg/wp/wp-content/uploads/2015/05/Beckman- Paper-2015-ILA-ASIL-Taiwan-draft-19-May.pdf.

———. "The UN Convention on the Law of the Sea and the Maritime Disputes in the South China Sea." *American Journal of International Law* 107 (January 2013): 142–63.

Bello. "The Dragon and the Gringo: Latin America's Shifting Geopolitics." *Economist*, 17 January 2015, http://www.economist.com/news/americas/21639549-latin -americas-shifting-geopolitics-dragon-and-gringo.

Bender, Jeremy. "Putin: Russia's Military Strength Is Unmatchable." *Business Insider*, 20 February 2015, http://www.businessinsider.com/putin-russias-military-strength -is-unmatchable-2015-2.

Berglund, Andrew. "'Maneuver-5' Exercise Focuses on Improving Distant Seas Com- bat Capabilities." U.S.-China Economic and Security Review Commission Staff Report, 16 December 2013, http://www.uscc.gov/sites/default/files/Research/Staff %20Report_Maneuver-5%20Exercise%20Focuses%20on%20Improving %20Distant%20Seas%20Combat%20Capabilities.pdf.

Berthelsen, John. "Trouble Could Be Brewing over China Development Loans." *Asia Sentinel*, 19 June 2015, http://www.asiasentinel.com/econ-business/trouble-china -development-loans/.

Bird, Mike. "China's New Development Bank Is Becoming a Massive Embarrassment for Obama." *Business Insider*, 31 March 2015, http://www.businessinsider.com /us-allies-joining-asian-infrastructure-investment-bank-aiib-embarrassment -2015-3.

Blanchard, Ben. "China Says Changing Position on Sea Dispute Would Shame Ances- tors." Reuters, 27 June 2015, http://www.reuters.com/article/2015/06/27/us -southchinasea-china-idUSKBN0P708U20150627.

———. "China's First Aircraft Carrier Completes South China Sea Drills." Reuters, 1 January 2014, http://www.reuters.com/article/us-china-carrier-idUSBREA 0101P20140102.

Blanchard, Ben, and Michael Gold. "Beijing Warns Taiwan Opposition as It Names Presidential Candidate." Reuters, 15 April 2015, http://www.reuters.com/article /2015/04/15/us-china-taiwan-idUSKBN0N60XK20150415.

Blanchard, Ben, and Manuel Mogato. "China Says U.S. 'Militarizing' South China Sea." Reuters, 30 July 2015, http://www.reuters.com/article/2015/07/30/us-south chinasea-china-usa-idUSKCN0Q415N20150730.

Blasko, Dennis J. "An Analysis of China's 2011 Defense Budget and Total Military Spending: The Great Unknown." *China Brief* 11, no. 4 (11 March 2011), http:// www.jamestown.org/programs/chinabrief/single/?tx_ttnews[tt_news]=37631& cHash=45e8b93079c0a07f#.VvKZ7Ed_e4M.

——. *The Chinese Army Today*, 2nd ed. London: Routledge, 2013.

——. "Corruption in China's Military: One of Many Problems." *War on the Rocks*, 16 February 2015, http://warontherocks.com/2015/02/corruption-in-chinas-military-one-of-many-problems/.

——. "PLA Special Operations Forces: Organizations, Missions and Training." *China Brief* 15, no. 9 (1 May 2015), http://www.jamestown.org/single/?tx_ttnews%5Btt_news%5D=43867&no_cache=1#.VZ1Pquu4n_Q.

——. "Ten Reasons Why China Will Have Trouble Fighting a Modern War." *War on the Rocks*, 18 February 2015, http://warontherocks.com/2015/02/ten-reasons-why-china-will-have-trouble-fighting-a-modern-war/.

Bodeen, Christopher. "China Hosts 10-Nation ASEAN Amid South China Sea Tensions." Associated Press, 16 October 2015, https://www.yahoo.com/news/chinese-military-reaches-amid-south-china-sea-tensions-084757965.html.

Boersama, Tim, and Kevin Foley. *The Greenland Gold Rush: Promise and Pitfalls of Greenland's Energy and Mineral Resources*. Energy Security Initiative. Washington, D.C.: Brookings Institution, September 2014.

Bondoc, Jarius. "China's Own Ancient Maps Disprove Beijing Sea Claim." *Philippine Star* (Manila), 22 October 2014, http://www.philstar.com/opinion/2014/10/22/1383005/chinas-own-ancient-maps-disprove-beijing-sea-claim.

Boudreau, John. "Japan to Give Vietnam Boats, Equipment Amid China Buildup." Bloomberg, 15 September 2015, http://www.bloomberg.com/news/articles/2015-09-16/japan-to-give-vietnam-boats-equipment-amid-china-s-buildup.

Bower, Ernest Z. "China Reveals Its Hand on ASEAN at Phnom Penh." *Southeast Asia from the Corner of 18th and K Streets* (newsletter) 3, no. 14 (July 19, 2012), http://csis.org/publication/southeast-asia-corner-18th-and-k-streets-china-reveals-its-hand-asean-phnom-penh.

Bran, Philippa. "China Pledges $46 Billion for Pakistan, but Will Beijing Deliver?" *Interpreter*, 21 April 2015, http://www.lowyinterpreter.org/post/2015/04/21/China-pledges-$46-billion-for-Pakistan-but-will-Beijing-deliver.aspx.

Brendon, Piers. *The Decline and Fall of the British Empire, 1781–1997*. New York: Knopf, 2008.

Brown, David G., and Kevin Scott. "China-Taiwan Relations: Cross-Strait Relations on Hold." *Comparative Connections* 16, no. 4 (January 2015) 3, http://csis.org/files/publication/1403qchina_taiwan.pdf.

Browne, Andrew. "Tiny Reef Poses a Big Hazard." *Wall Street Journal*, 20 May 2015, http://www.pressreader.com/china/the-wall-street-journal-asia/20150520/281612418985349/TextView.

Brunnstrom, David. "Images Show Vietnam Reclaiming Land in South China Sea." Reuters, 8 May 2015, http://www.reuters.com/article/2015/05/08/us-southchinasea-vietnam-idUSKBN0NT04820150508.

Buckley, Chris. "Communist Leadership Approves Security Goals for China." *New York Times*, 23 January 2015, http://www.nytimes.com/2015/01/24/world/asia/communist-leadership-approves-security-goals-for-china.html?_r=0.

Buckley, Michael. "The Price of Damming Tibet's Rivers." *International New York Times*, 30 March 2015, http://www.nytimes.com/2015/03/31/opinion/the-price-of-damming-tibets-rivers.html?_r=0.

Burke, Jason. "India and China Announce Trade Deals During Xi Visit to Delhi." *Guardian*, 18 September 2014, http://forces.us4.list-manage.com/track/click?u=44344175675c5e23c1145191d&id=6fae420b94&e=172e972f85.

Burman, Dennis. "Giant Appetite." *Wall Street Journal Asia*, 27 August 2015, http://www.pressreader.com/china/the-wall-street-journal-asia/20150827/2818 48642355259/TextView.

Butler, Simon. "Oceans on the Brink of Ecological Collapse." *Climate and Capitalism*, http://climateandcapitalism.com/2013/10/14/oceans-brink-ecological-collapse/.

Cai Penghong. "China's Evolving Overseas Interests and Peaceful Competition." In *Beyond the Wall: Chinese Far Sea Operations*, edited by Peter A. Dutton and Ryan D. Martinson, 63–72. Newport, R.I.: China Maritime Studies Institute, Naval War College, 2015, https://www.usnwc.edu/getattachment/667e7ff9-b1e4-46cb -b709-555d151d5c3f/WEB_CMS13.pdf.aspx.

Calamur, Krishnadev. "China's President Promises Pakistan $45B in Investment." National Public Radio (NPR), 21 April 2015, http://www.npr.org/sections/the two-way/2015/04/21/401263470/in-pakistan-visit-chinas-president-announces -45b-in-investment.

Capaccio, Anthony, and David Tweed. "U.S. Says Chinese Sub That Can Hit U.S. on Patrol Soon." Bloomberg, 23 September 2015, http://www.bloomberg.com/news /articles/2015-09-24/pentagon-says-chinese-sub-that-can-hit-u-s-to-go-on -patrol-soon.

Carlson, Benjamin. "The World According to Xi Jinping." *Atlantic*, 21 September 2015, http://www.theatlantic.com/international/archive/2015/09/xi-jinping-china -book-chinese-dream/406387/.

Cavas, Christopher P. "China's Navy Makes Strides, But Work Remains to Be Done." *Defense News*, 25 May 2015, http://www.defensenews.com/story/defense/ naval/2015/05/24/chinese-china-navy-naval-plan-warships-shipbuilding -construction-propulsion-power-plant-submarine-aircraft-carrier-destroyer -frigate/27725003/.

Cha Chun-ming. "Chinese Navy Heads Toward Modernization." *Ta Kung Pao* (Hong Kong), 11 April 1999, B6, in Foreign Broadcast Information Service-China (FBIS-CHI)-1999-0418.

Chang, Felix K. "Even Indonesia: Concerns over China's Reach in South China Sea." Foreign Policy Research Institute, 21 October 2014, http://www.fpri.org/article /2014/10/even-indonesia-concerns-over-chinas-reach-in-the-south-china-sea/.

Chase, Michael. "Xi in Command: Downsizing and Reorganizing," Asia Maritime Transparency Initiative, 11 September 2015, http://amti.csis.org/xi-in-command -downsizing-and-reorganizing-the-peoples-liberation-army-pla/.

Chase, Michael S., Jeffrey Engstrom, Tai Ming Cheung, Kristen A. Gunness, Scott Warren Harold, Susan Puska, and Samuel K. Berkowitz. *China's Incomplete Military Transformation: Assessing the Weaknesses of the People's Liberation Army (PLA)* (Santa Monica, Calif.: Rand, 2015), http://origin.www.uscc.gov/sites /default/files/Research/China%27s%20Incomplete%20Military%20 Transformation_2.11.15.pdf.

Chen, Dingding. "Defining a 'New Type of Major Power Relations.'" *Diplomat*, 8 November 2014, http://thediplomat.com/2014/11/defining-a-new-type-of-major -power-relations/.

Ch'en, Jerome, and Nicholas Tarling. *Studies in the Social History of China and South-East Asia: Essays in Memory*. New York: Cambridge University Press, 2009.

Chen Li and Du Mingjun. "Advanced Passenger Ro-Ro Ship Launched in Shenyang MAC." *China Military Online*, 20 January 2012, http://en.people.cn/90786/7710454.html.

Chen, Zhiwu. "China's Dangerous Debt: Why the Economy Could Be Headed for Trouble." *Foreign Affairs* 94, no. 4 (May–June 2015), https://www.foreignaffairs.com/articles/china/2015-04-20/chinas-dangerous-debt.

Chen Weidong. "Is There Trouble in Sino-Russian Paradise?" *Caixin Online*, 17 October 2014, http://english.caixin.com/2014-10-17/100739871.html.

Cheng, Jonathan, and Gordon Lubold. "South Korea Calls for South China Sea Rights." *Wall Street Journal*, 2 November 2015, http://www.wsj.com/articles/south-korea-calls-for-south-china-sea-rights-1446461006.

Chin, Gregory T. "China in a Changing Global Monetary System: Rising Influence and Followership." Paper presented at University of Pennsylvania CSCC conference "China in a Changing World," Philadelphia, 30 April–1 May 2015, https://cscc.sas.upenn.edu/events/2015/April/CSCC_3rd_Annual_Conference (cited with author's permission).

Chipman, John. *Military Balance 2015* (London: International Institute for Strategic Studies, 11 February 2015).

Christensen, Thomas J. "Obama and Asia: Confronting the China Challenge." *Foreign Affairs* 94, no. 5 (September–October 2015), https://www.foreignaffairs.com/articles/asia/obama-and-asia.

Chu, Shulong. "China's View on U.S. Policy in the South China Sea." In *Perspectives on the South China Sea: Diplomatic, Legal, and Security Dimensions of the Dispute*, edited by Murray Hiebert, Phuong Nguyen, and Gregory B. Poling, 13–19. Washington, D.C.: Center for Strategic and International Studies, http://csis.org/files/publication/140930_Hiebert_PerspectivesSouthChinaSea_Web.pdf.

Chubb, Andrew. "China's Expansion of 'Regular Rights Defense Patrols' in the South China Sea." *Southsea Conversations* (blog), 4 September 2014. https://southseaconversations.wordpress.com/2014/09/04/chinas-expansion-of-regular-rights-defense-patrols-in-the-south-china-sea-a-map-courtesy-of-cctv/.

Chung, Chris P. C. "Drawing the U-Shaped Line: China's Claim in the South China Sea, 1946–1974." *Modern China*, 11 August 2015, 1–35, doi:10.1177/0097700415598538.

Chung, Lawrence. "'One Country, Two Systems' Right Formula for Taiwan, Xi Jinping Reiterates." *South China Morning Post*, 27 September 2014, http://www.scmp.com/news/china/article/1601307/one-country-two-systems-right-formula-taiwan-xi-jinping-reiterates.

Clemens, Morgan. "The Maritime Silk Road and the PLA: Part One." *China Brief* 15, no. 6 (19 March 2015), http://www.jamestown.org/single/?tx_ttnews%5Btt_news%5D=43676&no_cache=1#.Vakon-u4k6g.

Clover, Charles. "China's Military Goes to War on Corruption." *Financial Times*, 6 July 2015, http://www.ft.com/intl/cms/s/0/62c7cb6c-23c0-11e5-9c4e-a775d2b173ca.html#axzz3fDUi3OiQ.

———. "China Raises Prospect of South China Sea Air Defense Zone." *Financial Times*, 27 May 2015, http://www.ft.com/int/cms/s/0.bd40ff7a-0447-11e5-a5c3 -00144feabdc0.html#axzz3bSz9rjox.

———. "Chinese Media Confirm Second Aircraft Carrier." *Financial Times*, 10 March 2015, http://www.ft.com/intl/cms/s/0/0339399a-c6f7-11e4-9e34-00144feab7de .html#axzz3fDUi3OiQ.

Cohen, David. "China Examines Military Strategy." *China Brief* 14, no. 3 (7 February 2014), http://www.jamestown.org/programs/chinabrief/single/?tx_ttnews [tt_news]=41932&tx_ttnews[backPid]=758&no_cache=1#.VvKpTUd_e4M.

Cohen, Paul A. *Discovering History in China: American Historical Writing on the Recent Chinese Past*. New York: Columbia University Press, 1984.

Cole, Bernard D. *Asian Maritime Strategies: Navigating Troubled Waters*. Annapolis, Md.: Naval Institute Press, 2013.

———. "China's Carrier: The Basics." *USNI News*, 27 December 2012, http://news .usni.org/2012/11/27/chinas-carrier-basics.

———. "China's Maritime Strategy." In *People's Liberation Army After Next*, edited by Susan M. Puska, 279–328. Carlisle, Pa.: Strategic Studies Institute of the Army War College, 2000.

———. "China's Navy Prepares: Domestic Exercises 2000–2010." In *Learning by Doing: The PLA Trains at Home and Abroad*, edited by Roy Kamphausen, David Lai, and Travis Tanner, 24–27. Carlisle, Pa.: U.S. Army War College, 2012.

———. *The Great Wall at Sea: China's Navy in the Twenty-First Century*. 2nd ed. Annapolis, Md.: Naval Institute Press, 2010.

———. "Island Chains and Naval Classics." U.S. Naval Institute *Proceedings* 140/11/ 1,341 (November 2014): 68–73.

———. "Reflections on China's Maritime Strategy: Island Chains and the Classics." Paper delivered at EMC Conference, Naval War College, Newport, R.I. March 2012, https://www.usnwc.edu/Academics/Faculty/Derek-Reveron/Workshops /Maritime-Security,-Seapower,—-Trade/Maritime-Working-Papers/cole-island -chains.aspx.

———. *Sea Lanes and Pipelines: Energy Security in Asia*. Westport, Conn.: Praeger, 2008.

Cole, J. Michael. "Watch: China's Shocking New Military Recruitment Video." *National Interest, The Buzz* (blog), August 13, 2015, http://nationalinterest.org/ blog/the-buzz/watch-chinas-shocking-new-military-recruitment-video-13573.

Collins, Gabe. "How Much Do China's Warships Actually Cost?" *Diplomat*, 18 June 2015, http://thediplomat.com/2015/06/how-much-do-chinas-warships-actually -cost/.

Collins, Gabe, and Andrew S. Erickson. "China Peak Oil: 2015 Is the Year." *China Signpost*, 7 July 2015, http://www.chinasignpost.com/2015/07/07/china-peak-oil -2015-is-the-year/.

———. "Implications of China's Military Evacuation of Citizens from Libya." *China Brief* 11, no. 4 (10 March 2011), http://www.jamestown.org/programs/chinabrief /single/?tx_ttnews[tt_news]=37633&cHash=7278. .#.VSrG8ZPMePU.

———. "Tank Watch: What Do China's November 2014 SPR Data Tell Us?" *China Sign Post*, 24 November 2014, http://www.chinasignpost.com/2014/11/24/tank-watch-what-do-chinas-november-2014-spr-data-tell-us/.

Collins, John M. *Military Geography for Professionals and the Public.* 1998. Reprint, Provo, Utah: Repressed Publishing, 2012.

Crispin, Shawn W. "Thai Coup Alienates U.S., Giving China New Opening." *YaleGlobal*, 5 March 2015, http://yaleglobal.yale.edu/content/thai-coup-alienates-us-giving-china-new-opening.

Currier, Carrie Liu. "China and the Global Surge for Resources." In *Ashgate Research Companion to Chinese Foreign Policy*, edited by Emilian Kavalski, 163–78. London: Ashgate, 2014.

Davis, Julie Hirschfeld, and Michael R. Gordon. "Japan and U.S. Set New Rules for Military Cooperation." *New York Times*, 27 April 2015, http://www.nytimes.com/2015/04/28/world/asia/japan-and-us-set-new-rules-for-military-cooperation.html.

Daxecker, Ursala and Brandon Prins. "Financing Rebellion through Maritime Piracy." *Political Violence @ A Glance* (blog), 20 August 2015, http://politicalviolenceataglance.org/2015/08/20/financing-rebellion-through-maritime-piracy/.

Deal, Jacqueline Newmyer. "PLA Strategy and Doctrine: A Close Reading of the 2013 Science of Military Strategy." Paper presented at the NBR-SSI Conference on the PLA, March 2015. Carlisle, Pa.. Publication forthcoming by NBR and the U.S. Army War College, SSI, 2016.

Dean, Cornelia. "Report Warns of 'Global Collapse' of Fishing." *New York Times*, 2 November 2006, http://www.nytimes.com/2006/11/02/science/03fishcnd.html?_r=0.

Demick, Barbara. "Judging China's One-Child Policy." *New Yorker*, 30 October 2015, http://www.newyorker.com/news/news-desk/chinas-new-two-child-policy.

Dempsey, Lauren. "7th Fleet Commander Kicks Off CARAT Cambodia 2014." *Navy News*, 27 October 2014, http://www.navy.mil/submit/display.asp?story_id=84017.

———. "USS Fort Worth Conducts CUES with Chinese Navy." *Navy News*, 26 February 2015, http://www.navy.mil/submit/display.asp?story_id=85767.

Deng Zhenghui. "Origins of Misperceptions between China and the U.S." PacNet no. 19. Center for Strategic and International Studies, 1 April 2015, http://csis.org/publication/pacnet-19-origins-misperceptions-between-china-and-us.

Denyer, Simon. "One Child Is Enough: Chinese Families Lukewarm Over Easing of One-Child Policy. *Washington Post*, 23 January 2015, https://www.washingtonpost.com/world/asia_pacific/one-is-enough-chinese-families-lukewarm-over-easing-of-one-child-policy/2015/01/22/bdfeff1e-9d7e-11e4-86a3-1b56f64925f6_story.html.

Desai, Raj M., and James Raymond Vreeland. "What the New Bank of BRICS Is All About." *Washington Post*, 17 July 2014, http://www.washingtonpost.com/blogs/monkey-cage/wp/2014/07/17/what-the-new-bank-of-brics-is-all-about/.

Desker, Barry. "ASEAN Integration Remains an Illusion." *East Asia Forum*, 2 April 2015, http://www.eastasiaforum.org/2015/04/02/asean-integration-remains-an-illusion/.

Ding, Ding, W. Raphael Lam, Shanaka J. Peiris. "Future of Asia's Finance: How Can It Meet Challenges of Demographic Change and Infrastructure Needs?" International Monetary Fund working paper WP/14/126 (2014), https://www.imf.org/external/pubs/ft/wp/2014/wp14126.pdf.

Dobbins, James, John G. McGinn, Keith Crane, Seth G. Jones, Rollie Lal, Andrew Rathmell, Rachel M. Swanger, and Anga R. Timilsina. *America's Role in Nation Building: From Germany to Iraq*. Santa Monica, Calif.: Rand, 2003.

Dollar, David. "China's Rise as a Regional and Global Power: The AIIB and the 'One Belt, One Road.'" *Horizons*. Washington, D.C.: Brookings Institution, Summer 2015, http://www.brookings.edu/research/papers/2015/07/china-regional-global-power-dollar.

Dolven, Ben, Jennifer K. Elsea, Susan V. Lawrence, Ronald O'Rourke, and Ian E. Rinehart. "Chinese Land Reclamation in the South China Sea: Implications and Policy Options." Congressional Research Service Report R44072, 18 June 2015. Washington, D.C.: Congressional Research Service, http://www.fas.org/sgp/crs/row/R44072.pdf.

Dominguez, Gabriel. "Beijing 'Setting Precedent' in South China Sea." *DW*, 23 June 2014, http://www.dw.de/beijing-setting-precedent-in-south-china-sea/a-17729200.

Dornbusch, Rudiger. "Purchasing Power Parity." NEBR Working Paper no. 1591, March 1985, http://www.nber.org/papers/w1591.pdf.

Downs, Erica S. "Business and Politics in the South China Sea: Explaining HYSY-981's Foray into Disputed Waters." Brookings, 24 June 2014, http://www.brookings.edu/research/articles/2014/06/24-business-politics-south-china-sea-downs.

———. "The Chinese Energy Security Debate." *China Quarterly*, no. 177 (March 2004): 21–41.

———. "Mission Mostly Accomplished: China's Energy Trade and Investment Along the Silk Road Economic Belt." *China Brief* 15, no. 6 (19 March 2015), http://www.jamestown.org/programs/chinabrief/single/?tx_ttnews%5Btt_news%5D=43677&cHash=61c6d57411956c3eb8e0ac9448f25076#.VbERoeu4mL8.

Duchâtel, Mathieu, Oliver Brauner, and Zhou Hang, "Protecting China's Overseas Interests: The Slow Shift away from Non-Interference." Stockholm International Peace Research Institute Policy Paper 41 (June 2014), http://books.sipri.org/files/PP/SIPRIPP41.pdf.

Duchâtel, Mathieu, and Bates Gill. "Overseas Citizen Protection: A Growing Challenge for China." Stockholm International Peace Research Institute, 12 February 2012, http://www.sipri.org/media/newsletter/essay/february12.

Dunn, Candace. "China Will Soon Surpass South Korea, Russia, and Japan in Nuclear Generating Capacity." EIA, 20 July 2015, http://www.eia.gov/todayinenergy/detail.cfm?id=22132.

Durden, Tyler. "Where Does China Import Its Energy From?" *Zero Hedge*, 20 January 2014, http://www.zerohedge.com/news/2014-01-20/where-does-china-import-its-energy-and-what-means-petroyuan.

Dutton, Peter. "An Analysis of China's Claim to Historic Rights in the South China Sea." In *Major Law and Policy Issues in the South China Sea: European and American Perspectives*, edited by Y. Song and K. Zou, 57–74. Surrey, U.K.: Ashgate, 2014.

Dzurek, Edward J. "The Spratly Islands: Who's on First?" International Boundary Research Unit. *Maritime Briefing* 2, no. 1 (1996).

Eberling, George G. *Future Oil Demands of China, India, and Japan.* New York: Lexington, 2014.

Elferink, Alex G. Oude. "The Islands in the South China Sea: How Does Their Presence Limit the Extent of the High Seas and the Area and the Maritime Zones of the Mainland Coasts?" *Ocean Development and International Law* 32, no. 2 (2001): 169–90, doi:10.1080/00908320151100307.

Erdbrink, Thomas, and Chris Buckley. "China and Iran to Conduct Joint Naval Exercises in the Persian Gulf." *New York Times,* 21 September 2014, http://www.nytimes.com/2014/09/22/world/middleeast/china-and-iran-to-conduct-joint-naval-exercises-in-the-persian-gulf.html.

Erickson, Andrew S. *Chinese Anti-Ship Ballistic Missile (ASBM) Development: Drivers, Trajectories, and Strategic Implications.* Washington, D.C.: Jamestown Foundation, May 2013. http://www.andrewerickson.com/wp-content/uploads/2014/01/China-ASBM_Jamestown_2013.pdf.

———. "CMSI Conference—'China's Naval Shipbuilding—Progress and Challenges'—My Personal Summary of the Discussion." *Andrew S. Erickson: China Analysis from Original Sources* (blog), 9 July 2015, http://www.andrewerickson.com/2015/07/quick-look-report-on-cmsi-conference-chinas-naval-shipbuilding-progress-and-challenges/.

———. "Revelations on China's Maritime Modernization." *Diplomat,* 16 April 2015, http://thediplomat.com/2015/04/revelations-on-chinas-maritime-modernization/.

Erickson, Andrew S., and Gabe Collins. "Beijing's Energy Security Strategy: The Significance of a Chinese State-Owned Tanker Fleet." *Orbis* 51, no. 4 (2007): 665–84. doi:10.1016/j.orbis.2007.08.009.

Erickson, Andrew S., Lyle Goldstein, and William S. Murray. *Chinese Mine Warfare: A PLA Navy "Assassin's Mace" Capability.* Chinese Maritime Studies, no. 3. Newport, R.I.: China Maritime Studies Institute, Naval War College, 2009, https://www.usnwc.edu/Research—-Gaming/China-Maritime-Studies-Institute/Publications/documents/CMS3_Mine-Warfare.aspx.

Erickson, Andrew S., and Conor M. Kennedy. "Tanmen Militia: 'China's Maritime Rights Protection' Vanguard." *National Interest,* 6 May 2015, http://nationalinterest.org/feature/tanmen-militia-china%E2%80%99s-maritime-rights-protection-vanguard-12816.

Erickson, Andrew S., and Adam P. Liff. "China's Military Spending Swells Again Despite Domestic Headwinds." *Wall Street Journal,* 5 March 2015, http://blogs.wsj.com/chinarealtime/2015/03/05/chinas-military-spending-swells-again-despite-domestic-headwinds/.

Erickson, Andrew S., and Austin Strange. "China's Blue Soft Power: Antipiracy, Engagement, and Image Enhancement." *Naval War College Review* 68, no. 1 (Winter 2015): 71–91.

———. "China's Global Maritime Presence: Hard and Soft Dimensions of PLAN Antipiracy Operations." *China Brief* 15, no. 9 (1 May 2015), http://www.jamestown.org/programs/chinabrief/single/?tx_ttnews%5Btt_news%5D=43868&cHash=41e27d4081351e4e8e357eb95cce0294#.Vfh9fLS4nUo.

———. *No Substitute for Experience: Chinese Antipiracy Operations in the Gulf of Aden.* CMSI No. 10 (Newport, R.I.: Naval War College, 2013), https://www.us nwc.edu/Research—Gaming/China-Maritime-Studies-Institute/Publications /documents/CMS10_Web_2.aspx.

Fedyszen, Thomas R. "Renaissance of the Russian Navy." U.S. Naval Institute *Proceedings* 138/3/1/1,309 (March 2012), http://www.usni.org/magazines/proceedings /2012-03/renaissance-russian-navy.

Feng, Bree. "China Backpedals on Shale Gas." *Chemical and Engineering News* 93, no. 3 (19 January 2015): 22–23, http://cen.acs.org/articles/93/i3/China-Backpedals -Shale-Gas.html.

Feng, Bree, and Edward Wong. "Iraq Keeps a Close Eye on Oil Interests in Iraq." *New York Times, Sinosphere: Dispatches from China* (blog), 17 June 2015, http:// sinosphere.blogs.nytimes.com/2014/06/17/china-keeps-a-close-eye-on-oil -interests-in-iraq/?_r=0.

Feng Zhaokui, "What Are China's Core Interests?" *China-US Focus.* 21 October 2014. http://www.chinausfocus.com/foreign-policy/what-are-chinas-core-interests-2/.

Finkelstein, David. "China's National Military Strategy." In *Rightsizing the PLA*, edited by Roy Kamphausen, and Andrew Scobell, 69–140. Carlisle, Pa.: U.S. Army War College, 2007. http://www.strategicstudiesinstitute.army.mil/pdffiles /PUB784.pdf.

———. "2015 Should Be an Exciting Year for PLA Watching." Arlington, Va.: Center for Naval Analyses, 8 April 2015.

Fisher, Richard D., Jr., and James Hardy. "China Practices Taiwan Invasion with Civilian Ferries, Bomber Flights in Bashi Channel." *IHS Jane's Defence Weekly*, 16 June 2015, http://www.janes.com/article/52268/china-practices-taiwan-invasion -with-civilian-ferries-bomber-flights-in-bashi-channel.

Fitzsimmons, Scott. "Evaluating the Masters of Strategy: Comparative Analysis of Clausewitz, Sun Tzu, Mahan, and Corbett." *Innovations* 7 (2007), http://www .ucalgary.ca/innovations/files/innovations/fitzsimmons-evaluatingthemaster sofstrategy.pdf.

Forsythe, Michael. "As China Prospers, the Military Recruiter's Job Gets Harder." *New York Times, Sinosphere: Dispatches from China* (blog), 20 March 2015, http:// sinosphere.blogs.nytimes.com/2015/03/19/as-china-prospers-the-military -recruiters-job-gets-harder/.

Franckx, Erik. "Chinese Claims in the East China Sea and South China Sea: A Legal Assessment of Cartographic Evidence." In *The Asian Century: What International Norms and Practices?*, edited by Françoise Nicolas, Céline Pajon and John Seaman, 22–32. Paris: French Institute for International Relations (Ifri), 2014, http://www .ifri.org/sites/default/files/atoms/files/ifri_conference_proceedings_12sept 2014_asian_century_norms_and_practices.pdf.

Frankel, Jeffrey. "Chinese Currency Manipulation Not a Problem." *East Asia Forum*, 9 March 2015, http://www.eastasiaforum.org/2015/03/09/chinese-currency -manipulation-not-a-problem/.

Fravel, M. Taylor. "China's New Military Strategy." *China Brief* 15, no. 13 (23 June 2015), http://www.jamestown.org/programs/chinabrief/single/?tx_ttnews%5Btt_news %5D=44072&cHash=c403ff4a87712ec43d2a11cf576f3ec1#.Vd2ZdLS4k0o.

——. "China's Strategy in the South China Sea." *Contemporary Southeast Asia* 33, no. 3 (2011): 292–319.

——. *Strong Borders, Secure Nation*. Princeton, N.J.: Princeton University Press, 2008.

Fravel, M. Taylor, and Christopher P. Twomey. "Projecting Strategy: The Myth of Chinese Counter-intervention." *Washington Quarterly* 37, no. 4 (Winter 2015): 171–87, doi:10.1080/0163660X.2014.1002164.

Freeman, Charles W., III. "Fear and Loathing in China's New Economic Normal." Brookings, November 13, 2014, http://www.brookings.edu/research/opinions/2014/11/13-fear-loathing-china-new-normal-freeman.

Freeman, Chas. "China and the Economic Integration of Europe and Asia." Remarks to the Summer Roundtable of the Pacific Pension Institute (23 June 2015), http://chasfreeman.net/china-eurasia-integration/.

Friedberg, Aaron L. "'Going Out': China's Pursuit of Natural Resources and its Implications for Grand Strategy." National Bureau of Asian Research, September 2006, http://www.nbr.org/publications/issue.aspx?id=66.

——. "The Sources of Chinese Conduct: Explaining Beijing's Assertiveness." *Washington Quarterly* 37, no. 4 (2015): 133–50, doi:10.1080/0163660X.2014.1002160.

Gabuev, Alexander. "Another BRIC(S) In the Great Wall." Carnegie Moscow Center, 7 July 2015, http://carnegie.ru/commentary/?fa=60628.

——. "Sino-Russian Trade after a Year of Sanctions." Carnegie Moscow Center, 11 September 2015, http://carnegie.ru/commentary/?fa=61240.

——. "Smiles and Waves: What Xi Jinping Took away from Moscow." Carnegie Moscow Center, 29 May 2015, http://carnegie.ru/commentary/?fa=60248.

Gady, Franz-Stefan. "Japan Will Permanently Join U.S.-India Naval Exercises." *Diplomat*, 13 October 2015, http://thediplomat.com/2015/10/confirmed-japan-will-permanently-join-us-india-naval-exercises/.

——. "Vietnam Commissions Two Subs Capable of Attacking China." *Diplomat*, 6 August 2015, http://thediplomat.com/2015/08/vietnam-commissions-two-new-subs-capable-of-attacking-china/.

Gan, Nectar. "Retired Generals Point to 'Horrible' Graft in PLA." *South China Morning Post*, 10 March 2015, http://www.scmp.com/news/china/article/1734592/retired-generals-point-horrible-graft-pla.

Gao Zhiguo, Song Yann-Huei, Hu Dekin, ZhuFeng, statements in "Highlights of a Cross-Strait Conference on Jointly Safeguarding Rights/Interest in the South China Sea: Both Sides of the Taiwan Strait Join Hands to Offer Policy Advice on the South China Sea." *China Ocean News*, 13 February 2015, http://epaper.oceanol.com/shtml/zghyb/20150213/77382.shtml (discontinued; accessed 10 July 2015).

Garamone, Jim. "Greenert Discusses U.S. Maritime Strategy Shift." *DoD News*, 4 November 2015, http://www.defense.gov/news/newsarticle.aspx?id=123561.

Gardiner, Beth. "Asia Pushes Hard for Clean Energy." *New York Times*, 18 November 2014, http://www.nytimes.com/2014/11/19/business/energy-environment/asia-pushes-hard-for-clean-energy.html.

Garver, John W. *Foreign Relations of the People's Republic of China*. Englewood Cliffs, N.J.: Prentice Hall, 1993.

———. "Sino-Russian Relations." In *China and the World*, edited by Samuel S. Kim, 114–31. Boulder, Colo.: Westview, 1998.

Geng Yansheng. "Defense Ministry's Regular Press Conference on April 30, 2015." PRC Ministry of National Defense, 30 April 2015, http://eng.mod.gov.cn/Press /2015-04/30/content_4582738.htm.

Gindarsah, Iis. "Indonesia and the South China Sea: A Two-fold Strategy." RSIS Commentary no. 158/2015 (27 July 2015), http://www.rsis.edu.sg/wp-content /uploads/2015/07/CO15158.pdf.

Givens, John Wagner. "Fleshing Out the Third Plenum: The Direction of China's Legal Reform." *China Brief* 14, no. 6 (21 March 2014): 10–13, http://www.james town.org/programs/chinabrief/single/?tx_ttnews%5Btt_news%5D=42128&tx _ttnews%5BbackPid%5D=758&no_cache=1#.VyOtWmM4kXo.

Glaser, Bonnie S. "A Big Deal: China Reveals Its South China Sea Strategy." *National Interest*, 24 April 2015, http://nationalinterest.org/blog/the-buzz/big-deal-china -reveals-its-south-china-sea-strategy-12720.

———. "China's Maritime Actors, Coordinated and Directed from the Top." *Asia Maritime Security Initiative*, Washington, D.C.: CSIS, 14 January 2015, http:// amti.csis.org/chinas-maritime-actors-coordinated-and-directed-from-the-top/.

———. "China's Maritime Rights Protection Leading Small Group—Shrouded in Secrecy." Asia Maritime Transparency Initiative, 11 September 2015, http:// amti.csis.org/chinas-maritime-rights-protection-leading-small-group-shrouded -in-secrecy/.

———. "Conflict in the South China Sea: Contingency Planning Memorandum Update." Council on Foreign Relations, April 2015, http://www.cfr.org/asia-and -pacific/conflict-south-china-sea/p36377.

———. "People's Republic of China Maritime Disputes." Testimony before the U.S. House Armed Services Subcommittee on Seapower and Projection Forces and the House Foreign Affairs Subcommittee on the Asia Pacific, 14 January 2014, http://csis.org/files/attachments/ts140114_glaser.pdf.

Glaser, Bonnie, and Deep Pal. "China's Periphery Diplomacy Initiative: Implications for China's Neighbors and the United States." *China-US Focus*, 17 November 2013, http://www.chinausfocus.com/foreign-policy/chinas-periphery-diplomacy -initiative-implications-for-china-neighbors-and-the-united-states/.

Glaser, Bonnie, and Philip Saunders. "Chinese Civilian Foreign Policy Research Institutes: Evolving Roles and Increasing Influence." *China Quarterly* 171 (September 2002): 597–616.

Glaser, Bonnie, and Jacqueline Vitello. "Xi Jinping's Great Game: Are China and Taiwan Headed towards Trouble?" *National Interest*, 16 July 2015, http://national interest.org/feature/xi-jinpings-great-game-are-china-taiwan-headed-towards -13346.

Goldstein, Lyle J. *Five Dragons Stirring up the Sea: Challenge and Opportunity in China's Improving Maritime Enforcement Capabilities.* China Maritime Study No. 5 (Newport, R.I.: Naval War College Press, April 2010), http://www.usnwc .edu/Research—-Gaming/China-Maritime-Studies-Institute/Publications /documents/CMSI_No5_web1.pdf.

———. "The Real Military Threat from China: Anti-Ship Cruise Missiles." *National Interest*, 22 January 2015, http://nationalinterest.org/feature/the-real-military-threat-china-anti-ship-cruise-missiles-12085.

Gordon, Deborah, Yevgen Sautin, and Wang Tao. "China's Oil Future." CEIP Carnegie Endowment for International Peace, 6 May 2014, http://carnegieendowment.org/2014/05/06/china-s-oil-future.

Gordon, Michael R. "U.S. Eases Embargo on Arms to Vietnam." *New York Times*, 2 October 2014, http://www.nytimes.com/2014/10/03/world/asia/us-eases-embargo-on-arms-to-vietnam.html.

Gowen, Annie. "Troops Face Off at India-China Border as Nations' Leaders Meet." *Washington Post*, 18 September 2014, https://www.washingtonpost.com/world/troops-face-off-at-india-china-border-as-leaders-of-nations-meet/2014/09/18/a86e7b8a-1962-4446-b80c-f038a57527f3_story.html.

Graham, Euan. "Energy Competition in the South China Sea: A Front-burner Issue?" *RSIS Commentary*, no. 179 (11 September 2014), http://www.rsis.edu.sg/wp-content/uploads/2014/09/CO14179.pdf.

———. "Maritime Security and Threats to Energy Transportation in Southeast Asia." *RUSI Journal* 160, no. 2 (April–May 2015): 20–31.

Grudgings, Stuart. "Insight: China's Assertiveness Hardens Malaysia's Stance in Sea Dispute." Reuters, 26 February 2014, http://uk.reuters.com/article/2014/02/26/uk-malaysia-china-maritime-insight-idUKBREA1P1Z020140226.

Grudgings, Stuart, and Ben Blanchard. "Malaysia Navy Chief Denies Chinese Incursion." Reuters, 29 January 2014, http://www.reuters.com/article/2014/01/29/us-malaysia-china-navy-idUSBREA0S0B020140129.

Haas, Benjamin. "Beijing Rebukes U.S. over South China Sea Islands Row." *China Post*, 1 May 2015, http://www.chinapost.com.tw/china/national-news/2015/05/17/436213/Beijing-rebukes.htm.

Hackett, James. *Military Balance 2016* (London: International Institute for Strategic Studies, 11 February 2015).

Hammond, Joshua. "Malabar 2014 Kicks Off." *Navy News*, 24 July 2014, http://www.navy.mil/submit/display.asp?story_id=82388.

Hand, Marcus. "Malacca Strait Traffic Hits an All Time High in 2014." *Seatrade Maritime News*, 20 June 2015, http://www.seatrade-maritime.com/news/asia/malacca-strait-traffic-hits-an-all-time-high-in-2014-vlccs-and-dry-bulk-lead-growth.html.

Hartnett, Daniel. "The Father of the Modern Chinese Navy." Center for International Maritime Security, 8 October 2014, http://cimsec.org/father-modern-chinese-navy-liu-huaqing/13291.

Heath, Timothy. "Diplomacy Work Forum: Xi Steps up Efforts to Shape a China-Centered Regional Order." *China Brief* 13, no. 22 (7 November 2013), http://www.jamestown.org/programs/chinabrief/single/?tx_ttnews%5Btt_news%5D=41594&cHash=a803315cd93291ad8b1043771111270b#.VerqRbS4mgQ.

Herberg, Mikkal. "China's Search for Oil and Gas Security: Prospects and Implications." NBR Special Report #47. In *China's Energy Crossroads: Forging a New Energy and Environmental Balance*, edited by Philip Andrews-Speed, 19–28.

Seattle: National Bureau of Asian Research, November 2014, http://www.nbr .org/publications/element.aspx?id=791.

Hille, Kathrin. "Putin Aims to Cement China Links as Ties with West Fray." *Financial Times*, 10 November 2014, http://www.ft.com/intl/cms/s/0/31e95c5e-68b8-11e4 -af00-00144feabdc0.html#axzz3goxLBxfc.

Hornby, Lucy. "Wanted List Reveals Nature of Chinese Corruption." *Financial Times*, 23 April 2015, http://www.ft.com/intl/cms/s/0/4a465994-e993-11e4-a687-00144 feab7de.html#axzz3k982GCbI.

Hornby, Lucy, and Andres Schipani. "China Tilts towards Liberal Latin American Economies." *Financial Times*, 11 May 2015, http://www.ft.com/intl/cms/s/0/b73a 606c-f46b-11e4-bd16-00144feab7de.html#axzz3g41lEakR.

Horta, Loro. "Brazil-China Relations." RSIS Working Paper no. 287 (10 March 2015), http://www.rsis.edu.sg/wp-content/uploads/2015/03/WP287.pdf.

Hsiao, Russell. "Military Delegates Call for National Maritime Strategy to Protect Expanding Interests." *China Brief* 11, no. 4 (10 March 2011), http://www.james town.org/single/?no_cache=1&tx_ttnews%5Btt_news%5D=37629&tx_ttnews% 5BbackPid%5D=7&cHash=79f56b556ae0003e6afc755934e1fa54.

Hu, Zep, and Y. F. Lo. "Taiwan, China Sign Taxation, Flight Safety Pacts." *China News Agency*, 25 August 2015, http://focustaiwan.tw/news/acs/201508250024.aspx.

Huang, Kaixi, "Closer Look: Why Official Goals for Natural Gas Use Are in Doubt." *CaixinOnline*, 23 November 2015, http://english.caixin.com/2015-11-23/1008 77612.html.

Huber, Peter, and Mark Mills. "Oil, Oil, Everywhere." Manhattan Institute, 27 January 2005, http://www.manhattan-institute.org/html/_wsj-oil_oil.htm.

Hwang, Jaeho. "The ROK'S China Policy Under Park Geun-Hye: A New Model of ROK-PRC Relations." Brookings Institution Center for East Asia Policy Studies, August 2014, http://www.brookings.edu/~/media/research/files/papers/2014/08 /south-korea-china-policy-hwang/south-korea-china-policy-hwang-working -paper.pdf.

Ikeshima, Taisaku. "China's Dashed Line in the South China Sea: Legal Limits and Future Prospects." *Waseda Global Forum*, no. 20 (2013): 17–50, https://dspace. wul.waseda.ac.jp/dspace/bitstream/2065/41466/1/WasedaGlobalForum_10 _Ikeshima.pdf.

iMan, Luke. "Chinese Media Takes Aim at J-15 Fighter." *GreenDef* (blog), September 2013, http://greendef.blogspot.com/2013/09/chinese-media-takes-aim-at-j-15 -fighter.html.

Information Office of the State Council of the PRC. "China's Ethnic Policy and Common Prosperity and Development of All Ethnic Groups." *Chinese Journal of International Law* 9, no. 1 (March 2009): 221–59, doi:10.1093/chinesejil/jmp037.

Innismay, Michelle. "Search for Missing Malaysia Airlines Jet Uncovers Shipwreck's Remnants." *New York Times*, 13 May 2015, http://www.nytimes.com/2015/05/14/ world/asia/malaysia-airlines-mh370-search-shipwreck-seabed-ocean-find .html?_r=0.

Jaffe, Amy Myers, Kenneth B. Medlock III, and Meghan L. O'Sullivan. "China's Energy Hedging Strategy: Less Than Meets the Eye for Russian Gas Pipelines." National

Bureau of Asian Research, 9 February 2015, http://www.nbr.org/research/activity.aspx?id=530.

Jakobson, Linda. "China's Foreign Policy Dilemma." Lowy Institute for International Policy, 5 February 2013, http://www.lowyinstitute.org/publications/chinas-foreign-policy-dilemma.

———. "China's Unpredictable Maritime Security Actors." Lowy Institute for International Policy, December 2014, http://www.lowyinstitute.org/files/chinas-unpredictable-maritime-security-actors_3.pdf.

———. "The PLA and Maritime Security Actors." In *PLA Influence on China's National Security Policymaking*, edited by Phillip C. Saunders and Andrew Scobell, 300–323. Stanford, Calif.: Stanford University Press, 2015.

Ji Guoxing. "Maritime Jurisdiction in the Three China Seas." IGCC Policy Paper 19 (1995), http://www.spratlys.org/contents/solutions/11.htm.

Jiang, Julie, and Chen Ding. "Update on Overseas Investments by China's National Oil Companies: Achievements and Challenges Since 2011." Partner Country series. Paris: International Energy Agency, 2014, https://www.iea.org/publications/freepublications/publication/PartnerCountrySeriesUpdateonOverseasInvestmentsbyChinasNationalOilCompanies.pdf.

Johnson, Christopher K. "Sweeping Reforms Announced at Third Plenum." Center for Strategic and International Studies, 15 November 2013, http://csis.org/publication/china-announces-sweeping-reform-agenda-plenum.

Johnson, Christopher K., with Ernest Z. Bower, Victor D. Cha, Michael J. Green, and Matthew P. Goodman. *Decoding China's Emerging 'Great Power' Strategy in Asia.* Washington, D.C.: Center for Strategic and International Studies, June 2014, http://csis.org/files/publication/140603_Johnson_DecodingChinasEmerging_WEB.pdf.

Johnson, Steve. "Capital Economics Claims GDP Deflator Miscalculated Across Emerging Markets." *Financial Times*, 8 June 2015, http://www.ft.com/intl/cms/s/3/3c6337b8-0b79-11e5-8937-00144feabdc0.html#axzz3fnvKnm9w.

Johnston, Alastair Iain. "How New and Assertive Is China's New Assertiveness?" *International Security* 37, no. 4 (Spring 2013): 7–48, http://belfercenter.ksg.harvard.edu/files/IS3704_pp007-048.pdf.

Johnston, Alastair Ian, and Robert S. Ross, eds. *Engaging China: The Management of an Emerging Power.* London: Routledge, 1999.

Jones, Andrew. "The Day the Chinese People Stood Up." *GB Times*, 1 October 2013, http://gbtimes.com/world/day-chinese-people-stood.

Kaiman, Jonathan. "Japan's Abe and China's Xi Hold Ice-breaking Meeting as APEC Starts." *Guardian*, 10 November 2014, A14, http://www.theguardian.com/world/2014/nov/10/xi-jinping-shinzo-abe-ice-breaking-meeting-apec-starts.

Kallender-Umezu, Paul. "Tokyo to Challenge China on Fiery Cross Reef." *Defense News*, 19 July 2015, http://www.defensenews.com/story/defense/policy-budget/2015/07/19/japan-china-fiery-cross-reef-artificial-island/30235685/.

Kapoor, Kanupriya, and Linda Sieg. "Indonesian President Says China's Main Claim in South China Sea Has No Legal Basis." Reuters, 23 Marcy 2015, http://www.reuters.com/article/2015/03/23/us-indonesia-china-southchinasea-idUSKBN0MJ04320150323.

Karsten, Joshua. "US 7th Fleet, Singaporean, Malaysian, and Indonesian Navies Meet to Enhance Multilateral Cooperation." *Navy News*, 7 May 2015, http://www.navy .mil/submit/display.asp?story_id=86971.

Kato, Yoichi. "AIIB on Track to Attract 70-plus Members, Chief Says." *Nikkei Asian Review*, 10 September 2015, http://asia.nikkei.com/Politics-Economy/Economy /AIIB-on-track-to-attract-70-plus-members-chief-says.

———. "U.S. Commander Says China Aims to be a 'Global Military' Power." *Asahi Shimbun*, 28 December 2010, http://www.china-defense-mashup.com/ us-commander-says-china-aims-to-be-a-global-military-power.html.

Kaufman, Alison, and Tamara Hemphill. "PRC Foreign Policy under Xi Jinping: An Initial Assessment." Arlington, Va.: Center for Naval Analyses (ICP-2014-U-008327-Final), August 2014, 1–5.

Kazianis, Harry. "China's Ten Red Lines in the South China Sea." *Diplomat*, 7 July 2014, http://thediplomat.com/2014/07/chinas-10-red-lines-in-the-south-china -sea/.

Keck, Zachary. "China Tests New Unmanned Mini-Sub." *Diplomat*, 1 July 2014, http:// thediplomat.com/2014/07/china-tests-new-unmanned-mini-sub/.

———. "The Submarine Race in the Malaccan Strait." *Diplomat*, 16 July 2015, http:// thediplomat.com/2013/07/the-submarine-race-in-the-malaccan-strait/.

Keliher, Macabe, and Hsinchao Wu. "How to Discipline 90 Million People." *Atlantic*, 7 April 2015, http://www.theatlantic.com/international/archive/2015/04/xi -jinping-china-corruption-political-culture/389787/.

Kennedy, Paul. *The Rise and Fall of the Great Powers: Economic Change and Military Conflict from 1500 to 2000*. Boston: DC Heath, 1987.

Kiani, Khaeeq. "6,600MW Put on Back Burner." *Pakistan Engineering Review* 40 (15 August 2015), http://www.dawn.com/news/1161417.

Knowler, Greg. "Investment Floods into China's One Belt, One Road Strategy." *JOC. com*, 3 July 2015, http://www.joc.com/international-trade-news/investment -floods-china's-one-belt-one-road-strategy_20150703.html.

Ko Hirano. "Mekong States Aim to Maintain Balance Between Japan, China." *Kyodo*, 5 July 2015, https://english.kyodonews.jp/news/2015/07/361995.html.

Koh Swee Lean Collin. "Westward Ho: Expanding Global Role for China's Navy?" RSIS Commentary no. 005/2014 (7 January 2014), http://www.rsis.edu.sg/rsis -publication/idss/2130-westward-ho-expanding-global/#.VZ7_C-u4n_Q.

Kraska, James. "Confidence Building Regimes." Paper presented at Maritime Security in the Asia-Pacific conference. Washington, D.C., March 2015.

Kraska, James, and Michael Monti. "The Law of Naval Warfare and China's Maritime Militia." *International Law Studies* 91 (Newport, R.I.: Naval War College, 2015).

Kristensen, Hans M. "China's Noisy Nuclear Submarines." Federation of American Scientists, 21 November 2009, http://fas.org/blogs/security/2009/11/subnoise/.

Kristensen, Hans M., and Robert S. Norris. "Chinese Nuclear Forces, 2015." *Bulletin of Atomic Scientists*, 18 June 2015, doi:10.1177/0096340215591247.

Krutikhin, Mikhail. "East or West, Home Is Best." Carnegie Moscow Center, 15 October 2014, http://carnegie.ru/eurasiaoutlook/?fa=56936.

Kuhn, Anthony. "One County Provides Preview of China's Looming Aging Crisis." NPR, *All Things Considered*, 14 January 2015, http://www.npr.org/sections

/parallels/2015/01/14/377190697/one-county-provides-preview-of-chinas-looming-aging-crisis.

Kuhn, Robert Lawrence. "Xi Jinping's Dream." *New York Times*, 4 June 2013, http://www.nytimes.com/2013/06/05/opinion/global/xi-jinpings-chinese-dream.html.

Kuo, Lily. "The Shortcomings of Electricity as the Chinese Indicator of Choice." *Quartz*, 18 October 2012, http://qz.com/17174/the-shortcomings-of-electricity-the-chinese-indicator-of-choice/.

Kuo, Lily, and Heather Timmins. "China Is Building a $46 Billion Railroad through Pakistan's Insurgency." *Defense One*, 20 April 2015, http://www.defenseone.com/technology/2015/04/china-building-46b-railroad-through-pakistans-insurgency/110536/.

Kynge, James, and Christian Oliver. "Li Keqiang Pushes for China-Europe Investment Treaty." *Financial Times*, 29 June 2015, http://www.ft.com/intl/cms/s/0/f0b923c0-1e67-11e5-ab0f-6bb9974f25d0.html#axzz3g41lEakR.

Laeng, Jennifer. "China Coast Guard Vessel Found at Luconia Shoals." *Borneo Post Online*, 3 June 2015, http://www.theborneopost.com/2015/06/03/china-coast-guard-vessel-found-at-luconia-shoals/.

LaGrone, Sam. "New Chinese Nuclear Sub Design Includes Special Operations Mini-Sub." *USNI News*, 25 March 2015, http://news.usni.org/2015/03/25/new-chinese-nuclear-sub-design-includes-special-operations-mini-sub.

Lai, David. Introduction to *The PLA at Home and Abroad: Assessing the Operational Capabilities of China's Military*, edited by Roy Kamphausen, David Lai, and Andrew Scobell. Carlisle, Pa.: Strategic Studies Institute, 2010, http://www.strategicstudiesinstitute.army.mil/pdffiles/PUB995.pdf.

Lam, Willy. "The Generals' Growing Clout in Diplomacy." *China Brief* 15, no. 7 (3 April 2015), http://www.jamestown.org/programs/chinabrief/single/?tx_ttnews%5Btt_news%5D=43750&cHash=9f47f10a7531e5f9b9d2428f61c275c5#.Ve3lyrS4mgQ.

———. "White Paper Expounds Civil-Military Relations in Xi Era." *China Brief* 15, no. 12 (19 June 2015), http://www.jamestown.org/programs/chinabrief/single/?tx_ttnews%5Btt_news%5D=44059&cHash=98a51f9293591b93a3f83bc5993a4131#.Vfh08LS4mgQ.

Lampton, David M. "How China Is Ruled." *Foreign Affairs* 93, no. 1 (January–February 2014): 74–85.

———. "The U.S. and China: Sliding from Engagement to Coercive Diplomacy." Pac-Net no. 63, Center for Strategic and International Studies, 4 August 2014, http://csis.org/publication/pacnet-63-us-and-china-sliding-engagement-coercive-diplomacy.

Lannin, Sue. "South China Sea Tensions Deter Oil Exploration," *ABC News* (Australia), 11 August 2015, http://www.abcnet.au/news/2015-08-11/south-china-sea-tensions-deter-oil-exploration/6688988.

Lee, John. "China's Geostrategic Search for Oil." *Washington Quarterly* (Summer 2012): 75–92.

Leffler, Melvyn P. *A Preponderance of Power: National Security, the Truman Administration, and the Cold War*. Stanford, Calif.: Stanford University Press, 1992.

Lelyveld, Michael. "Doubts Rise on Russia-China Gas Deal." Radio Free Asia, 4 June 2015, http://www.rfa.org/english/commentaries/energy_watch/doubts-rise-on-russia-china-gas-deal-04062015110032.html.

Leung, James. "Xi's Corruption Crackdown." *Foreign Affairs* 94, no. 4 (May–June 2015), https://www.foreignaffairs.com/articles/china/2015-04-20/xis-corruption-crackdown.

Lewis, John, and Xue Litai. "China's Search for a Modern Air Force." *International Security* 24, no. 1 (Summer 1999): 64–94.

Li Daguang, and Ma Zheng. "The Complexity of the Maritime Military Struggle Calls for a Powerful Navy." China National Defense University. Translated by the China Maritime Studies Institute. Newport, R.I.: Naval War College, July 2015.

Li, Fion. "IMF Official Says Yuan No Longer Undervalued Amid Reserve-Status Push." Bloomberg, 26 May 2015, http://www.bloomberg.com/news/articles/2015-05-26/imf-says-yuan-is-no-longer-undervalued-amid-reserve-currency-bid.

Li, Jujun. "Traditional Military Thinking and the Defensive Strategy of China." An address at the U.S. [Army] War College. Letort Paper no. 1, 29 August 1997. http://www.strategicstudiesinstitute.army.mil/pubs/download.cfm?q=82.

Li Keqiang. *Report on the Work of the Government*. Delivered at the Third Session of the 12th National People's Congress, 5 March 2015. Available at *Xinhuanet*, 16 March 2015, http://news.xinhuanet.com/english/china/2015-03/16/c_134071473.htm.

Li, Mingjiang. "International Status: China's Pursuit of a Comprehensive Superpower Status." In *Ashgate Research Companion on Chinese Foreign Policy*, edited by Emilian Kavalski, 33–46. London: Ashgate, 2012.

Li, Nan. "The Evolution of China's Naval Strategy and Capabilities: From 'Near Coast' and 'Near Seas' to 'Far Seas.'" *Asian Security* 5 no. 2 (May 2009): 144–69.

Li, Niu. "Major Challenges Facing China's Economy in 2015." *China-US Focus*, 18 March 2015, http://www.chinausfocus.com/finance-economy/major-challenges-facing-chinas-economy-in-2015/.

Li Ruohan. "AIIB Appoints Jin Liqun as Its First President." *Global Times*, 25 August 2015, http://english.jschina.com.cn/20322/201508/t2346110.shtml.

Liang, Xiaodeng. "India's Accession to the Shanghai Cooperation Organization." National Bureau of Asian Research, 20 August 2015, http://www.nbr.org/research/activity.aspx?id=595.

Liebenberg, David M. "How a 120-Year-Old War is Driving China's Military Modernization." *Diplomat*, 2 February 2015, http://thediplomat.com/2015/02/how-a-120-year-old-war-is-driving-chinas-military-modernization/.

Liff, Adam P., and G. John Ikenberry, "Racing toward Tragedy?" *International Security* 39, no. 2 (Fall 2014): 52–91.

Lin, Jeffrey, and P. W. Singer. "China's Getting Ready to Turn on Asian's Biggest Warship." *Popular Science*, 4 June 2015, http://www.popsci.com/cruiser-test-rig-nears-completion.

Liu Hua. "Xi Jinping and Recep Tayyip Erdoğan Together Attend the China-Turkey Business Forum." *Xinhua*, 30 July 2015, http://hr.china-embassy.org/eng/gnxw/t1286481.htm.

LLD and AEF. "Chinese Official Acknowledges the Economic Data Fraud." BBC Chinese, 4 March 2015, http://www.bbc.co.uk/zhongwen/simp/china/2015/03 /150304_cn_economic_data.

Lu, Verna. "China Offers First Glimpse of Sweeping National Security Law." *South China Morning Post Online* (Hong Kong), 7 May 2015, http://www.scmp.com /news/china/policies-politics/article/1788339/release-chinas-draft-security -law-sparks-fears-further.

Lubold, Gordon, and Adam Entous. "U.S. Says Beijing Is Building Up South China Sea Islands." *Wall Street Journal*, 9 May 2015, http://www.wsj.com/articles/u-s -says-beijing-building-up-south-china-sea-islands-1431109387.

Luo, Baozhen. "China Will Get Rich Before It Gets Old." *Foreign Affairs* 94, no. 3 (May–June 2015), https://www.foreignaffairs.com/articles/china/2015-04-20 /china-will-get-rich-it-grows-old?gp=140810%3A1fe52990555a12cd&CID=E MC-FARelease-baozhen-luo-042115.

Lynch, David J. "Carter Warns China That U.S. Will Go Wherever Global Law Permits." Bloomberg, 27 May 2015, http://www.bloomberg.com/politics/articles /2015-05-27/carter-warns-china-that-u-s-will-go-wherever-global-law-permits.

Ma, Damian. "Rebalancing China's Energy Strategy." Paulson Papers on Energy and Environment. Washington, D.C.: Paulson Institute, 6 January 2015, http://www .paulsoninstitute.org/think-tank/2015/01/06/rebalancing-chinas-energy-strategy/.

Ma Zhancheng. "Xi Eyes More Enabling Int'l Environment." *Xinhua*, 30 November 2014, http://news.xinhuanet.com/english/china/2014-11/30/c_133822694_4.htm.

Mackinder, Halford. *Democratic Ideals and Reality: A Study in the Politics of Recon-struction*. London: Constable and Company, 1919; reprint, London: Forgotten Books, 2012.

———. "The Geographic Pivot of History." A paper of the Royal Geographic Society. London: Royal Geographic Society, 1904.

Magnier, Mark, Lingling Wei, and Ian Talley. "Economy Expanded 7.4% in 2014." *Wall Street Journal*, 19 January 2015, http://www.wsj.com/articles/china-gdp -growth-is-slowest-in-24-years-1421719453.

Mahan, Alfred Thayer. *The Influence of Sea Power upon History, 1660–1783*. London: Sampson Low, Marston, 1890.

Martinson, Ryan. "China's Second Navy." U.S. Naval Institute *Proceedings* 141/4/1,346 (April 2015): 24–29.

———. "Here Comes China's Great White Fleet." *National Interest*, 1 October 2014, http://nationalinterest.org/feature/here-comes-chinas-great-white-fleet-11383.

———. "A Salt Water Perspective on China's New Military Strategy." *Real Clear Defense*, 2 June 2015, http://www.realcleardefense.com/articles/2015/06/02/a _salt_water_perspective_on_chinas_new_military_strategy_107997.html.

Mastro, Oriana Skylar. "China's Military Is About to Go Global!" *National Interest*, 18 December 2014, http://nationalinterest.org/feature/chinas-military-about-go -global-11882.

———. "Why Chinese Assertiveness Is Here to Stay." *Washington Quarterly* 37, no. 4 (Winter 2015): 151–70, https://twq.elliott.gwu.edu/sites/twq.elliott.gwu.edu /files/downloads/Mastro.pdf.

Matthew, Francis. "China Working to Dominate Sea Routes as US Loses Interest." *Gulf News*, 22 August 2014, http://gulfnews.com/opinions/columnists/china -working-to-dominate-sea-rtes-as-us-loses-interest-1.1374556.

Mattis, Peter. "Army Day Coverage Stresses Continuity of Reform." *China Brief* 14, no. 16 (22 August 2014), http://www.jamestown.org/programs/chinabrief /single/?tx_ttnews%5Btt_news%5D=42765&cHash=0f561d7f3dfcc8075847911 690aadb5e#.VZ6YFuu4k0o.

McCauley, Adam. "The Most Dangerous Waters in the World." *Time*, 22 September 2014, http://time.com/piracy-southeast-asia-malacca-strait/.

McCauley, Kevin. "President Xi Clears the Way for Military Reform: PL, Clique Breaking and Making, and Personnel Shuffle." *China Brief* 15, no. 3 (4 February 2015), http://www.jamestown.org/single/?tx_ttnews%5Btt_news%5D=43498 &tx_ttnews%5BbackPid%5D=7&cHash=3c905ec80c598bc9668e6324ed19 4a01#.VZ6UPuu4k0o.

McCurry, Justin. "China Lays Claim to Okinawa as Territory Dispute with Japan Escalates." *Guardian*, 15 May 2013, http://www.theguardian.com/world/2013/ may/15/china-okinawa-dispute-japan-ryukyu.

———. "China Warns U.S. Plane to Leave Airspace over Disputed Islands." *Guardian*, 21 May 2015, http://www.theguardian.com/world/2015/may/21/china-warns -us-plane-to-leave-airspace-over-disputed-islands.

McDevitt, Michael A. "The PLA Navy Anti-Access Role in a Taiwan Contingency." Paper prepared for the 2010 Pacific Symposium "China's Naval Modernization: Cause for Storm Warnings." National Defense University, Washington D.C., 10 June 2010.

———. "The South China Sea: Assessing U.S. Policy and Options for the Future." Occasional Paper. Arlington, Va.: CNA Corporation, October 2014.

Mearsheimer, John. "The Rise of China Will Not Be Peaceful at All." *Australian*, 18 November 2004, http://mearsheimer.uchicago.edu/pdfs/A0034b.pdf.

———. *The Tragedy of Great Power Politics*, updated ed. New York: W. W. Norton, 2014.

Medcalf, Rory, and James Brown. "Defense Challenges 2035: Securing Australia's Lifelines." Lowy Institute, November 2014, http://www.lowyinstitute.org/files/ defence-challenges-2035.pdf.

Medeiros, Evan S. *China's International Behavior: Activism, Opportunism, and Diversification*. Santa Monica, Calif.: Rand, 2009.

Mehta, Aaron. "U.S. Providing Vietnam $18M for Coast Guard Vessels." *Defense News*, 1 June 2015, http://www.defensenews.com/story/defense/policy-budget/budget /2015/06/01/us-providing-vietnam-18m-in-coast-guard-vessels/28290871/.

Merrigan, Justin. "Chinese Ministry Plans to Consolidate Its Shipyards." *Sea Breezes*, 18 January 2012, http://www.seabreezes.co.im/index.php?option=com_content &view=article&id=777:chinese-ministry-plans-to-consolidate-its-shipyards &catid=29:asia-pacific&Itemid=50.

Meyer, Eric. "With Oil and Gas Pipelines, China Takes a Shortcut Through Myanmar." *Forbes*, 9 February 2015, http://www.forbes.com/sites/ericrmeyer/2015/02/09 /oil-and-gas-china-takes-a-shortcut/.

Miller, Alice. "The CCP Central Committee Leading Small Groups." *China Leadership Monitor*, no. 26 (Palo Alto, Calif.: Hoover Institute, September 2008), http://www.hoover.org/sites/default/files/uploads/documents/CLM26AM.pdf.

———. "More Already on the Central Committee's Leading Small Groups." *China Leadership Monitor*, no. 44 (Palo Alto, Calif.: Hoover Institute, July 2014), http://www.hoover.org/sites/default/files/research/docs/clm44am.pdf.

———. "The PLA in the Party Leadership Decisionmaking System." In *PLA Influence on China's National Security Policymaking*, edited by Philip C. Saunders and Andrew Scobell, 58–83. Stanford, Calif.: Stanford University Press, 2015.

Minnick, Wendell. "Chinese Carrier's Purported Air Wing Deemed Plausible but Limited." *John's Navy and Other Marine or Military News* (blog), 10 September 2014, https://rnzngunners.wordpress.com/2014/09/10/chinese-carriers-purported-air-wing-deemed-plausible-but-limited/.

Mitchell, Tom. "China Rail Group Signs $12b Nigeria Deal." *Financial Times*, 20 November 2014, http://www.ft.com/intl/cms/s/0/259e9c42-7098-11e4-8113-00144feabdc0.html#axzz3g41lEakR.

Mogato, Manuel. "Philippines, Vietnam Upgrade Ties in Show of Unity Against China." Reuters, 29 January 2015, http://www.reuters.com/article/2015/01/29/us-philippines-vietnam-idUSKBN0L21JP20150129.

Morris, Lyle. "Taming the Five Dragons? China Consolidates Its Maritime Law Enforcement Agencies." *China Brief* 13, no. 7 (28 March 2013), http://www.jamestown.org/programs/chinabrief/single/?tx_ttnews%5Btt_news%5D=40661&cHash=c3c1a5a4ce04d29db680c8a092843afd#.VZ8KWOu4n_Q.

Morrison, Charles E. "China's Economic Rise: History, Trends, Challenges, Implications for the United States." Congressional Research Service Report RL 33534, 21 October 2015. Washington, D.C.: Congressional Research Service, https://www.fas.org/sgp/crs/row/RL33534.pdf.

Mulvenon, James. "Chairman Hu and the PLA's New Historic Missions." *China Leadership Monitor*, no. 27 (9 January 2009), http://media.hoover.org/documents/CLM27JM.pdf.

———. "Military Themes from the 2013 National People's Congress." *China Leadership Monitor*, no. 41 (spring 2013), http://www.hoover.org/sites/default/files/uploads/documents/CLM41JM.pdf.

Murphy, Martin. "Deepwater Oil Rigs as Strategic Weapons." *Naval War College Review* 66, no. 2 (Spring 2013): 110–14, https://www.usnwc.edu/getattachment/3453d037-02ec-48e6-a6b3-d710e21c2e89/Deepwater-Oil-Rigs-as-Strategic-Weapons.aspx.

Myer, Eric. "With Oil and Gas Pipelines, China Takes Shortcut Through Myanmar." *Forbes*, 9 February 2015, http://www.forbes.com/sites/ericrmeyer/2015/02/09/oil-and-gas-china-takes-a-shortcut/.

Nachemson, Andrew. "China Seen as Launching Plan to Revamp Global Economic Order." *Washington Times*, 16 June 2015, http://www.washingtontimes.com/news/2015/jun/16/china-seen-as-launching-plan-to-revamp-global-econ/.

Nash, Paul. "China's 'Going Out' Strategy." *Diplomatic Courier*, 10 May 2012, http://www.diplomaticcourier.com/news/regions/brics/181-china-s-going-out-strategy.

Nathan, Andrew J., and Robert S. Ross. *The Great Wall and the Empty Fortress*. New York: W. W. Norton, 1997.

Newton, Jem. "Greece Sets Deadlines for Port Privatization." *JOC.com*, 20 August 2015, http://www.joc.com/port-news/european-ports/port-piraeus/greece-sets-deadlines-port-privatization_20150820.html.

Ng, Jason, and Trefor Moss. "Malaysia Toughens Stance with Beijing Over South China Sea." *Wall Street Journal*, 8 June 2015, http://www.wsj.com/articles/malaysia-toughens-stance-with-beijing-over-south-china-sea-1433764608.

Noel, Pierre. "Asia's Energy Supply and Maritime Security." *Survival* 56, no. 3 (June–July 2014): 201–16.

Noor, Farish A. "How China Sees Itself and Its Role in Asia." RSIS Commentary no. 230/2014 (19 November 2014), https://www.rsis.edu.sg/rsis-publication/rsis/co14230-how-china-sees-itself-and-its-role-in-asia/#.VgBUELS4mgQ.

O'Brian, Robert C. "The Navy's Hidden Crisis: It's Too Small—And Getting Smaller." *Politico Magazine*, 5 February 2015, http://www.politico.com/magazine/story/2015/02/navy-hidden-crisis-114943.html#.VOj-Wim4mL0.

Odom, Jonathan G. "Freedom of the 'Far Seas': A Maritime Dilemma for China." *China Maritime Studies* 13 (5 May 2015), http://papers.ssrn.com/sol3/papers.cfm?abstract_id=2604469.

O'Dowd, Edward. *China's Military Strategy in the Third Indochina War: The Last Maoist War*. London: Routledge, 2007.

Okeowo, Alexis. "China in Africa: The New Imperialists?" *New Yorker*, 12 June 2013, http://www.newyorker.com/news/news-desk/china-in-africa-the-new-imperialsts.

Oleson, Alexa. "Experts Challenge China's 1-Child Policy Claim." *Boston.com*, 27 October 2011, http://www.boston.com/news/world/asia/articles/2011/10/27/chinas_touting_of_1_child_rules_draws_challenges/.

O'Rourke, Ronald. "China Naval Modernization: Implications for U.S. Navy Capabilities." Congressional Research Service Report RL33153, 1 June 2015. Washington, D.C.: Congressional Research Service, https://fas.org/sgp/crs/row/RL33153.pdf.

Osawa, Jun. "China' ADIZ over the East China Sea: A 'Great Wall in the Sky'?" Brookings, 17 December 2013, http://www.brookings.edu./research/opinions/2013/12/17-china-air-defense-identification-zone-osawa.

Osborne, Kris. "Report: Chinese Navy's Fleet Will Outnumber U.S. by 2020." *DefenseTech*, 3 December 2014, http://defensetech.org/2014/12/03/report-chinese-navys-fleet-will-outnumber-u-s-by-2020/.

Osnos, Evan. "Born Red." *New Yorker*, 6 April 2015, http://www.newyorker.com/magazine/2015/04/06/born-red.

O'Sullivan, Meghan L. "China-Russia Gas Pact Is No Big Deal." Bloomberg, 14 November 2014, http://www.bloombergview.com/articles/2014-11-14/new-chinarussia-gas-pact-is-no-big-deal.

O'Sullivan, Stephen. "LNG Import Infrastructure: Overbuilt and Underused." *Trusted Sources*, 26 February 2015, http://www.trustedsources.co.uk/blogs/china/lng-import-infrastructure-overbuilt-and-underused.

Owens, Mackubin Thomas. "In Defense of Classical Geopolitics." *Naval War College Review* 52, no. 4 (Autumn 1999): 59–76.

Ozawa, Harumi. "Japan Approves Biggest Defense Budget Ever." AFP, 14 January 2015, http://www.businessinsider.com/afp-japan-approves-biggest-ever-defence-budget-amid-asia-tensions-2015-1.

Page, Jeremy. "China Puts Conciliatory Slant on Land Reclamation." *Wall Street Journal*, 1 May 2015, http://www.wsj.com/articles/china-puts-conciliatory-slant-on-land-reclamation-1430466637.

———. "Chinese Ships Approach Malaysia." *Wall Street Journal Online*, 28 March 2013, http://onlinewsj.com/article/SB100014241278873246851045783860526 90151508.html.

———. "Deep Threat: China's Submarines Add Nuclear-Strike Capability, Altering Strategic Balance." *Wall Street Journal*, 24 October 2014, http://www.wsj.com/articles/chinas-submarine-fleet-adds-nuclear-strike-capability-altering-strategic-balance-undersea-1414164738.

———. "In Pacific Drills, Navies Adjust to New Arrival: China." *Wall Street Journal*, 17 July 2015, http://www.wsj.com/articles/in-rimpac-naval-drills-off-hawaii-militaries-adjust-to-new-arrival-china-1405527835.

Page, Jeremy, and Gordon Lubold. "Chinese Navy Ships Come to within 12 Nautical Miles of U.S. Coast." *Wall Street Journal*, 4 September 2015.

Page, Jeremy, and Lingling Wei. "Takedown of Generals Amid Rampant Buying of Ranks Raises Concerns over Combat Readiness." *Wall Street Journal*, 12 March 2015, A8.

Panda, Ankit. "China's HD-981 Oil Rig Returns, Near Disputed South China Sea Waters." *Diplomat*, 27 June 2015, http://thediplomat.com/2015/06/chinas-hd-981-oil-rig-returns-to-disputed-south-china-sea-waters/.

———. "Implications of China's Military Evacuation of Citizens from Libya." *Diplomat*, 6 April 2015, http://thediplomat.com/2015/04/china-evacuates-foreign-nationals-from-yemen/.

Parameswaran, Prashanth. "China Blasts ASEAN Head for South China Sea Remarks." *Diplomat*, 12 March 2015, http://thediplomat.com/2015/03/china-blasts-asean-head-for-south-china-sea-remarks/.

———. "Playing It Safe: Malaysia's Approach to the South China Sea and Implications for the United States." Center for a New American Security, Maritime Strategy series, 23 April 2015, http://www.cnas.org/sites/default/files/publications-pdf/CNAS%20Maritime%206_Parameswaran_Final.pdf.

———. "Vietnam Lodges a Submission at The Hague and Rejects Chinese Position Paper on the South China Sea." *Diplomat*, 12 December 2014, http://thediplomat.com/2014/12/vietnam-launches-legal-challenge-against-chinas-south-china-sea-claims/.

———. "Will China Have a Mini-US Navy by 2020?" *Diplomat*, 30 July 2015, http://thediplomat.com/2015/07/will-china-have-a-mini-us-navy-by-2020/.

———. "Why the 'New' U.S. Trilateral Dialogue with Japan and India Matters." *Diplomat*, 1 October 2015, http://thediplomat.com/2015/10/why-the-new-us-trilateral-dialogue-with-japan-and-india-matters/.

Parfitt, Tom. "Russia-China Clinch Tightens with Joint Navy Exercises in Mediterranean." *Telegraph*, 11 May 2015, http://www.telegraph.co.uk/news/worldnews/europe/russia/11596851/Russia-China-clinch-tightens-with-joint-navy-exercises-in-Mediterranean.html.

Parry, Chris. *Super Highway: Sea Power in the 21st Century*. London: Elliott and Thompson, 2014.

Paton, James, and Aibing Guo. "Russia, China Add to $400 Billion Gas Deal." Bloomberg, 9 November 2014, http://www.bloomberg.com/news/articles/2014-11-10/russia-china-add-to-400-billion-gas-deal-with-accord.

Pearson, Natalie Obiko. "China Breaks India Monopoly on Nepal Economy as Investment Grows." Bloomberg, 14 December 2014, http://www.bloomberg.com/news/articles/2014-12-14/china-breaks-india-monopoly-on-nepal-economy-as-investment-grows.

Pedrozo, Raul. "China versus Vietnam: An Analysis of Competing Claims." Foreword by Michael A. McDevitt (Arlington, Va.: Center for Naval Analyses, August 2014), https://southeastasiansea.files.wordpress.com/2014/08/china-versus-vietnam-an-analysis-of-the-competing-claims-in-the-south-china-sea.pdf.

———. "Responding to Ms. Zhang's Talking Points on the EEZ." *Chinese Journal of International Law* 10, no. 1 (2011): 207–23.

Peng Guangqian, and Yao Youzhi, eds. *The Science of Military Strategy*. Beijing: Military Science Publishing House, 2005.

———, eds. *The Science of Military Strategy*. Beijing: Academy of Military Sciences, Military Press, 2013.

Peng, Han. "China Discovers Major Natural Gas Field in South China Sea." China National Television (CNTV), 15 September 2014, http://english.cntv.cn/2014/09/15/VIDE1410771244300916.shtml.

Perlez, Jane. "Images Show China Building Aircraft Runway in Disputed Spratly Islands." *New York Times*, 16 April 2015, http://www.nytimes.com/2015/04/17/world/asia/china-building-airstrip-in-disputed-spratly-islands-satellite-images-show.html?_r=0.

———. "Leader Asserts China's Importance on Global Stage." *New York Times*, 30 November 2014, http://www.nytimes.com/2014/12/01/world/asia/leader-asserts-chinas-growing-role-on-global-stage.html?_r=0n.

———. "Rescue Mission in Yemen Proves to Be Boon for Chinese Military's Image." *New York Times*, *Sinosphere: Dispatches from China* (blog), 8 April 2015, http://sinosphere.blogs.nytimes.com/2015/04/08/rescue-mission-in-yemen-proves-to-be-boon-for-chinese-militarys-image/?_r=0.

———. "Xi Jinping of China Calls for Cooperation and Partnerships in UN Speech." *New York Times*, 27 September 2015, http://www.nytimes.com/2015/09/29/world/asia/china-xi-jinping-united-nations-general-assembly.html?_r=0.

Pettis, Michael. "What Multiple Should We Give China's GDP Growth? Balance Sheet Fragility." *Michael Pettis' China Financial Markets* (blog), 17 May 2015, http://blog.mpettis.com/2015/05/what-multiple-should-we-give-chinas-gdp-growth/.

Philipp, Joshua. "China Claims Airspace over Its Self-Made Islands." *Epoch Times*, 20 May 2015, http://www.theepochtimes.com/n3/1350957-china-claims-airspace-over-its-self-made-islands-says-its-entitled/.

Phoenix Weekly. "Chinese Overseas Investment Hindered by Lack of Experience, Political Opposition in Host Countries." *Global Times*, 14 September 2015, http://www.globaltimes.cn/content/942349.shtml.

Pillsbury, Michael. *The Hundred-Year Marathon: China's Secret Strategy to Replace America as the Global Superpower*. Boston: Henry Holt, 2015.

Pinchuk, Denis, Svetlana Burmistrova, and Katya Golubkova. "Russia Could Postpone Gas Pipe to China Touted by Putin." Reuters, 18 March 2015, http://www.reuters.com/article/2015/03/18/us-russia-gas-china-idUSKBN0ME19120150318.

Poling, Gregory B. "The South China Sea in Focus: Clarifying the Limits of Maritime Dispute." Center for Strategic and International Studies, July 2013, http://csis.org/files/publication/130717_Poling_SouthChinaSea_Web.pdf.

Pollack, Jonathan D. "Is Xi Jinping Rethinking Korean Unification?" Brookings, 20 January 2015, http://www.brookings.edu/research/presentations/2015/01/20-xi-jinping-korean-unification-pollack.

Pomfret, John. "U.S. Takes a Tougher Tone with China." *Washington Post*. 30 July 2010, http://www.washingtonpost.com/wp-dyn/content/article/2010/07/29/AR2010072906416.html.

Press Trust of India. "India, Vietnam Ink Seven Pacts, Call for 'Freedom of Navigation.'" *Indian Express*, 15 September 2014, http://indianexpress.com/article/world/asia/india-vietnam-ink-7-pacts-call-for-freedom-of-navigation/.

Przystup, James J. "Japan-China Relations: A Handshake at the Summit." *Comparative Connections* 16, no. 3 (January 2015), http://csis.org/files/publication/1403qjapan_china.pdf.

Qi Jianguao. "Article on International Security Affairs," trans. James A. Bellacqua and Daniel M. Hartnett. Arlington, Va.: CNA Corporation, March 2013.

————. "Pondering and Understanding the Impact of the Unprecedented Great Changing Situation on the Strategic Configuration of the World and on Our National Security Environment." *Study Times*, 21 January 2013.

Qin Anmin. "China Is Actively Exploring International Oil Markets." *Xinhua*, 19 July 1999, 4.

Qing, Dai. "Relaxing China's One-Child Policy." *New York Times*, 12 June 2015, http://www.nytimes.com/2015/06/13/opinion/relaxing-chinas-one-child-policy.html?_r=0.

Rajagopalan, Megha. "China Sends Four Oil Rigs to South China Sea Amid Regional Tensions." Reuters, 20 June 2014, http://www.reuters.com/article/2014/06/20/us-china-southchinasea-rigs-idUSKBN0EV0WG20140620.

Raustiala, Kal, and Christopher Sprigman. "Fake It till You Make It: The Good News about China's Knockoff Economy." *Foreign Affairs* 92, no. 4 (July–August 2013): 25–30, https://www.foreignaffairs.com/articles/china/2013-06-11/fake-it-till-you-make-it.

Reed, John. "How Effective Will China's Carrier-Based Fighters Be?" *Defensetech*, 25 April 2012, http://defensetech.org/2012/04/25/how-effective-will-chinas-carrier-based-fighters-be/.

Renz, Patrick M., and Frauke Heidemann. "China's Coming 'Lawfare' and the South China Sea." *Diplomat*, 8 May 2015, http://thediplomat.com/2015/05/chinas-coming-lawfare-and-the-south-china-sea/.

Rinehart, Ian, and Bart Elias. "China's Air Defense Identification Zone (ADIZ)." Congressional Research Service Report R43894, 30 January 2015. Washington, D.C.: Congressional Research Service, http://www.fas.org/sgp/crs/row/R 43894.pdf.

Roach, J. Ashley. "China's Shifting Sands in the Spratlys." *Insights* 19, no. 15 (15 July 2015), http://www.asil.org/insights/volume/19/issue/15/chinas-shifting-sands -spratlys.

Robson, Seth. "Japan, New Zealand Joining Talisman Saber for First Time." *Stars and Stripes*, 28 May 2015, http://www.stripes.com/news/pacific/japan-new-zealand -joining-talisman-saber-for-1st-time-1.349078.

Rose, Adam, and Chen Aizhu. "Iran Oil Officials in Beijing to Discuss Oil Supplies, Projects." Reuters, 7 April 2015, http://economictimes.indiatimes.com/news /international/business/iran-oil-officials-in-beijing-to-discuss-oil-supplies -projects/articleshow/46833911.cms.

Rosen, Mark. "U.S. Slams Chinese 9 Dashed Line Claim." *Maritime Executive*, 12 December 2014, http://www.maritime-executive.com/article/Submission-US -Slams-Chinese-9-Dashed-Line-Claim-2014-12-12.

Rosenberg, Matthew. "Building of Islands Is Debated, but China and U.S. Skirt Conflict at Talks." *New York Times*, 30 May 2015, http://www.nytimes.com/2015/05/31 /world/asia/building-of-islands-is-debated-but-china-and-us-skirt-conflict-at -talks.html?_r=0.

Rubel, Robert C. "Navies and Economic Prosperity: The New Logic of Sea Power." *Corbett Paper* no. 11. London: The Corbett Center for Maritime Security Studies of King's College, October 2012, http://www.kcl.ac.uk/sspp/departments/dsd /research/researchgroups/corbett/corbettpaper11.pdf.

Ruwitch, John. "Satellites and Seafood: China Keeps Fishing Fleet Connected in Disputed Waters." Reuters, 27 July 2014, http://www.reuters.com/article/2014 /07/28/us-southchinasea-china-fishing-insight-idUSKBN0FW0QP20140728.

RWZ and AEF. "CCDI Identified Three Key 'Black Holes' of Central Government Owned Companies." *Xinhua*, 20 June 2015, http://news.xinhuanet.com/ yuqing/2015-06/20/c_127934581.htm.

Ryan, Mark A., David M. Finkelstein, and Michael A. McDevitt, eds. *Chinese Warfighting: The PLA Experience since 1949*. Armonk, N.Y.: ME Sharpe, 2003.

Sabonis-Helf, Theresa. "Russia and Energy Markets." In *New Realities: Energy Security in the 2010s and Implications for the U.S. Military*, edited by John R. Deni, 15–46. Carlisle, PA: Strategic Studies Institute and U.S. Army War College Press, 2013.

Samaranayake, Nilanthi. "After the Visit." *Pragati*, 29 October 2014, http://pragati .nationalinterest.in/2014/10/after-the-visit/.

———. "The Long Littoral Project: Bay of Bengal: A Maritime Perspective on Indo-Pacific Security." CNA, September 2012, https://cna.ocanCNA_files/PDF/IRP -2012-U-002319-Final.pdf.

Sanusi, Lamido. "Africa Must Get Real about Chinese Ties." *Financial Times*, 11 March 2013, http://www.ft.com/intl/cms/s/0/562692b0-898c-11e2-ad3f-00144feabdc0 .html#axzz3g41lEakR.

Saunders, Philip. "China's Juggling Act: Balancing Stability and Territorial Claims." PacNet no. 33. Center for Strategic and International Studies, 29 April 2014, http://csis.org/files/publication/Pac1433.pdf.

Saunders, Philip C., and Andrew Scobell, eds. *PLA Influence on China's National Security Policymaking.* Stanford, Calif.: Stanford, 2015.

Schreer, Benjamin. "China's Development of a More Secure Nuclear Second-Strike Capability: Implications for Chinese Behavior and U.S. Extended Deterrence." *Asia Policy*, no. 19 (January 2015), doi:10.1353/asp.2015.0010.

Schurtenberger, Erwin. "Reassessing China's Economic Growth Potential." ECO Rep 2_2015 (May 2015).

Scott, Richard. "China-Owned Ships: A Rapid Rise to Become One of the World's Largest Fleets." *International Shipping News*, reprinted in *Hellenic Shipping News*, 17 March 2015, http://www.hellenicshippingnews.com/china-owned-ships-a -rapid-rise-to-become-one-of-the-worlds-largest-fleets/.

Sempa, Francis P. "Geography and World Power at 100." *Diplomat*, 25 April 2015, http://the diplomat.com/2015/04/geography-and-world-power-at-100/.

Shambaugh, David. "China's Soft Power Push: The Search for Respect." *Foreign Affairs* 94, no. 4 (July–August 2015), https://www.foreignaffairs.com/articles/ china/2015-06-16/china-s-soft-power-push.

———. "The Illusion of Chinese Power," Brookings, 25 June 2014, http://www.brook-ings.edu/research/opinions/2014/06/23-chinese-power-shambaugh.

Sharman, Christopher H. "China Moves Out: Stepping Stones toward a New Maritime Strategy." *China Strategic Perspectives 9* (Washington, D.C.: National Defense University Press, 2015, https://archive.org/stream/ChinaStrategicPerspectives 9-nsia/China%20Strategic%20Perspectives%209_djvu.txt.

———. "Closing the Information Deficit: Strategic Implications of Chinese Naval Exercises in the Western Pacific 2004–2014." Paper written at the National War College, Washington, D.C., 2015.

Shear, David. "Statement of David Shear, Assistant Secretary of Defense for Asian & Pacific Security Affairs before the Senate Committee on Foreign Relations." 13 May 2015, http://www.foreign.senate.gov/imo/media/doc/051315_Shear_ Testimony.pdf.

Shen Dingli. "Will China Replace U.S. as Global Superpower?" *People's Daily* (Bei-jing), 9 February 2015, http://en.people.cn/n/2015/0209/c98649–8847610.html.

Shi Xiaoqin. "The Boundaries and Directions of China's Seapower." In *Twenty-First Century Seapower: Cooperation and Conflict at Sea*, edited by Peter Dutton, Robert Ross, and Oystein Tunsjo, 65–84. London: Taylor & Francis: 2012.

Shobert, Benjamin. "China Will Get Old Well before It Gets Rich." CNBC, 10 October 2013, http://www.cnbc.com/2013/10/10/china-will-get-old-well-before-it-gets -rich.html.

Shu Guang Zhang. *Mao's Military Romanticism: China and the Korean War, 1950– 1953.* Lawrence: University Press of Kansas, 1995.

Shukman, David. "What Is Fracking and Why Is It Controversial?" BBC, 27 June 2013, http://www.bbc.com/news/uk-14432401.

Singh, Abhijit. "A 'PLA-N' for Chinese Maritime Bases in the Indian Ocean." PacNet no. 7. 26 January 2015, Center for Strategic and International Studies, http://csis.org/publication/pacnet-7-pla-n-chinese-maritime-bases-indian-ocean.

Slavin, Erik. "Japan Defense Report Criticizes China, Supports U.S. Base Realignment." *Stars and Stripes*, 21 July 2015, http://www.stripes.com/news/japan-defense-report-criticizes-china-supports-us-base-realignment-1.358964.

———. "US, Japan Announce Expansion of Defense Ties." *Stars and Stripes*, 8 April 2015, http://www.stripes.com/news/pacific/japan/us-japan-announce-expansion-of-defense-ties-1.338920.

Smith, Paul J. "The Senkaku/Diaoyu Island Controversy: A Crisis Postponed." *Naval War College Review* 66, no. 2 (Spring 2013): 27–44.

Snyder, Scott, and See-won Byun. "China-Korea Relations: Beijing Ties Uneven with Seoul, Stalled with Pyongyang." *Comparative Connections* 16, no. 3 (January 2015), http://www.isn.ethz.ch/Digital-Library/Publications/Detail/?lang=en&id=188287.

Solis, Mireya. "China Flexes Its Muscles at APEC with the Revival of FTAAP," *East Asia Forum*, 23 November 2014, http://www.eastasiaforum.org/2014/11/23/china-flexes-its-muscles-at-apec-with-the-revival-of-ftaap/.

Spitzer, Kirk. "New Head of the U.S. Pacific Command Talks to TIME about the Pivot to Asia and His Asian Roots." *Time*, 25 May 2015, http://time.com/3895434/admiral-harry-harris-us-pacific-command-china-japan-asia/.

Spykman, Nicolas John. *America's Strategy in World Politics: The United States and the Balance of Power.* New York: Harcourt Brace, 1942.

Steinberg, James, and Michael E. O'Hanlon. *Strategic Reassurance and Resolve: U.S.-China Relations in the Twenty-First Century.* Princeton, N.J.: Princeton University Press, 2014.

Stephens, Philip. "Now China Starts to Make the Rules." *Financial Times*, 28 May 2015, http://www.ft.com/cms/s/0/9dafcb30-0395-11e5-a70f-00144feabdc0.html#axzz43vvWWgFG.

Storey, Ian. "China's Malacca Dilemma." *China Brief* 6, no. 8 (12 April 2006), http://www.jamestown.org/programs/chinabrief/single/?tx_ttnews[tt_news]=31575&no_cache=1#.VvSMFUd_et4.

———. "Conflict in the South China Sea: China's Relations with Vietnam and the Philippines." *Asia-Pacific Journal* (30 April 2008), http://www.japanfocus.org/-ian-storey/2734/article.html.

Stout, Kristi Lu. "Is Xi Jinping's 'Chinese Dream' a Fantasy?" CNN, 16 July 2013, http://www.cnn.com/2013/05/26/world/asia/chinese-dream-xi-jinping/.

Street, Chriss W. "China's National Effort in Oil and Natural Gas Fracking Fails." *Breitbart*, 18 August 2014, http://www.breitbart.com/national-security/2014/08/18/china-s-national-effort-in-oil-gas-fracking-fails/.

Su Jijuan, Wu Yongliang, and Zhu Qingming. "China's Maritime Security Challenges and Opportunities." Translated by CMSI (June 2015). *National Defense Science Technology Industry* (June 2015), 42–44.

Sun, Oh Ei. "South China Sea Disputes: KL's Subtle Shift on China?" RSIS Commentary no. 142/2015 (19 June 2015), http://app.getresponse.com/click.html?x=a62b&lc=XZfrE&mc=l9&s=CEoZU&u=jcU&y=e&.

Sun, Yun. "China and the Changing Asian Infrastructure Bank." PacNet no. 43. Center for Strategic and International Studies, 28 July 2015, http://csis.org/publication /pacnet-43-china-and-changing-asian-infrastructure-bank.

———. "China's New Calculations in the South China Sea." *Asia-Pacific Bulletin*, no. 267 (10 June 2014), http://www.eastwestcenter.org/publications/china's-new -calculations-in-the-south-china-sea.

———. "Chinese National Security Decision-Making: Processes and Challenges." Brookings, May 2013, http://www.brookings.edu/research/papers/2013/05/ chinese-national-security-decision-making-sun.

Supriyanto, Ristian Atriandi. "Indonesia's Natuna Islands: Next Flashpoint in the South China Sea?" RSIS (17 February 2015), https://www.rsis.edu.sg/rsis-publication/ rsis/co15033-indonesias-natuna-islands-next-flashpoint-in-the-south-china -sea/#.Vf_3-bS4mgQ.

Sutter, Robert G. "Asia's Importance, China's Expansion and U.S. Strategy: What Should Be Done?" *Asia-Pacific Bulletin*, no. 283. Washington, D.C.: East-West Center, 28 October 2014, http://www.eastwestcenter.org/publications/asia's -importance-china's-expansion-and-us-strategy-what-should-be-done.

———. *China's Rise in Asia: Promises and Perils*. Lanham, Md.: Rowman & Littlefield, 2005.

Sutter, Robert G., and Chin-Hao Huang. "China–Southeast Asia Relations: Beijing Sets Positive Agenda, Plays Down Disputes." *Comparative Connections* 16, no. 3 (January 2015), http://csis.org/publication/comparative-connections-v16-n3 -china-southeast-asia.

Suzuki, Takahiro. "China Plans to Build a New Base for Keeping an Eye on the Senkaku Islands." *Yomiuri Shimbun*, 14 June 2015, http://news.asiaone.com/ news/asia/china-plans-build-new-base-keeping-eye-senkaku-islands.

Swaine, Michael D. "China's Assertive Behavior, Part One: On Core Interests." *China Leadership Monitor*, no. 34 (15 November 2010), http://carnegieendowment .org/2010/11/15/china-s-assertive-behavior-part-one-on-core-interests.

———. "Chinese Views and Commentary on the East China Sea Air Defense Identification Zone (ECS ADIZ)." *China Leadership Monitor*, no. 43 (Spring 2014), http://www.hoover.org/sites/default/files/uploads/documents/CLM43MS.pdf.

———. "Chinese Views and Commentary on the 'One Belt, One Road' Initiative." *China Leadership Monitor*, no. 47 (14 July 2015), http://www.hoover.org/research /chinese-views-and-commentary-one-belt-one-road.

———. "Chinese Views and Commentary on Periphery Diplomacy." *China Leadership Monitor*, no. 44 (28 July 2014), http://www.hoover.org/sites/default/files /research/docs/clm44ms.pdf.

———. "Chinese Views Regarding the Senkaku/Diaoyu Islands Dispute." *China Leadership Monitor*, no. 41 (7 June 2013), http://www.hoover.org/research/chi- nese-views-regarding-senkakudiaoyu-islands-dispute.

———. "Xi Jinping's Address to the Central Conference on Work Relating to Foreign Affairs: Assessing and Advancing Major-Power Relationships with Chinese Characteristics." *China Leadership Monitor*, no. 46 (Winter 2015), http://www .hoover.org/sites/default/files/clm46ms.pdf.

Szczudlik-Tatar, Justyna. "China's New Silk Road Diplomacy." *Policy Paper* no. 34. Warsaw: Polish Institute of International Affairs. December 2013, http://www .pism.pl/files/?id_plik=15818.

Tajima, Yukio. "Japan, South Korea to Resume Defense Exchanges." *Nikkei Asian Review*, 31 May 2015, http://asia.nikkei.com/Politics-Economy/International -Relations/Japan-South-Korea-to-resume-defense-exchanges.

Takahashi, Kosuke. "Japan Mulling Plans for QRF Units Based on Southwest Islands." *IHS Jane's Defence Weekly*, 28 May 2014, 5, http://www.janes.com/article/38204 /japan-mulling-plans-for-qrf-units-based-on-southwest-islands.

Takeda, Jun'ichi. "China's Rise as a Maritime Power: Ocean Policy from Mao Zedong to Xi Jinping." *Review of Island Studies*, 23 April 2014, http://islandstudies.oprf -info.org/research/a00011/. Translated from "Chugoku no kaiyo seisaku," *Tosho Kenkyu Journal* 2 no. 2 (April 2013): 73–95.

Tanner, Murray S., and Peter W. Mackenzie, *China's Emerging National Security Interests*. Arlington, Va.: CNA, January 2015.

Tate, Andrew. "China Building Mobile Landing Platform, New Ro-Ro PLA Support Ship." *IHS Jane's Navy International*, 3 June 2015, http://www.janes.com/article /51984/china-building-mobile-landing-platform-new-ro-ro-pla-support ship.

———. "China Converting Old Frigates into Coast Guard Cutters." *IHS Jane's Navy International*, 27 July 2015, http://www.janes.com/article/53248/china-converting -old-frigates-into-coastguard-cutters.

TGS and AEF. "Downward Pressure Continues and Greater Difficulties Lie Ahead." *People's Daily*, 14 April 2015, http://politics.people.com.cn/n/2015/0412/c1024 -26831938.html.

———. "Xi Jinping: The Nuclear Industry Is a Cornerstone of China's National Security." *Xinhua*, 15 January 2015, http://news.xinhuanet.com/politics/2015-01/15/ c_1114011173.htm.

TGS, NNL, and AEF. "PLA Strategist: China's Rise Requires Great Wisdom." *China-scope*, 30 July 2015, http://chinascope.org/main/content/view/7314/92/.

Thayer, Carlyle A. "Can Vietnam's Maritime Strategy Counter China?" *Diplomat*, 29 September 2014, http://thediplomat.com/2014/09/can-vietnams-maritime -strategy-counter-china/.

———. "No, China Is Not Reclaiming Land in the South China Sea." *Diplomat*, 7 June 2015, http://thediplomat.com/2015/06/no-china-is-not-reclaiming-land-in-the -south-china-sea/.

———. "The Philippines and Vietnam Forge a Strategic Partnership." *Diplomat*, 10 March 2015, http://thediplomat.com/2015/03/the-philippines-and-vietnam -forge-a-strategic-partnership/.

———. "South China Sea: What Are the Prospects for Joint Development?" *Thayer Consultancy Background Brief*, 8 January 2015.

———. "Vietnam's East Sea Strategy and China-Vietnam Relations." Paper delivered to the 2nd International Conference on China's Maritime Strategy. Macau, 19–20 September 2014, http://www.theasanforum.org/vietnam-among-the-powers -struggle-cooperation/.

Tiezzi, Shannon. "China Nixes South China Sea Discussions at Defense Meeting." *Diplomat*, 18 February 2015, http://thediplomat.com/2015/02/china-nixes-south-china-sea-discussions-at-defense-meeting/.

———. "China to Showcase Never-Before-Seen Weapons and Equipment in Military Parade." *Diplomat*, 22 August 2015, http://thediplomat.com/2015/08/china-to-showcase-never-before-seen-weapons-and-equipment-in-military-parade/.

———. "Chinese Admirals Spill the Beans on New Aircraft Carrier." *Diplomat*, 12 March 2015, http://thediplomat.com/2015/03/chinese-admirals-spill-the-beans-on-new-aircraft-carrier/.

———. "In New Plan, China Eyes 2020 Energy Cap." *Diplomat*, 20 November 2015, http://thediplomat.com/2014/11/in-new-plan-china-eyes-2020-energy-cap/.

———. "Taiwan Will Have a Female President in 2016." *Diplomat*, 18 June 2015, http://thediplomat.com/2015/06/taiwan-will-have-a-female-president-in-2016/.

———. "Three Goals of Beijing's Military Diplomacy." *Diplomat*, 30 January 2015, http://thediplomat.com/2015/01/3-goals-of-chinas-military-diplomacy/. Originally in *China Review News*, 2 February 2015.

Till, Geoffrey. "Close Encounters of the Maritime Kind." In *Major Law and Policy Issues in the South China Sea*, edited by Yuan-huei Song and Keyuan Zou, 177–91. Burlington, Vt.: Ashgate, 2014.

Ting Shi. "Li's Silk Road Trip Marks China's Advance on Russia's Patch." Bloomberg, 14 December 2014, http://www.bloomberg.com/news/articles/2014-12-14/li-s-silk-road-trip-marks-china-s-growing-sway-on-russia-s-patch.

Torode, Greg. "PLA Navy Amphibious Task Force Reaches Malaysia 'to Defend South China Sea.'" *South China Morning Post*, 27 March 2013, http://www.scmp.com/news/asia/article/1200564/pla-navy-amphibious-task-force-reaches-james-shoal-near-malaysia.

———. "Vietnam Buys Submarine-Launched Land Attack Missiles to Deter China." Reuters, 30 April 2015, http://uk.reuters.com/article/uk-vietnam-military-id UKKBN0NL0B220150430.

Trenin, Dmitri. "From Greater Europe to Greater Asia? The Sino-Russian Entente." Carnegie Moscow Center, 9 April 2015, http://carnegieendowment.org/files/CP_Trenin_To_Asia_WEB_2015Eng.pdf.

Tunsjo, Oystein. *Security and Profit in China's Energy Policy*. New York: Columbia University Press, 2013.

Tweed, David, and Chris Blake. "China Reserves Right to Declare Air Zone over South China Sea." Bloomberg, 8 May 2015, http://www.bloomberg.com/news/articles/2015-05-08/china-reserves-right-to-declare-air-zone-over-south-china-sea.

United Nations Report on Somalia Piracy. UN Report S/2015/776. 12 October 2015. http://oceansbeyondpiracy.org/sites/default/files/attachments/SecGen%20Report%202015.pdf.

U.S. Census Bureau. "China's Population to Peak at 1.4 Billion Around 2026." News release, 15 December 2009, https://www.census.gov/newsroom/releases/archives/international_population/cb09-191.html.

U.S. Department of Defense. *Annual Report to Congress: Military and Security Developments Involving the People's Republic of China 2013*. Washington, D.C.: Office of the Secretary of Defense, 2014. http://www.defense.gov/Portals/1/Documents/pubs/2013_China_Report_FINAL.pdf.

U.S. Department of State, Office of Ocean Affairs, Bureau of Oceans and International Environmental and Scientific Affairs. "Limits in the Seas: Straight Baseline Claim: China." No. 117, 9 July 1996, http://www.state.gov/documents/organization/57692.pdf.

U.S. Energy Information Administration. "China: International Energy Data and Analysis." 14 May 2015, http://www.eia.gov/beta/international/analysis_includes/countries_long/China/china.pdf.

———. "South China Sea." Last updated 7 February 2013, http://www.eia.gov/beta/international/analysis_includes/regions_of_interest/South_China_Sea/south_china_sea.pdf.

van der Kley, Dirk. "The China-Vietnam Standoff: Three Key Factors." *Interpreter*, 8 May 2014, http://www.lowyinterpreter.org/post/2014/05/08/China-Vietnam-standoff-Three-key-factors.aspx.

Vogel, Ezra. "Xi Jinping Compared to Deng Xiaoping: Two Consequential Leaders of China." *ASAN Forum* 3, no. 5 (15 October 2015), http://www.theasanforum.org/xi-jinping-compared-to-deng-xiaoping-two-consequential-leaders-of-china/.

Voigt, Kevin, and Natalie Robehmed. "Explainer: South China Sea—Asia's Most Dangerous Waters." CNN, 29 June 2011, http://www.cnn.com/2011/WORLD/asiapcf/06/25/south.china.sea.conflict/.

Vu Trong Khanh and Nguyen Anh Thu. "Vietnam, China Trade Accusations of Vessel-Ramming Near Oil Rig." *Wall Street Journal*, 24 June 2014, http://www.wsj.com/articles/vietnam-china-trade-accusations-of-vessel-ramming-near-oil-rig-in-south-china-sea-1403608970.

Vu, Truong-Minh, and Nguyen Thanh Trung. "Deference or Balancing Act: Whither Vietnam's Foreign Policy Tilt?" Center for Strategic and International Studies, 2 September 2014, http://cogitasia.com/deference-or-balancing-act-whither-vietnams-foreign-policy-tilt/.

Vuving, Alexander. "Did China Blink in the South China Sea?" *National Interest*, 27 July 2015, http://nationalinterest.org/feature/did-china-blink-the-south-china-sea-10956.

Wachman, Alan M. *Why Taiwan? Geostrategic Rationales for China's Territorial Integrity*. Stanford, Calif.: Stanford University Press, 2007.

Waldmeir, Patti, and Gabriel Wildau. "China Graft Probe Uncovers Falsified Revenues at Large SOEs." *Financial Times*, 29 June 2015, http://www.ft.com/intl/cms/s/0/91b7855c-1d85-11e5-ab0f-6bb9974f25d0.html#axzz3fnvKnm9w.

Walt, Vivienne. "China Makes a Big Play to Buy a Strategic Greek Port." *Fortune*, 10 April 2015, http://fortune.com/2015/04/10/china-goes-after-greek-port/.

Wang, Adrian. "Xi Jinping Urges China's Military to Create 'Information Warfare' Strategy." *South China Morning Post*, 30 August 2014, http://www.scmp.com/news/china/article/1582004/xi-jinping-urges-chinas-military-create-information-warfare-strategy.

Wang, Ben Yunmo. "China Going out 2.0: Dawn of a New Era for Chinese Investment Abroad." *Huffington Post*, 11 April 2015, http://www.huffingtonpost.com/china -hands/china-going-out-20-dawn-o_b_7046790.html.

Wang, Honggang. "How to Implement China's Foreign Strategy in 2015." *Contemporary International Relations* 25, no. 2 (March–April 2015): 97–101.

Wang Min. "Letter Dated 22 May 2014 from the Charge d'affaires of the Permanent Mission of China to the United Nations addressed to the Secretary General." United Nations A/68/887, http://www.un.org/ga/search/view_doc.asp ?symbol=a/68/887.

Wang Qian and Zhang Yunbi. "Network Planned to Cope with Sea Disasters." *China Daily*, 19–21 December 2014, http://www.chinadaily.com.cn/china/2014-12/19 /content_19121397.htm.

Wang, Xiaobing, Futoshi Yamauchi, Keijiro Otsuka, and Jikun Huang. "Wage Growth, Landholding, and Mechanization in Chinese Agriculture." *Policy Research Working Paper* 7138, Development Research Group, Agriculture and Rural Development Team, December 2014, https://openknowledge.worldbank.org/bitstream /handle/10986/21134/WPS7138.pdf?sequence=1.

Wang Xiaoxuan. "Cooperation between the Maritime Forces of US, Japan, and Australia and Its Impact on China." Translated by CMSI. *Military Digest*, no. 8 (2015): 10–13.

Wang, Yi. "ASEAN: China Makes 10 New Proposals." *Xinhua*, 6 August 2015, http:// www.chinadailyasia.com/nation/2015-08/06/content_15300588.html.

Wang Yusheng. "Rethinking the 'Strategic Crossroads.'" *China-US Focus*, 6 July 2015, http://www.chinausfocus.com/foreign-policy/rethinking-the-strategic-cross roads/.

Wang, Zhongmin. "China's Elusive Shale Gas Boom," *Paulson Papers on Energy and Environment*. Washington, D.C.: Paulson Institute, March 2015, http://www .paulsoninstitute.org/think-tank/2015/03/12/chinas-elusive-shale-gas-boom/.

Watson, Bruce W. "The Evolution of Soviet Naval Strategy." In *The Future of the Soviet Navy: An Assessment to the Year 2000*, edited by Bruce W. Watson and Peter M. Dunn, 113–29. Boulder, Colo.: Westview Press, 1986.

Watson, Cynthia A., Mark Mohr, and Riordan Roett. "Enter the Dragon? China's Presence in Latin America." Washington, D.C.: Woodrow Wilson Center, n.d. https://www.wilsoncenter.org/sites/default/files/EnterDragonFinal.pdf.

Watts, Jake Maxwell. "Up to 20 Countries Waiting to Join China-Led AIIB, President-Designate Says." *Wall Street Journal*, 19 September 2015, http://www.wsj.com /article_email/up-to-20-countries-waiting-to-join-china-led-aiib-president -designate-says-1442666572-lMyQjAxMTA1MjIzMTEyODEyWj.

Wei, Lingling. "Chinese Firms Turn to Foreign Investors to Borrow." *Wall Street Journal*, 23 April 2014, http://www.wsj.com/articles/SB10001424052702304788 404579519092610644698.

———. "China Moves to Devalue Yuan." *Wall Street Journal*, 10 August 2015, http:// www.wsj.com/articles/china-moves-to-devalue-the-yuan-1439258401.

Welizkin, Paul. "With China in the Lead, Asia Pacific Poised to be Richest Region." *China Daily*, 16 June 2015, http://usa.chinadaily.com.cn/us/2015-06/16/content _21023188.htm.

Western, Jon, and Joshua S. Goldstein. "R2P." *Foreign Affairs*, 26 March 2013, https://www.foreignaffairs.com/articles/syria/2013-03-26/r2p-after-syria.

Wezeman, Pieter D., and Siemon T. Wezeman. "Trends in International Arms Transfers, 2014." SIPRI Fact Sheet (March 2015), http://www.sipri.org.

Wheatley, Jonathan. "China Applies to Join EBRD to Build Ties with Europe." *Financial Times*, 25 October 2015, http://www.ft.com/intl/cms/s/0/b34d5a78-7994-11e5-933d-efcdc3c11c89.html#axzz3phW89CvE.

Wishik, Anton Lee. "An Anti-Access Approximation: The PLA's Active Strategic Counterattacks on Exterior Lines." *China Security*, no. 19 (2011): 37–48, http://www.chinasecurity.us/index.php?option=com_content&view=article&id=48.

Wong, Chun Han. "China to Expand Naval Operations Amid Growing Tensions with U.S." *Wall Street Journal*, 26 May 2015, http://www.wsj.com/articles/china-shifts-maritime-military-focus-to-open-seas-1432648980.

Wong, Edward. "China Opens Corruption Inquiry into Sinopec President." *New York Times*, 28 April 2015, A13, http://www.nytimes.com/2015/04/28/world/asia/china-opens-corruption-inquiry-into-sinopec-president.html.

———. "China Says It Could Add Defense Zone over Disputed Waters." *New York Times*, 31 May 2015, http://www.nytimes.com/2015/06/01/world/asia/china-says-it-could-set-up-air-defense-zone-in-south-china-sea.html?nlid=58270588&_r=0.

———. "China Sees Long Road to Cleaning Up Pollution." *New York Times*, *Sinosphere Dispatches from China* (blog), 2 June 2014, http://sinosphere.blogs.nytimes.com/2014/07/02/china-sees-long-road-to-cleaning-up-pollution/?_r=0.

Wood, Peter. "China Plays Helo Card to Shift Military Balance in East China Sea Dispute." *China Brief* 15, no. 5 (6 March 2015), http://www.jamestown.org/programs/chinabrief/single/?tx_ttnews%5Btt_news%5D=43621&cHash=85f4b59a11e2b4e7581f4312449a6d19#.VZ6QBeu4k0o.

———. "China's 'Eternal Prosperity': Is Island Expansion a Precursor to South China Sea ADIZ?" *China Brief* 14, no. 20 (23 October 2014), http://www.jamestown.org/programs/chinabrief/single/?tx_ttnews%5Btt_news%5D=42994&cHash=74f2e12df680fd3ce142ebe2722e47ae#.VPiu1Cm4nfY.

Wortzel, Larry M. *Dictionary of Contemporary Chinese Military History*. Westport, Conn.: Greenwood Press, 1999.

Wright, Mary Clabaugh. *The Last Stand of Chinese Conservatism: The T'ung-Chih Restoration, 1862–1874*. Stanford, Calif.: Stanford University Press, 1957.

Wu Jiao. "Deal Signed to Expand Sino-Kazakh Pipeline." *China Daily*, 7 April 2013, http://www.chinadaily.com.cn/china/2013-04/07/content_16379084.htm.

Wu Jiao and Zhang Yunbi, "Xi in Call for Building New 'Maritime Silk Road.'" *China Daily*, 4 October 2013, http://usa.chinadaily.com.cn/china/2013-10/04/content_17008940.htm.

Wu Shengli. "Learn Profound Historical Lessons from the Sino-Japanese War of 1894–1895 and Unswervingly Take the Path of Planning and Managing Maritime Affairs, Safeguarding Maritime Rights and Interests, and Building a Powerful Navy." *China Military Science*. Translated by CMSI (April 2014), 1–4.

Wu Shicun. "Gains and Losses for U.S. in the South China Sea." *ChinaFocus*, 25 June 2015, http://www.chinausfocus.com/peace-security/u-s-ambivalence-in-south -china-sea/.

———. *Solving Disputes for Regional Cooperation in the South China Sea: A Chinese Perspective*. Cambridge, U.K.: Chandos, 2013.

Wylie, J. C. *Military Strategy: A General Theory of Power Control*. Annapolis, Md.: Naval Institute Press, 1953.

Wyne, Ali. "The American World Order and China's New Bank." *War on the Rocks*, 7 April 2015, http://warontherocks.com/2015/04/the-american-world-order-and -chinas-new-bank?singlepage=1.

Xi Jinping. "Working Together toward a Better Future for Asia and the World." Keynote Speech at the Boao Forum, 7 April 2013, http://www.fmprc.gov.cn/ce /ceie/eng/ztlt/diplomacy/t1075089.htm.

Xia Hongping, Wei Bing, and Shi Binxin. "Standardization, an Urgent Issue for 'System of Systems' Operations." *Jiefangjun Bao*, 10 December 2013.

Xu Xaoshi. "The 'New Normal' and the Future of China's Economy." *China-U.S. Focus Digest*, 15 July 2015, http://www.chinausfocus.com/finance-economy/the -new-normal-and-the-future-of-chinas-economy/.

Xu, Xiaobo, Cheng Meng, and Xu Li. "Analysis and Implications of the Accidents in the Singapore Strait." Paper submitted to the Annual Meeting of Transportation Research Board, Singapore, National University, 2012, http://trrjournalonline .trb.org/doi/abs/10.3141/2273-13.

Yang Yujun, "Xi Jinping: China to Cut Troops by 300,000." *Xinhua*, 3 September 2015, http://www.chinadaily.com.cn/world/2015victoryanniv/2015-09/03/content _21782967.htm.

Yap, Chuin-wei, and Brian Spegele. "China's First Advanced Nuclear Reactor Faces More Delays." *Wall Street Journal*, 15 January 2015, http://www.wsj.com/articles /chinas-first-advanced-nuclear-reactor-faces-more-delays-1421297393.

Yeo, Mike. "Chinese Carrier Fighter Now in Serial Production." *USNI News*, 10 November 2014, http://news.usni.org/2014/11/10/chinese-carrier-fighter-now-serial -production.

Yifei, Chen. "China to Launch 'World's Largest' Coastguard Patrol Vessel." *South China Morning Post*, 17 December 2014, http://www.scmp.com/news/china -insider/article/1663219/china-coastguard-poised-take-delivery-over-worlds -largest-patrol.

Youwei. "The End of Reform in China." *Foreign Affairs* 94, no. 4 (May–June 2015), https://www.foreignaffairs.com/articles/china/end-reform-china.

Yu Bin. "China–Russia Relations: Russia's Pride and China's Power." *Comparative Connections* 16, no. 3 (January 2015), http://csis.org/files/publication/1403qchina _russia.pdf.

Yu, Jeanny. "China Yuan Moving up the World Currency Ranks and Shifting to a Strengthening Trend." *South China Morning Post*, 28 June 2014, http://www .scmp.com/business/banking-finance/article/1542085/yuan-surges-currency -rankings.

Yuan, Luo, "Philippines' Illegal Occupation of Ren'ai Reef Must Be Ended with Determination." *Global Times*, 21 July 2015, http://www.globaltimes.cn/content /933053.shtml.

Yung, Christopher D., and Ross Rustici. "'Not an Idea We Have to Shun': Chinese Overseas Basing Requirements in the 21st Century." *China Strategic Perspectives* 7 (October 2014), http://ndupress.ndu.edu/Portals/68/Documents/stratperspec- tive/china/ChinaPerspectives-7.pdf.

Zenn, Jacob. "Future Scenarios on the New Silk Road." *China Brief* 15, no. 6 (19 March 2015), http://www.jamestown.org/programs/chinabrief/single/?tx_ttnews %5Btt_news%5D=43675&tx_ttnews%5BbackPid%5D=25&cHash=2e8543858d 1d72191a08f683044105f2#.VakqG-u4k6g.

Zhang Haiwen. "Is It Safeguarding the Freedom of Navigation or Maritime Hege- mony of the United States?" *Chinese Journal of International Law* 9 (2010): 31–47.

Zhang, Hongzhou. "China's Global Resources Drive." RSIS Commentary no. 152/ 2014, 31 July 2014, https://www.rsis.edu.sg/rsis-publication/idss/chinas-global -resources-drive-a-market-oriented-strategy-for-food/#.Vafzy-u4k6.

Zhang Hongzhou and Arthur Guschin. "China's Silk Road Economic Belt: Geo- political Challenges in Central Asia." RSIS Commentary no. 099/2015, 24 April 2015, https://www.rsis.edu.sg/rsis-publication/rsi/co15099-chinas-silk-road -economic-belt-geopolitical-challenges-in-central-asia/#.VVfSReu4k_U.

Zhang Junshe. "The New U.S. Maritime Strategy Shows Its Two Sides to China." *People's Daily*, 19 March 2015, http://en.people.cn/n/2015/0319/c98649-8865473 .html.

Zhang Xiaolin, and Cao Yang. "Promote the Transformation of Naval Strategy, Safeguard Maritime Security." Naval Command Academy. Translated by Ryan Martinson, CMSI. July 2015.

Zhang Wenmu. "Sea Power and China's Strategic Choices." *China Security* (Summer 2006): 17–31, http://dspace.cigilibrary.org/jspui/bitstream/123456789/20626/1 /Sea%20Power%20and%20Chinas%20Strategic%20Choices.pdf?.

Zhang, Yulian, ed. *Science of Campaigns* (Beijing: National Defense University Press, 2016). Chinese only.

Zhang Yunbi. "FM: China Will Watch over Waters." *China Daily*, 29 June 2015, http:// usa.chinadaily.com.cn/epaper/2015-06/29/content_21133287.htm.

———. "Nansha Islands Construction 'Befits China's International Responsibilities.'" *China Daily*, 27 May 2015, http://www.chinadaily.com.cn/china/2015-05/27 /content_20827819.htm.

Zhang, Yunling. "One Belt, One Road." *Global Asia* 10, no. 2 (Fall 2015): 8–12.

Zhao Jingfang. "Managing Crises in Sino-US Relations," *Zhongguo Pinglun*, no. 193: 40–43.

Zhao Lei. "FTZ to Allow Foreign Private Players in Shipping Industry." *China Daily*, 4 September 2014, http://www.chinadaily.com.cn/business/2014-09/04/content _18544704.htm.

———. "Maritime Efforts 'to Help Others.'" *China Daily*, 4 May 2015, http://www .chinadaily.com.cn/china/2015-05/04/content_20608747.htm.

——. "Navy Stages Live-Ammo Drill in S. China Sea." *China Daily*, 3 August 2015, http://www.chinadaily.com.cn/china/2015-08/03/content_21483771.htm.

Zhao Rui, Stephen Hynes, and Guang Shun He. "Blue Growth in the Middle Kingdom: An Analysis of China's Ocean Economy." Working Papers. Paper 3. http://cbe.miis.edu/cbe_working_papers/3.

Zhao Shengnan. "Stay Vigilant over Taiwan Separatists, Build Ties: Xi." *China Daily*, 5 March 2015.

Zhao Shengyang and Zhang Yunbi. "China Pledges to Protect Maritime Sovereignty." *China Daily*, 29 June 2012, http://europe.chinadaily.com.cn/china/2012-06/29/content_15533513.htm.

Zheng Wang. "The Nine-Dashed Line: 'Engraved in Our Hearts.'" *Diplomat*, 25 August 2014, http://thediplomat.com/2014/08/the-nine-dashed-line-engraved-in-our-hearts/.

Zheng Zhihua. "Why Does China's Maritime Claim Remain Ambiguous?" AMTI Brief (Washington, D.C.: CSIS, 12 June 2015), http://amti.csis.org/why-does-chinas-maritime-claim-remain-ambiguous/.

Zhong Nan. "Key Pact Sealed with Australia." *China Daily*, 18 June 2015, http://usa.chinadaily.com.cn/epaper/2015-06/18/content_21042345.htm.

Zhou, Guangzhao. "Scientist Outlines Five Challenges for PRC in 21st Century." *Xinhua*, 24 May 2000.

Zhu, Charlie, and David Stanway. "'Made in China' Nuclear Reactors a Tough Sell in Global Market." Reuters, 6 March 2015, http://www.reuters.com/article/2015/03/06/us-china-nuclear-idUSKBN0M20ID20150306.

Zhu Feng. "Beijing's Successful Agenda-Setting." *China Daily*, 14 November 2014, http://usa.chinadaily.com.cn/epaper/2014-11/14/content_18916158.htm.

Zimmerman, James. "Beijing's Negative Stance on Investment." *Wall Street Journal*, 1 April 2015, http://www.wsj.com/articles/james-zimmerman-beijings-negative-stance-on-investment-1427908711.

Zoellick, Robert. "Remarks on AUSFTA." United States Studies Centre, 2 July 2015, http://ussc.edu.au/news-room/Remarks-by-Robert-Zoellick-on-AUSFTA.

Zou Keyuan. "China and Maritime Boundary Delimitation: Past, Present, and Future." In *Conflict Management and Dispute Settlement in East Asia*, edited by Ramses Amer and Zou Keyuan, 149–70. Burlington, Vt.: Ashgate, 1988.

ZYH and AEF. "Chinese Think Tank Releases Report on the Security of China's Perimeter." *Xinhua*, 16 January 2015, https://chinascope.org/main/content/view/6901/81/.

——. "U.S. Invites Japan to patrol the South China Sea, Fulfilling Japan's Wishes." *People's Daily*, 17 June 2015, http://chinascope.org/main/content/view/7221/40/.

INDEX

About the Author

Capt. Bernard D. Cole, USN (Ret.), is professor emeritus at the National War College. During his Navy career he commanded USS *Rathburne* (FF 1057) and Destroyer Squadron 35, and also served as a naval gunfire liaison officer with the 3rd Marine Division in Vietnam from June 1967 to July 1968. He earned a PhD in history from Auburn University and was named the Naval Institute Press "Author of the Year" in 2015. This is his eighth book on Asian energy security and maritime affairs.

The Naval Institute Press is the book-publishing arm of the U.S. Naval Institute, a private, nonprofit, membership society for sea service professionals and others who share an interest in naval and maritime affairs. Established in 1873 at the U.S. Naval Academy in Annapolis, Maryland, where its offices remain today, the Naval Institute has members worldwide.

Members of the Naval Institute support the education programs of the society and receive the influential monthly magazine *Proceedings* or the colorful bimonthly magazine *Naval History* and discounts on fine nautical prints and on ship and aircraft photos. They also have access to the transcripts of the Institute's Oral History Program and get discounted admission to any of the Institute-sponsored seminars offered around the country.

The Naval Institute's book-publishing program, begun in 1898 with basic guides to naval practices, has broadened its scope to include books of more general interest. Now the Naval Institute Press publishes about seventy titles each year, ranging from how-to books on boating and navigation to battle histories, biographies, ship and aircraft guides, and novels. Institute members receive significant discounts on the Press' more than eight hundred books in print.

Full-time students are eligible for special half-price membership rates. Life memberships are also available.

For a free catalog describing Naval Institute Press books currently available, and for further information about joining the U.S. Naval Institute, please write to:

Member Services
U.S. NAVAL INSTITUTE
291 Wood Road
Annapolis, MD 21402-5034
Telephone: (800) 233-8764
Fax: (410) 571-1703
Web address: www.usni.org